Programming Web Services with Perl

Programming Web Services with Perl

Randy J. Ray and Pavel Kulchenko

O'REILLY®

Beijing • Cambridge • Farnham • Köln • Paris • Sebastopol • Taipei • Tokyo

Programming Web Services with Perl
by Randy J. Ray and Pavel Kulchenko

Copyright © 2003 O'Reilly & Associates, Inc. All rights reserved.
Printed in the United States of America.

Published by O'Reilly & Associates, Inc., 1005 Gravenstein Highway North, Sebastopol, CA 95472.

O'Reilly & Associates books may be purchased for educational, business, or sales promotional use. Online editions are also available for most titles (*safari.oreilly.com*). For more information, contact our corporate/institutional sales department: (800) 998-9938 or *corporate@oreilly.com*.

Editor:	Nathan Torkington
Production Editor:	Mary Anne Weeks Mayo
Cover Designer:	Pam Spremulli
Interior Designer:	David Futato

Printing History:

    December 2002:   First Edition.

Nutshell Handbook, the Nutshell Handbook logo, and the O'Reilly logo are registered trademarks of O'Reilly & Associates, Inc. Many of the designations used by manufacturers and sellers to distinguish their products are claimed as trademarks. Where those designations appear in this book, and O'Reilly & Associates, Inc. was aware of a trademark claim, the designations have been printed in caps or initial caps. The association between the image of a flying dragon and the topic of programming web services with Perl is a trademark of O'Reilly & Associates, Inc.

While every precaution has been taken in the preparation of this book, the publisher and authors assume no responsibility for errors or omissions, or for damages resulting from the use of the information contained herein.

ISBN: 0-596-00206-8
[M]

Table of Contents

Preface . . . . **ix**

1. Introduction to Web Services **1**
   History   2
   The Web Services Dream   3
   The Web Services Cold Shower   4
   Who to Believe?   5
   Web Services in the Real World   6

2. HTTP and XML Basics **9**
   HTTP   9
   XML   13
   XML Schema   22

3. Introduction to XML-RPC **32**
   History of XML-RPC   32
   Example Client: Meerkat   42
   Limitations of XML-RPC   49

4. Programming XML-RPC **52**
   Perl Toolkits for XML-RPC   52
   RPC::XMLSimple   53
   XMLRPC::Lite   59
   RPC::XML   67

5. Introduction to SOAP **83**
   Background   83
   XML Definitions   84

	RPC over SOAP	108
	SOAP Transport	111
	Further Reading	113
6.	**Programming SOAP**	**114**
	A Toolkit Approach	114
	DevelopMentor's SOAP Module	115
	The SOAP::Lite Module	119
	Other SOAP-Related Modules	136
7.	**Serving SOAP over HTTP**	**138**
	Basic SOAP::Lite Servers	138
	The Application	139
	Designing the Server	140
	Tying the Interface Code to SOAP	146
	Improving the Code and the Service	152
	Ideas for Further Exploration	158
8.	**SOAP Services Without HTTP**	**160**
	Choosing a Protocol	160
	Authentication	161
	Transports with Server and Client	165
	Standalone Protocols	173
	Creating New Transport Modules	177
9.	**Service Description with WSDL**	**185**
	Basic WSDL	185
	WSDL Programming	211
10.	**Service Advertising and Discovery with UDDI**	**214**
	Defining UDDI	214
	Programming with UDDI::Lite	231
11.	**REST: Representational State Transfer**	**237**
	Defining REST	237
	REST Principles	240
	Programming REST	246

12. Advanced Web Services Topics 262

Message Routing 263
Packaging 267
Security 271
Services Discovery 287
Reliable Messaging 289
Business Process Management 291
Implementation Considerations 298
WS-Next 302

A. XML-RPC Toolkit Programming Reference 303

B. SOAP::Lite Programming Reference 327

C. XML-RPC Example Code 360

D. SOAP Example Code 377

E. WSDL and UDDI Examples 415

F. Bibliography and References 434

Index 439

Preface

Web services make distributed computing easy. Through standardized protocols for locating, describing, and making remote procedure calls, it's possible to have components of an application written by different groups in different programming languages running on different machines that run different operating systems.

That's not to say that *writing* a web service is necessarily easy. There's a maze of jargon and acronyms to get through, and if you're truly masochistic, you'll spend days with the dense specifications trying to get your head around the XML you're expected to produce and consume. And even if you let a toolkit handle the XML for you, the toolkit must still work within the limitations of the protocol, so unless you understand the protocol (even at a high level), you'll be confused.

This book will help you cut through the confusion. Whether you're creating and parsing XML yourself or using a toolkit to do it, this book cuts through the jargon and acronym soup to give you what you need to get the job done. The main web service systems and specifications (XML-RPC, SOAP, WSDL, UDDI, and REST) are covered both at the XML level and at the toolkit level.

Audience for This Book

If you're a Perl programmer approaching web services either from curiosity or necessity, you're the person for whom we wrote this book. You'll learn not only what the protocols are and how to use the various Perl toolkits built around them, but how to design your own applications with web services in mind.

This book covers an intersection of XML, networking, and Perl. Your Perl skills should be at the intermediate level; we assume you know how to create and manipulate data structures and create object-oriented modules. Our sample programs use references and objects without comment. The good news is that we don't assume you've already used any of the toolkits we describe—LWP, SOAP::Lite, among others.

We explain all the XML you'll need for the rest of the book in Chapter 2, so you don't need prior XML exposure (though it might help to make the heavy XML bolus that is SOAP easier to swallow). In terms of networking, we assume you know about IP addresses and ports, but because the various modules we use hide the nasty details of networking, you don't need prior network programming.

Structure of This Book

The book is divided into 12 chapters and 6 appendixes. To help you focus on just the web services aspects of the sample programs, chapters include and discuss fragments of code; the full source is available in several appendixes.

Chapter 1, *Introduction to Web Services*, gives you the big picture, telling you what's covered and why it's important.

Chapter 2, *HTTP and XML Basics*, gets you up to speed with the open foundations that web services are built on.

Chapter 3, *Introduction to XML-RPC*, is an introduction to the XML and HTTP of XML-RPC.

Chapter 4, *Programming XML-RPC*, shows you how to develop your own XML-RPC applications using three popular toolkits.

Chapter 5, *Introduction to SOAP*, is an introduction to the XML and HTTP of SOAP.

Chapter 6, *Programming SOAP*, is an introduction to writing SOAP clients and servers in the two SOAP toolkits.

Chapter 7, *Serving SOAP over HTTP*, focuses on using the SOAP::Lite toolkit to write SOAP clients with HTTP as a transport.

Chapter 8, *SOAP Services Without HTTP*, uses SOAP::Lite over transports, such as SMTP (email) and Jabber (instant messaging).

Chapter 9, *Service Description with WSDL*, shows how to describe web services interfaces.

Chapter 10, *Service Advertising and Discovery with UDDI*, explains the leading way to discover services dynamically.

Chapter 11, *REST: Representational State Transfer*, is an introduction to the web services philosophy that is often seen as a simpler alternative to XML-RPC and SOAP.

Chapter 12, *Advanced Web Services Topics*, surveys the leading edge of web services technology for security, discovery, reliability, transactions, and internationalization.

Appendix A, *XML-RPC Toolkit Programming Reference*, provides a reference to the three XML-RPC toolkits discussed in Chapter 4.

Appendix B, *SOAP::Lite Programming Reference*, is a definitive guide to the `SOAP::Lite` toolkit used heavily in Chapters 4 through 10.

Appendix C, *XML-RPC Example Code*, contains the full program listings for the applications developed in Chapters 3 and 4.

Appendix D, *SOAP Example Code*, contains the full program listings for the applications developed in Chapters 6, 7, and 8.

Appendix E, *WSDL and UDDI Examples*, contains the full program listings for the examples developed in Chapters 9 and 10.

Appendix F, *Bibliography and References*, gathers the bibliography and references used in the writing of the book.

Conventions Used in This Book

The following typographic conventions are used in this book:

Italic
> Used for email addresses and URLs, as well as for new terms where they are defined.

`Constant width`
> Used for code listings and for keywords, variables, function names, command options, module names, directories, filenames, parameters, utilities, program names, and XML elements where they appear in the text.

`Constant width bold`
> Used to highlight key fragments of a larger code example, or to show the output of a piece of code.

`Constant width italic`
> Used as a general placeholder to indicate terms that should be replaced by actual values in your own programs.

> This icon designates a note, which is an important aside to the nearby text.

> This icon designates a warning relating to the nearby text.

Comments and Questions

Please address comments and questions concerning this book to the publisher:

O'Reilly & Associates, Inc.
1005 Gravenstein Highway North
Sebastopol, CA 95472
(800) 998-9938 (in the United States or Canada)
(707) 829-0515 (international or local)
(707) 829-0104 (fax)

We have a web page for this book, where we list errata, examples, or any additional information. You can access this page at:

http://www.oreilly.com/catalog/pwebserperl

To comment or ask technical questions about this book, send email to:

bookquestions@oreilly.com

For more information about our books, conferences, Resource Centers, and the O'Reilly Network, see our web site at:

http://www.oreilly.com

Acknowledgments

Randy

First and foremost I would like to thank Nat Torkington, editor and friend. He brought this opportunity to me, and was amazingly patient as I struggled to get up to speed with the materials I was given. My friends Paul and Ami Echeverri, both tech writers, didn't help with the book so much as keep me sane and entertained while fielding the occasional question about writing.

Ryan Dietrich introduced me to XML-RPC (and Radiohead's "Kid A" CD) while he was contracting to Red Hat. I'm also grateful to Kevin Greene, Stephen Nelson, Mike Reynolds, and Sky Schultz from my time as a contractor at Hewlett-Packard, and to Matt Lanier, Paul Lindner, Jason Miller, Garth Webb, Tom Lancaster, Eric Chen, and Bob Moss from my time at Red Hat.

Thanks to all the technical reviewers, and especially to Pavel Kulchenko, who not only reviewed but contributed, and who also was quick to answer a barrage of questions as I was writing the chapters on SOAP::Lite.

Finally, I'd like to acknowledge the Perl community, in particular the perl5-porters community. Not for the creation and maintenance of Perl, as you might assume, but for the community they've built around it. It is because of this sense of community that I was able to grow from just another programmer using the language, to being able to contribute modules to CPAN and eventually write this book.

Pavel

I owe a debt of gratitude to many people who one way or another made this book possible.

I would like to thank to my wonderful coauthor, Randy Ray, who was the pleasure to work with. Special thanks to Tony Hong, Stephen Friedl, Igor Dvoeglazov, and others who reviewed the draft of the book for their sound technical advice and valuable feedback.

Thanks are due to the people in the Perl and SOAP communities; their enthusiastic support, contributions, comments, and insistence on clarity have all made some difference to the book.

Thanks to our wonderful technical editor, Nathan Torkington, who was gently persistent in his effort to get this book happen and contributed his knowledge and experience to make it great.

And last, but definitely not the least, I wouldn't be able to finish the writing without my family's patience and love (or maybe I would, but what would be the point). Even though they have no interest in the content of the book (at least for now), my son Daniil and my wife Alena provided the support and encouragement I needed. Thank you!

CHAPTER 1
Introduction to Web Services

The world is full of useful data and services offered by computer programs. But most of that data and most of those services are locked away. Web sites, designed for access by people and not programs, bury the information in an ever-changing morass of HTML. Communication protocols have been specific to applications and sometimes to operating systems. Precompiled libraries are useful only for particular programming languages on the system they were compiled for.

If you want to write a program to book a flight, check how much paid time off you have accrued, or find all the shows on TV that feature the stars of *Buffy the Vampire Slayer*, you're facing an uphill battle. All that data exists, but it's effectively inaccessible.

Sure, you could screenscrape HTML from web sites such as *expedia.com* and *tvguide.com*, but that puts you at the mercy of the web designers of those sites. Every time they decide to make their pages look prettier, you'll have to rewrite your screenscraper.

You might be able to wangle access to the machine that runs the payroll system, but it's unlikely. You might even know the programming language the payroll software was written in. But can you figure out the database structure?

Web services are all about enabling computers to communicate with each other, opening up services and data. Built on open standards, the way that the Web is, web services offer convenient standard ways to open up the functionality of your applications to other applications.

In this chapter you'll learn a bit about the history of web services and the current lie of the land—what systems you can choose from, where the hype exceeds reality, and so on.

History

Web services didn't spring full-formed from the collective forehead of Microsoft, IBM, and Sun. Systems such as SOAP, XML-RPC, and WSDL are merely the latest iteration in a long series of distributed computing initiatives. Ever since there were two computers, people have been trying to make them work together.

The web services we have today trace their ancestry back to the Sun Remote Procedure Call (RPC) system. This provided a standard way for a client to interact with a server, using the model of a procedure call. A server might offer many services (procedures, identified by name), and a client would tell the server which service to use and what values to pass it (parameters). The server would send back a value (the return value) from the service.

The problem at the time was that the binary representation of values varied depending on the operating system, hardware, and programming languages that created the value. The Sun RPC system solved the problem by specifying how to encode the values in the parameters—a standard binary format. Representing data can still be a problem, but webservers solve it by representing values in XML (Extensible Markup Language).

Microsoft offered the next major step forward, with its Component Object Model (COM). COM was based on language independence, interoperability, a strong focus on reusable components, and extensibility. The ability to develop components and object libraries that would be accessible over varying platforms and by multiple languages removed some old hurdles in areas of rapid application development and system integration. While RPC dealt only in procedures, COM was designed to exist in a world of objects and method calls.

Microsoft extended this model with DCOM, the *Distributed* Component Object Model. DCOM overcame many of the limitations of data and interface specifications. Remote objects could be accessed as though they were local, and you could even extend a remote interface. DCOM has never really taken off outside the Microsoft world, though.

The leading competitor to DCOM (and its successor, COM+) is the Common Object Request Broker Architecture, known as CORBA. Also object-oriented, CORBA has recognition and acceptance at high levels within large-scale development projects. At the heart of a CORBA implementation is an Object Request Broker (ORB), which takes incoming requests and dispatches them to the appropriate server. Programmers use the Interface Design Language (IDL) to describe the functions that a service offers, and then a translator program takes the IDL and emits source code to handle the interaction with the ORB.

The Web Services Dream

From this melting pot of history came web services. Dissatisfaction with various aspects of Sun RPC, COM, and CORBA lead programmers to look for glue that had the best parts of all of these systems (cross-platform, high-level, interlanguage) and left behind the drawbacks (complex ORB systems, proprietary ownership, and confusing IDLs).

Web services escape being shackled to particular hardware or languages by using the Extensible Markup Language (XML) to represent data. There are XML parsers available for everything from embedded systems to supercomputers, and almost every conceivable programming language (including Perl!). The ubiquity of XML parsers and the platform neutrality of the XML standard means that web services designers don't have to worry about the issues of byte ordering and datatype size that were a major hurdle for the Sun RPC designers.

To get away from the complexity of ORBs, sockets, and all manner of connectivity hassles, web services are built on top of the Hypertext Transfer Protocol (HTTP). HTTP is also ubiquitous, with web servers available for almost every platform. A server is identified by a URL, and managing communication simply becomes a problem of mapping a procedure call onto an HTTP request and response (this mapping is quite natural, as we'll see in Chapter 2).

XML-RPC was the first web service protocol, forked from the early development of SOAP (Simple Object Access Protocol). As the name XML-RPC suggests, it only tries to encode procedure calls. It defines a standard way to encode data, method calls, and exceptions. It's quite simple, and has gained popularity in the world of scripting languages such as Perl and Python, because its type system is very similar to those of most scripting languages. Chapters 3 and 4 show how to develop XML-RPC servers and clients in Perl.

SOAP attempts to solve more problems than XML-RPC. It introduces headers for extensibility, which opens the door to security, routing, and other concepts. It separates somewhat from HTTP so that you can use other systems, such as instant messaging or low-level network connections, to pass messages between servers and clients. You can have requests without responses (in an asynchronous environment you may never get a response) and responses without requests (continually broadcasting temperature data, for example). It can also be used in document style, in which servers and clients exchange XML documents that don't necessarily represent method calls and responses (invoices and receipts, for example).

The increased power of SOAP comes at a price, though: complexity. As you'll see in Chapter 5, the SOAP standard is considerably harder to grasp than XML-RPC. But the power of SOAP has attracted many in corporate and enterprise programming, where SOAP is often used for systems integration. Chapters 6, 7, and 8 show how to develop SOAP clients and servers in Perl.

Web services designers tried hard not to throw out the baby with the bathwater, though. CORBA's IDL, from which glue code is automatically generated, has a counterpart in the Web Services Description Language (WSDL). A WSDL document is an XML file that describes the interfaces (method names, parameters, return values) offered by a service. While primarily the realm of statically typed precompiled languages such as Java and C++, Perl can produce and consume WSDL. Chapter 9 explains more about this.

"If we have a lot of similar services, and machine-readable descriptions of their interfaces," went the next web services brainwave, "why not have our client programs find and use a service at runtime instead of hardwiring a particular server and interface in at compile-time?" The Universal Description, Discovery, and Integration (UDDI) project provides a system to do just this kind of *loose coupling* of server and client. It's like a search engine for web services, so your program only has to know which UDDI server(s) to learn the details of any service it wants to talk to. UDDI is the focus of Chapter 10.

The Web Services Cold Shower

The previous section showed the positive side of web services—open standards, cross-platform interoperability, and loose coupling. But it's only half the story. As web services are more widely deployed, developers have found holes and shortcomings in systems described earlier.

The XML-RPC specification, for instance, has no standardized error system. Sure, there's a way for a server to say "something went wrong," and it can even return an error string and number, but there are no standard values for the string and number. Each application invents its own error codes. (There is an effort outside the XML-RPC specification to come up with some standard error codes, and this is described in Chapter 3).

The SOAP standard uses advanced features of XML, such as namespaces and XML Schema types (Chapter 2 introduces these if you've never met them before). This eliminates some parsers, which can't handle namespaces, and increases the processing overhead.

There are some who say that XML-RPC and SOAP promote a misleading view of distributed computing; that any complex application built around remote procedure calls is inevitably going to be poorly designed and ineffectively implemented. The Representational State Transfer (REST) philosophy of web services offers a completely different view of how you should design your web services. You'll see REST in detail in Chapter 11.

The web services world is so fractious that even REST has its detractors. They say REST is too academic, it is theory that's difficult to translate into practice, and it avoids the hard problems of standardized encodings that XML-RPC and SOAP are designed to solve.

UDDI is arguably the biggest example of the web-services hype. At one point there were predictions of artificially intelligent (AI) programs that would discover and connect web services automatically, from standardized descriptions of functionality offered and wanted. However, there are no standardized descriptions of functionality, UDDI covered only a very small part of the business relationship that most large-scale web services needed to express, and ultimately nobody has felt the need for this kind of Holy Grail strongly enough to implement it.

In addition, all the web services protocols are easily criticized on grounds of performance. HTTP is far from an optimal transfer protocol, and XML isn't an economical encoding system. Custom systems and even the older systems, such as Sun RPC and CORBA, can out-perform a web services protocol such as XML-RPC or SOAP (though obviously a lot depends on your ORB, the types of messages you're exchanging, and so on).

As if that wasn't bad enough, there are critics of the standards process at the World Wide Web Consortium (W3C), which oversees the development of SOAP, WSDL, and an ever-increasing set of standards built on top of them. Those critics say that the standards process is driven by big vendors such as Microsoft and IBM, who are less concerned with finding the right solution to the problem than coming up with something that they can build a marketing campaign around and sell. A cynic would say that there's a large industry in manufacturing XML solutions to overinflated problems.

Who to Believe?

Reality, as always, lies somewhere between the optimist and the cynic. There are real advantages to using web services instead of systems such as CORBA, as well as real drawbacks.

The toolkits for SOAP and XML-RPC are far more convenient to use than CORBA or COM, and convenience matters. Perl programmers know that you don't have to run the fastest, just fast enough. (As the old joke says, I don't have to outrun the bear, I just have to outrun you). In a world in which development cycles are shrinking, and deadline pressures are growing, convenience leads to quicker development, which means higher profits.

Web services succeed in being lightweight, in the sense that it's easier to implement an HTTP server and client than it is to write an ORB or talk to one. As a result, there are SOAP and XML-RPC libraries for languages that don't have ORBs, and web services have spread further than CORBA, COM, and Sun RPC ever did.

While the AI pipe dream of UDDI servers reducing programming problems to a set of XML transformations has gone up in smoke, UDDI isn't a complete bust. For domain-specific applications, UDDI is still useful. For example, in bioinformatics you don't care which human genome server you search, so long as it has the data. A UDDI registry of searchable databases has been proposed to let programs say "I want to search the human genome" and respond by automatically finding a current list of servers.

Interoperability does remain a bugbear, though. The web-services standards are long and often nebulous, so it's quite easy to write a server or client that appears to conform to the standards but actually doesn't. There are interoperability suites and periodic "bakeoffs" in which toolkit implementers run extensive tests against one another to ensure interoperatability. However, there are many toolkits that have some interoperability problems, and the promise of transparent interoperability is still just that.

Web Services in the Real World

Let's look at the applications in this book and see how they lend themselves to the web-services protocol they illustrate.

Chapter 3 gives a quick example of writing an XML-RPC client for the Meerkat news service from nothing more than an XML parser and an HTTP library. XML-RPC lends itself to this because there's no innate object orientation to the design of the news service, and the main audience for the news service is the programmers of the scripting languages that happen to best support XML-RPC.

Chapter 4 reimplements the Meerkat client using the three Perl XML-RPC toolkits to show how much simpler life is with a toolkit to do the heavy lifting for you. Each toolkit also implements another example, fetching an entry from one of several quote databases. This is a more complex example, with an API to implement as both server and client.

Here is a simple program that fetches and prints five Perl stories from Meerkat using the XMLRPC::Lite toolkit:

```perl
#!/usr/bin/perl -w

use XMLRPC::Lite;

$client = XMLRPC::Lite
  ->proxy('http://www.oreillynet.com/meerkat/xml-rpc/server.php')
  ->on_fault(sub { die "Transport error: " . $_[1]->faultstring });

$resp = $client->call('meerkat.getItems',
                    { 'search'      => '/[pP]erl/',
                      num_items     => 5,
                      descriptions  => 75 })->result();
```

```
foreach $story (@$resp) {
  print $story->{description}, "\n";
  print "  ", $story->{link}, "\n";
  print "\n";
}
```

This is the kind of output it produces:

```
Deploy USE_GNOMENG infrastrcuture o USE_REINPLACE instead of PERL o Mark
  http://www.FreshPorts.org/audio/freebirth/

Support for merging, speed improvements, support for XTMPath, and LTM.
  http://www.garshol.priv.no/download/xmltools/prod/XTMBase.html

Michael Stevens compares two popular mail filtering tools, both written in
  http://www.perl.com/pub/a/2002/08/27/filtering.html

Directory layouts of py-gtk and py-gnome packages have been changed, so tha
  http://www.FreshPorts.org/mail/pmail/

Directory layouts of py-gtk and py-gnome packages have been changed, so tha
  http://www.FreshPorts.org/editors/moleskine/
```

As you can tell from the program, the `XMLRPC::Lite` module encodes and decodes Perl values (we got back an array of hashes), sending the request via HTTP and parsing the response. The `call()` and `result()` methods hide the tricky stuff.

Chapter 6 shows two SOAP toolkits accessing the same web service, which translates numbers into words. Here's the `SOAP::Lite` client:

```
#!/usr/bin/perl -w
  use strict;
  use SOAP::Lite;

  my $num = shift; $num =~ /^\d+$/ or die "USAGE: $0 num\n";
  my $endpoint = 'http://www.tankebolaget.se/'
                .'scripts/NumToWords.dll/soap/INumToWords';
  my $method_uri = 'urn:NumToWordsIntf-INumToWords';

  my $num2words = SOAP::Lite
    ->new(uri => $method_uri, proxy => $endpoint);
  my $response = $num2words
    ->NumToWords_English(SOAP::Data->name(aNumber => $num));

  die $response->faultstring if $response->fault;
  print "$num may be expressed as ", $response->result, "\n";
```

While more complex than the XML-RPC example, this shows fault handling (if (`$response->fault`)), method calls, and how to hardcode the type of a piece of data (the `SOAP::Data` object). If the `SOAP::Lite` methods look a lot like the `XMLRPC::Lite` methods, it's because they're built from a single framework.

The extended application developed in Chapter 7 is a shopping-cart system, which illustrates real-world issues of authentication, database abstraction, and interface design. Chapter 8 runs the shopping-cart system on transports other than HTTP (such as the Jabber message system) and shows how to do in other transports what you get for free with HTTP.

Chapter 9 builds a WSDL file to describe the shopping-cart API. You'll see how the APIs we designed in Chapter 7 translate to WSDL. We don't revisit the shopping cart for Chapter 11 on REST, though; instead, we develop a simple book catalog system to illustrate the principles of REST. Chapter 12 is an overview of the advanced topics in web services, such as security and performance.

CHAPTER 2
HTTP and XML Basics

The web-services technologies described in this book are built primarily from XML and HTTP. While toolkits don't demand an intimate knowledge of these techniques, having a basic understanding of these low-level elements will lead to better grasp of the more complex concepts presented later in this book.

This chapter presents overviews of HTTP (with some discussion of HTTP/S), XML, and a little coverage of the XML Schema language. The goal of this chapter is to present these topics if you aren't yet familiar with them, without straying too far from the main focus of the book. The discussion of these concepts will focus on their application to XML-RPC and SOAP, with references to other books and web sites if you want to learn more.

HTTP

Anyone who has surfed the Web has used the Hypertext Transfer Protocol; it's the dominant protocol for fetching web pages from a server. The name is now something of a misnomer because the protocol is used for more than HTML web pages. URLs (Uniform Resource Locators, or web addresses) that start with *http* indicate a page that is fetched through HTTP.

HTTP was originally developed as a layer over the TCP protocol to simplify applications that exchanged HTML data. Since then, it's been adopted and standardized by the World Wide Web Consortium (W3C) into the form currently in use. The current HTTP standard is at Version 1.1, which supports a number of optimizations over the 1.0 specification that had been the standard for some time.

Fortunately, as will be illustrated later, because there are excellent programming toolkits available for Perl that simplify using HTTP, it isn't necessary to have an intimate knowledge of HTTP details and internals.

The Request/Response Cycle

HTTP is based on a simple model of a request/response conversation. A client sends a request to a target server, possibly with some amount of data accompanying the request. The server always gives a response, even if it's an error. There are even ways for the server to report to the client that it is completely unable to handle the client's request.

Figure 2-1 shows a simple layout of the request sent by a client and the corresponding response. Note the similarities between the two.

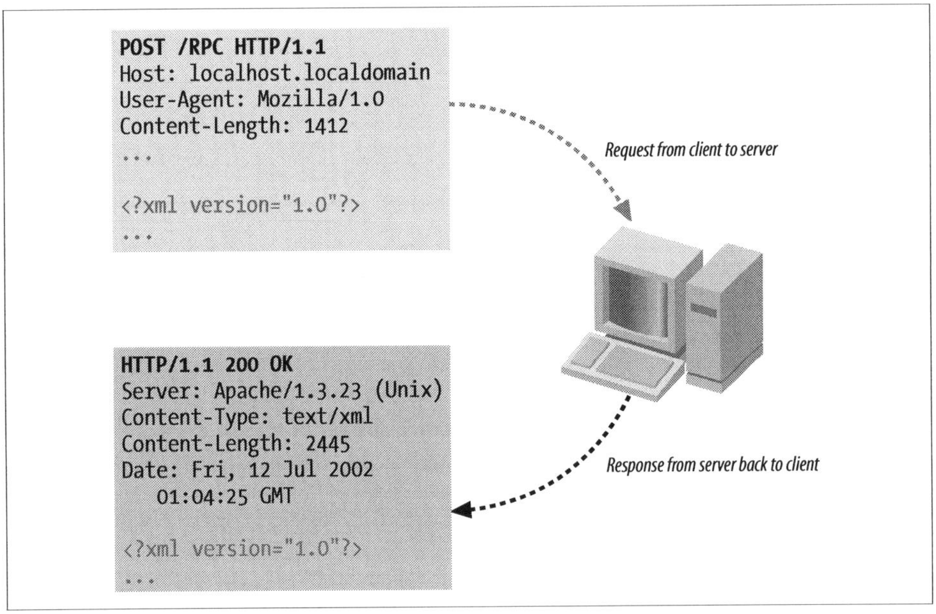

```
POST /RPC HTTP/1.1
Host: localhost.localdomain
User-Agent: Mozilla/1.0
Content-Length: 1412
...

<?xml version="1.0"?>
...
```
Request from client to server

```
HTTP/1.1 200 OK
Server: Apache/1.3.23 (Unix)
Content-Type: text/xml
Content-Length: 2445
Date: Fri, 12 Jul 2002
    01:04:25 GMT

<?xml version="1.0"?>
...
```
Response from server back to client

Figure 2-1. Basic request/response model

Both ends of the conversation communicate a lot of their information in message headers, which are similar in style to those used by electronic mail and Internet news servers.

HTTP Message Structure

The structure of an HTTP message is basically the same for requests and responses, except for the first line. Both messages start with a line specific to the message type (a *request line* or a *response line*), followed by a series of zero or more *headers* and a blank line to denote the end of headers (or just the blank line if there are no headers). Following the blank line is the *message body*.

Examining the request

The most important part of the request is the first line, known as the request line. This line defines the type of operation being requested by virtue of the command (or *verb*, as it is often called in HTTP terminology) present. In Figure 2-1, the verb used was POST, which along with the more common GET, entails the vast majority of requests.

The general structure of a request line looks like this (the parentheses and question mark indicate that the space and the protocol string are optional):

    verb SPACE resource (SPACE protocol)?

The verb is followed by some amount of blank space (spaces or tab characters but not newline or linefeed characters) and the desired resource. The resource is a URL, generally without the initial protocol and hostname information. They are removed because the connection is already made to the host and is being made via HTTP, so the protocol name and hostname are redundant at this point.*

Optionally, more space may follow the resource and then be followed by a protocol identifier. Referring again to Figure 2-1, the protocol request was for HTTP/1.1, which tells the server that the client is expecting support for elements of HTTP from the 1.1 standard. This implies that HTTP 1.0 may not be sufficient to handle the request.

Table 2-1 shows the common HTTP verbs. The verb of the request influences which headers are required versus optional. POST requests, for example, communicate the data of the request in the message body, which immediately follows the header information. In order for the server to know how much information there is to be read, the headers must tell the server what it needs to know. In HTTP 1.0, the only way to do this was to provide a header called Content-Length, which held the size (in bytes) of the content as an integer. HTTP 1.1 introduced more flexible approaches, mainly to support streaming media. Content-Transfer-Encoding and Content-Type are also commonly used to convey this kind of information. The latter header is generally required for POST requests so that the server knows whether it is receiving form data, a file upload, etc.

Table 2-1. HTTP request commands (verbs)

Command	Meaning
HEAD	A HEAD request is used to get the headers and response only for a given resource. It can check server availability or check the timestamp on cached data.
GET	The GET request is the most common for general web access. The URL contains all the information for the request, and the body is presumed empty (and ignored).

---

* The URL can be complete, but full URLs are usually seen only when the server also acts as a proxy, in which case any URL that isn't local is interpreted as a proxy request.

Table 2-1. HTTP request commands (verbs) (continued)

Command	Meaning
POST	A POST request sends data to an address that is generally not a document, but rather an application. Its use is almost certainly familiar to anyone who's written form-based CGI applications.

Most web-service models built upon HTTP use POST to send requests, simply because requests involve sending some data (the routine or method to be called, parameters to be passed, etc.). This shouldn't be taken as discounting the GET approach altogether. Some later examples will show how effective GET can be when dealing with a service that is built to suit that model.

Examining the response

When a server gets a request like the format described earlier, it must provide a response of some sort. The first line of the response indicates the status, and its structure is much simpler, though more free-form in some ways, than the first line of the request.

A response line looks like this:

    protocol SPACE status_code SPACE status_message

Here, the protocol portion of the response line usually reflects the same element from the request line (assuming it was present there at all). The protocol as specified in the response informs the client what type and version of communication is in use; the client can then interpret headers in the correct fashion.

Following the protocol is the *status code*, and after it, the *status message*. The codes and messages are defined in the HTTP specification, with allowances for locally defined codes in case no existing code fits a given situation. The message portion is less important than the numeric code and is more of a convenience to the human reader. Codes are all three digits long and are categorized by the leading digit. Table 2-2 explains the five groups of response codes.

Table 2-2. The five HTTP response code groups

Codes	Group	Examples
1xx	Informational	Code 100 indicates that the initial part of a request has been read, and the client should now continue with the remainder.
2xx	Successful client request	Most common is code 200, the general "success" code.
3xx	Redirected request (further action needed)	The 301 response code is frequently used to redirect browsers to a new URL.
4xx	Request incomplete or unsuccessful	404 is an all-too-familiar response when a page can't be found. The 401 code is also common; it signals the need for authentication to access a resource.
5xx	Server-side errors	This group is for cases in which the problem is a failure within the server; the most familiar code in this group is 500.

As with request messages, a response immediately follows the first line with any informational headers that are to be a part of the response. The range of headers is just as broad as for the request, with some names in both lists, `Content-Type` and `Content-Length`. Where the request is generally expected to identify itself with a `User-Agent` header, most servers can be relied upon to identify themselves with a `Server` header.

After the sequence of headers, the content of the response is presented. When the request is for a simple document, the response is generally just that document, with little or no modification. In fact, the content can really be anything the controllers of the server desire it to be. For applications, the content may be an HTML page, or some sort of data ranging from plain text to (in the case of most web services) XML-encoded data. The `Content-Type` header in the response identifies the type of data in the response body to the client.

Reading More About HTTP and LWP

The web site for the World Wide Web Consortium (*http://www.w3.org*) catalogs current specifications on almost all WWW-related technologies (all that they are developing or endorse), including many links to standards documents relating to HTTP. For more coverage, try *HTTP: The Definitive Reference* by David Gourley and Brian Totty, and *HTTP Pocket Reference* by Clinton Wong, both by O'Reilly.

Another O'Reilly title that may be of interest to developers of web services, in particular from the client side, is *Perl and LWP* by Sean M. Burke. This looks in-depth at programming HTTP applications using the powerful `LWP` (Library for WWW Programming in Perl) module. This book uses LWP only a little, as the toolkits handle the communications for you.

XML

The Extensible Markup Language, or XML, is arguably one of the most useful and important technologies to emerge as a result of HTML and the World Wide Web. While the basic concepts and theories behind it aren't very complicated, it has proven to be a critical tool in solving numerous problems, from providing neutral data representation between very different architectures, to bridging the gap between software systems with minimal effort.

Self-Describing Data

XML is often referred to as "self-describing data," because the XML version of the data contains information you'd otherwise use to describe the data format including: element/parameter names, structural relationships between elements, hierarchical relationships, and so forth. If the element tags (names) are chosen so as to be meaningful and descriptive, the resulting XML can often be read and reasonably understood separate from the applications that use it.

At the simplest level, understanding XML is a matter of understanding the definitions and roles of the three primary building blocks: elements, attributes, and data. There are other things that can appear in an XML file, and they're also explained in the following sections.

This XML fragment shows elements (book), attributes (isbn), and data ("Programming Web Services with Perl"):

```
<book isbn="0596002068">Programming Web Services with Perl</book>
```

Elements and namespaces

Elements are the building blocks of XML. To those familiar with HTML, elements are what make XML look like HTML at first glance. However, XML is very different from HTML, and much of the difference is in the rules governing the elements.

An element (also referred to interchangeably as a *tag*) is a name, or symbol, made up of alphabetic, numeric, and a handful of special characters (hyphens, underscores or periods). The very first character of an element name must be either alphabetic or an underscore; numbers or the other special characters can't start an element name. Also, the leading three characters can't be XML, in any combination of case. These are reserved for the W3C's use. Unlike HTML, the case of the letters is important: <Start>, <start> and <StArT> are all different tags in an XML document, and each would have matching closing tags </Start>, </start>, </StArT>, respectively. (But using tags so similar to each other is a good way to confuse others who use the data, so it isn't recommended.)

An element either contains data or is an *empty element*. An empty element is a special subtype of element that is defined from the outset to not contain any data (plain data or other elements). HTML introduced several empty tags: <img> for images, <hr> for horizontal rules, and <br> to force line breaks. Empty elements in XML look slightly different. They are denoted by putting the / character, which usually denotes the closing tag, before the closing > character; for example, the XHTML equivalents of the previous tags (XHTML is a reengineering of HTML4 in XML) look like: <img/>, <hr />, and <br/>. The presence or absence of a space between the tag name and the /> sequence is completely up to you—a matter of readability. It has no effect on the syntax of the element itself.

In the previous paragraph, XHTML was defined as a *use* of XML, which is also called an *application*. This is a case where the terminology of XML can sometimes be confusing. Programmers are used to the word "application" meaning a piece of software, a program (or collection of programs) that runs to provide some service or functionality. Here, it means a specific use of XML. Saying that XHTML is an XML application is the same as saying that it is an application of XML, in this case to the problem of defining HTML with the inherent strictness of XML.

An element isn't identified only by its name. Elements (and attributes, as will be shown in the next section) may also have a *namespace* associated with them. Namespaces associate tag names with specific XML applications especially in cases in which tag names might conflict with each other. An XML file may contain data expressed using elements from any number of different XML applications. The namespace prefixes are what keep the elements different enough to manage.

Namespaces are defined by declaring them within an opening tag. They may be associated with a specific prefix, which is then used on all elements governed by the namespace; or a default namespace may be declared. When a prefix is declared, the namespace is applied to an element by joining the prefix and the element name with a ":" character. An element may declare several namespaces at once, but may only declare one default. The snippet in Example 2-1 shows the declaration of two namespaces, including a default, and their application to different elements.

Example 2-1. Declaring namespaces within elements

```
<message xmlns="urn:namespace:example"
         xmlns:xsd="http://www.w3.org/2001/XMLSchema">
  <messageStructure>
    <xsd:schema>
      ...
    </xsd:schema>
  </messageStructure>
  <messageBody>
    ...
  </messageBody>
<message>
```

In this simple fragment, the opening tag, message, declares both a labeled namespace and a default. The default namespace applies to all tags that don't have a specific namespace label. The second namespace is associated with the label xsd, and uses the URI *http://www.w3.org/2001/XMLSchema*. All the elements with names that start with the characters xsd: are considered associated with that namespace. In the example, the schema element is linked to this namespace. Without the prefix, it would be in the same namespace as message, and the distinction between the description of a message and the declaration of a schema fragment might be lost.

If a tag doesn't declare a default namespace, it either inherits a default from the parent tag, or (if there is no default defined at any higher level) it's said to have an empty namespace. Likewise, it's not unusual to see XML documents that don't use default namespaces at all but instead declare their namespaces and explicitly qualify every element. This is common in SOAP messages, as you'll see in later chapters.

Attributes

Attributes provide information about an element, as opposed to the information the element itself provides (either in its contents, or merely by its presence). This is another case in which XML strays from the familiar ground of HTML; XML attributes always have a name and a value.

An attribute's name must follow the same rules as an element name; alphabetic, numeric, and a few special characters are all that are allowed. Just like elements, the leading character of an attribute must be alphabetic or an underscore. The value of an attribute must always be quoted, with either single or double quotes.

It is considered a good design principle to keep attributes focused on the element to which they are attached. Table 2-3 shows some examples of attributes, including some that violate this principle.

Table 2-3. Examples of attributes

Element and attribute	Notes
`<Text lang="english">`	Good; `lang` clearly refers to the language the content (text) of the element is in.
`<age units="years">`	Also good; the attribute assists applications in interpreting the content.
`<cost purch_order="3554">`	Dubious; the relevance of a purchase order number in a cost field is questionable. It represents data that probably should be associated with a higher-level element.
`<img src="a.gif" noborder />`	Bad; while empty tags are capable of having attributes, and `src` is a valid attribute, attributes can't be "empty" in the sense of having no value component, so `noborder` is invalid.

Besides the limitation of not using XML as the leading three characters of a name, there are some attribute names that are reserved in XML to have special meaning. These are shown in Table 2-4. An attribute may appear in a given element only once, but aside from that, their use and content are very flexible. XML entities (explained in the next section) expand within attribute values.

Table 2-4. Reserved attributes in XML

Attribute	Function
`xml:lang`	Specifies the (human) language the content of the element is in, such as en for English.
`xml:space`	Used to specify how the XML parser treats whitespace in an element's data.
`xml:link`	This conveys information to an XLink processor. XLink is a type of XML processing, beyond the scope of this book.
`xml:attributes`	Also related to XLink processing, this is used to remap attributes in cases in which there could be a conflict between names XLink is expecting to see. (This may be changed to `xlink:attributes` in a future revision of the relevant specifications.)

Attributes aren't generally given namespace qualification, unless the reference is to an attribute from a completely different XML application. In the previous examples of reserved attributes, all are prefixed with `xml:`, which is an indication that they belong to the core XML definition. In the previous explanation of namespaces, the declaration of a given namespace looked like an attribute whose name was `xmlns`.

Declaring a prefix for an attribute is a matter of using `xmlns` itself as a "prefix" for an attribute whose name is the desired prefix name, and whose value is the URI of the namespace:

```
xmlns:xsd="http://www.w3.org/2001/XMLSchema"
```

This example declares xsd as a prefix, but syntactically it can be confusing, given the fact that it looks more like an attribute itself. The later chapters on SOAP show elements using attributes from other sources to declare the datatype of an element by referencing a type attribute from the XML schema namespace, and in many cases by providing a value that is namespace-qualified into a related (but different) namespace.

Data

Data, the text within elements, is pretty much self-explanatory. The format and layout are up to the person who designed the XML structure. Data is the content between opening and closing tags of an element, minus specialized pieces such as processing instructions, comments, etc.

In many XML applications, data and elements aren't mixed as content. That is, element hierarchy is designed such that an element either contains data or other elements, but not both. The syntax of UDDI (Universal Description, Discovery and Integration, a technology related to SOAP and covered in a later chapter) is a good example of this sort of design. As a counter example, the DocBook XML application defines a wide range of elements, only some of which don't allow a mixture of data and other elements as their content.

A special kind of data is the XML *entity reference*. This is also a familiar syntax to those experienced with HTML. An entity reference is a sequence that starts with & and ends with ; with no space in between. While HTML supports a large number of entities, there are only five predefined entities in XML, shown in Table 2-5. XML allows the expression of characters using the entity syntax, with the Unicode value for the character as the contents between the delimiters. It may be in hexadecimal or decimal. These are also shown in Table 2-5.

Table 2-5. XML entities

Entity	Character	Notes
&amp;	&	Not allowed inside a processing instruction (see next section)
&lt;	<	Use inside attributes quoted with " " characters, to avoid processing problems
&gt;	>	Use after]] in ordinary text and inside processing instructions
&quot;	"	Can be used inside attributes quoted with " "

Table 2-5. XML entities (continued)

Entity	Character	Notes
&apos;	'	Can be used within attributes quoted with " "
&#*nnn*;	Variable	The character whose decimal Unicode value is *nnn* (with no leading zeros) is returned
&#x*nnn*;	Variable	The character whose hexadecimal Unicode value is *nnn* (with no leading zeros) is returned

A common mistake often made by people moving from HTML to XML is to assume all the same entities (such as é for é) are available. Depending on the parser and the application using it, the results may be a fatal error or the unknown entities discarded.

Comments, processing instructions, and specialized content

No language is complete without the ability to provide notes to the reader that don't interfere with the processing of the file itself, and XML is no exception to this rule. Comments in XML follow the same syntax as in HTML; they start with the sequence <!--, and end with the sequence -->.

Comments don't nest. A comment will end at the first occurrence of the closing sequence the parser finds, but the opening sequence may occur within the scope of the comment (and will be considered a part of the comment's text).

Processing instructions are special sequences that provide information to the application that is processing the XML document. They specify the type of processor that should receive the instruction, so an instruction for a XSLT (Extensible Stylesheet Language Template) processor is clearly marked as such and can then be discarded by an ordinary XML processor. A processing instruction looks like this:

    <?xml-stylesheet href="oreillystyle.xsl" type="text/xsl"?>

Note the special syntax of the opening and closing delimiters; <? and ?> are what denote a processing instruction. The string immediately following the opening delimiter is called the *target* of the instruction, and everything else is the *data*. The data is usually made up of attributes, like an ordinary element. But it doesn't have to be, and the instruction may have no data.

This instruction is the first line of most XML documents:

    <?xml version="1.0" encoding="iso-8859-1"?>

It tells the XML processor that the document requires the 1.0 version of the XML specification, and that the character set (or *encoding*) used to express the document is the ISO 8859-1 set, also known as "Latin-1." XML documents can use any recognizable character set, and the character set is what defines alphabetic and numeric characters, so <café> would be a valid element name in the given character set.

Lastly, there are some specialized sequences used in XML documents. Most are rarely, if ever, seen in the context of web services. However, they deserve mention.

One of these is the document type-declaration, <!DOCTYPE>. This is most often used when declaring a Document Type Declaration (DTD), but can also be used to declare entities. DTDs and entity declarations are covered in the next section.

Another type of specialized content is the CDATA section, which is used to express a segment of the document that shouldn't get any special processing. Within a CDATA section, entities aren't expanded, and elements aren't noted as anything other than character data. A CDATA section is initiated with the (complex) sequence, <![CDATA[, and continues until it sees the ending sequence,]]>.

Describing XML with DTD and XML Schema

XML documents have two levels of correctness: *well-formed* and *valid*. Well-formed simply means that the document is structurally sound, that all opening tags have matching closing tags, that elements don't overlap each other, and so forth. Most parsers will generate errors otherwise (depending on whether the parser is built to be tolerant of the faults). Being valid is a different subject completely.

An XML document may be associated with a description document, a metadocument of sorts, against which it can be validated. Validation ensures that the elements that appear are allowed in the XML application the document supposedly represents, and that the order in which they appear is also permitted. Validation checks attributes and if data content is and isn't permitted.

There are different methods for expressing the valid syntax of an XML document, and this section will address the two most common: the DTD and the XML Schema representation.

The DTD

Initially, the Document Type Declaration was the only tool for describing an XML application. The DTD is an inherited syntax from XML's (and HTML's) roots in SGML, the Standard Generalized Markup Language. DTDs have the advantage of a wide range of SGML-oriented tools already in the marketplace.

A DTD can declare elements, attributes, and entities. Further, the way entities are declared and used often make DTDs more clear and concise. Example 2-2 shows a sample DTD.

Example 2-2. A typical DTD layout

```
<!ENTITY % container '(name, version?, hidden?, signature+,
                       help?, package?, code)' >

<!ELEMENT  proceduredef   %container; >
<!ELEMENT  methoddef      %container; >
<!ELEMENT  functiondef    %container; >
```

Example 2-2. A typical DTD layout (continued)

```
<!ELEMENT    name           (#PCDATA) >
<!ELEMENT    version        (#PCDATA) >
<!ELEMENT    hidden         EMPTY >
<!ELEMENT    signature      (#PCDATA) >
<!ELEMENT    help           (#PCDATA) >
<!ELEMENT    code           (#PCDATA) >
<!ATTLIST    code           language (#PCDATA) >
```

This example doesn't use all the features that a DTD may exhibit. The first declaration defines an entity, similar in nature to the &, which is already familiar to HTML developers. Like the character entities, container acts as a macro expansion. In the next three declarations, three elements are defined. Each can have the same sort of content, the sequence of elements defined by the container entity. This gives the visual effect of "defining" these elements as "containers." In fact, they are meant as the three choices for the document's top-most element, hence the association.

Example 2-2 is meant only to provide a rough overview of the syntax. The DTD is fading in popularity against the XML Schema language. Many books specifically on XML still cover DTD syntax in its entirety, however, such as *XML in a Nutshell* by Elliotte Rusty Harold and W. Scott Means (O'Reilly).

XML Schema

The XML Schema language is a much more flexible, and therefore much more complex, method of describing document content. It is covered in greater detail in a later section; here are some of the reasons for choosing it over DTD syntax.

First and foremost, XML Schema is a complete XML application, unlike the DTD syntax. A schema document can be parsed and processed as XML, whereas the tools for handling DTDs are confined mainly to the SGML world. This means that the same tools being used by the software application itself can also manage the syntax description. This is reason enough in many cases.

As an XML application, XML Schema also integrates more easily with other XML applications. SOAP uses XML Schema datatypes as the basis for data modeling in remote method calls. WSDL, the Web Services Definition Language (covered in a later chapter), uses XML Schema directly within WSDL files to provide the description of complex elements and datatypes used within the service description.

XML Schema isn't the only post-DTD description format, but it has the endorsement and backing of the W3C organization, which has lent it a great deal of momentum and credibility. The syntax and structure of XML Schema is covered later in this chapter.

XML Modules and Tools for Perl

Perl has a multitude of XML-related tools. In many cases, the challenge isn't whether a module exists to solve a given task, but rather which of the available modules would be the best choice. Since this book is less focused on XML itself, this section will just briefly examine some of the parsing-related tools. In fact, the toolkits for XML-RPC and SOAP that are available on CPAN abstract the underlying XML parser from the user, freeing the programmer to focus on other issues.

XML::Parser

This parser was the first XML parser for Perl. Larry Wall, Perl's author, developed its earlier incarnations. Over the years, the responsibility for its maintenance has changed hands several times, but it remains a very fast parser. It is built around the Expat parser library for C written by James Clark.

The parser itself suffers from certain drawbacks and limitations. It doesn't have full namespace support because these weren't part of the XML suite of specifications when Expat was written. It uses an event model that was designed before XML experts settled on the SAX (Simple API for XML) and SAX2 models. Thus, while the event model is similar, it isn't fully compatible with SAX or SAX2. Furthermore, the parser don't validate; it detects only whether a document is well-formed or not.

This shouldn't be taken as a condemnation, however. Many XML-based packages on CPAN are built around this parser, and it has become more and more portable as time has gone on. This parser is a useful tool that will continue to be used for some time to come.

XML::LibXML and XML::LibXSLT

The new kid on the XML parsing block is the XML::LibXML module. This is a validating parser built around a C library for parsing XML called simply libxml2. The C library itself integrates smoothly with a second library called libxslt, which applies XSLT transformations to XML based on stylesheet inputs. As such, the XML::LibXSLT package is usually also installed at the same time XML::LibXML is.

This parser is also very fast, and forms the basis for a SAX/SAX2 package available through CPAN. More and more tools are being built around this parser due to the more advanced features offered through libxml2 over Expat. The interface offered by this package gives the user a choice of parsing based on either DOM (the Document Object Model) or SAX events.

XML::SAX

Where the XML::LibXML parser supports a parsing style that emits SAX or SAX2 events, the XML::SAX package provides a more thorough implementation of the SAX and SAX2 models for developers to use. It can use the XML::LibXML parser as its basis, shoring it up with packages to manage namespaces. It also provides a pure-Perl implementation of a SAX-compliant parser programs can fall back on if the faster parser isn't available.

XML::XPath, XML::Simple, and others

There are modules that offer alternatives to the SAX-based approaches to XML parsing. The W3C defined the XPath syntax as a way of referencing data within large XML documents using a path syntax based on the element names and attributes. The `XML::XPath` module implements the XPath syntax completely, while attempting to provide a means for other packages to add in extensions. It uses `XML::Parser` as the base parsing engine for the documents themselves.

Another XML module worth noting is the `XML::Simple` package. This package provides one of the most simple, basic interfaces to XML available. It converts XML data to a hash-table structure, maintaining as much of the inherent nature of the data as it can. Though not suitable for more intense projects, such as handling SOAP messages, this package manages to meet the needs of many software projects.

This only scratches the surface of the XML tools available in Perl. The `XML::RSS` package was referred to earlier in the LWP programming example, and later chapters cover XML-based modules for XML-RPC and SOAP. Full details about parsing XML with Perl are provided in the book *Perl & XML* by Erik T. Ray and Jason McIntosh (O'Reilly).

Using XML in an application means trading off efficiency in speed and memory for such flexibility. Most XML parsers add significantly to the size and performance of an application, and XML data itself is larger in storage size than the same data would be if maintained in a more compact, application-specific format. XML is best used in those places where the benefits outweigh the drawbacks, such as sharing data between several different applications or languages.

XML Schema

The XML Schema language is the specification that the W3C organization developed to replace the DTD as the preferred way to describe the content and structure of XML documents. While the DTD still has a well-established place in XML technologies, schemas are being used by more and more applications. The overall acceptance of the XML Schema format continues to grow at a steady pace.

In general, you have to read this section only if you're planning to read the chapters detailing the low-down and dirty details of SOAP, WSDL, and UDDI. Those three standards build heavily on the XML Schema Language. If you're planning on letting toolkits do all the heavy lifting for you, you can flip straight past this to Chapter 3 and enjoy the simple life.

Why Replace the DTD?

The main argument against the DTD is simple: it isn't XML. The DTD structure was inherited from HTML's roots in SGML, which itself is designed to solve a much wider range of problems. Thus, the syntax and structure of the DTD has to manage and support this flexibility that XML itself doesn't use or need.

The DTD still has some benefits over XML Schema:

- A DTD is generally simpler and smaller in size than the schema describing the same structure.
- XML Schema don't provide a way to define named text entities, such as é for the character é.
- While being an XML application is a boon for XML Schema, the selection of available tools still heavily favors DTD. This factor can be expected to change over time, however.

The main area in which XML Schema wins out over the DTD is in expressing more complex structures and relationships. While a DTD can express the same level of complexity, the complexity of the DTD itself grows at an alarming rate. The XML Schema language has very rich support not just for defining elements and types themselves, but also for defining them by extending and expanding upon existing structures.

The schema approach also can define the format and constraints on the data in elements. Beyond simply stating whether an element contains character data, other elements, or a mix, this ability means putting specific limitations on what is allowed for a element's content. For example, if an element is declared as being of type integer (one of the predefined basic types, covered later), this means that if a document is validated against the schema, the content must contain a numerical value with no decimal (or fractional) parts. Types may define their constraints and conditions using a wide range of techniques.

Document structure versus data structure

A schema can define not only the components of the overall document structure but can also describe complex structured data. The data structures may then be used to describe the document itself. These definitions are distinct from each other, making it possible to have both a dataRecord that is an element, and a dataRecord that describes a complex data structure.

It is this data-centric approach that truly separates schemas from DTDs. With a DTD, the structural relationship can be described, but the distinction between data and description is lost. There is nothing that classifies the elements themselves within a DTD, so all definitions are treated exactly the same way.

Understanding more about XML Schema

The rest of the material in this chapter covers the high points of the schema language, but a complete coverage is beyond the scope of the book, let alone a single chapter. The schema specifications are on the W3C's web site (*http://www.w3c.org*), and in addition to this there is an O'Reilly book devoted exclusively to the topic, *XML Schema*. The actual coverage of the schema language in this book is limited to the topics related to SOAP and its aggregate technologies such as WSDL (covered in more detail in Chapter 9).

Schema Components

A schema is built up from a collection of components. These components are classified in the formal specification as belonging to one of three groups, as illustrated in Table 2-6. The primary components are those most often seen in practice, but depending on the role the schema is intended to play, not all the primary components may be present.

Schemas can be used with other technologies such as WSDL to provide definitions of datatypes without actually defining the overall document structure. In fact, WSDL uses a schema description to describe its overall document layout but defers the definitions of types to an XML application outside of WSDL, such as XML Schema itself.

Table 2-6. Groups of XML Schema components

Group	Types of components
Primary components	Simple type definitions
	Complex type definitions
	Attribute declarations
	Element declarations
Secondary components	Attribute group definitions
	Identity-constraint definitions
	Model group definitions
	Notation declarations
"Helper" components	Annotations
	Model groups
	Particles
	Wildcards
	Attribute uses

A schema document uses a top-level container element called schema and a namespace http://www.w3.org/2001/XMLSchema. Some schema documents may refer to the earlier namespace that was used, http://www.w3.org/2000/10/XMLSchema, but the newer should be used for any new descriptions being written.

The predefined simple types

Before exploring the tools by which a schema author defines a document structure, you need to understand the basic types that XML Schema provides. All other definitions, whether they describe elements or attributes or new types, must reference some existing type (either supplied by XML Schema or declared elsewhere within the document). All new types are *extensions of*, or *restrictions upon*, existing types.

The specification for XML Schema has two parts, the second of which[*] is focused specifically on the datatypes that are provided as a starting point. The types themselves reflect the general functionality of a broad set of programming languages and tools. They exist both as components to be used directly within a schema and as building blocks from which to derive more specific types as the need presents itself.

The full list of predefined basic types is too long to reproduce here in full. Table 2-7 highlights the list of types, showing both obvious basic concepts (numeric variations) and the more detailed and specialized types (date expressions, URIs).

Table 2-7. A subset of types defined by XML Schema

Type	Example	Description
string	Any character-based sequence	The `string` type covers the range of character data, allowing for facets that define properties such as minimum or maximum length, etc.
boolean	true, false, 1, 0	The `boolean` type illustrates a primitive that is an enumeration, allowing only the four values shown as examples.
decimal	123.456, –5, +100.0	The `decimal` is one of three primitive numerical types (the other two being `float` and `double`). It defines numbers in terms of digits to the left and right of a decimal point, and an optional sign. Exponential notations aren't permitted; they're left instead to the other numerical primitives.
dateTime	2002-07-19T09:16:58	The `dateTime` is one of the more detailed type specifications. It provides for dates in ISO 8601 format.
anyURI	http://www.oreilly.com	The `anyURI` field is just that: a kind of string that describes a URI, whether relative or absolute. It may include fragment specifications (reference parts), etc.
base64Binary	(No example; imagine a really large, Base64–encoded PNG image)	This type allows for defining elements that are used to contain binary data encoded using the well-known Base64 algorithm.
integer int	1, 32768, etc.	These show two generations of derivation from the previous `decimal` type. The `integer` type is a restriction of `decimal` that has no decimal point or following digits. The `int` type further restricts this by limiting the range to between 2147483647 and –2147483648, inclusive. This is the range of a signed, 32-bit integer (the C `int`).

---

[*] http://www.w3.org/TR/xmlschema-2/

Table 2-7. A subset of types defined by XML Schema (continued)

Type	Example	Description
NMTOKEN	_Name, longerName, soap:Envelope	The NMTOKEN is an expression of that type from the XML specification itself. This is a derivation of token, which is a derivation of normalizedString, which is derived from string. It represents the same type of name that the NMTOKEN specification in a DTD does.

Note that the last two rows of examples represented derivations of earlier types. The specification of schema types provides 19 primitive types, and 25 types derived from these primitives. Each type represents some important basic form from the perspective of XML or XML Schema. While some may seem to be redundant at first glance, a closer look reveals that they each have a distinct role to play.

Primary components

The primary components are those that define elements, attributes, and types (both simple and complex). Type declarations aren't required to have names, but attributes and elements must be named.

Each type of components may be considered *local* or *global*, depending on where they fall within the schema document. Items that are direct children of the top-level schema element are considered global. Any components that are nested within other structures are considered local to their containing structure. Whether to make a particular component global or local is as much a part of the design process as choosing content itself. Global parts may be referenced and reused within other parts of the schema, where local parts can't. Global elements also have the advantage of being candidates for the top-level element in any document based on the schema. Likewise, keeping an element local instead of global may be a method of keeping it from being used as a top-level container.

Attributes

Attributes are declared with the attribute element, which itself uses attributes to provide the basic information about the new component. The attribute's name, type, and use are the most commonly seen attributes in these definitions, with the addition of ref, which serves a special function. The name and type attributes define the name of the new attribute, as well as its type. The type must be one of the simple types available to the schema, either from the basic set provided by the XML Schema specification or one defined elsewhere in the schema itself.

The name must conform to what is known as a NCName in schema terms. That is simply a name (following the usual character limitations) that don't contain a colon (:) anywhere within. This prevents conflict with the name possibly being referenced by full namespace qualification at some future point.

The use attribute defines the nature of the attribute's use within the element it (eventually) gets associated with: a value of optional (the default) means that the attribute's presence in the element is optional. A value of required is the opposite, requiring that the attribute always be present on the given element. The last value is prohibited, which keeps an attribute from being inherited when a new type is being derived from some existing type (normally, as with class inheritance, all the class information would propagate to the new derived class, or type as in this case).

The ref attribute allows a complex definition to refer to attributes defined in other parts of the schema. Example 2-3 illustrates how ref defines an attribute only once, while actually using it in many places. This attribute can also define elements and types, so it will be seen in several places.

Elements

Elements are defined using a tag called element. They also feature name and type attributes, as well as a host of others (that aren't usually present in simple WSDL or SOAP applications). It may also use the ref attribute to define a local instance of a globally defined element. The name must also be a NCName, as with attribute declarations. The other attributes that warrant mentioning are used to define elements: minOccurs and maxOccurs.

When an element is defined as a local part of a type declaration, these attributes can specify minimum or maximum times the element can occur. If minOccurs is 0, the element isn't required to be present. If maxOccurs is set to unbounded, the element may appear as many times as desired.*

Since elements are generally expected to be more complex than attributes, the type of an element may be any defined type in the schema. This includes the basic types provided by the specification as well as any defined within the schema itself. The type attribute may be skipped if the type information is going to be given within the element block itself.

Simple and complex types

Defining types is necessarily more complex than defining elements or attributes. There are two categories of type definition: *simple* and *complex*. Simple types don't allow attributes or nested elements within them. Complex types may have attributes, elements, data or any combination of those components. Complex types may even be built up from other complex or simple types.

Simple types have one aspect to them complex types don't: a simple type is always a derivation of some sort, based on a previous type. A new simple type may be defined

---

* In earlier versions of XML Schema, the character * was also used to express an unbounded value for maxOccurs.

by declaring itself a *restriction* of an existing type. This is much like subclassing. Alternately, the new type may be defined as a list of some other type, or a union of several types. A single named type can be defined in terms of only one of these three derivations. But a type may be defined, then derived from using any or all of the three methods in other type declarations.

Types, simple or complex, aren't required to have names if the definition is made at a local level. Global types must have names, and these names may then be used to define the type of attributes or elements or even as the basis for defining other types. Like elements and attributes, the type declaration tags (`simpleType` and `complexType`) use an attribute called name to define this part of the component.

Complex types are at once more and less difficult than simple types. Less difficult in that a complex type can be smaller than a simple type in the number of elements that declare it. However, you can do much more with complex types, so a complex type definition can easily be larger than a simple type.

A complex type can also define itself as a restriction of a base type (which must be a complex type as well). A new complex type may also define itself as an *extension* of an existing type, a concept that has no counterpart in simple types. Where a restriction generally narrows the scope of what a type can express, an extension adds more content to a complex type. Still, both are very similar in nature to the relationship between parent classes and subclasses in object-oriented programming languages, which was the intent of the developers of XML Schema.

A complex type is declared in some cases where it would seem that the type should be simple, such as when attributes are going to be part of the data representation. The `complexType` container has a child element called `simpleContent` that is used in these cases, when the main goal is to overcome the limitation of `simpleType` without defining an overly complex structure. A `simpleContent` container may declare itself as extending a base (simple) type, or restricting one.

When it comes to defining a complex type in terms of complex content, there are a range of elements that can be used. These are summarized in Table 2-8.

Table 2-8. Complex type declaration elements

Element	Role	Notes
sequence	Defines a list (sequence) of content parts that are ordered with regards to each other.	While the order within a sequence is a part of the definition of it, elements within it may still be defined with minOccurs of 0, allowing for individual elements to be optional.
Choice	Defines a component that will be one of a set of specified choices. Only one choice appears at a time.	One at a time, but the element itself typed with the choice declaration may appear multiple times.

Table 2-8. Complex type declaration elements (continued)

Element	Role	Notes
all	Like sequence, this declares a set of parts that appear together. However, order isn't mandated here, and each part may only appear exactly once or not at all.	The all content description is meant for cases in which other types would be too unwieldy. It has other restrictions besides the number limitation; the parts listed within an all may be only elements, not other types or other core components.

Three elements may not seem to present an intimidating number of combinations, until you consider the fact that all these may appear as subdescriptions within the types being declared by any other format (even all, which can only contain element components, may have elements with anonymous type declarations).

A unified example schema

Example 2-3 shows the use of elements, attributes, and cross references between them. It partially describes a XML syntax for expressing Concurrent Version Control (CVS) operations. Remember that this is only a fraction of the full expressiveness of XML Schema, but more than this is outside the scope of the book.

Example 2-3. XML Schema syntax samples

```
<?xml version="1.0"?>
<xsd:schema targetNamespace="urn:schema-samples"
            xmlns:xsd="http://www.w3.org/2001/XMLSchema">

  <!-- A basic attribute declaration -->
  <xsd:attribute name="lang" type="xsd:string" />
  <!-- An attribute with local (anonymous) typing -->
  <xsd:attribute name="lines">
    <xsd:simpleType>
      <xsd:restriction base="xsd:unsignedInt">
        <xsd:maxInclusive value="256000" />
      </xsd:restriction>
    </xsd:simpleType>
  </xsd:attribute>
  <!-- A simple type using enumeration -->
  <xsd:simpleType name="programming.lang">
    <xsd:restriction base="xsd:string">
      <xsd:enumeration value="C" />
      <xsd:enumeration value="Perl" />
      <xsd:enumeration value="PHP" />
      <xsd:enumeration value="Java" />
    </xsd:restriction>
  </xsd:simpleType>
  <!-- A more complex type, using some of the above -->
  <xsd:complexType name="SoftwareModule">
    <xsd:simpleContent>
      <xsd:attribute name="code.language"
                     type="programming.lang" />
```

Example 2-3. XML Schema syntax samples (continued)

```
      <xsd:attribute name="comment.language" type="lang" />
      <xsd:attribute ref="lines" />
    </xsd:simpleContent>
  </xsd:complexType>
  <!-- Defining an element using the previous type at this
       level allows for a document referencing this schema
       to use the element as a top-level container -->
  <element name="code" type="CodeModule" />
  <!-- Now define an even more complex type -->
  <xsd:complexType name="CVS.Checkin">
    <xsd:sequence>
      <xsd:element name="module" type="xsd:string" />
      <xsd:element name="credentials">
        <xsd:complexType>
          <xsd:choice>
            <xsd:element name="pserver "
                         type="xsd:string" />
            <xsd:sequence>
              <xsd:element name="name" type="xsd:string" />
              <xsd:element name="password"
                           type="xsd:string" />
            </xsd:sequence>
          </xsd:choice>
        </xsd:complexType>
      </xsd:element>
      <xsd:element name="file" type="xsd:string" />
      <xsd:element ref="code" />
    </xsd:sequence>
  </xsd:complexType>
  <element name="checkin" type="CVS.Checkin" />
</xsd:schema>
```

While the example is admittedly contrived, it does show how the various components can work together. Example 2-4 shows a simple XML document that follows this schema

Example 2-4. A CVS operation in XML

```
<?xml version="1.0"?>
<checkin xmlns="CVS-Schema.xsd">
  <module>perl-web-examples</module>
  <credentials><pserver>...</pserver></credentials>
  <file>perl/server.pl</file>
  <code code.language="Perl" comment.language="en-US">
    # The Perl code would go here
  </code>
</checkin>
```

Both the code and checkin elements are declared at the top level, making them global definitions. The type declarations that define the elements are also global. The type that defines the code.language attribute, programming.lang, is defined as an enumeration. This means that "perl" would not have been acceptable as a value for the attribute.

Note the nesting that takes place around the definition of the `credentials` element: the content of this element will be one of an element called `pserver` that contains a string or a sequence of two elements (`name` and `password`, both strings). Using the `choice` construct here also contributes to future flexibility: if the set of choices is extended to include SSH (Secure SHell) key information or digest-authentication tokens, the existing choices are still valid in all the documents that already exist.

XML Schema in SOAP and Related Areas

XML Schema is important not just because of the momentum it has in the effort to replace the DTD. The SOAP specification uses basic datatypes from the schema specifications. Service descriptions written using WSDL relegate the description of datatypes to an external application without specifying a specific one. In practice, though, XML Schema is the dialect of choice for WSDL type detail. Even the basic types in XML-RPC are based on the same precursor documents that led to XML Schema, such as the XML Data specification.

Fortunately, the core elements of schema declarations tend to be clear and self-explanatory. The specification also allows for a documentation element, called `annotation`, to be present at almost all levels of a schema document.* While there are a lot of pieces to the schema puzzle that aren't covered here, the basics that were presented should help you through the majority of schemas in general, and a good part of the structure of more complex schemas (even if repeated referencing of the W3C specifications are necessary).

Schemas aren't limited to SOAP and WSDL in their use. More and more, XML applications are being defined in terms of schema rather than DTD. The Electronic Business XML (ebXML) initiative, an alternative approach to web services (in place of SOAP) between businesses, uses multiple schema documents to define the structure of its multitiered architecture.

---

* Subject, of course, to the limited inclination of developers to comment their code.

CHAPTER 3
Introduction to XML-RPC

XML-RPC is a web services protocol that implements remote procedure calls over HTTP. While it doesn't have the advanced feature set of SOAP or CORBA, its simplicity makes it easy to implement and use.

This chapter introduces the main concepts and limitations of XML-RPC, and describes how XML-RPC uses XML and HTTP. If you plan to use a toolkit, you need to read only the first part of the chapter about the concepts in XML-RPC. If you're going to do it all yourself, read not only the concepts sections but also the XML and HTTP sections, and the sample client section about the Meerkat service.

History of XML-RPC

XML-RPC was designed primarily by Dave Winer of UserLand Software, Inc. He was one of the designers working on the SOAP specification and became frustrated with the mounting complexity. He wanted something to use immediately, but SOAP was taking a long time to coalesce. So he forked off what was then an early working draft of the SOAP protocol, and this became what is now known as XML-RPC.

The first implementation of the specification was in Userland's Frontier product, a content management system with scripting, object database, and server capabilities. This was introduced in April 1998, and eventually the specification was published to encourage the development of other compliant toolkits. Currently, there are 65 implementations in languages ranging from AppleScript to Zope. There are toolkits for Lisp, Ruby, Eiffel, Scheme, Dylan, and an impressive seven different implementations for PHP. Perl features three different implementations, which will be covered in-depth in Chapter 4.

The web site for XML-RPC, *http://www.xmlrpc.com*, is a good source for more history of the specification. It also features links to various toolkits and the current specification as well.

The XML in XML-RPC

XML-RPC uses a simple XML application to express function calls (requests) and returned values (responses) between clients and servers. The heart of an XML-RPC message is the way data is encoded into XML.

Data encoding

Data is at the core of any interface, since the first and foremost goal is to send information between two points. XML-RPC supports six basic datatypes in messages (seven, technically, since i4 and int may be considered distinct), and also supports serialization of arrays and structures (name/value pairs just like Perl's hashes). The data types are explained in Table 3-1.

Table 3-1. The XML-RPC datatypes

Name/Tag	Sample value	Description
`<int>` or `<i4>`	12, -1, 65536, etc.	The int and i4 types express 32-bit signed integer values. They are functionally the same, but if a server is expecting one of the two, it may not always accept the other encoding.
`<double>`	-2.7182818284, 3.14159265358979	The double tag describes double-precision floating-point data. The expression may only consist of the sign, digits, and the decimal point. The specification doesn't provide for exponential notation.
`<string>`	"XYZ", etc.	Data marked with the string tag is meant to be unedited character data. The only characters not directly allowed are & and <, which are entity-encoded as & and <.
`<boolean>`	0 or 1	The boolean type expresses the typical boolean true/false range using the values 1 and 0, respectively. While Perl lets you test general scalars for truth/falseness, this isn't true of many other languages.
`<dateTime.iso8601>`	20020726T02:50:54	Date and time values are expressed according to the ISO 8601 standard, and the type used for this is called dateTime.iso8601. This is covered in depth later.
`<base64>`	Any Base64-encoded blob of data	The Base64 type was added to the spec in a later revision, to support binary data that doesn't fit easily into the others.

Aside from the base64 and dateTime.iso8601 types, the tags should be very self-explanatory. Some confusion may come from the int versus i4 tags, but these are only distinct in applications that check the actual encoding type information. Some servers are more strict about this than others, but those that are generally publish detailed descriptions of their interface, so the information is available to make the correct choice.

The base64 type was added in an update to the specification in early 1999. It allows for arbitrary data (images, digital audio, etc.) to be encoded using the widely accepted Base64 algorithm. The content between the opening and closing tags is considered to be the complete encoded entity (no allowance is made for breaking up large blobs into smaller chunks), not including any whitespace immediately before or after the data itself. Arbitrary whitespace can't appear within the Base64 data. If you ever need to process the Base64 data yourself, the `MIME::Base64` module for Perl provides functions to encode and decode strings. Since the toolkits all handle this transparently, it won't be covered here.

The choice of the `dateTime.iso8601` tag may seem curious at first, but the ISO 8601 standard allows for specification of dates and times in all time zones (by expressing them as offsets from UTC, Coordinated Universal Time). The syntax of that standard allows for partial specification of time only, date only, etc. It's a fairly flexible format with wide acceptance in the Web and Internet communities.

All the datatypes are expressed in XML using their tag name. None use any attributes, and none are valid as empty elements. The fragment in Example 3-1 shows each of the types in XML format:

Example 3-1. The XML-RPC datatypes in XML

```
<int>255</int>

<i4>-2147483648</i4>

<double>3.14159265358979</double>

<string>XML-RPC &amp; Perl</string>

<boolean>0</boolean>

<dateTime.iso8601>20020726T02:50:54</dateTime.iso8601>

<base64>
  SnVzdCBBbm90aGVyIFBlcmwgQm9vaw==
</base64>
<!-- What did that say? "Just Another Perl Book" -->
```

Note that the string example decodes as `XML-RPC & Perl`. Data elements of type string may contain any characters, including nonprintable and null characters. The XML-RPC layer defines the string as the contents between the opening and closing tags (not including leading and trailing whitespace). This doesn't change the fact that if one end of the conversation is written in a language that stumbles over unusual characters (such as C might with embedded null characters), a problem can then arise. These things can't be mandated away by the specification, however, and must instead be handled by the toolkit authors when (and where) necessary.

Arrays and structures

The array and struct datatypes are how XML-RPC expresses complex data. These constructions can serialize almost any array or hash table Perl can produce (except for objects). Both structures allow for recursive embedding of structures, so an array's element may be a struct with a member element that contains yet another array, and so on.

The array element serializes data when the only distinguishing factor between two elements is their place within the order. Elements in an array don't have to all be of the same type. An array element contains one child, a data element. Even when an array has zero actual elements, the data container must be present.

Within the data container are zero or more value elements, each of which contains one item of data. Example 3-2 shows a basic array structure.

Example 3-2. A simple array structure

```
<array>
  <data>
    <value><int>255</int></value>
    <value><double>3.14159265358979</double></value>
    <value><i4>-2147483648</i4></value>
    <value><string>XML-RPC &amp; Perl</string></value>
    <value>
      <array>
        <data>   <!-- An array with zero elements -->
        </data>
      </array>
    </value>
    <value>A string with no wrapping tag</value>
  </data>
</array>
```

In this example, an empty array was embedded in at what would be element 4 (assuming the count starts at 0). The example also showed a shortcut that the specification permits: within a value element, if the type of data being serialized is string, the type-specific tags are optional. In Perl, this array looks like this:

```
@array = (255, 3.14159265358979, -2147483648, 'XML-RPC & Perl', [],
          'A string with no wrapping tag');
```

Expressing the struct type of data isn't much more complex than the array. The main difference is that the elements of a struct are named key/value pairs, just like Perl's hashes. A struct contains zero or more instances of a container called member. A member container holds two elements, the first, called name, and the second, called value. The value element is treated just as it is within an array, as you saw earlier. The name element is functionally the same as a string, but it isn't explicitly typed as such. The specification defines no limitations on the characters that can appear within the name element.

As with Perl's hashes, the order of the key/value pairs isn't guaranteed, so nothing about the order of the serialization should be assumed to mean anything to the actual data itself. Example 3-3 shows a simple struct expression.

Example 3-3. A simple sample struct expression

```
<struct>
  <member>
    <name>pi</name>
    <value><double>3.14159265358979</double></value>
  </member>
  <member>
    <name>min.signed.int</name>
    <value><i4>-2147483648</i4></value>
  </member>
  <member>
    <name>publisher</name>
    <value>O'Reilly &amp; Associates</value>
  </member>
  <member>
    <name>nested array</name>
    <value>
      <array>
        <data>
        </data>
      </array>
    </value>
  </member>
  <member>
    <name>nested struct</name>
    <value>
      <struct></struct>
    </value>
  </member>
</struct>
```

Unlike the array expression, an empty struct has no elements within it. Example 3-3 matches the following Perl:

```
%hash = (pi => 3.14159265358979, `min.signed.int' => -2147483648,
         publisher => "O'Reilly & Associates", `nested array' => [],
         `nested struct' => {});
```

Making a request

Data is useful, but data alone doesn't constitute a request. When a client makes a request to a service, it must inform the server at the other end what remote procedure (or *method,* in the language of the XML-RPC specification) it wishes to call. Within the call, any parameters that need to be passed as arguments to the procedure are encoded.

Requests are also expressed in simple XML structure. The top-level element of the XML document is methodCall when encoding a request. It has one required child element and one optional element. The required element is methodName, and it contains the name of the method being called on the remote server. The name may contain only alphanumeric characters, underscore (_), period (.), colon (:), and slash (/)

characters. As with other identifiers, the leading character of the name must be either an alphabetic character or an underscore. Many XML-RPC services use the period to denote namespaces, so seeing method names such as system.listMethods is common.

The optional element is called params; it's used when the procedure call has one or more parameters. It may be present even when there are no parameters, because the specification allows params to be empty. Toolkits for XML-RPC must allow for the case of an empty parameter list in their deserialization.

Within params are zero or more containers called param. Within each param container is exactly one value element, governed by the same rules as before. Example 3-4 illustrates this.

Example 3-4. A simple request message

```
<?xml version="1.0"?>
<methodCall>
  <methodName>user.create</methodName>
  <params>
    <param>
      <value>
        <struct>
          <member>
            <name>user_id</name>
            <value>rjray</value>
          </member>
          <member>
            <name>password</name>
            <value>bad_password!</value>
          </member>
          <member>
            <name>age</name>
            <value><int>34</int></value>
          </member>
        </struct>
      </value>
    </param>
    <param>
      <value>www.blackperl.com</value>
    </param>
  </params>
</methodCall>
```

In the example, a routine called user.create is called with two parameters, a struct and a string. The struct has three members in it, the first two of which are string types, while the third is an int. In this example, the data represents new user information in the structure, followed by the host or domain in the second argument. The indentation is purely for readability; most toolkits don't make any effort to maintain indention levels in the XML they generate. Also, the initial line required by an XML document is present in this example. Since an XML-RPC message must be valid XML, this line must always be present.

Even as the number of parameters and their complexity increases, the request will still look basically like Example 3-4. This simplicity in XML-RPC is what has given it a strong following, even after the SOAP specifications were unveiled and updated over time.

Creating a response

In any client/server model, the request is only half of the story. Fortunately, as simple as the request XML structure itself is, the response structure is even simpler.

The response is much more straightforward because the response format is stricter than the request. Requests have to specify the remote procedure or method name, and they must contend with specifying lists of arguments. A response always returns exactly one value. There are no responses with no return parameter (the equivalent of a C function returning void, for example).

The single return value is passed back to the client within a methodResponse top-level element, which contains a params element with a single param container. Example 3-5 shows a simple response message.

Example 3-5. A typical XML-RPC response

```
<?xml version="1.0"?>
<methodResponse>
  <params>
    <param>
      <value><int>1</int></value>
    </param>
  </params>
</methodResponse>
```

While it is true that the structure of the response message contains several elements that may seem redundant, it allows for a simpler definition of content bodies by keeping the placement and role of params consistent across both requests and responses. Though the XML-RPC specification provides neither a formal DTD or schema, several other parties have crafted their own for use with other XML-related tools, and the structure of the messages lend themselves to clear and simple expression.

Of course, while a return value may only be a single item, it can be a structure or array value. And as with requests, the contents of a structure or array may be arbitrarily deep and complex. Later in the chapter, the value of this rule will be demonstrated when discussing overloading of methods (procedures) and server-side call management.

Sending an error response

Needless to say, not every procedure will run without error. Such errors have to be easily distinguished from successful calls. In the next section, which discusses the HTTP communication, you'll see how the HTTP response code can't be used to signal a procedure-level error. Instead, XML-RPC has a syntax for marking a response as an error. This is called a *fault*. Since a client can't request a fault (obviously), this only applies to response messages.

Example 3-6 illustrates a typical fault message.

Example 3-6. A fault message for XML-RPC

```
<?xml version="1.0"?>
<methodResponse>
  <fault>
    <value>
      <struct>
        <member>
          <name>faultCode</name>
          <value><int>404</int></value>
        </member>
        <member>
          <name>faultString</name>
          <value><string>Resource not found</string></value>
        </member>
      </struct>
    </value>
  </fault>
</methodResponse>
```

When a server returns a fault response, the `fault` structure replaces the `params` structure from a successful response. If an application uses XPath notation to process the response XML, for example, it can use the same query path regardless of fault or success, and then examine the child element's name to determine the nature of the response (fortunately, as will be seen in Chapter 4, toolkits do this so the application doesn't have to deal with it directly).

The `fault` structure is simply a container element with a single child, a `value` element. Unlike other value specifications, in this instance the only allowable content is a `struct` with exactly two `member` children. One of these must be named `faultCode` and have an `int` value. The other must be called `faultString` and have a value that is a `string`. The order of these two isn't important, because the `struct` doesn't preserve member order. But the naming is important, and must be followed. The `fault` structure can't contain extra members. The XML-RPC specification doesn't detail any sort of basic fault messages or codes. The strings and integers used are entirely up to the servers providing the service.

Client and Server Communication

All communication in XML-RPC is done over HTTP. For strict adherence to the specification, all communication must further be limited to HTTP 1.0, because the specification explicitly calls for the presence of a Content-Length header in both the request and response. Many of the toolkits don't adhere to this level of strictness and will accept "chunked" content-encoding on the server end of things. All toolkits provide the Content-Length header on responses, as far as is known. Their client implementations may also allow for HTTP 1.1–style content encoding as well, but it isn't safe to assume this.

Clients make their requests using the POST verb of HTTP, hence the requirement for the Content-Length headers. In theory, the simpler data elements can be provided in the URL as query arguments, but applying this to the complex types (structures and arrays) is unnecessarily complex. Instead, the specification states that requests are sent as the body of a POST request, regardless of length.

The communication of important information between client and server is done through the HTTP headers. The specification requires that the headers shown in Table 3-2 be present in both requests and responses. This is another detail that is generally handled at the toolkit level, and as such is probably not something an application developer needs to worry about. A toolkit developer, on the other hand, should ensure that they are capable of dealing with any other XML-RP-compliant tools.

Table 3-2. HTTP headers required for XML-RPC

Header	Role
Content-Length	An integer value giving the length in bytes of the content of the message (not including the headers).
Content-Type	This value must always be text/xml. Note that the HTTP specification for headers and their values allows a server to provide additional information, as long as this value is present and clear.
Host	(Required for requests only.) The name of the host the client is trying to connect with, in case multiple virtual hosts are being managed by the same server application.
Server	(Required for responses only.) A text string that identifies the server in some way, usually identifying the server software rather than just the hostname.
User-Agent	(Required for requests only.) A string that identifiers the client application making the request. The use of the User-Agent header is inherited from the header's role in the tradition role of the Web.

Both requests and responses provide the content-related headers. The requesting client has the additional requirement of providing the Host and User-Agent headers, while the responding server only needs to provide a Server header.

When a client sends a request to a server and receives an XML-RPC response, the HTTP involvement in the conversation has been successful regardless of whether the response itself is a fault or not. The reasoning for this is simple: the XML-RPC functionality could very well be coexisting with an ordinary web server, and that server has no native understanding of success versus failure in XML-RPC terms. An HTTP server only knows if it was able to successfully handle a request and send a valid response. HTTP error codes in the 400 (request incomplete) or 500 (server error) ranges can indicate only that the HTTP server had problems, not the XML-RPC code.

Any time a server receives a request and can give a response, the HTTP response code must be 200, the basic HTTP success indicator. This holds true for faults as well as successful returns, which is why faults are used to communicate problems. The range of fault types for XML-RPC is theoretically unbounded, but the range of error codes for HTTP is finite. Additionally, not all servers can attach arbitrary documents to error messages. In other words, HTTP error codes just wouldn't work. So, unless the URL is invalid, or the server is down, the HTTP layer reports success.

Example 3-7 shows the same response message as Example 3-5, but with server-side headers and the HTTP response line added. The content is abbreviated, and depending on the server in use, the complete set of headers may be much longer.

Example 3-7. XML-RPC response with HTTP headers

```
HTTP/1.1 200 OK
Connection: close
Content-Length: 138
Content-Type: text/xml
Date: Sun, 28 Jul 2002 11:20:13 GMT
Server: Apache/1.3.23 (Unix) mod_perl/1.26

<?xml version="1.0"?>
<methodResponse>
  <params>
    <param>
      <value><int>1</int></value>
    </param>
  </params>
</methodResponse>
```

In Chapter 4, when toolkits are discussed, we will cover the merits of using an Apache server with `mod_perl` enabled. Suffice it to say, `mod_perl` can make an XML-RPC environment even more efficient, when coded and configured properly.

Method Signatures and Overloading

By design, XML-RPC treats the remotely executable procedures as strongly typed. While languages such as Perl or PHP may operate fine with arbitrary parameters passed in, languages such as Java and C are much more demanding about the integrity of their arguments list. Many server implementations address this by tracking the number, order, and type of parameters a procedure or method may accept. This is often referred to as the *signature* of the remote call.

Method signatures aren't a part of the XML-RPC specification. They are implemented at the server level in many of the toolkits offered for application development. Signatures are most often used by the server to determine if it can actually send the input data to the appropriate procedure without generating a fatal exception or error. Most languages have some sort of exception-handling facility (such as Perl's eval and die functions), but some don't. These languages can encounter problems if passed a string when expecting an integer, for example. Depending on the language and how the software was written, the result of these problems can range from just returning errors to stack-buffer overflows.

A method's *signature* is defined as the sequence of the return parameter's type, followed by the types of all input parameters. For example, using the messages from Example 3-4 and Example 3-8 as the input and response of the same method, that method's signature would be:

    (int, struct, string)

Note that the first input parameter is the struct, and that nothing in the signature indicates (or mandates) any of the underlying structure in that parameter.

This is one reason why the return values from methods must always be single values. There would be no way to discern the earlier signature from one that indicates a single input of string, with an output of int followed by struct. In order to fully support languages such as Java or C++ that allow multiple interfaces to methods (sometimes called *overloaded* methods), it is necessary to distinguish between the different calling signatures. If an XML-RPC server is exposing routines from a library written in C, this isn't an issue. But Java, C++, and many other languages (including Perl) can have more than one way to call a given routine.

How a server manages method signatures and how (or even if) it imparts that information to client applications is entirely up to the developers of the server toolkits and developers of the servers themselves.

Example Client: Meerkat

Before moving to Chapter 4 and diving straight into the different Perl toolkits for XML-RPC, let's look at a simple example of a client* to give you a feel for the phases in the XML-RPC request/response lifecycle. The example is fairly rudimentary, so that it can be done without using any of the available toolkits. But even so, it's complex enough that it also serves as an incentive for you to read Chapter 4, which shows how much the toolkits can simplify an application.

---

* Illustrating server development will be left for the introduction of toolkits in Chapter 4 because such code would be long and unwieldy if written from scratch.

The Meerkat Service

Meerkat is an open wire service offered by O'Reilly & Associates, Inc. It offers application-level access to news stories in an array of channels and covers a large variety of topics. Meerkat demonstrates the early success of XML-RPC as an API layer.

Users register an account at *http://meerkat.oreillynet.com* and then customize the way the news content is presented. From the browser interface, it is possible to select not only the channels themselves but also to fine-tune the set of stories that are chosen for display by applying a search pattern (which can in fact be a regular expression) as a filter against the list. For example, a filter of "perl" against the stories from the "Scripting News" channel limits the results to just the stories that mention Perl.

Users may save a choice of channels to browse and a search pattern. To get started, Meerkat offers a set of ready-to-use basic profiles for the more common and popular topics. Figure 3-1 shows a screenshot of Meerkat displayed with the Mozilla browser running under Linux. The profile used for the contents that are displayed gathers items from most of the Perl-related channels, plus a few others such as the popular Slashdot news portal. All stories are searched for the word "perl," so that only the ones that actually mention Perl directly are displayed.

In addition to being able to save preferences, users can tune the search parameters within the URL itself. The documentation for the service explains this in greater detail, but basically all the form elements on the page may instead appear in the URL. Furthermore, the format of the data returned can also be tuned to a certain degree, including the generation of XML rather than HTML. In fact, a suitable web services client can be built using just this form of the search interface.

However, Meerkat also provides an XML-RPC interface. All the data-retrieval and searching functionality available to the web browser is also available at the API level. The user-level personalization and customization aren't available to the programmatic interface, but a client program can easily manage its own layer of preferences control.

From Meerkat Query to HTML Sidebar

Our first example that uses XML-RPC is a simple utility that takes the output from a query and converts it to an HTML segment suitable for inclusion in a larger page. In essence, this is the sort of task one might do with an ordinary RSS feed, only in this case the application can use different queries to construct different feeds.

The example doesn't use any of the XML-RPC toolkits available for Perl just yet, which means the code is much more complex than it would otherwise be. This helps to draw a comparison to the code in Chapter 4, in which the tools are introduced and demonstrated. Instead, the example uses the LWP module (a set of classes for HTTP clients, available from the Comprehensive Perl Archive Network) directly as a

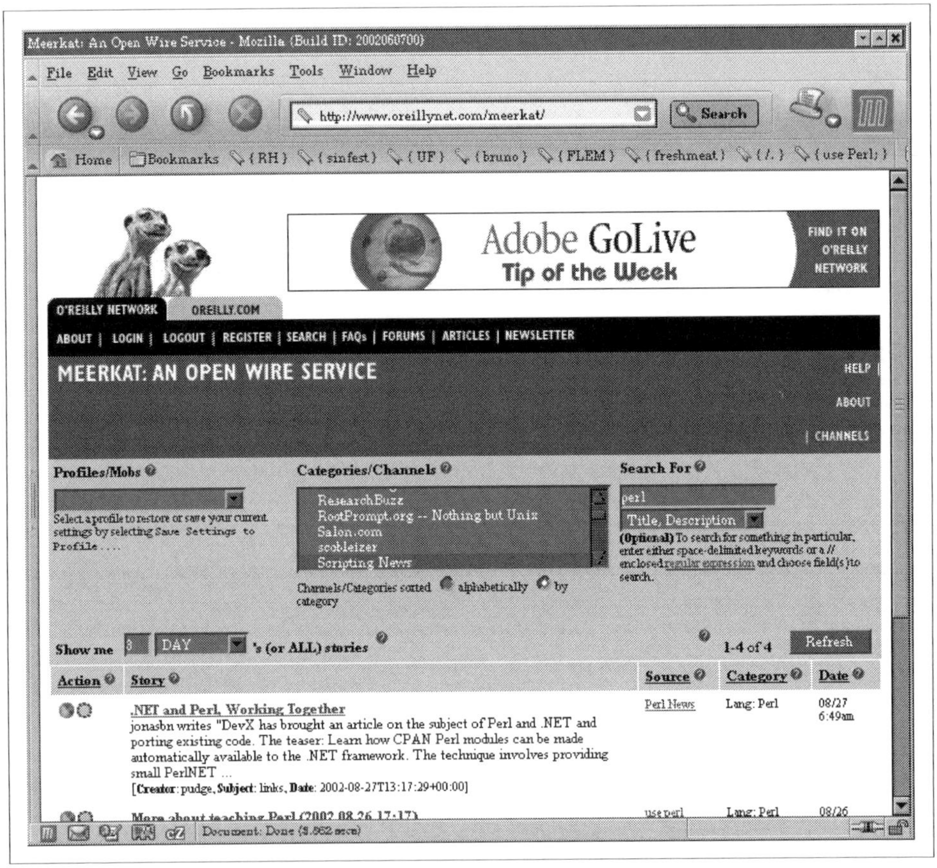

Figure 3-1. A sample Meerkat page

way to communicate with the Meerkat server and uses the XML::XPath module to parse and process the responses the server provides. In the case where the application reading the response is this specialized, the XPath language provides a much easier solution than having to process the entire document with a package like XML::Parser.

The code for the utility is given in Example 3-8. Remember, this is no small script, because we're doing everything by hand. Using a toolkit from Chapter 4 makes the program considerably smaller, as we'll see. In practice, you'd only do things at this low a level if the toolkits were not available. This is meant to demonstrate how helpful the toolkits are.

Example 3-8. The meer2html sample utility

```
#!/usr/bin/perl -w

use strict;
use vars qw($chan $cat $num $data $UA $request);
```

Example 3-8. The meer2html sample utility (continued)

```perl
use LWP::UserAgent;
use HTTP::Request;
use XML::XPath;

use constant MEERKAT =>
    'http://www.oreillynet.com/meerkat/xml-rpc/server.php';
use constant XPATH_TO_STRUCTS =>
    '/methodResponse/params/param/value/array/data/value' .
    '/struct';

if ($ARGV[0] =~ /^-ch/) {
    $chan = $ARGV[1];
    $num  = $ARGV[2] || 15;
} elsif ($ARGV[0] =~ /^-ca/) {
    $cat = $ARGV[1];
    $num = $ARGV[2] || 15;
}

unless (($chan or $cat) and ($num =~ /^\d+$/)) {
    die "USAGE: $0 { -channel str | -category str } [ n ]";
}

$UA = LWP::UserAgent->new();
$request = HTTP::Request->new(POST => MEERKAT);
$request->content_type('text/xml');

$data = $chan ? data_from_chan($chan, $num) :
                data_from_cat($cat, $num);
show_data($data);

exit;

sub data_from_chan {
    my ($chan, $num) = @_;

    $chan = resolve_name($chan, 'Channels')
        unless ($chan =~ /^\d+$/);
    get_data(channel => $chan, $num);
}

sub data_from_cat {
    my ($cat, $num) = @_;

    $cat = resolve_name($cat, 'Categories')
        unless ($cat =~ /^\d+$/);
    get_data(category => $cat, $num);
}

sub show_data {
    my $data = shift;

    my $xp = XML::XPath->new(xml => $$data);
    my $nodes = $xp->find(XPATH_TO_STRUCTS);
```

Example 3-8. The meer2html sample utility (continued)

```perl
    my @stories = ();
    for my $struct ($nodes->get_nodelist) {
        my $tmp = {};
        for my $key (qw(title link description)) {
            my $node = $xp->find(qq(member[name="$key"]),
                                 $struct);
            $tmp->{$key} =
                $xp->find('value/string',
                          $node->get_node(1))
                    ->string_value;
        }
        push(@stories, $tmp);
    }
    print STDOUT qq(<span class="meerkat">\n<dl>\n);
    for (@stories) {
        print STDOUT <<"END_HTML";
<dt class="title"><a href="$_->{link}">$_->{title}</a></dt>
<dd class="description">$_->{description}</dd>
END_HTML
    }
    print STDOUT qq(</dl>\n</span>\n);
}

sub resolve_name {
    my ($str, $name) = @_;

    $name = "meerkat.get${name}BySubstring";
    my $xml = <<"END_XML";
<?xml version="1.0"?>
<methodCall>
  <methodName>$name</methodName>
  <params>
    <param><value>$str</value></param>
  </params>
</methodCall>
END_XML

    $request->content($xml);
    my $resp = $UA->request($request);
    die "resolve_name: transport error: " . $resp->message
        if $resp->is_error;
    my $xp = XML::XPath->new(xml => $resp->content);
    my $nodeset = $xp->find(XPATH_TO_STRUCTS);
    die "resolve_name: $str returned more than 1 match"
        if ($nodeset->size > 1);
    my $node = $nodeset->get_node(1);
    $node = $xp->find('member[name="id"]', $node);

    $xp->find('value/int', $node->get_node(1))
        ->string_value;
}
```

Example 3-8. The meer2html sample utility (continued)

```
sub get_data {
    my ($key, $val, $num) = @_;

    my $xml = <<"END_XML";
<?xml version="1.0"?>
<methodCall>
  <methodName>meerkat.getItems</methodName>
  <params>
    <param><value>
      <struct>
        <member>
          <name>$key</name>
          <value><int>$val</int></value>
        </member>
        <member>
          <name>time_period</name>
          <value><string>7DAY</string></value>
        </member>
        <member>
          <name>num_items</name>
          <value><int>$num</int></value>
        </member>
        <member>
          <name>descriptions</name>
          <value><int>200</int></value>
        </member>
      </struct>
    </value></param>
  </params>
</methodCall>
END_XML

    $request->content($xml);
    my $resp = $UA->request($request);
    die "resolve_name: transport error: " . $resp->message
        if $resp->is_error;
    my $content = $resp->content;
    return \$content;
}
```

One of the first things to notice in this application is the amount of space occupied by the inline-coded XML blocks. In this tool, there are only two such blocks to build. The application itself is very difficult to retarget to a different kind of XML-RPC server, because it makes some specific assumptions about the layout of the responses to the queries.

The application starts by defining the usual pragmas and loading some key libraries. The `LWP::UserAgent` and `HTTP::Request` are parts of the `LWP` package that were briefly touched on in Chapter 2. The `XML::XPath` module provides the implementation of the W3C's XPath query syntax. Finally, two constant values are defined (using the constant pragma) for the URL of the Meerkat service itself and for a particularly long XPath expression that is used in a few different places.

Processing the command-line arguments with this tool is straightforward. The user is required to specify either a category or channel, using -category and -channel, respectively (which can be abbreviated as short as -ca or -ch). The argument is checked for validity later. Following this is an optional numeric argument to specify how many items to fetch. This defaults to 15 if not given explicitly. After the command line has been deemed valid, the application creates a LWP::UserAgent object and a HTTP::Request object. The request object is then set to have a Content-Type header of text/xml.

Getting the data is very direct. There are two data-fetching routines defined, one each for channels and categories. This allows the application to specify how to resolve the user-specified value if it isn't already numeric. Because Meerkat uses numeric identifiers, the application allows the user to specify the channel or category by name (by substring, in fact). This value is used to call either the getChannelsBySubstring or getCategoriesBySubstring routine. Luckily for the application, these are both virtually identical in syntax, except for the actual remote procedure name. That simplifies the resolve_name routine, which can plug the type into the XML string it builds, and parse the results the same way regardless of which is called. If the substring match returns more than one hit, the application stops.

With a numeric channel or category ID, the get_data routine makes the ultimate call to the service to get the actual story data. As with resolve_name, the structure of the call is virtually identical in both cases, differing by only one segment of the XML string. By using the frontend routines data_from_chan and data_from_cat, it is easier to avoid repeated tests to tell which type the user provided. The content returned by the call to Meerkat's getItems routine is then returned as a scalar reference (to avoid repeated copying of so large a string on the stack).

Processing the data is also simple. For the sake of the example, the application is designed to generate a block of HTML within a span element that contains a description list. The list uses the title value from a given data record for the dt tag, and the link value as the target of a hyperlink. The data in the description field of the structure is plugged into the dd element.

The XPath expressions used here are simple, but because XPath will be set aside in favor of toolkits, there is no need to explain them in detail. The tool itself, while a very basic example, can be used as-is for generating segments of HTML. These segments can be created from a task scheduler such as the Unix cron command and included as server-side elements in HTML pages. Of course, if used in such a "production" environment, it would be better to make more of the settings (such as how far back in time to search) controllable by parameters.

The real power of the interface is realized when the application is much more flexible in the messages it can send and the results it can process. Meerkat allows access to almost every search aspect present at the web level from the XML-RPC level. Not only can the searches be more detailed and refined, the nature and content of the results can also be tuned to meet the needs of any given application.

Limitations of XML-RPC

As flexible and powerful as XML-RPC is, it does suffer from a number of very significant limitations. None of these limitations prevent it from being usable, and there are some very useful systems built with XML-RPC. In some cases the use of XML-RPC is a supplementary feature, while in others it is a basic aspect of the system. However, understanding the limitations of the protocol make it easier to avoid pitfalls or traps when designing applications to use it.

Status of the Specification

Probably the most limiting aspect of XML-RPC is within the specification itself. No, this doesn't mean that the protocol is the source of the limitation. Rather, the specification as it stands is frozen. Because there is no version specification within the base definitions, the author of the protocol has thus far chosen to not implement any changes or extensions to the specification. This is primarily out of a concern for maintaining a strict sense of compatibility at the wire level between implementations.

The definition of XML-RPC is intentionally simple and clear. The specification at *http://www.xmlrpc.com* is the single and definitive source for evaluating a claimant to the stamp of XML-RPC compatibility.

Some toolkits (in various languages) have strayed off of the path in small steps, primarily in terms of being more flexible at the transport level. The most common example of this is when a toolkit chooses to allow HTTP 1.1 chunked transfer encoding. When this style of content-transmission is used, it isn't always necessary to provide a Content-Length header. This method is often used with streaming content models such as multimedia types, but it can also be used in cases in which an application wants (or needs) to start the transmission of data before the complete length of the response is known.

If an application or toolkit does something like this, it still bears the responsibility of being completely compatible with even the strictest servers and clients. Otherwise, it can't refer to itself as being an implementation of XML-RPC.

As an example, at least two of the Perl XML-RPC toolkits (XMLRPC::Lite and RPC::XML, both detailed in Chapter 4) can compress messages with the popular GNU Zip compression algorithm. These toolkits do this only after confirming that the recipient of the message can correctly understand the compressed content. They confirm using standard HTTP headers beyond those used directly by the XML-RPC specification. Thus, both implementations maintain compatibility with other toolkits and applications.

Among the most-requested additional features is a type that is functionally equivalent to C's void or Perl's undef. While it is true that these aren't types in the strictest sense of the word, they are often used to denote that a function has no return value or express a value that is demonstrably different than the boolean false.

As it stands, there is no way to express a remote procedure that doesn't return some sort of value. Every procedure call is expected to return something, even if the value is immediately discarded. Proponents of a <nil/> or <null/> type argue that having such an option would not only make more syntactic sense than returning a throwaway integer or boolean, it would also be several bytes shorter.

Another common request is for more flexibility in the HTTP coupling that the specification exhibits. In particular, because the specification calls out explicitly to the Content-Length header and the POST HTTP verb, the alternatives offered by HTTP 1.1 (and in some cases available as extensions to HTTP 1.0) can't be easily applied to XML-RPC conversations. It is difficult to take advantage of optimizations such as persistent or asynchronous connections, or streaming transfer methods. In addition to this, there are those in favor of completely decoupling XML-RPC from HTTP to allow for lighter-weight transports, such as TCP, or attachment to newer technologies such as BEEP (the Blocks Extensible Exchange Protocol).

The specification-level limitations are difficult, but XML-RPC remains useful in its present form. You can work around the shortcomings by adjusting interfaces and using Base64 to send data that doesn't otherwise fit the available model.

XML-RPC and Interoperability

The XML-RPC specification itself doesn't provide any degree of well-defined interoperability between clients and servers from different implementations. There are some efforts on the parts of individuals and development teams, but all of these are left up to voluntary compliance. Interoperability, were it to be formalized, would need to cover at least two areas: the nature and structure of error or diagnostic messages and the way in which services and capabilities are discovered and shared.

Thus far, very little has been done in the XML-RPC community about consistency in error and diagnostic codes and messages. The numeric codes are actually more important from the vantage point of standardization because depending on exact text message isn't only unreliable, it fails to take into account issues of internationalization. The participants of an XML-RPC mailing list undertook such an effort at standardization, and the current state of that project may be read at the URL:

http://xmlrpc-epi.sourceforge.net/specs/rfc.fault_codes.php

This particular set came to be the chosen list as a result of the persistence and effort of the author, who regularly solicited feedback as he developed the document.

In the area of service description and discovery, the most popular effort towards interoperability derives from an interface developed as part of the PHP toolkit, upon which the Meerkat XML-RPC service described earlier was built.

This discovery interface provides access to information about the methods a server provides. It lists the procedure names, as well as calling-syntax details and documentation (when available). The original designer chose names for the routines that started with the sequence system so as to avoid collision with other procedure names. As with the proposed standard regarding error codes, this is only a suggestion to service designers, but one that has caught on in at least one of the Perl toolkits. The three main methods are:

system.listMethods
Provides a list (array) of local procedure/method names as string-type values.

system.methodHelp
For a given method name (which is passed as a parameter to the call), this returns any help text (or documentation) for the method.

system.methodSignature
Returns an array of arrays, listing the known signatures for the method given as an argument. Recall from earlier that the signature is defined as the promised return value's type followed by the types of any arguments. A method/procedure can be called in more than one way, which is what the purpose of defining signatures is meant to distinguish.

Some toolkits provide more than this, while some toolkits provide no predefined methods at all. It is still necessary for client developers to have some knowledge of the servers they are dealing with. They can also try sending requests for these methods and see what happens.

Choosing XML-RPC over SOAP

The single biggest advantage XML-RPC has over SOAP is the size of the specification, or more accurately, the compactness of it. XML-RPC can be implemented much more simply than SOAP. As more and more applications are being targeted towards embedded platforms and other targets, memory or processing overhead (or both) may be at a premium.

Even when memory or other such resources aren't an issue, the fact remains that XML-RPC is a much simpler protocol than SOAP. As such, it introduces less complexity into a software system than SOAP would. Many applications need the functionality and scope that SOAP offers. In cases where it isn't needed, however, there is no reason to introduce extra overhead.

CHAPTER 4
Programming XML-RPC

Web services toolkits hide the XML and HTTP protocol details and let you, the applications programmer, focus on the application you're building. In this chapter we look at three XML-RPC toolkits for Perl. Each offers different features and a different interface, with different advantages and drawbacks for the programmer.

This chapter shows how to use each toolkit, and develops the same pair of applications in all three. You'll see the relative strengths and weaknesses of each toolkit and be able to select and use the right toolkit for your application.

Perl Toolkits for XML-RPC

This chapter presents the toolkits from oldest to newest. The first XML-RPC toolkit was the Frontier::RPC2 package by Ken MacLeod. The name refers to the original system the package was intended to support, the Frontier content management system from UserLand Software, the source of the XML-RPC specification itself. In mid-2002, the package was taken over by a new maintainer. The time proved right for renaming the modules, and now the module is known as RPC::XMLSimple.

Following this module was the XMLRPC::Lite component of the SOAP::Lite package for Perl. Support for XML-RPC was added at a later point than the SOAP components themselves, but the functionality builds on the framework that the author, Pavel Kulchenko, had already created to support the SOAP standards. As a result, it integrates very smoothly, and benefits from elements already present in SOAP::Lite, such as a pure-Perl XML parser that can be used when none of the CPAN-based XML modules are available.

The newest addition to the Perl/XML-RPC family is the RPC::XML package. Like the RPC::XMLSimple package, this module requires that the XML::Parser module from CPAN be installed. It doesn't provide a native XML parser the way XMLRPC::Lite does. It relies on the LWP package for client transport, but on the server side it can work with the HTTP::Daemon package (from LWP), the Net::Server package (from CPAN), or with Apache and mod_perl directly as a mod_perl location-handler.

In each toolkit we'll create the same client and server applications. This side-by-side comparison lets you see the strengths and weaknesses of each, to help you choose the best solution for your project.

It should be noted that in many of the code examples given throughout this chapter, the code shown will be restricted to relevant sections that illustrate the technology and concepts being discussed at that point. The full source of the examples in this chapter is provided in Appendix C.

RPC::XMLSimple

The RPC::XMLSimple module provides support code for the client and server classes, RPC::XMLSimple::Client and RPC::XMLSimple::Daemon. An application will include only the server or client code, as needed. Both of those modules already include the core elements.

Installation of the module is very simple because it is available through CPAN and has only a few simple dependencies. It does require the XML::Parser module to handle the XML data, and the LWP module for both client communications and server functionality.

Client Example: meer2html.pl

Let's reimplement the meer2html.pl tool from Chapter 3 using the toolkit instead of building and parsing XML-RPC requests and responses manually. Comparing just the length in lines of the two versions of the utility (with comments and blank lines excluded), the Frontier version is less than half the length of the manual version.

Example 4-1 shows the relevant parts of the meer2html-Frontier.pl code. The sections shown are those that differ significantly from the original version.

Example 4-1. The meer2html-Frontier.pl script

```
use RPC::XMLSimple::Client;

$client = RPC::XMLSimple::Client->new(url => MEERKAT);

sub show_data {
    my $data = shift;

    print STDOUT qq(<span class="meerkat">\n<dl>\n);
    for (@$data) {
        print STDOUT <<"END_HTML";
<dt class="title"><a href="$_->{link}">$_->{title}</a></dt>
<dd class="description">$_->{description}</dd>
END_HTML
```

Example 4-1. The meer2html-Frontier.pl script (continued)

```perl
    }
    print STDOUT qq(</dl>\n</span>\n);
}

sub resolve_name {
    my ($str, $name) = @_;

    $name = "meerkat.get${name}BySubstring";
    my $resp = $client->call($name, $str);
    die "resolve_name: $str returned more than 1 match"
        if (@$resp > 1);

    $resp->[0]{id};
}

sub get_data {
    my ($key, $val, $num) = @_;

    $client->call('meerkat.getItems',
                  { $key         => $val,
                    time_period  => '7DAY',
                    num_items    => $num,
                    descriptions => 200 });
}
```

The first difference is that rather than "use"ing three modules for XML management and transport, only one is needed (RPC::XMLSimple::Client). As a result, the only object created for communication with Meerkat is $client, an object of the RPC::XMLSimple::Client class.

The example then skips forward to the show_data routine. In the previous version, this routine extracted data from the XML that Meerkat returns. That isn't necessary with RPC::XMLSimple, because the toolkit has already converted the return message from the server into a native Perl data structure. Because the data returned from Meerkat is in an array of structures, the Perl data received here is an array reference, each element of which is a hash reference.

The resolve_name routine is also considerably simpler. The most significant difference is the absence of hardcoded XML. The call method of the RPC::XMLSimple::Client class handles the creation of the XML block behind the scenes. Both remote routines return an array of structures, even if the number of structures is just one. So the return value of the call is made by dereferencing the first element and then pulling the id key from it.

Finally, the get_data is also significantly shorter and simpler. It, too, benefits from not needing to explicitly construct the XML for the main data-retrieval request. The space saved is even more notable because the original sported a fairly lengthy and involved XML block. The other benefit is that the return value comes back as an array reference containing hash references. There is no need to preprocess this data at all before it gets handed to the next part of the pipeline, so the invocation of the call method acts as the return value as well.

When errors occur, this package throws exceptions in the form of die statements. In this script, the only thing that would be done with an error would be to die as well, so no effort is made to trap these.

The RPC::XMLSimple::Client Class in Detail

The RPC::XMLSimple::Client class is designed to abstract from the application all the overhead and work of maintaining the user agent and other objects from the LWP class that are used in managing the actual communications to and from the remote server. In addition to that, it provides some utility functionality to ease the expression of data in a format that the toolkit can correctly turn into an XML-RPC message.

Client creation is with a new method, which may take any of five parameters as input (or a hash reference using these keys and their values):

url
: The value for this key is the URL of the server to which the client is to connect.

proxy
: If necessary, a proxy URL may be passed with this parameter, which will be used to route all communications to the server URL.

encoding
: If the outgoing messages are to be encoded in a character set other than UTF-8 (the default for XML), this parameter allows for specifying the desired encoding.

use_objects
: If this parameter has a value that evaluates to true, calls to the server return data as object instances rather than native Perl values. Useful when a string value might look like an integer or some other type.

debug
: If set to a true value, this parameter dumps the request and response messages to the controlling terminal.

The client object actually makes the remote call to the server using the call method. It takes the remote procedure name as a first argument, and any parameters to the call as subsequent arguments. Like all the toolkits here, the client is able to do a good job of converting Perl scalars to the appropriate XML-RPC datatypes. There are data-conversion routines available for those cases where a value could fit more than one type.

The class methods boolean, date_time, base64, int, double, and string all take their single argument and return an object. The objects may be used to fetch or set the underlying values using a method called value. If called with no argument, the method returns the object's current value. If an argument is passed, it is set as the new value. When one object is passed to call, it is guaranteed to be properly encoded in the outgoing message. When use_objects is set on the client, these are the types of objects that will be returned from calls to the server. Each object class has a name, as shown in Table 4-1.

Table 4-1. The data classes in RPC::XMLSimple

XML-RPC datatype	RPC::XMLSimple data class
Int	RPC::XMLSimple::Integer
Double	RPC::XMLSimple::Double
String	RPC::XMLSimple::String
Boolean	RPC::XMLSimple::Boolean
dateTime.iso8601	RPC::XMLSimple::DateTime::ISO8601
base64	RPC::XMLSimple::Base64

The client class correctly handles XML-RPC arrays and structures when passed in a Perl array reference or hash reference. When the return value from a server call is an array or structure, the client object returns an array or hash reference. If use_objects is set, the low-level simple data values will be objects.

When any type of error occurs, whether a localized runtime error (such as transport or socket errors) or a fault returned from the server, the client object throws an exception in the form of a die call. The text of the error message will contain some detail about what caused the exception, including the fault code and fault string, when the cause is a <fault> from the server. Unfortunately, there is no finer-grained method of catching or handling faults.

A Server Example: Providing "Fortunes"

Let's build a simple service that wraps the *fortune* program. To make it more interesting and challenging, rather than just simply running the program on the server and sending the text back to the client, the service lets the client take advantage of the functionality present in the modern implementations of *fortune*. Clients can choose from various books of quotes, as well as the ability to manipulate the statistical probability of any given book being chosen as the source. Current versions of the program can do even more than this, but these features will be enough for the example.

This example uses a simple package of code called *XRFortune.pm*, for "XML-RPC Fortune," to handle the interaction with the *fortune* program. The XRFortune module is described in the sidebar "The XRFortune.pm Module," and its source is given in Appendix C.

The example server script is short enough to show in its entirety and is given in Example 4-2.

The XRFortune.pm Module

This module wraps the well-known *fortune* application. The syntax of the commands is based on the GNU version of the program, as distributed by Red Hat Linux. You can download the GNU *fortune* program from *ftp.gnu.org* if you don't have it.

There are three routines in the XRFortune package: books, fortune, and weighted_fortune.

- The books routine can be called in one of three ways: with no arguments, with a single string, or with an array reference of strings. With no arguments, it returns a list of the books *fortune* has access to, as an array reference. With one string or a list of strings, it validates the strings as known books, returning an array reference of the ones that are valid. The return value is always an array reference.

- The fortune routine takes an optional argument, either a single book or a list of books as an array reference. If any arguments are passed, they are given to the invocation of fortune to restrict the selection to just those books. Otherwise, it is called with no arguments, allowing the choice to come from any of the known books.

- The weighted_fortune routine allows for control over the likelihood that a fortune will come from a given book. There are two ways this is done: "pass an array reference" means to equally weight all the (valid) books in the array (the default within fortune is to weigh them by their size relative to the whole). The second way is to pass a hash reference whose keys are book names and whose values are the integer weights the books should have. The list has invalid books pruned out, then the remaining weights are totaled up, and must equal 100 exactly, or a fault is returned. The books and their weights are then converted to the appropriate command-line sequence for the call to fortune.

Both fortune and weighted_fortune return the lines of text as an array reference, with newline characters chopped off. This avoids confusion on systems with different interpretations of newlines.

Example 4-2. The fortune-Frontier.pl server

```
#!/usr/bin/perl -w

use strict;

use XRFortune;
use RPC::XMLSimple::Daemon;

RPC::XMLSimple:Daemon->new(
        LocalPort => 9000,
        ReuseAddr => 1,
        methods => {
            books              => \&XRFortune::books,
            fortune            => \&XRFortune::fortune,
```

Example 4-2. The fortune-Frontier.pl server (continued)

```
            weighted_fortune => \&XRFortune::weighted_fortune
    });

exit;
```

The `RPC::XMLSimple::Daemon` instance is created using the commonly named new constructor. As will be explained later, the only one of the arguments it actually cares about is the methods key and the hash reference passed as its value. The hash reference is expected to provide a mapping of internal subroutines to names by which they may be remotely called. The keys of the hash table are the external names, and the values are subroutine references. Thus, they may also be anonymous subroutines or closures.

The `LocalPort` and `ReuseAddr` parameters are passed to the parent class of `RPC::XMLSimple::Daemon` and are used to bind the server to port 9000, as well as to set a parameter on the underlying socket structure that enables binding even if there are left-over sockets from a previous execution.

The RPC::XMLSimple::Daemon Class in Detail

The `RPC::XMLSimple::Daemon` class is a subclass of `HTTP::Daemon` from the `LWP` module, which in turn is a subclass of `IO::Socket::INET`. The initial two parameters in Example 4-2 are actually parameters to the constructor for the socket class. Both the RPC and HTTP subclasses create their objects by first calling the super-class constructor, then adding extra material to the newly created object.

This package provides one of the lightest-weight daemon implementations of the XML-RPC choices. As can be seen in Example 4-2, the constructor goes straight into the typical socket-based connection loop. The call to new doesn't actually return unless there is an error in object creation (in which case it simply returns undef).

The daemon doesn't make any effort to track or enforce method signatures for the methods it publishes. Incoming calls are sent to the matching subroutine reference with the list of parameters that accompanied the request. The return value of the subroutine call is serialized into the response. If a routine returns a list of values, only the first one is sent back to the client, since the protocol expects a return value to be a scalar (which covers list references and structure/hash references).

As it is currently implemented (based on `Frontier::RPC` Version 0.06 and `RPC::XMLSimple` Version 1.0), the server object not only goes directly into the accept loop without offering the application any direct control, but it uses a hardcoded path for the requests it is willing to accept. The server expects all incoming RPC requests to be on the URL path /RPC2, a value that is coded directly into the server class itself. This is likely to change in a future version.

XMLRPC::Lite

The XMLRPC::Lite package is part of the SOAP::Lite suite, written by one of the authors of this book, Pavel Kulchenko. It shares much of the same underlying architecture and structure as the SOAP package. As a result, it also supports some transport protocols that aren't officially part of XML-RPC, such as TCP/IP and the POP3 protocol. This package is also the only one of the three toolkits that can be used without dependency on an external XML parser. It will use the faster XML::Parser if it is available, however.

Installation of this module takes place as a part of the larger installation of SOAP::Lite itself. That installation process is described in greater detail in Chapter 6 so it won't be covered here.

Client Example: meer2html.pl

Example 4-3 shows how Chapter 3's Meerkat application looks with XMLRPC::Lite.* Notice how similar it appears to the RPC::XMLSimple version of this application (Example 4-1). The interface design of all the XML-RPC toolkits are very similar, which should simplify switching between them, if need be. As always, full code is available in Appendix C.

Example 4-3. The meer2html-Lite.pl client

```
use XMLRPC::Lite;

$client = XMLRPC::Lite->proxy(MEERKAT)
         ->on_fault(sub { die "Transport error: " .
                             $_[1]->faultstring });
sub show_data {
    my $data = shift;

    print STDOUT qq(<span class="meerkat">\n<dl>\n);
    for (@$data) {
        print STDOUT <<"END_HTML";
<dt class="title"><a href="$_->{link}">$_->{title}</a></dt>
<dd class="description">$_->{description}</dd>
END_HTML
    }
    print STDOUT qq(</dl>\n</span>\n);
}

sub resolve_name {
    my ($str, $name) = @_;
```

---

* Only the different parts are shown in this example, not the perl -w or other elements shared with the RPC::XMLSimple version of the utility.

Example 4-3. The meer2html-Lite.pl client (continued)

```perl
    $name = "meerkat.get${name}BySubstring";
    my $resp = $client->call($name, $str)->result;
    die "resolve_name: $str returned more than 1 match"
        if (@$resp > 1);

    $resp->[0]{id};
}

sub get_data {
    my ($key, $val, $num) = @_;

    $client->call('meerkat.getItems',
                  { $key         => $val,
                    time_period  => '7DAY',
                    num_items    => $num,
                    descriptions => 200 })->result;
}
```

Again, only one module needs to be included in order to get the necessary range of XML-RPC support. Creating the client object is different in the XMLRPC::Lite package: while there is a new( ) method that can be explicitly called, the structure of the methods is such that most of them automatically create an object when called without an object reference. So, calling the proxy method as a static method has the side effect of creating the object. The return value from proxy is the object reference, which is then chained to a call to on_fault, a method that sets the callback to be used when an error occurs in an XML-RPC call.

The proxy method has a slightly misleading name, but it comes from the SOAP::Lite roots of XMLRPC::Lite in which the meaning of a URI is more complex than in XML-RPC. Here, it is used to set the URL of the XML-RPC server that the client expects to communicate with (MEERKAT is a constant defined earlier in the program).

XMLRPC::Lite does exception handling through use of the die keyword in Perl but will use a callback instead if one is provided. For this application, the callback is set using the on_fault method. The error handler simply dies, using the error message from SOAP::Lite.

The show_data subroutine is unchanged from the RPC::XMLSimple version. Because the toolkits all convert the information received from the server into native Perl data structures, there is no need for this part of the application to be any different from the RPC::XMLSimple rendition.

Both resolve_name and get_data use the $client object to make the actual remote calls. The method used here is named call and takes as an argument the name of the remote procedure to call. In both cases, the data that is being passed to the remote call can easily be properly identified for serialization into the XML-RPC syntax. Were some of the data not so clear (such as using 101 as a <string> instead of an <int>), there are methods that specify the way in which XMLRPC::Lite serializes it.

One way in which this toolkit handles data differently from the other two is that the calls through the client object to the remote server don't return native Perl data. They return an object reference in a special class called XMLRPC::SOM, which is described later. For now, know that the values returned by call need to be used to call another method called result. This method takes the XMLRPC::SOM object and converts it to a native Perl value.

The XMLRPC::Lite Class in Detail

The XMLRPC::Lite class is a subclass of SOAP::Lite, which will be covered in a later chapter. The XML-RPC code benefits from this relationship in terms of functionality and debugging support.

An XMLRPC::Lite client object can be created directly with the new method of the class, or indirectly by calling most of the class' methods as static methods (also called class methods). In Example 4-3, the proxy method was called as a static method. This method returns an object reference on success, and in this case the reference was immediately used to call the on_fault method to set up a callback for catching run-time errors and XML-RPC faults. As with proxy, this method returns the object reference on success, and this is the value that is ultimately stored in $client. The proxy method supplies the URL of the XML-RPC server with which the client communicates. The method may be used as often as needed to retarget the client object when desired.

When the client object calls a remote procedure on the server, it can be done in one of two ways: either by calling the remote name as a method on the object itself or by using the call method provided within the XMLRPC::Lite class. The call method intervenes when there are one or more characters in the procedure's name that aren't legal in Perl subroutine names, such as in Example 4-3 (the "." in meerkat.getItems). When a remote call is successful, the returned value is an object in the XMLRPC::SOM class.

The XMLRPC::SOM objects encapsulate the deserialized return from an XML-RPC call. The class inherits from SOAP::SOM, and as such contains a lot of functionality XML-RPC users don't need to worry about (covered in Chapter 6). From the perspective of XML-RPC, the main methods that need to be understood are result, fault, faultcode, and faultstring.

The result method returns the value returned by the server as native Perl data. It returns undef if the response was a fault. When that is the case, the fault method returns the full structure of the <fault> element itself as a Perl hash reference. An application can use this to retrieve the faultCode and faultString keys, or it may use the faultcode and faultstring methods on the XMLRPC::SOM object directly.

As an alternative to handling potential server-side faults directly within the logic of the client, XMLRPC::Lite allows an application to configure a callback on the client object that will be invoked if a fault is read in the response. This was demonstrated in Example 4-3 with the on_fault method. If this is configured, the callback is invoked as a method on the client object and given one of two inputs: either the XMLRPC::SOM object when a fault is read from the server or the special Perl variable $@ when an exception has been thrown within the client library itself. The on_fault method may be used at creation time (as in Example 4-3) or at any time during the life of the client object. In Example 4-3, the method is called with an anonymous subroutine that simply calls die with the value from the faultstring method on the data object.

When calling a remote method, the client object takes the parameters for the call as ordinary Perl data and attempts to resolve any ambiguity using regular-expression matching. This doesn't always work, of course, as there may be times when the application means to pass 10 as a string rather than an int. The XMLRPC::Data class assists by allowing an application to specify the type associated with a data parameter. Like the other classes here, it inherits a lot of functionality that isn't relevant to XML-RPC. It is useful in this environment because it creates objects that can be passed to the call method (or through the direct-calling syntax):

```
$string = XMLRPC::Data->type(string => 10);
...
$client->call(someMethod => $string);
```

XMLRPC::Lite is pretty adept at deriving int and double data, so this form of explicit typing should be necessary only for string values that look like something else or the boolean and dateTime.iso8601 types.

Debugging

XMLRPC::Lite has a powerful tracing functionality that lets you follow program flow from the creation and destruction of objects up to the XML messages that get sent over the wire. Enable tracing when the module is loaded with:

```
use XMLRPC::Lite +trace => 'all';
```

There are a number of specifiers that may follow the trace keyword. These are often referred to as *signals* in the SOAP::Lite documentation, and are shown in Table 4-2. The use line enables all the trace points and is also the default behavior if no arguments are given.

Table 4-2. The trace signals

Keyword	Meaning
transport	(Client-side only) Triggered by the client right before a request is sent and right after the response is received. Each time the argument passed is the object used, a HTTP::Request or HTTP::Response reference as appropriate.
dispatch	(Server-side only) When the method (server-side) has been resolved from the call to a local name, this signal is called with the resolved name. Currently (as of SOAP::Lite 0.55) disabled.

Table 4-2. *The trace signals (continued)*

Keyword	Meaning
parameters	(Server-side only) This signal is triggered before a method call is finally dispatched. The arguments are the parameters to the server-side method after they have been converted from XML to Perl data.
result	(Server-side only) After the method has been run on the server-side, this signal is triggered with the results passed back from the call (before serialization).
headers	(Server-side only) The headers signal is designed to trigger on the headers of an incoming request. It is currently (as of SOAP::Lite 0.55) disabled.
objects	This signal notes the creation and destruction of the internal objects within the classes.
method	When the serializer (the component used to turn Perl data into an XML representation) builds a message around a method name (such as for a request), it sends this signal.
fault	As earlier, but this is the signal called when the serializer is building a fault message.
freeform	As with the previous two, but this signal is used for general cases that don't fit the method or fault models.
trace	This signal marks the entry-point of most functions in the classes. However, not all methods send the signal.
debug	This signal is used in transport modules to track the contents of requests or responses.

The tracing facility is very thorough, and further explanation may be found in Appendix B, which covers the SOAP::Lite toolkit classes in detail. It is possible to provide customized callbacks for any or all the signals listed in the table. Also see the SOAP::Trace section of the SOAP::Lite manpage for more information.

Auto-Dispatch

Another very useful feature of the client class is something called *auto-dispatching*. With this feature, a client application can configure the XMLRPC::Lite client to intercept your Perl function calls and instead transparently make remote method calls. This works only if all the calls are to method names that are valid Perl identifiers (no illegal characters such as ".") in them).

When XMLRPC::Lite is initially loaded, it is possible to set some of the class parameters to values that will later be used as defaults for the creation of new objects. It is also possible to instruct the client class to use Perl's auto-loading functionality to intercept unknown function calls and attempt to resolve them remotely, before giving up and signaling an error. Methods such as proxy and on_fault can be specified in the use line, just as trace was earlier:

```
use XMLRPC::Lite proxy => 'http://localhost:9000';
```

Any client object that is created but given no explicit proxy value will use this default when it tries to call a remote function. With another special keyword, autodispatch, an internal client object can use that same proxy value to automatically look up any unknown functions that are called:

```
use XMLRPC::Lite +autodispatch =>
                 proxy => 'http://localhost:9000';
...
$a = remoteMethod($arg);
```

Of course, using auto-dispatch can lead to code that is more difficult to trace because it hides the remote nature of some of the calls. Auto-dispatch is also unable to call routines whose names contain characters Perl would not recognize in a subroutine name. However, it can make a small-size to mid-size script more readable. The balance between compactness and maintainability is different for different circumstances and can't be dictated as an absolute rule.

The Fortune Server Using XMLRPC::Lite

Implementing the fortune server isn't much more complex using the XMLRPC::Lite classes. In fact, were the underlying code object-oriented rather than procedural, it would be virtually identical. Example 4-4 shows this version of the fortune server.

Example 4-4. The fortune-Lite.pl daemon

```
#!/usr/bin/perl -w

use strict;

use XRFortune;
use XMLRPC::Transport::HTTP;

BEGIN {
    no strict 'refs';

    for my $method qw(books fortune weighted_fortune) {
        *$method = sub { shift; XRFortune::$method(@_) };
    }
}

XMLRPC::Transport::HTTP::Daemon
    ->new(LocalPort => 9000, ReuseAddr => 1)
    ->dispatch_to(qw(books fortune weighted_fortune))
    ->handle;

exit;
```

The first thing to notice is that the package used by Perl isn't the same name used to create the server object. The XMLRPC::Lite::Transport module contains several server classes to choose from. In Example 4-4, the class selected is one that uses an HTTP::Daemon instance behind the scenes to provide the actual server functionality. Unlike the server class provided in the RPC::XMLSimple kit, this class isn't a subclass of HTTP::Daemon but instead transparently routes the relevant methods to the contained object.

The next area worth examining is the BEGIN block that creates local (to the main:: namespace) versions of the three functions that the XRFortune.pm module provided. The loop construct is a shorthand for creating the three subroutines without having three nearly identical declarations. This allows the server object to present them as simple names, rather than requiring that clients use a package name to fully qualify them. However, it isn't enough to import them into the local namespace (assuming XRFortune.pm exports them).

The XMLRPC::Lite server implementations assume that they are dealing with object-oriented code or methods in the traditional sense. Because of this, when the routine is actually entered, the first argument to it will be the package name because all calls are essentially static method invocations. So instead of importing (or aliasing) the routines, the BEGIN block creates simple frontend calls to each routine that strip the initial parameter from the arguments list before calling the true code.

Creating the server object itself is straightforward: a constructor (new) is called with arguments (LocalPort and ReuseAddr) that will eventually be passed to the creation of the HTTP::Daemon object. The return value from the constructor is the new object reference, which is then used to call the dispatch_to method to set up what server-side functionality is being made available to clients. This, too, returns the server object reference upon success, at which point the handle method is called to enter the accept/dispatch loop of the server.

The XMLRPC::Lite Server Classes

The server functionality provided by XMLRPC::Lite is much broader than that of RPC::XMLSimple. Several different classes are provided from which to create a server object. They can also be subclassed, allowing application-specific derivatives to intercede in areas such as authentication or URI mapping. Basic classes are provided for HTTP transport via HTTP::Daemon, ordinary CGI dispatch, and Apache integration. Other server classes include raw TCP/IP transport and support for using a POP3 server as a source of requests. As with the client functionality described earlier, much of the server capabilities are derivative of the SOAP::Lite classes they inherit from.

The server classes generally follow the same behavior in terms of the methods they handle. The primary differences are in how the objects themselves are created. Table 4-3 illustrates the various server classes and the specifics of their constructor syntax. The first column is the module that an application would have to load, and the second column represents the class within that module. Hence, an application would use XMLRPC::Transport::POP3 and then instantiate from the XMLRPC::Transport::POP3::Server class.

Table 4-3. XMLRPC::Lite server classes

Module	Class	Constructor
XMLRPC::Transport::HTTP	Daemon	Arguments to the constructor for this class are mainly passed to the creation of an HTTP::Daemon object. The selection and syntax are the same as for IO::Socket::INET, the parent of that class. These include LocalPort, ReuseAddr, etc. Other arguments are described later.
	CGI	This class provides XML-RPC server functionality as an ordinary CGI application on a webserver. The constructor's arguments are described later.

Table 4-3. XMLRPC::Lite server classes (continued)

Module	Class	Constructor
	Apache	Just as the CGI class provides an XML-RPC layer for ordinary CGI, this class implements some additional hooks and functionality to operate in cooperation with Apache and mod_perl.
XMLRPC::Transport::POP3	Server	The constructor takes a string that represents the POP3 server to poll. It's a pseudo-URL of the form pop3://pop.server.com. It can also include user authentication information.
XMLRPC::Transport::TCP	Server	The raw TCP/IP server class uses an IO::Socket::INET object behind the scenes, and thus the arguments to the constructor are those that would be passed to the creation of the socket, such as LocalAddr, LocalPort, Listen, etc.

Each server class has its own specialized arguments that it recognizes, but all the server classes are ultimately derived from SOAP::Server, which also has a set of arguments it will handle. These arguments are actually a syntax for having the new object call other class methods before the new object reference is returned.

Any of the following methods may appear as an argument to the constructor, immediately followed by what would have been the argument(s) to the method (a list is passed in this syntax as a list reference):

dispatch_to
    This method sets up the known set of methods/routines to be made available to clients. The arguments to this method are each any one of the following:

    Directory path (/usr/local/perl, etc.)
        If the value appears to be a directory path, it is added to the search path for loading modules on demand. Note that the server classes clear out the @INC array for the sake of security. This facility allows the adding (or re-adding) of directories after this has happened.

    Class name (Class::Sub, etc.)
        When the string matches a known class, it makes all methods in that class (or, if you prefer, all functions in the namespace) available. Clients request them using XML-RPC's notion of class-qualified names, Class.Sub.method, for example.

    Subroutine name (Class::Sub::method, local_method, etc.)
        When the value matches a known subroutine name (possibly including the class name), the method or routine is made available. As with specifying a class, the client will have to refer to the subroutine using the full class name, as specified here.

    This method may take just one such option, or as many as the application sees fit to pass at once.

options
    This sets options on the server object. Currently, the only supported option at the XML-RPC level is compress_threshold followed by an integer value. The

server classes use compression if the client indicates support for it and if the `Compress::Zlib` module is available. This option sets the minimum size in bytes a message must be before being compressed. The default is to never compress.

The server classes all have a `handle` method, as well. The Apache-based class also has an alias for `handle` under the name `handler`, so that it is more easily used as a location handler under `mod_perl`. The way `handle` behaves is dependent on the server class. For the `Daemon` class, it enters a loop in which the server waits for incoming requests on the socket and serves each in turn, only exiting when interrupted by a signal. The `CGI` and `Apache` classes handle one request each time the method is invoked and expect the relevant request information to be passed as arguments. The `TCP` class behaves in a similar fashion to the `Daemon` class, while the `POP3` class handles all request messages in the specified POP3 mail folder before returning to the caller.

All the server classes call their local subroutines as if they were methods, passing the class (or package) name in as the first parameter. This works fine for publishing an API that is already a set of class methods. However, when the code to be published isn't object-oriented, such as in the Fortune module, it requires a bit of extra work, as you saw with the BEGIN block in Example 4-4.

RPC::XML

The last of the XML-RPC toolkits discussed here is the `RPC::XML` package, developed by one of the authors of this book, Randy J. Ray. This package isn't quite as independent as the `XMLRPC::Lite` implementation; it requires an external XML parser (currently the `XML::Parser` package from CPAN).

This package gives you a lot of flexibility in creating server applications. The main server class, `RPC::XML::Server`, can function as a standalone server using either the `HTTP::Daemon` class from the `LWP` package or the `Net::Server` package from CPAN. This latter package supports several different multiprocess models and provides all the background operation for whichever model the application chooses to use. Applications can even choose a model on-the-fly, rather than being locked into a specific one. The `RPC::XML` package also provides a server class designed especially to act as a content handler for Apache and `mod_perl`.

In addition to these choices in server management, the package comes with a set of server-side methods that implement the introspection interface pioneered by the PHP XML-RPC suite that was used in building the Meerkat API. This introspection interface was described in Chapter 3.

Client Example: meer2html.pl

The RPC::XML version of the Meerkat example isn't significantly different from the other toolkits' versions. Example 4-5 shows the relevant parts of this version of the script. Appendix C lists the full program.

Example 4-5. The meer2html-RPC::XML.pl script

```
use RPC::XML::Client;

$client = RPC::XML::Client
            # Remember that MEERKAT was declared with "use constant"
            ->new(MEERKAT,
                error_handler =>
                sub { die "Transport error: $_[0]" });
sub show_data {
    my $data = shift;

    print STDOUT qq(<span class="meerkat">\n<dl>\n);
    for (@$data) {
        print STDOUT <<"END_HTML";
<dt class="title"><a href="$_->{link}">$_->{title}</a></dt>
<dd class="description">$_->{description}</dd>
END_HTML
    }
    print STDOUT qq(</dl>\n</span>\n);
}

sub resolve_name {
    my ($str, $name) = @_;

    $name = "meerkat.get${name}BySubstring";
    my $resp = $client->simple_request($name, $str);
    die "resolve_name: $str returned more than 1 match"
        if (@$resp > 1);

    $resp->[0]{id};
}

sub get_data {
    my ($key, $val, $num) = @_;

    $client->simple_request('meerkat.getItems',
                            { $key          => $val,
                              time_period   => '7DAY',
                              num_items     => $num,
                              descriptions  => 200 });
}
```

As with the previous toolkits, only one library is used to get the functionality needed for a client. The constructor for the class is slightly different from both previous toolkits. The first argument must be the URL of the server the client will be conversing with. The constructor can accept some other arguments as well, but in this case, all that gets passed is the error_handler key followed by a closure that is used as a callback when errors occur.

The way RPC::XML handles errors is to return an error message as a simple string, whereas most methods return references normally. Setting the callback in this case causes an error to immediately call die, without the code having to check every return value later on.

For the sake of completeness, the show_data routine is also included here, despite being completely identical to the version used for RPC::XMLSimple and XMLRPC::Lite. This just underscores the simplicity of the way in which all three toolkits make data available to the programmer.

The resolve_name and get_data routines are slightly different than either of the two previous client examples. First, the method the RPC::XML::Client class uses is called simple_request. In fact, the client class defines two methods for making remote requests, the other one being send_request. The one used here returns native Perl data, while the other form returns a data object, similar to the behavior of XMLRPC::Lite. You can choose whether you wish to get the returned data as an object that can be tested for failure and treated as a fault or if you want to let callbacks handle that and just get the Perl data directly.

The RPC::XML::Client Class in Detail

Instances of the RPC::XML::Client class are containers for other class instances, specifically LWP::UserAgent and HTTP::Request. The user-agent object manages the actual communication to and from the server. The request object is created ahead of time so that common elements, such as the majority of the HTTP headers, can be precomputed, rather than newly evaluated on every outgoing message.

The RPC::XML::Client class has a number of methods available to application developers, some of which are summarized here. Appendix A contains a full reference to the classes for all the XML-RPC toolkits covered in this chapter.

new
    This is the class constructor. It requires one initial argument, the URI of the server it will eventually connect to. In addition, these arguments are recognized:
    error_handler
        This key, followed by a subroutine reference, provides a callback routine to be invoked when an error occurs on the client side. It will be called with a single argument, the error message (usually the special Perl variable $@).
    fault_handler
        This is similar to the error callback but provides the callback when a fault is returned by the server (not to be confused with an actual server error or

client-side error). When it is invoked, it is given a single argument: the RPC::
XML::fault object containing the fault itself.

combined_handler
: This is a convenience parameter for setting both handlers to the same callback at once.

    Note that the callbacks don't get the client object in the argument list. See the callback-specific methods later for the alternative to specifying them at object creation.

send_request
: This is the more robust of the two methods for calling remote procedures. The arguments it accepts may be either the remote name followed by zero or more data arguments, or a precomputed RPC::XML::request object (described later). The return value is either a data object reference or an error string. If the return value isn't a reference, it is a local (not server-side) error. Otherwise, server-side errors are returned as RPC::XML::fault objects.

simple_request
: This method is functionally the same as send_request, with the difference that it returns native Perl data rather than a data-encapsulating object. This is meant to simplify smaller, shorter tasks. But it also means that the object can't be directly tested to see if it is a fault or not. The application must either use the callbacks or check that the return is a hash reference with only the keys faultCode and faultString. It is also difficult to discern an error message from the client code, unless the application was expecting a result that could not look like a text string. When using this method, the fault_handler and error_handler callbacks are strongly recommended.

uri
: When called with no arguments, this method returns the current URI the client is connecting to. When an argument is passed, it is assumed to be a new URI and replaces the old one. This actually calls the uri method of the underlying HTTP::Request object. As such, it checks the validity of the URI, returning undef if it is invalid. It also means that an object of the URI class (the URI module is an installation dependency for LWP, so it will be available to the application) may be given as an argument.

error_handler, fault_handler, combined_handler
: These methods get the current handler (when called with no arguments) or set a new handler (when called with an argument that is a code reference). The combined_handler method returns a two-element list because it is retrieving what may be two different callbacks.

    These methods are useful for setting callbacks that need to have access to the object itself. They can be given closures as new callbacks that contain lexically scoped references to the object.

The RPC::XML::Client class doesn't auto-dispatch methods the way XMLRPC::Lite does. It does offer helper functions for creating data objects in cases where the Perl interpreter might not be able to correctly guess the type. Table 4-4 lists the data classes and the related helper functions.

Table 4-4. The RPC::XML data classes and functions

Data class	Helper	Description
RPC::XML::int	RPC_INT	The class holds an int value, though the helper function is rarely needed because Perl can identify an integer distinctly.
RPC::XML::i4	RPC_I4	Because an XML-RPC server that checks signatures considers int and i4 as distinct, this class and helper are useful for expressing this type rather than defaulting to int.
RPC::XML::Double	RPC_DOUBLE	This class wraps a double value, which is also easily identified by Perl.
RPC::XML::String	RPC_STRING	This class and helper function are useful for expressing string values that could be mistaken for other types.
RPC::XML::Boolean	RPC_BOOLEAN	The boolean type can be created with any of true, false, yes, no, 1, or 0. When serialized, it conforms to the XML-RPC specification.
RPC::XML::datetime_iso8601	RPC_DATETIME_ISO8601	This class wraps a date string but doesn't make any effort to validate the format.
RPC::XML::base64	RPC_BASE64	The last of the classes (and helpers), this manages arbitrary chunks of data. The data is kept intact and only converted to Base64 for XML serialization.

All the helper functions take a single value as an argument and return an object reference from the appropriate class.

The classes themselves share a number of common methods:

new
> This is the class constructor. It takes a new value and returns an object reference that wraps the data so that other parts of the module can use it directly. The RPC::XML::base64 constructor recognizes a second parameter to the constructor, used to signify that the data is already encoded as Base64.

as_string
> Returns an XML fragment that expresses the object in a format that conforms to XML-RPC.

value
> This method returns the underlying Perl value that the object wraps. Note that for the Base64 data, this returns the real data, not the encoded format.

type
> Returns a simple identifier of the type for the object. Types are the names as defined in the XML-RPC specification (int, dateTime.iso8601, double, etc.).

is_fault
> This is a boolean test to determine if the value object represents a fault. This is a constant false value in all the data classes, except for the RPC::XML::fault class, in which it is overridden to return true.

These methods apply to the RPC::XML::array and RPC::XML::struct classes, as well. Helper functions aren't available for them, but RPC::XML can map them from list and hash references, respectively.

Faults are managed in a class called RPC::XML::fault, which is a subclass of the struct class (and it doesn't have a helper function either). Faults must be created using the class constructor, but the constructor has a few shortcut approaches available to the writer:

new(RPC::XML::struct)
> Creates the fault object from an existing RPC::XML::struct object.

new($int, $string)
> Creates the object from an integer and string, which are explicitly converted and assigned to the correct structure keys.

new(faultCode => $code, faultString => $string)
> In case the application chooses to be more explicit, this format is also supported. The two keys may be specified in either order.

As mentioned earlier, the fault class overrides the is_fault method to return true.

The Fortune Server Using RPC::XML::Server

As with previous implementations of the *fortune* example, the code in Example 4-6 is very simple. The RPC::XML::Server class version is longer than either of the previous two, however. This is because this server class doesn't provide a way to add local procedures by class or namespace as previous implementations do.

One thing that sets this server class apart from the previous two is that it manages and monitors the signatures associated with server-side routines. These are apparent in Example 4-6, and a client trying to connect to this server would have to form a valid request based on these specifications.

Example 4-6. The RPC::XML fortune server

```
RPC::XML::Server->new(port => 9000)
    ->add_proc({ name => 'books',
                 signature => [ 'array',
                                'array string',
                                'array array' ],
                 code => \&XRFortune::books })
    ->add_proc({ name => 'fortune',
                 signature => [ 'array',
                                'array string',
```

Example 4-6. The RPC::XML fortune server (continued)

```
                            'array array' ],
             code => \&XRFortune::fortune })
  ->add_proc({ name => 'weighted_fortune',
               signature => [ 'array',
                              'array string',
                              'array array' ],
               code => \&XRFortune::weighted_fortune })
  ->server_loop;
```

In this example, only the toolkit-specific lines are shown (the full code is given in Appendix C). The class constructor isn't that different in syntax or function from the previous examples. Like `XMLRPC::Lite`, most of the methods return the object reference upon success, allowing for methods to be chained together. Here, the `add_proc` method is called three times, adding one procedure each time. After the third call, the `server_loop` method handles the socket-accept logic until a signal of some kind causes it to exit, at which point the script also exits.

The design philosophy behind this server implementation is to exert more hands-on control over the methods and procedures that are published. It does this by allowing them to be added manually, loaded from a XML file (a format called "XPL," detailed later), or by loading entire directories of such files at a time. The XML file format will be discussed later, after we cover the basics of the server class itself.

The RPC::XML::Server Class in Detail

The `RPC::XML::Server` class is a container much like the server classes from `RPC::XMLSimple` and `XMLRPC::Lite`. Like those two, the basic functionality is found in the `HTTP::Daemon` class from the `LWP` package. But this server class can also use the `Net::Server` package from CPAN, if it is available. `Net::Server` provides a server framework with several different styles for the connection/service model. Besides the standard single-process and fork-per-request models, the package can also emulate Apache's preforking, multiple-child architecture. The package is worth evaluation independent of XML-RPC itself.

Server-side code is associated with a server object in one of three forms: a method, a procedure, or a function. The names distinguish the way the server interacts with the code when managing a request, as shown in Table 4-5.

Table 4-5. Types of server-side code

Style	Signatures	Server object
Procedure	Yes	No
Method	Yes	Yes
Function	No	No

A method (RPC::XML::Method) checks signatures but doesn't count the server object (which is passed as the first parameter when invoked) in the argument list. This allows the method itself to access the server object and its relevant data. A procedure (RPC::XML::Procedure) is almost the same as a method, but it doesn't get the server object. It does check signatures. Finally, the function (RPC::XML::Function) does no checking of signatures at all, and doesn't receive the server object.*

The constructor for the server class has a complex array of options available. These are summarized in Table 4-6. At present, much of the server functionality can be controlled only through these options. Not all have corresponding accessor methods for later modification.

Table 4-6. The options available to the RPC::XML::Server constructor

Option	Function
no_http	If this is passed with a non-false value, it prevents the constructor from allocating a HTTP::Daemon object. This is used by the Apache module or when the application wants to use Net::Server instead.
no_default	If passed and non-false, suppresses the loading of the interoperability methods provided by the package. These are detailed later.
host port queue	These four values may be used when the application wants to explicitly provide a hostname or address to bind to, port to bind to, or listen-queue size. They are used when creating the HTTP::Daemon object but may also be used with Net::Server, depending on other issues specific to that module.
path	By default, the daemon will not consider the path part of the URI used in the request. If this option is passed, the server handles requests only to the given path. This option has no meaning for the Apache module because it is configured to a specific location by Apache itself.
xpl_path	When adding methods or procedures by way of XPL files (covered later), this option allows you to specify additional directories to search for these files. Always takes a list reference as the argument.
timeout	The default time-out from the point when the server accepts a connection on the inbound socket until it expects to be able to read the full request is 10 seconds. This option can set a different value.
auto_methods	When this is passed and non-false, it allows the server to search for an unknown method by looking in the directories that can hold XPL files, for a file whose name matches the requested method. This is off by default, for obvious security reasons.
auto_updates	Like the previous option, this is off by default and applies only to code read from XPL files. If this is passed with a non-false value, then methods associated with an XPL file check the modification time of the file before being executed. If the file has been updated, it is reloaded before the request is dispatched.

Compared to the constructor, the remaining class methods are pretty simple and clear. Some of the more commonly used ones are:

add_method, add_proc
> Adds a new method (or procedure) to the server. The new code may be specified as an object of the appropriate class, as a hash reference, or as a filename. If the value is a hash reference, the name of the method used (add_method or

---

* As of Version 0.4 (the latest at the time of writing), there is no equivalent of RPC::XML::Function that includes the server object like a method does.

add_proc) determines the type of internal object used. Filenames are expected to be XPL files.

delete_method
: Removes a method/procedure/function from the server by its published name. Returns the internal object that represents the method, in case the application wishes to re-add it later.

get_method
: Gets the internal object for the method/procedure/function specified as an argument. The name requested must match the externally published name for the code.

add_methods_in_dir
: Adds all the XPL files in the specified directory. Provided as a matter of convenience, for applications that collect their code as XPL files in one location.

share_methods, copy_methods
: These methods allow two objects to share or copy method objects between them. Methods that are shared mean that each server has a reference to the same underlying object. Statistics gathered (such as call frequency) will be the same in both servers. Methods that are copied don't share any part except the code reference part within the internal object. This allows multiple server objects to use the same method code from XPL files without having to load them multiple times (which results in multiple anonymous subroutines from the same code block).

server_loop
: This method is the center of server functionality for the objects. It is here that the server enters the socket-accept loop and waits for client connections. The application can pass arguments as a hash table (not a hash reference). If the object has no HTTP::Daemon instance associated with it (no_http was specified at creation time), the hash table represents arguments that are passed to the run method of Net::Server. Otherwise, when using HTTP::Daemon, the only argument recognized is signal, whose value should be either a string specifying a signal by name or a list reference of more than one signal name. The signals specified are configured to act as interrupts for the accept loop.

As of Version 0.43 of the toolkit, RPC::XML::Server and the Apache subclass derived from it support compression using the Compress::Zlib module from CPAN, if available. The mechanics of expressing compression support in the message headers tries to be compatible with XMLRPC::Lite. In general, if the compression module is available and both ends of the conversation support compression, it should happen behind the scenes without any direct intervention on the part of the application.

Managing server-side code with XPL files

There have been numerous references to XPL files up to now. These files are a format originally created for expressing methods for the server. Since then, the syntax has been extended to distinguish methods, procedures, and functions. The actual code for the method may also be provided in multiple languages (though obviously only the Perl code matters to this server).

The goal of the format was to provide a way to exchange "bundles" of XML-RPC functionality with all the meta-data (signatures, help text, etc.) packaged as well. XPL originally referred to the file being a *.pl* wrapped in XML.

Example 4-7 shows a sample XPL file for one of the introspection routines the RPC::XML package includes. This example has the help text removed, as well as comment blocks, for brevity. The full example is listed in Appendix C.

Example 4-7. A sample XPL file, listMethods.xpl

```
<?xml version="1.0"?>
<!DOCTYPE methoddef SYSTEM "rpc-method.dtd">
<methoddef>
<name>system.listMethods</name>
<version>1.1</version>
<signature>array</signature>
<signature>array string</signature>
<help>
...
</help>
<code language="perl">
<![CDATA[
#!/usr/bin/perl
sub listMethods
{
    use strict;

    my $srv = shift;
    my $pat = shift;

    my @list = sort $srv->list_methods;

    # Exclude any that are hidden from introspection APIs
    @list = grep(! $srv->get_method($_)->hidden, @list);
    @list = grep(index($_, $pat) != -1, @list) if ($pat);

    \@list;
}

__END__
]]></code>
</methoddef>
```

The layout of the file is very basic. The outer tag is one of `methoddef`, `proceduredef`, or `functiondef`. The container tag therefore declares the type of procedure being defined (in terms of the three types explained earlier). Within this container must be a `name` tag that provides the published name of the routine, at least one `signature` tag with a space-separated signature (except in the case of `RPC::XML::Function` declarations), and the `code` container with the actual Perl code for the routine.

The source code can be encoded one of two ways: using an XML CDATA section, as done earlier, or by ensuring that any < or & characters are entity-encoded. By using the CDATA approach and including both the `#!perl` start-up line and `__END__` token at the end, the whole XPL file can be syntax-checked with `perl -cx`. (This doesn't validate the XML, it checks only the Perl syntax.)

In addition to the previous tags, the file can also define `version` (the version number/symbol of the code), `hidden` (an empty tag whose presence means the function should not be listed by the introspection API), and `help` (the minidocumentation text the introspection API uses when describing the routine to a client). These tags are all optional, and the `version` tag information isn't generally used anywhere except in the Apache status module, described later.

The application developer isn't left with the task of creating these files manually. The distribution of `RPC::XML` includes a utility script that can create the XPL files from files containing the Perl code and meta-data either in files or passed on the command line. The script, `make_method`, is documented and the distribution's `Makefile.PL` contains an example of integrating it into a build process. The distribution uses the XPL format to manage the introspection API routines that are provided. The make_method tool can build an XPL file from command-line data or from a meta-configuration file:

```
make_method --name=reboot --helpfile=reboot.help --code=reboot.pl \
            --signature=int --output=reboot.xpl

make_method --base=reboot
```

The Introspection Interface for Servers

Table 4-7 lists the server introspection routines, along with their calling syntax (signatures) and basic functionality.

Table 4-7. The server introspection routines

Procedure name	Signature(s)	What it does
system.identity	string	Returns the server's identity in the form of a "name/version" string.
system.introspection	array array array struct string	Returns an array of structures that completely describe all the routines the server has configured (minus any that are tagged to be hidden). If a single name is specified, returns just the one structure. If an array is given, returns the structure for just those names.

Table 4-7. The server introspection routines (continued)

Procedure name	Signature(s)	What it does
system.listMethods	array array string	Lists the methods known to the server (minus hidden ones). If a string is passed, only the names that contain it as a substring are returned.
system.methodHelp	string string array array	Returns the help text for a single named method as a string or an array of help strings if passed an array of names.
system. methodSignature	array string array array	Returns the array of signatures for the named method or an array of arrays when more than one name is passed. Each signature is represented by an array of types, with the first being the type of return value to expect.
system.multicall	array array	Takes an array of structures, each representing one remote call. Makes the remote calls and returns an array of the result values.
system.status	struct	Returns a structure containing various runtime statistics and status reports from the server.

Both the primary server class and the Apache-specific class (described next) default to loading these routines. Loading of the routines can be disabled by passing no_default => 1 in the constructor. Likewise, they can be added at a later time by calling a method on the server object called add_default_methods. The Apache server class has a slightly different version of system.status that reports additional information pertaining to the Apache environment.

Writing for Apache with Apache::RPC::Server

One distinct difference between the RPC::XML toolkit versus the others is the native support for running under Apache and mod_perl. The basic server class is subclassed in Apache::RPC::Server, which provides handlers for the PerlHandler and PerlChildInitHandler phases of the request/response lifecycle.

The handler and init_handler methods of the class are used as Apache location handlers, not as components of a script that would run under the Apache::Registry system. Instead, the Apache configuration maps a URI location (or more than one) to the XML-RPC subsystem. The objects of this class don't allocate HTTP listeners, operating instead on the request objects that Apache creates for handlers to access.

Configuring Server Objects

RPC server objects for the Apache environment are usually configured in a different manner than the other servers. In many cases, the configuration of the XML-RPC handler in Apache will be a simple PerlHandler directive:

```
<Location /rpc>
    SetHandler perl-script
    PerlHandler Apache::RPC::Server
</Location>
```

This configuration doesn't install any server-side code except for the introspection routines. To give the administrator the ability to control the Apache RPC environment at this level, the `Apache::RPC::Server` class allows for most of the configurable parameters to be set using location-based directives. The following fragment shows many of these in use, with in-line comments explaining them:

```
<Location /rpc>
    SetHandler perl-script
    # handler() doesn't have to be specified, but it can be
    PerlHandler Apache::RPC::Server->handler
    # define a name for the server, in case more than one
    # will be configured for this Apache host
    RpcServer rpc
    # add a directory to the list of dirs that methods are
    # kept in; may appear multiple times
    RpcServerDir /opt/rpc/methods
    # Add on specific method by file name; may also appear
    # multiple times
    RpcServerMethod /opt/rpc/extra/method.xpl
    # suppress loading the introspection API methods
    RpcDefMethods no
    # disable auto-loading of methods...
    RpcAutoMethods no
    # ...but allow existing methods to auto-update:
    RpcAutoUpdates yes
</Location>
```

There are more options detailed in the manpages for the class. When configured using `Location` directives, the server objects pick up their methods from a three-step sequence:

1. Unless specifically disabled, the introspection methods are loaded first.
2. Any `RpcServerDir` directives are treated, and all XPL files in each specified directory are loaded.
3. Any `RpcServerMethod` directives are processed, and the files are loaded.

Any methods can be overridden in this process by a adding a new method under the name of an existing one. Thus, a server can add all the routines in a given directory, then use one or more `RpcServerMethod` directives to selectively replace some of them.

For more direct control over the RPC server objects, Apache can be configured using `<Perl>` sections in the configuration file. Using this method, the server-side code can be controlled in finer detail. The configuration also has full access to the server operations, and multiple server objects can be configured to share common methods, rather than having multiple copies of the same code in memory simultaneously. This fragment shows a sample configuration with two servers, one of which is access-controlled; the other isn't:

```
<Perl>

# First, create and configure some Apache::RPC::Server
# objects

# One regular one, with the standard settings:
$main::defobj = Apache::RPC::Server->new(path => '/RPC',
                                         auto_methods => 1,
                                         auto_updates => 1);
# One version without the default methods, and no
# auto-actions
$main::secobj = Apache::RPC::Server->new(no_default => 1,
                                         path =>
                                             '/rpc-secured');
# Give the secured one access to server.status, for report
# gathering:
$main::secobj->copy_methods($main::defobj, 'system.status');

# Imagine that add_method and/or add_methods_in_dir has been
# used to add to the methods tables for those objects. Now
# assign them to locations managed by Apache:
$Location{'/RPC'} =
    {
        SetHandler  => 'perl-script',
        PerlHandler => '$main::defobj'
    };
$Location{'/rpc-secure'} =
    {
        SetHandler   => 'perl-script',
        PerlHandler  => '$main::secobj',
        AuthUserFile => '/etc/some_file',
        AuthType     => 'Basic',
        AuthName     => 'SecuredRPC',
        'require'    => 'valid-user'
    };

</Perl>
```

In the example, the password-protected RPC server chose not to load the default methods. However, there was a need for the system.status method to track the statistics of the server. This can be explicitly added with add_method, but by using share_ methods, the actual internal Perl code already present on the "open" server is used.

This approach has another advantage over the Location configuration method. When servers are configured using Perl sections, they are configured in the parent before the child processes are created. As a result, the children are created with the servers already in place and ready to operate. This is because the code sets the location handler to be an actual object reference, rather than a class name. When the handler is called for a request, it has the object there and ready, and doesn't have to first check for and retrieve a (possibly new) class instance to handle the request.

With the Location configuration, the objects aren't created until the first request is received, which keeps them from being shared between children.

The Apache::RPC::Status Monitor

The last topic for this chapter isn't an XML-RPC processor, but it works together with the Apache server class. Apache::RPC::Status is a status monitor modeled after the Apache::Status package that reports the statistics of configured XML-RPC servers controlled by the Apache server.

The Apache::RPC::Status package lets a server administrator check the status of the RPC servers configured on a given host. As Figures 4-1 through 4-3 illustrate, the monitor allows the view to go from a high-level view of the server (or servers) down to the numbers for a given procedure.

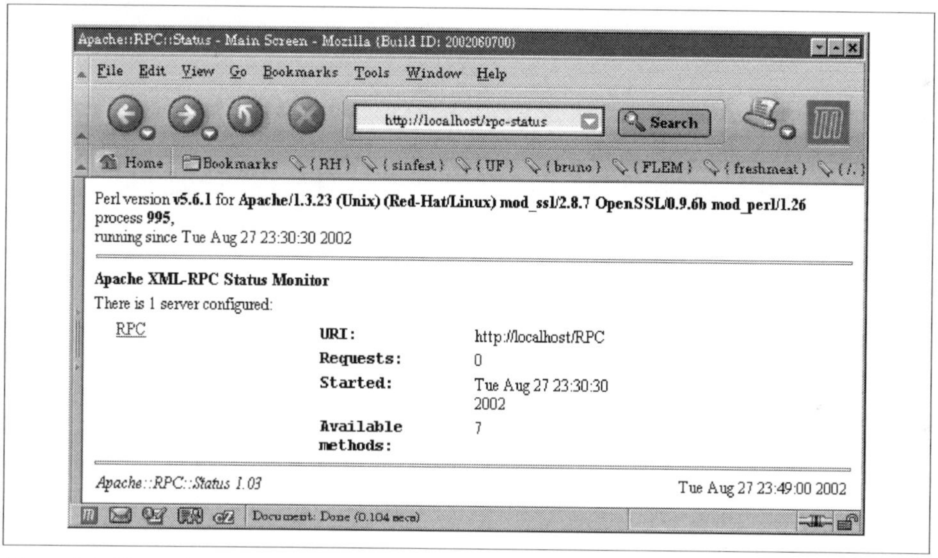

Figure 4-1. The main monitor page

Fortunately, configuring and enabling the status monitor is much less intensive than are the RPC servers themselves:

```
</Location /rpc-status>
    SetHandler perl-script
    PerlHandler Apache::RPC::Status
</Location>
```

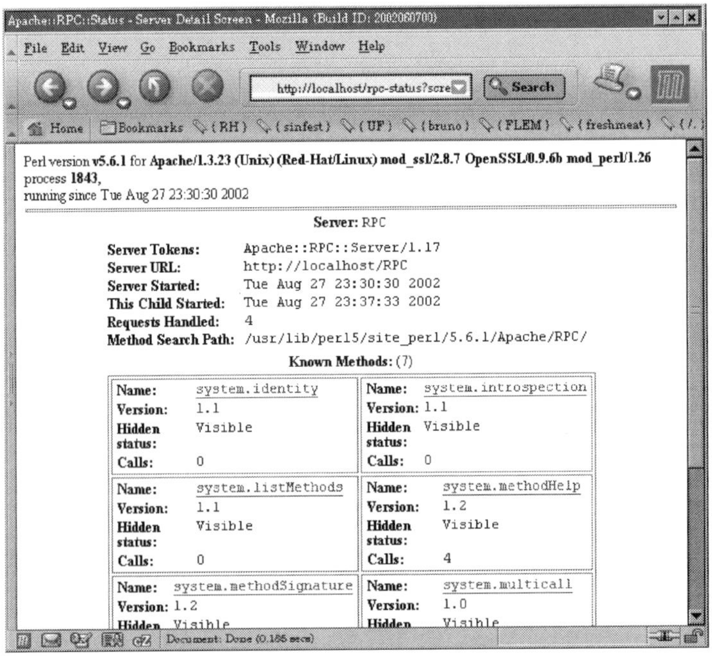

Figure 4-2. The server-level page, showing known methods

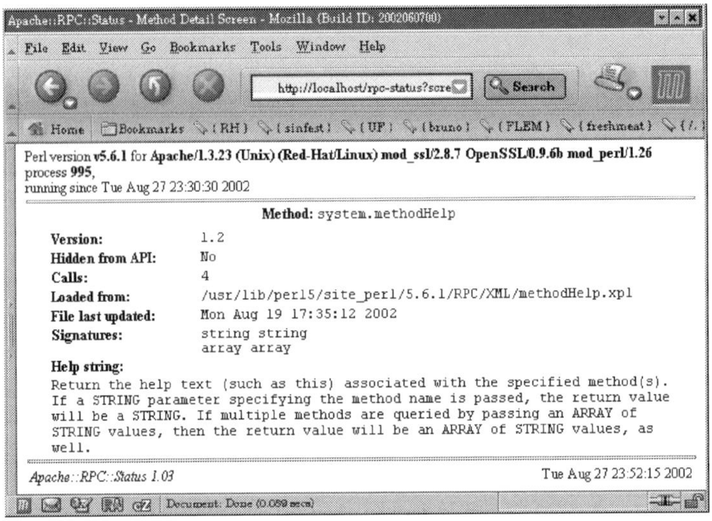

Figure 4-3. The method-level page, showing documentation

CHAPTER 5
Introduction to SOAP

The Simple Object Access Protocol (SOAP) is the basis for the W3C design for web services. The specifications that make up SOAP cover the expression of data, what to require for communication, and how to link messages with communication layers. When using toolkits (introduced in Chapter 6), it is often not necessary to know more than just the basic elements of SOAP. But the more thorough your understanding, the easier you can develop better, more efficient applications.

This chapter introduces the basic parts of SOAP, and illustrates how they work together to create a platform for distributed application development. The focus of this chapter is the XML that implements SOAP requests and responses and how the SOAP specification is built from other XML technologies, such as XML Schema. Later chapters build SOAP-enabled applications with toolkits, but to make full use of the toolkits, you must know the constraints of the SOAP protocol that they implement.

Background

Where CORBA and COM+ followed RPC, SOAP and XML-RPC are more like its contemporaries. While SOAP was going through a very thorough process of requirements gathering and design analysis, XML-RPC was spun off from an early draft of SOAP.

The time spent in design and planning was far from squandered. The resulting specification from the working group is very flexible and leaves a considerable amount of room for expansion of the protocol. Expansion and extension of the protocol may come from added XML applications bundled into the encoding layer, in either (or both) of the message header and body. Beyond this, the protocol itself is kept by version and maintained as a W3C *Technical Recommendation*, the term used by the W3C for standards that have been adopted.

At the time of this writing, the Technical Recommendation (TR) of the specification is at Version 1.1, with Version 1.2 currently very close to acceptance as the new current TR. By virtue of the clear definitions of versions and capabilities of the specification, an application (usually at the server end) can tell almost immediately whether it can handle a given request well before reading the entire message.

> As this chapter outlines the elements and structure of SOAP communications, there will occasionally be the need to highlight a significant difference between the two versions of the protocol. Look for such differences in paragraphs like this.

SOAP offers a lot more capability and expressiveness than XML-RPC. In addition to enabling remote procedure calls, it also supports a document model in which messages are more free-form and not as strictly defined in terms of a more typical call/response pattern. While it doesn't inherently do features such as security, authentication, transactions, etc., it allows these concepts to be layered over the basic SOAP elements.

SOAP allows for conversations to be designed around more than one server, or *node*, as they are often called in the specification. SOAP uses the concepts of *actors* (called *roles* in SOAP 1.2) and metadata to fine-tune the transition of messages through all stages of a conversation. Like XML-RPC, SOAP can express all the relevant data (method names, data, and parameters) as XML within the messages. Unlike XML-RPC, SOAP allows for more choice and flexibility in how encoding takes place, by allowing messages to specify the encoding rules they use. These topics are explored in greater detail in later sections.

XML Definitions

This chapter introduces the structure and mechanics of SOAP and SOAP messages. In practice, the majority of the work behind creating SOAP messages and disassembling them on the receiving end is done using a toolkit such as `SOAP::Lite`, which will be introduced in Chapter 6. Understanding the form and function of SOAP messages helps you understand the functionality of the toolkit components. This chapter is by no means a complete overview of SOAP. The number (and length) of books devoted to the topic of SOAP is a testimony to the depth of the subject.

Because SOAP is by its very nature a more complex protocol than XML-RPC, it should be no surprise that the depth of the XML it uses is appropriately more complex. One of the key differences between parsing SOAP messages as opposed to XML-RPC is the need for support of XML namespaces. SOAP not only uses namespaces for their original purpose of mixing document-type elements, it also uses them to distinguish between different versions of the specification.

Another important factor in processing a typical SOAP message is that the specification requires the message contain no DTD declaration or processing instructions (which includes XML comments). This may limit the ability to apply other technologies, such as XSLT, to either the request or response messages. The current draft proposals for SOAP 1.2 allow processing instructions to be present but mandate that receivers ignore them. This allows other processing, such as XSLT (XML Stylesheet Language Transforms), without burdening the servers.

Despite these minor differences, a SOAP message is still at its core just another XML document. As such, it is self-describing and (in most cases) very readable by the average viewer. Thoughtful and consistent labeling of the namespaces can also add to the readability.

The Basic Message Structure

In the simplest of terms, a SOAP message is made up of the following parts:

- The containing Envelope tag, with proper namespace qualification and declaration.
- An optional Header tag, which provides additional information directly to the server attempting to handle the message.
- The Body tag, within which is encoded the data ranging from details of the request being made, to the expression of any data that may be a part of a request.

Example 5-1 is a simple message with Envelope, Header, and Body.

Example 5-1. A basic SOAP message

```
<SOAP-ENV:Envelope xmlns:SOAP-ENV=
    "http://schemas.xmlsoap.org/soap/envelope/">
  <SOAP-ENV:Header>
    <auth:Authorize xmlns:auth=
        "http://auth.xmlsoap.org/auth/">
      <auth:type>user</auth:type>
      <auth:name>soapclient</auth:name>
      <auth:passwd>s0m3*th!ng</auth:passwd>
    </auth:Authorize>
  </SOAP-ENV:Header>
  <SOAP-ENV:Body>
    <call:getQuote xmlns:call=
        "http://bigtrade.com/soap/service/">
      ...detail of function call and data
    </call:getQuote>
  </SOAP-ENV:Body>
</SOAP-ENV:Envelope>
```

The message starts with the required Envelope tag. The tag is qualified as being in a namespace that is referenced by the URI *http://schemas.xmlsoap.org/soap/envelope/*. This particular namespace is what identifies the message as being SOAP 1.1, so the declaration does double-duty, both declaring the prefix and identifying the SOAP version.

The Header element is an optional part of the message. In this case it illustrates how a client might pass authentication credentials to the server. In a more complete example, there would likely be attributes in the Authorize tag that control how the server would respond if it did not understand what to do with the tag (discussed in more detail in the section "The Header Tag: Routing and More"). Here, it is enough to see how the child tags are required to be namespace-qualified as well, to set them apart from the SOAP-ENV space. Note that the child tags of Authorize use the same namespace as their parent. (We made up the namespace for the Authorize tag, despite the *xmlsoap.org* domain, so don't try to use it in your own programs!)

Because HTTP messages aren't encrypted, in practice you wouldn't send a password in the clear like this. The easiest way to secure it is to use a transport layer of HTTP over Secure Socket Layer (SSL). This is the *https* protocol used to implement secure web sites that handle credit card numbers and other data that shouldn't be sent unencrypted over the wire.

Following the Header is the mandatory Body element. As with the header part of the message, the immediate child tag within Body is expected to have a separate namespace from that of the SOAP envelope. Of course, the authorization and the function call could have used the same namespace, but the getQuote tag would still have had to declare it. At this point, the earlier declaration made for Authorize has gone out of scope.

The tag in the body of the message is the beginning of a common SOAP example, the stock trading-price quote.* The details of the call itself and the data within will be explained when we get to the Body element.

Because SOAP messages can become lengthy and complex, many of the examples through the rest of this book will be expressed as fragments, rather than whole and complete messages.

The Envelope Tag: Declaring Namespaces

In Example 5-1, the Envelope tag was used only to declare the basic SOAP namespace. In fact, a tag may be used to declare as many namespaces as the application needs to define at a given point, and the start of the message is often the choice. Some frequently used namespaces that get in SOAP messages are listed in Table 5-1. The table also shows the labels that are consistently used to identify them throughout the book.

---

* It may be taken on *very good* authority that this is the only reference to stock-quote applications to be found in this entire book.

Table 5-1. *The most common namespaces*

Namespace URI	Label
http://schemas.xmlsoap.org/soap/envelope/	SOAP-ENV (1.1)
http://www.w3.org/2002/06/soap-envelope	SOAP-ENV or env (1.2)
http://schemas.xmlsoap.org/soap/encoding/	SOAP-ENC (1.1)
http://www.w3.org/2002/06/soap-encoding	SOAP-ENC or enc (1.2)
http://www.w3.org/2001/XMLSchema	xs (sometimes xsd)
http://www.w3.org/2001/XMLSchema-instance	xsi

The SOAP-ENV and SOAP-ENC labels occur multiple times in the table because the namespace URI is also used to identify which version of the SOAP specification has been used for the message. In the working drafts for SOAP 1.2, we use the labels env and enc in place of SOAP-ENV and SOAP-ENC. The older labels are used by some toolkits and languages, regardless of the SOAP version. Within this and the chapters that follow, the newer and shorter labels will be used for SOAP 1.2 examples, while the longer labels will be retained for examples that are SOAP 1.1. The last two lines in the table correspond to XML Schema namespaces that SOAP messages use a lot in expressing data.

The SOAP-ENV label is familiar; it was used in Example 5-1. But what exactly is the SOAP-ENC label used to annotate? This label is used in the SOAP specification to define the namespace for the data encoding SOAP itself provides for convenience. Messages may often be able to express all data using these encodings, without having to use any XML Schema. Some messages may use multiple encodings. It isn't unusual to see a tag like that in Example 5-2, where several namespaces are declared at once.

Example 5-2. *Envelope tag with several declarations*

```
<SOAP-ENV:Envelope xmlns:SOAP-ENV=
    "http://schemas.xmlsoap.org/soap/envelope/"
    SOAP-ENV:encodingStyle=
    "http://schemas.xmlsoap.org/soap/encoding/"
    xmlns:xsd="http://www.w3.org/2001/XMLSchema"
    xmlns:xsi="http://www.w3.org/2001/XMLSchema-instance">

    ...rest of message

</SOAP-ENV:Envelope>
```

Besides specifying a namespace for the encoding rules, an envelope may define a default encoding style that should be assumed over all elements in the message that aren't explicitly assigned a different style. Later, other attributes will be discussed in the context of the header and body of the message.

The Header Tag: Routing and More

The Header tag is the only optional part of the basic SOAP message. Despite this, it is present more often than not. The header section of a message may include authentication credentials (as shown in Example 5-1), information about other servers the message will visit, transaction management, and so forth. Another way of looking at this is that headers provide metadata for the message, adding more detail and information.

Each tag that is a child element of header tag is considered to be a single *block*, considered independently of all others. Each block must be qualified by a namespace. There are no child elements defined for Header within the SOAP specification itself; thus, all blocks use tags imported from a different specification. You may see attributes from the SOAP environment on these tags because XML permits the mixing of attributes within a tag by way of namespace qualification, just as it does with the tags themselves.

Example 5-1 showed a single block within the Header element, a block that provided authentication credentials for the caller. Example 5-3 uses the same Header but adds some additional blocks.

Example 5-3. A header containing several blocks

```
<SOAP-ENV:Header>
  <auth:Authorize xmlns:auth=
      "http://auth.xmlsoap.org/auth/">
    <type>user</type>
    <name>soapclient</name>
    <passwd>s0m3*th!ng</passwd>
  </auth:Authorize>
  <p:priority xmlns:p="http://tasks.xmlsoap.org/priority"
      SOAP-ENV:mustUnderstand="0">
    <value xsi:type="xs:int">19</value>
  </p:priority>
  <tr:transaction xmlns:tr="soap-transaction"
      SOAP-ENV:mustUnderstand="1">
    <transactionID>141421</transactionID>
  </tr:transaction>
</SOAP-ENV:Header>
```

Taking the tags somewhat literally, it can be assumed that the second block acts to specify that the task may be run at a particular priority. It refers to a different namespace, and thus a completely separate specification from SOAP itself. Following the "priority" block is a third block that specifies a transaction identifier for the message. Its namespace is a relative URI computed against the namespace URI of the parent (Header) tag.

Both blocks also introduce a new piece of the SOAP picture. They each bear an attribute called mustUnderstand, that is qualified into the namespace that SOAP-ENV represents. The SOAP envelope provides two global attributes that may be used within blocks in the header: mustUnderstand and actor. In simple terms, actor associates blocks from the header with a specific step (or *node*, as will be defined soon) in the lifecycle of the message, while mustUnderstand defines whether the node that would handle a given block must do so. SOAP also provides the attribute introduced earlier, encodingStyle, that can choose a different encoding to express the actual information contained in those blocks.

The encodingStyle attribute

Looking back to Table 5-1, there are predefined namespaces for the basic encoding rules the SOAP specification provides. These are generally referenced in the Envelope tag, at the same point that the main namespaces are being declared. An encoding style may also be specified at the header-block level. This provides a different default encoding from that given in the Envelope tag and extends to the closing tag that matches the declaring tag.

Data encoding, and the differences in encoding styles themselves, are covered in greater detail later within this chapter.

Actors, roles, nodes, and responsibility

Before looking at the actor (called a role in SOAP 1.2) and mustUnderstand settings, it may help to understand what actors and nodes are, in the context of a SOAP message.

A SOAP transaction isn't limited to just one receiver, or endpoint. The more traditional model of the client/server system has the server as the single destination of a message, with the response that the client receives coming completely from that server. In the SOAP model, a message may pass through several hands before reaching a final destination. Each intermediate step may act on and alter some part of the message before passing control to the next. The response that the initiating client eventually receives may be a composite of response data from any number of the intermediaries involved.

Each step on such a path may be thought of as a *node*. There are always at least two nodes, each of which has exactly one role: it is either the initial sender of a request (the client) or it is the ultimate receiver of a request and responsible for generating the response (the server). In some cases, though, a node may be responsible for doing both. A request that it gets may only be making one of several stops. In these cases, the node must process those parts it has responsibility for, then send the message along to the next node in the chain.

SOAP manages these routes through the definition of actors and responsibility. An actor is merely a role played by a node along the trip. An *actor* is said to have responsibility for a block if the block refers to the current actor, or if the block refers to the anonymous actor, and the acting node is the ultimate receiver of the message. Actor roles are specified through attributes within the block's container element.

The actor/role attributes

There are two defined specific actors in SOAP 1.1, with a third one added to the specification with SOAP 1.2. The actor attribute is specified in the opening tag of a given block and must be qualified into the envelope namespace (as appropriate for the SOAP version). If there is no actor attribute in a block's tag, that block is said to be the responsibility of the *anonymous actor*. This actor represents the ultimate receiver of the message, regardless of the number of intermediate nodes involved.

> In SOAP 1.2, the actor attribute was renamed as role. The names "actor" and "role" should be considered identical in the rest of the text.

The second of the common actor roles is the *current actor*. This refers to the currently active node. The actor attribute is set to a particular URI, slightly different between Versions 1.1 and 1.2, which tells the node that it has responsibility for the given block. An actor will see this value of the attribute only if it was specifically set by the client from whom the message was received. However many nodes there are in the complete message lifespan, as soon as one of those nodes receives a header block with the actor set to this URI, that node will have to either process it, ignore it, or report an error. Whichever of these may be the case, if the message proceeds forward to a new node, the block is removed from the header.

With SOAP 1.2, a third predefined role was added to the specification: that of the *null actor*. If a sender of a message wishes to convey some information in the header that isn't intended to be explicitly processed at any point, it may signal this by defining an actor attribute with the appropriate URI. This prevents the final recipient of the message from wrongly trying to process the information while acting in the role of anonymous actor. In fact, the SOAP 1.2 specification makes it clear that a node must not process any block that specifies this actor role. There is no corresponding functionality in SOAP 1.1. However, this should only be needed when there is a chance that the data block might be mistaken for a block to be processed. If there is no such concern, the null actor specification is probably not needed.

Table 5-2 lists these predefined actor roles and the URIs that identify them in SOAP 1.1 and 1.2:

Table 5-2. The URIs that define actor roles

Actor role	Identifier
Current actor	http://schemas.xmlsoap.org/soap/actor/next (1.1)
	http://www.w3.org/2002/6/soap-envelope/role/next (1.2)

Table 5-2. The URIs that define actor roles (continued)

Actor role	Identifier
Null actor	http://www.w3.org/2002/6/soap-envelope/role/none
	(not defined for SOAP 1.1)
Some other actor	Any other valid URN

The third row is there to illustrate that the current actor, null actor, and anonymous actor are simply those explicitly defined by SOAP. The application (and application developer) is free to use this attribute in other ways. One common function is to explicitly provide the URI for the next node in the chain. In situations in which the locations are already known, the actor may simply be a unique identification of the next service that should receive the message. There is no requirement that the URI provided as the value of an actor attribute actually refers to a valid, reachable web server. The interpretation of these actor URI values is left to the implementation of the applications and servers themselves.

The mustUnderstand attribute

The mustUnderstand attribute is used to tell the actor currently processing the message whether the block bearing this attribute is something the application must handle. The values allowed for the attribute in SOAP 1.1 are either 0 or 1. In Version 1.2, those values are acceptable as well, and in addition the value may also be an instance of the boolean type from the XML Schema namespace (generally tagged with xs or xsd, refer to Table 5-1 earlier).

The interpretation of the value is simple: when the value is true (either the explicit boolean true, or 1), the block must be understood by the responsible party. Combining this with the actor attribute prevents other nodes from having to understand all elements. Referring back to Example 5-3, the priority block is specified as not being mandatory. If the application understands the block and acts on the information it provides, it's acceptable. But if it can't, the block can be safely disregarded. Conversely, the transaction block is marked as mandatory. If the server application can't act on it, it has to signal a failure to the requesting client. In Example 5-3, all the blocks are the responsibility of the same actor, the ultimate recipient of the message. If the transaction block also has an actor attribute present, only that actor has to honor the mustUnderstand attribute.

When this attribute isn't present at all, it is the same as having it present with a value of 0 (or false). In Example 5-3, the authorization block doesn't have a mustUnderstand, so the default is used. Because of this, if the application doesn't understand the block, it's free to ignore it.

Attribute placement and example

The global attributes are recognized only when associated with the outer tag of a block; that is, the immediate children of the Header tag. Both versions of the specification allow for the attributes to be present in deeper tags but instruct that the application must ignore them in such cases. Because of this, all the blocks in Table 5-3 are equivalent.

Table 5-3. Header blocks using mustUnderstand

Block	Reasoning

`<env:Header>`
  `<tr:transaction xmlns:tr=`
    `"soap-transaction>`
    `<transactionID>`
      `12217`
    `</transactionID>`
  `</tr:transaction>`
`</env:Header>`
	The specification says that when there is no `mustUnderstand` attribute given, the server must treat it as though it were explicitly set to the false value.

`<env:Header>`
  `<tr:transaction xmlns:tr=`
    `"soap-transaction"`
    `env:mustUnderstand="0">`
    `<transactionID>`
      `12217`
    `</transactionID>`
  `</tr:transaction>`
`</env:Header>`
	It is present, in a tag that is an immediate child of the Header tag. However, it's also set to the value both SOAP 1.1 and 1.2 (the case here, since env is used) consider `false`.

`<env:Header>`
  `<tr:transaction xmlns:tr=`
    `"soap-transaction">`
    `<transactionID`
      `env:mustUnderstand="1">`
      `12217`
    `</transactionID>`
  `</tr:transaction>`
`</env:Header>`
	The attribute is both specified and set to a type of `true` value that this version uses, but it isn't in an element that is an immediate child of Header. Thus it is ignored by the application.

With this ability, a client can, for example, specify a priority without the danger that a server might reject the request out-of-hand because of an inability to act on that part of the header.

Example 5-4 shows a larger header with many content blocks to tie all this material together. The header shown here will be traced through several stages of processing by multiple nodes.

Example 5-4. A complex header block, illustrating the attributes

```
<env:Header>
  <t:data xmlns:t="null" env:actor=
      "http://www.w3.org/2002/6/soap-envelope/role/none">
    <value id="timestamp">1014457345</value>
  </t:data>
```

Example 5-4. A complex header block, illustrating the attributes (continued)

```
    <crm:userUpdate xmlns:crm="x-schema:crm_structure.xml"
        env:mustUnderstand="true"
        env:actor=
        "http://www.w3.org/2002/6/soap-envelope/role/next">
      <crm:userIdNum><value>501</value></crm:userIdNum>
    </crm:userUpdate>
    <cert:checkSignature xmlns:cert="http://cert.ssl.org/cert"
        env:mustUnderstand="true"
        env:actor="http://soap.ssl.org/soap/checkSignature">
      <cert:signatureType>seeded-gpg</cert:signatureType>
      <cert:signatureSeed>
          <value href="#timestamp" />
      </cert:signatureSeed>
      <cert:pkKeySerial>128-4095-1014458368</cert:pkSerial>
      <cert:md5>823dd310c0d0842b2b5e1b4d28822db9</cert:md5>
    </cert:checkSignature>
    <crm:enactUpdate xmlns:crm="x-schema:crm_structure.xml"
        env:mustUnderstand="true"
        env:actor="http://soap.blackperl.com/crm/enactUpdate">
      <crm:userId>
        <value href="#userID" />
      </crm:userId>
      <crm:updateTokens>
        <value href="#data_in_body" />
      </crm:updateTokens>
    </crm:enactUpdate>
  </env:Header>
```

This header contains four subblocks within it:

- A <data> tag that refers to the null actor, thus ensuring that none of the nodes will attempt to directly process it.
- A <userUpdate> tag that starts the processing chain due to the fact that it is marked with the current actor URI, as specified in SOAP 1.2. It is given a namespace, crm, that is expressed as an XML Schema Language file, which it is assumed the relevant nodes have access to.
- A <checkSignature> block in the cert namespace of a fictional certification service at the *ssl.org* domain. Of all the blocks, this one contains the most in terms of child tags, which implies that processing it is probably not meant to involve the message body.
- Lastly, another tag from the crm namespace, this time <enactUpdate>. It too has some data tags within it, each of which refers to an identifier. The identifiers may be in the body, or they may be added by other steps along the way.

When the header is received, the node, filling the role of current actor, is responsible for the userUpdate block. For this example, assume that this node is expected to either verify that a valid user ID is present, or to retrieve one based on some information provided. Here, the numerical user ID is present as a <value> tag to userUpdate.

This node must turn this data into something useful to the ultimate recipient prior to passing along the message to the next node in the chain. Looking at the next block, it is meant to prove the message's validity through a digital signature. The current actor must eventually pass the message off to this next service at the URL given in that block's actor. In doing this, the acting node creates what is essentially a new message, with the header shown in the following code. Note that in this new header, the block that has already been processed is now removed, and a new block has been added to the end of the chain. Additionally, the actor attribute for the next block has been set so that the receiving node will know that it is responsible for handling that block. Once all this is done, the intermediary is then responsible for routing this new message, based on the URL from the actor. The changed elements are emphasized as follows:

```
<env:Header>
    <t:data xmlns:t="null" env:actor=
        "http://www.w3.org/2002/6/soap-envelope/role/none">
      <value id="timestamp">1014457345</value>
    </t:data>
    <cert:checkSignature xmlns:cert="http://cert.ssl.org/cert"
        env:mustUnderstand="true"
        env:actor=
        "http://www.w3.org/2002/6/soap-envelope/role/next">
      <cert:signatureType>seeded-gpg</cert:signatureType>
      <cert:signatureSeed>
          <value href="#timestamp" />
      </cert:signatureSeed>
      <cert:pkKeySerial>128-4095-1014458368</cert:pkSerial>
      <cert:md5>823dd310c0d0842b2b5e1b4d28822db9</cert:md5>
    </cert:checkSignature>
    <crm:enactUpdate xmlns:crm="x-schema:crm_structure.xml"
        env:mustUnderstand="true"
        env:actor="http://soap.blackperl.com/crm/enactUpdate">
      <crm:userId>
          <value href="#userID" />
      </crm:userId>
      <crm:updateTokens>
          <value href="#data_in_body" />
      </crm:updateTokens>
    </crm:enactUpdate>
    <t:data xmlns:t="null" env:actor=
        "http://www.w3.org/2002/6/soap-envelope/role/none">
      <value id="userID">rjray</value>
    </t:data>
</env:Header>
```

The assumption here is that the process of checking the digital signature will immediately respond with an error notification (called a fault within SOAP, and discussed later in this chapter) back to the sender if the signature doesn't pass validation. Note that this block uses the data in the first header block, the one tagged with the null actor. Taking it on faith that the signature is valid, the key-service node creates a new message with the third-generation header as shown here:

```
<env:Header>
  <data env:actor=
      "http://www.w3.org/2002/6/soap-envelope/role/none">
    <value id="timestamp">1014457345</value>
  </data>
  <crm:enactUpdate xmlns:crm="x-schema:crm_structure.xml"
      env:mustUnderstand="true"
      env:actor=
      "http://www.w3.org/2002/6/soap-envelope/role/next">
    <crm:userId>
      <value href="#userID" />
    </crm:userId>
    <crm:updateTokens>
      <value href="#data_in_body" />
    </crm:updateTokens>
  </crm:enactUpdate>
  <t:data xmlns:t="null" env:actor=
      "http://www.w3.org/2001/12/soap-envelope/actor/none">
    <value id="userID">rjray</value>
  </t:data>
  <cert:data xmlns:cert="http://cert.ssl.org/cert">
    <cert:messageString>signature: good</cert:messageString>
    <cert:messageCode>200</cert:messageCode>
  </cert:data>
</env:Header>
```

With this final version of the header, it can be assumed that the node handling it is going to do the actual requested operation, if it can. It may be guessed that the functionality the enactUpdate tag represents required the signature verification from a trusted service, such as the one used here.

Through this example, all the changes that were enacted by intermediaries took place within the header itself. In fact, the various nodes may add tag blocks to both the header or the body.

The Body Tag: Anatomy of a Message

The chained examples just shown managed to illustrate a complex, multinode process that made little use of the message's body. According to the specification, the Body tag is still a required element. It also marks the end of the message because the Envelope tag is expected to close after the Body tag does.

> There is a subtle but significant distinction between SOAP Versions 1.1 and 1.2. In SOAP 1.1, it wasn't explicitly stated that the Body tag was the end of the envelope. As such, it silently permitted additional tags following Body. This loophole is closed in SOAP 1.2, which explicitly states that no other tags may follow the body. A SOAP 1.2 application that plans to handle SOAP 1.1 messages would have to watch for this.

As with the Header tag, the Body tag is required to be qualified with the same namespace as the Envelope tag. The opening tag of a message body doesn't provide any attributes itself. There is no purpose for any of the common SOAP attributes at this level. All child elements of the body may utilize the encodingStyle attribute. However, neither actor nor mustUnderstand have any relevance to the child blocks of a message body. In essence, all parts of the body are given over to the same ultimate recipient. This is the same node that fills the role of the anonymous actor for the header blocks that don't specify an actor.

Like the header of the message, the contents of the body must all bear namespace qualifiers. But unlike the header, the specification does provide one tag within the envelope's namespace that may appear within a body. This is the Fault tag, which is used in error reporting. Faults themselves are covered in detail later. The body isn't required to have any child elements. The only limitation on child elements is that only one Fault element can be present in a Body.

So what role does the body of the message play? It carries information, just as the Header does (and to a lesser degree, the Envelope as well). The message body enjoys the distinction of always being present, and always being the responsibility of the ultimate recipient of the message. Intermediaries may add to the body of a message, but they are expected to not actually try to process any part of it in any way.

Depending on the nature of the application itself, the body of the message may be little more than a storehouse of information. In the extended set of header blocks that were traced in Examples 5-4 through 5-6, all the functionality of the request was contained in the headers of the message. Each of these tasks were directed by a header block: the look up of a username through numerical ID, the validation of the message against a digital signature, and the actual request to update the user information against whatever system was being modeled. The body of the message is used only to provide the data the update action utilizes. In that extended example, none of the intermediaries updated the body itself. Both intermediate operations—the ID lookup and the signature check—appended their information to the header.

There are other ways this could have been done. For example, the digital signature application might have taken as part of its specification the element ID of one of the body's child elements. Applications on either side of the signature function could then have added their data to the body without interfering with the signature. The signature application itself didn't have to worry about changing the body because the signature was already computed and evaluated. All these choices were open to the designers of the applications involved. Their only responsibility was to provide clear and accurate specification of their interfaces when dealing with each other.

Of course, the body can be responsible for much more than just carrying data. Encapsulation of RPC within SOAP can use the body to provide the remote call being marshaled, for example. The part of the header that provides the actual update can be placed within the body, instead of in the header. Bodies can contain many child elements, ranging from multiple application instructions to complex serialized objects.

Expressing and Encoding Data

Messages necessarily demand the ability to communicate data. The encoding of data was a major issue in the cross-platform compatibility of the early RPC implementations. The XML-RPC protocol provides a simple yet flexible encoding that covers the same ranges the original RPC implementations did (and more than most).

Encoding (often called *serialization*) of data within SOAP is considerably more complex than in XML-RPC. As such, trying to comprehend it just from the specification by itself can be an intimidating task. This is made even more complex by the fact that a message may use an encoding other than the basic SOAP encoding. In fact, a message may use several different encodings at various places within the envelope. Specifying these encodings is the role of the `encodingStyle` attribute described earlier.

XML Schema and encoding

The SOAP encoding model is based primarily on the XML Schema Language, generally referred to as XML Schema. This is convenient because it provides many of the most-common "basic" types as building blocks from which more complex data descriptions are constructed.

However, SOAP also requires that a message be manageable without forcing the recipient to process any schemas. Because of this, all attributes that are parts of data definitions must be present; they can't be assumed to be inherited from the corresponding schema.

The encoding schema that describes the data serializations provided by SOAP is the one specified earlier in Table 5-1, in which the commonly used namespace labels were introduced. Refer to those URIs (for SOAP 1.1 and 1.2), as well as the URIs that are associated with the namespace labels `xsi` and `xsd` (the SOAP 1.2 specification uses `xs` in place of `xsd`). While the URI is necessarily different for the basic SOAP encoding itself, both versions of SOAP use the same namespace URIs for the XML Schema declarations.

Simple types, values and enumerations

Through XML Schema, SOAP provides some very familiar simple types, listed in Table 5-4.

Table 5-4. Simple types available

Type	Example
int	4294967295, –1, 2600
float	2.7182818284590452354, –6.28318, 3.40282347E+38
negativeInteger	–212, –32768
string	Just about anything you want

Unlike XML-RPC, SOAP data is expressed in the form of *named parameters*. Take the following construct:

    <Name>James</Name>

This doesn't refer to `Name` as a type. `Name` is the parameter itself, and the string "James" is its value. It is presumed that the schema that describes the document this parameter appears in has defined `Name` as a string (or some other possibilities, that will be explored soon).

The XML Schema specification provides the definitions of these types, and attributes that may be used in qualifying elements that contain such data. However, no tags are provided by XML Schema directly. To aid in encoding values in places and situations in which the type may not be immediately known, the SOAP encoding schemas provide tags in their namespaces as a convenience. The previous fragment can also be written as follows:

    <Name><SOAP-ENC:string>James</SOAP-ENC:string></Name>

Within SOAP terminology (and borrowing from XML Schema), a simple type categorizes a set (or class) of simple values. A simple value is like that in earlier examples. Simple values don't have named parts or even multiple parts.

Likewise, one of the XML Schema types can also be provided in an attribute:

    <Lang xsi:type="xsd:string">Greek</Lang>

This naming of data elements is what SOAP calls accessors. Accessors are explained in greater detail in a later section, but for now it is enough to understand that the name by which data is referred to is its accessor. When the type of the data a name refers to can be changed from one instance to the next using the type attribute, that is what SOAP considers polymorphic. To Perl, of course, it seems like an ordinary scalar.

One simple type remains, the *array of bytes*. This is a type provided as a "catch-all" of sorts, for data that doesn't conveniently fit into the other types, such as audio or image data. While the encoding isn't mandated as such, the recommended encoding is base64, as defined in XML Schema (and generally familiar outside of XML Schema, as well). The SOAP encodings provide a corresponding subtype for this, as well. An example of an array of bytes might look like this:[*]

```
<picture xsi:type="SOAP-ENC:base64">
  aG93IG5vDyBicm73biBjb3cNCg==
</picture>
```

The general definition of the "base64" encoding includes limits on line length that aren't enforced in the context of SOAP values. Lines may be broken (or not broken) at any point convenient to the application.

Compound types and values

SOAP and XML Schema provide for more complex data expression through *compound types*, types that are built up by creating associations of several other values under one name. Compound types come in two forms: the *structure* (sometimes referred to simply as *struct*) and the *array*.

The structure is a familiar concept. In terms of Perl, this may be thought of as similar to the hash table, in which the named values that make up the parts of the compound type are the key/value pairs, and the hash table itself represents the container. Any elements in a compound type may refer to a simple type or another compound type. Here's an example of a simple structure:

```
<Book xmlns="http://www.loc.gov/schema">
  <title>Perl Guidebook, The</title>
  <isbn>01-55677-1234</isbn>
</Book>
```

This corresponds to the simple hash:

```
%Book = (
         title => 'Perl Guidebook, The',
         isbn  => '01-55677-1234'
        );
```

As with the simple types, compound types are described using the XML Schema syntax. A schema fragment to describe the previous structure might look like this:

```
<xs:element name="Book" type="tns:Book"/>
<xs:complexType name="Book">
  <xs:element name="title" type="xs:string"/>
  <xs:element name="isbn" type="xs:string"/>
</xs:complexType>
```

---

[*] If this looks familiar, it's because it's the example from the specification itself. Because the Base64 format is fairly reader-unfriendly, it's what almost all authors use as an example of this type.

Accessors, scoping, and reference

The introduction of the structure also means introducing the concept of the data *accessor*. The term is used in this context to mean the retrieval of a part of a compound value such as a structure or an array. This is potentially confusing, as the "accessor" already has a place in object-oriented programming. The usage in this context is similar but not completely the same. The SOAP usage is presented here because the specifications use the word in this role consistently, and this is meant to help avoid confusion.

An accessor in the SOAP sense of the word is the way a specific data element is uniquely referred to. In more traditional object-oriented terms, an accessor is generally a type of method that provides access to internal ("protected") class elements without exposing those elements directly. A SOAP accessor isn't a routine or method. In a structure, the name of the structure element is the accessor. This can mean that the accessor is a combined sequence of element names when referring to a deeply nested data element. In an array, the position within the array itself is the accessor.

The *scoping* of an accessor is important when a specific accessor isn't unique throughout the entire message. For example, if a message body contains two or more instances of the same structure with the containing tags at the same depth within the Body content, an accessor can refer to either structure, unless there is enough information to narrow it down to one specific structure. But when the focus is already within a structure, an accessor to a piece of data contained within is valid, even though the same accessor points to a different value in a different structure. This is what is known as the scope of an accessor and isn't unlike the concept of scope within Perl.

Another type of accessor is the *reference*. References in the XML sense aren't really new, either. Any opening tag may bear an `id` attribute whose value is a unique (within the message) string. Other tags may then refer to that element using the `href` attribute and providing the name as the value, as in Example 5.5.

Example 5-5. Defining references between values

```
<enc:string id="question-1">
  What is the answer to life, the universe and
  everything?
</enc:string>
<enc:int id="answer-1">42</enc:int>

<q:TestItem xmlns:q="http://testgiver.org/basic">
  <q:Question href="#question-1"/>
  <q:Answer href="#answer-1"/>
</q:TestItem>
```

Both versions of the SOAP specification strongly encourage that references be used only on data that is being referred to at least twice. If data is being referred to in only one place, it should be directly embedded within the containing tags, rather than being given a reference. The TestItem tag of Example 5-5 should have been expressed as follows:

```
<q:TestItem xmlns:q="http://testgiver.org/basic">
  <q:Question>
    What is the answer to life, the universerse and
    everything?
  </q:Question>
  <q:Answer>42</q:Answer>
</q:TestItem>
```

Using references in such a simple fragment may not seem obvious, but references don't have to refer to the current document. A reference can point to an external resource, just as the href attribute often does within HTML. The TestItem tag may wish to refer to the answers externally, away from the prying eyes of XML-skilled students:

```
<q:TestItem xmlns:q="http://testgiver.org/basic">
  <q:Question href="#question-1"/>
  <q:Answer href="http://test.server.edu/test-1#answer-1"/>
</q:TestItem>
```

Recall that the header blocks in Example 5-4 also used references, both to refer between the header and the body and to refer to data provided by intermediary processes.

Arrays and partial arrays

As was mentioned earlier, arrays are regarded as compound types in which the ordering of the elements provides the accessors, not the names, of the elements. Arrays may contain elements of any variety of types, including structures and other arrays. Arrays may also be constrained to a certain subset of types by proving type information in the opening tag or in the schema that defines the namespace being used. The arrayType attribute provided by the SOAP encoding namespace is the mechanism used to provide this information.

The value of the arrayType attribute is a type identifier. That value is generally from the XML Schema namespace, but can also be other namespace-qualified types. Example 5-6 illustrates three arrays.

Example 5-6. Different kinds of arrays

```
<enc:Array enc:arrayType="xs:int[3]">
  <enc:int>1</enc:int>
  <enc:int>2</enc:int>
  <enc:int>3</enc:int>
</enc:Array>
```

Example 5-6. Different kinds of arrays (continued)

```
<a:AnyThingGoes xmlns:a="something.xml"
    enc:arrayType="xs:anyType[4]">
  <enc:int>27</enc:int>
  <enc:string>Three-cubed</enc:string>
  <enc:float>3.14159</enc:float>
  <enc:anyURI>http://www.oreilly.com</enc:anyURI>
</a:AnyThingGoes>

<loc:Booklist xsi:type="enc:Array"
    xmlns:loc="http://www.loc.gov/schema"
    enc:arrayType="loc:Book[2]">
  <loc:Book>
    <loc:title>Perl Guidebook, The</loc:title>
    <loc:isbn>01-55677-1234</loc:isbn>
  </loc:Book>
  <loc:Book>
    <loc:title>Perl Primer, The</loc:title>
    <loc:isbn>01-55832-4321</loc:isbn>
  </loc:Book>
</loc:Booklist>
```

The first of these is just an array of integers, while the second shows an array in which elements are different types. The third array uses the Book structure definition from an earlier fragment to define the element types. It also uses a tag taken from the same namespace to serialize the array itself.

In this example, the second array used a named parameter tag provided by a namespace that was defined in the opening tag. In the third example, the tag was again a named parameter, but the type was provided in an inline fashion, using the xsi:type attribute. The second array also illustrated how different types are encoded into a single array. When the type provided for arrayType has derivatives (such as a signed subtype of int), a derivative value is allowed to appear in the array. This is like Java or other strongly typed object languages in which a subclass instance may be passed in a place where the parameter had been typed as an ancestor class.

The arrayType attribute provides not only the type for the data, but the size of the array as well. The specifications define the format of the arrayType value using a set of rules similar to the style used for parser definitions. In simple terms, an array type definition has two parts: the element type and the dimension. The *dimension* is given in the last set of square brackets ([and]), and may be zero or more integers separated by commas. The *element type* may also be followed by a pair of brackets, which indicates that each array element is itself also an array. This inner set of brackets doesn't have any numbers in it, but has commas to show multiple dimension. It is the responsibility of the arrays in the data to provide their specific size information when they are serialized. Additionally, if the dimension of the array itself isn't given, that means the application should determine size by inspecting the data. Table 5-5 shows some declarations with their explanations.

Table 5-5. Sample arrayType values and explanations

Value	Type	Dimension	Explanation
int[10]	Int	[10]	One row of integers, 10 elements in length
string[][3]	string[]	[3]	One row of 3 elements, each an array of strings
int[,][]	Int[,]	[]	One row of elements, each of which is a 2D array of integers, with the size of the outer array to be determined from the data
anyType[5,5]	anyType	[5,5]	A 5-by-5 matrix whose elements may be of any type that includes other arrays

The special type specifier anyType is the XML Schema equivalent of the Object type in Java or SmallTalk. It may be thought of as the true Perl scalar of the SOAP encoding mechanism. It simply means that any type may occur as an element.

You may have noticed that an array's size may be left to examination only in the case of single-dimensional arrays. A serialized array specifies elements only in a linear sequence. Thus, an array of dimension two or higher must explicitly provide the sizes of the dimensions. This is a change from C or Perl, in which secondary and later dimensions were implemented as arrays of references or pointers. In other words, the type int[5,5] isn't the same as int[5][5]. The latter isn't a valid type definition, for one thing, and the first declaration results in a series of 25 integer values being serialized, not 5 occurrences of a further 5-element array. The following 2×2 array shows this in more detail:

```
<enc:Array enc:arrayType="xs:string[2,2]">
    <xs:string>Row 1, Column 1</xs:string>
    <xs:string>Row 1, Column 2</xs:string>
    <xs:string>Row 2, Column 1</xs:string>
    <xs:string>Row 2, Column 2</xs:string>
</enc:Array>
```

This may seem like an unusual approach, but it becomes more clear when encoding partial arrays and sparse arrays.

Partial and sparse arrays are similar, but aren't identical. A *partial* array is one that isn't sent in its entirety. The elements that are sent are still considered to be ordered; they just don't represent a complete array, and they may not start at the very first element. The attribute offset provides the information as to where in the array the data starts. This fragment encodes elements 3 and 4 of a 5-element array:

```
<enc:Array enc:arrayType="xs:int[5]" enc:offset="[2]">
    <xs:int>3</xs:int>
    <xs:int>4</xs:int>
</enc:Array>
```

In contrast, a *sparse* array is one in which some number of elements are sent, but there is no guarantee about the relative positions of any of the elements. The elements that are sent have an attribute called position, which provides the placement within the whole for that element, as follows:

```
<enc:Array enc:arrayType="xs:string[10,10]">
  <xs:string enc:position="[2,4]">Row 3, Col 5</xs:string>
  <xs:string enc:position="[7,9]">Row 8, Col 10</xs:string>
</enc:Array>
```

Using the position attribute, only two of the 100 elements are passed, but the receiver knows exactly which two they are.

References may also be used within arrays, including partial and sparse ones. The references may refer to individual data elements or to other arrays that are used to fill in when the datatype for the referencing array allows:

```
<enc:Array enc:arrayType="xs:int[][10]">
  <enc:Array enc:arrayType="xs:int[10]">
    <xs:int position="[9]">-1</xs:int>
    <xs:int position="[0]">3</xs:int>
  </enc:Array>
  <enc:Array enc:position="[3]" href="#array-3"/>
</enc:Array>
```

The fragment defines a sparse array with 10 arrays of integers. The first slot (slot 0, since the opening tag had no offset, and the first child tag had no position attribute) has data for its slots 0 and 9. The fourth slot of the outer array is a reference elsewhere in the document, to what will presumably be an array whose type matches what is expected.

Structures and generic compound types

Returning briefly to the subject of structures, the encoding rules aren't limited to structures that have all their accessors known in advance. It is possible and permitted to have structures in which the accessors are known only by inspection of the serialized data itself. Any accessors that contain data whose type can't be derived in advance still must provide the type information by means of an xsi:type attribute.

To further support generic compound data, the rules also allow for compound types that mix together accessors that are distinguished by type and accessors distinguished by ordinal position, as in Example 5-7.

Example 5-7. A compound type with mixed accessors

```
<newUserList xmlns="http://linux.com/userSchema">
  <ShellUser>
    <name>rjray</name>
    <shell>/bin/tcsh</shell>
    <password xsi:type="md5pw">
      8be3d7e3ccf03a98026acfce9dcc6487
    </password>
  </ShellUser>
  <CvsUser>
    <name>rjray</name>
    <commitAccess xsi:type="xs:boolean">true</commitAccess>
    <password xsi:type="md5pw">
```

Example 5-7. A compound type with mixed accessors (continued)

```
        8be3d7e3ccf03a98026acfce9dcc6487
    </password>
  </CvsUser>
  <CvsUser>
    <name>guest</name>
    <commitAccess xsi:type="xs:boolean">false</commitAccess>
    <password xsi:type="md5pw">
        473640010efda30acaedea407ab4aa64
    </password>
  </CvsUser>
</newUserList>
```

The SOAP root attribute

When a serialization contains multiple values and structures that are all children of the Body tag, SOAP generally assumes that the first one is the root of the object graph. This isn't always the case, especially when there are references involved in the serialization. To allow an application greater control over data expression, SOAP provides an attribute in the encoding namespace called root. This attribute is of type xs:boolean.

All elements have an implied value of false (or 0) for this attribute, except for the element considered to be the graph root. Changing the consideration of the root requires only that the attribute be explicitly provided in the true root. It is a good idea to include the attribute with a false value in other elements that might otherwise be considered possible root candidates (such as cases where the first element will not be the root).

The element that is considered the root may in some cases affect the way the message is deserialized for the server application. This is a very rarely used feature, and no examples were found in the specifications or related documents to clarify the functionality.

Signaling a Problem: Faults

The last of the XML and serialization topics to be covered is the SOAP Fault. In the simplest terms, faults are errors. The Fault tag was referred to earlier when discussing the Body tag. It has the distinction of being the only preprovided child element for Body as defined by the SOAP specifications. If one of the SOAP nodes has a problem with the message, this is the mechanism for communicating the problem back to the original client.

In practice, a fault child element looks just like a structured datatype. The biggest difference is that the permitted members are predefined, as is their order. The tag itself must be qualified into the same namespace as the Body, Header, and Envelope tags.

Fault elements

The elements within the `Fault` tag are strictly defined both in name and in order. The first two of the four are mandatory; they must be present in all fault messages. The third and fourth elements are optional and serve to provide greater detail on the nature of the error at hand. These elements are defined in Table 5-6 (with columns for SOAP 1.1 and 1.2, which use different names). Note that the types given for the elements are from XML Schema.

Table 5-6. The element tags of a fault

Tag name (1.1)	Tag name (1.2)	Type	Role
faultcode	Code	Qname (SOAP 1.2 uses subelements)	This is a qualified name that identifies the specific type of fault that has occurred. SOAP has a small number of predefined fault codes for certain common situations.
faultstring	Reason	string	The string provided by this element is meant to be a human-readable representation of the error. It should be a relatively brief phrase, similar in nature to the text responses of HTTP itself.
faultactor	Role	anyURI	This element is intended to specify which node in the message path is the source of the fault. Any node that isn't the ultimate receiver, but is generating the fault, must set this.
detail	Detail	tag blocks	Conveys the application-specific fault information. The contents of this element are zero or more tag elements. This element may also have an attribute, the familiar encodingStyle (which propagates to the child tags).

The SOAP 1.2 specification for faults also includes a fifth element, called `Node`. This identifies at which node the fault occurred, if the data is relevant. The updated specification also changes the content of the `Code` element, so that it uses child elements called `Value` and `Subcode` (the latter is optional). More information on SOAP 1.2 faults can be found in the specifications.

The detail element can be an important piece of content. If the nature of the fault is a failure to process the message body, the `detail` element must be present, even if it contains no child tags. Likewise, the absence of this element can be safely interpreted as meaning that the fault was not related to the message body at all. No information on header-related errors may appear within `detail`. Any information on header-based errors must be provided in the header of the response.

Each of the child elements present in a `detail` block may be namespace-qualified and may have their own `encodingStyle` attribute for more localized encoding.

> The SOAP 1.1 specification explicitly allows for additional elements within a `Fault`, providing that all added elements are namespace-qualified. The SOAP 1.2 specification, however, makes no mention of this. Unless later drafts clarify, this stands as another potential trap when providing SOAP 1.1 compatibility in a SOAP 1.2 application.

Predefined faults

The designers of SOAP recognized that consistency in fault codes is an important aspect of interoperability between different clients and varying servers. It isn't enough to rely on the `faultstring` accessor, for several reasons:

- Developers may not phrase the same thought using the exact same words.
- Trying to deduce the nature of an error from the string completely ignores any and all issues of localization and language.
- Errors naturally fall into *categories*, whether those categories are defined in terms of system resources ("IO Error," "Out of Memory," etc.) or protocol definitions ("404 Not Found," "500 Server Error," etc.).
- The point of having two cooperating values is so that the code defines the general fault, with the string providing detail specific to the error itself.

Both SOAP 1.1 and 1.2 define sets of fault codes to use as a basis for generating these diagnostics. Neither specification expects their list to be exhaustive or restrictive. The goal is to provide for consistency in reporting the most common faults.

> Of the changes between SOAP 1.1 and SOAP 1.2, this is the most radical. The fault codes defined for SOAP 1.1 were completely removed and replaced with different codes in SOAP 1.2. Each of the faults from 1.1 has a corresponding entry in the 1.2 table, while the 1.2 table defines an additional one.

Table 5-7 presents the fault codes for SOAP 1.1. In this version of the specification, the intent was to have the codes be the first element of a sequence of two or more elements linked with "." characters. The part of the code to the left of the first period specifies the class of the fault, and the portion to the right provides more specific classification of the fault itself.

Table 5-7. The predefined faults for SOAP 1.1

Code	Meaning
`VersionMismatch`	The processing node found a namespace (SOAP version) it can't process.
`MustUnderstand`	A child element of the `Header` that specified a `mustUnderstand` attribute of 1 can't be handled.
`Client`	The `Client` errors were used to describe errors in which the problem was in the encoding or specification of the data as it was received from the client.
`Server`	In contrast to the `Client` errors, `Server` errors were defined as those that came from problems the server encountered while processing an otherwise valid, correct request.

Based on the model that SOAP 1.1 described, the previous codes would have appeared in forms more like `VersionMismatch.SOAP1-1Required`, or `Client.MalformedBodyContent`. The longer text of the error would be left to the `faultstring` field, with the other fields used where appropriate and required.

SOAP 1.2 provides a more complete fault model. Part of this is replacing the dotted-groups with qualified names. Another part is to give more detail in the definition of the predefined faults. Table 5-8 lists the SOAP 1.2 faults.

Table 5-8. The predefined faults for SOAP 1.2

Code	Meaning
`VersionMismatch`	The meaning and use of this is the same as in SOAP 1.1.
`MustUnderstand`	As above, this matches the SOAP 1.1 fault of the same name.
`DataEncodingUnknown`	A header or body element that the current node is responsible for processing specified an encoding (via `encodingStyle`) the node doesn't support.
`Sender`	This fault corresponds to the `Client` code from SOAP 1.1. It causes the `detail` part of the fault to be required in the response.
`Receiver`	As with `Sender`, this corresponds to the `Server` code from SOAP 1.1. It, too, will make the `detail` element of the fault necessary.

The two codes that are the exact same "name" as their SOAP 1.1 counterparts shouldn't be interpreted as exactly the same. The SOAP 1.2 definitions and restrictions are much more specific with regards to these predefined values.

As was mentioned earlier, the SOAP 1.2 specification also goes into more depth on the exact contents of the remaining elements of a `Fault` block, depending on the error itself. Rather than reproduce all that here, when the specification is still in revision, you should check the sections of the SOAP 1.2 specification that deal with faults. One unfortunate reality of developing complex software is the need to provide clear, intuitive, and specific error messages.[*]

RPC over SOAP

One of the most common applications of SOAP is to provide Remote Procedure Call (RPC) functionality. While SOAP goes beyond the goals of either XML-RPC or the original RPC itself, it is a simple fact that a large number of existing systems built around the RPC model are still in use. New applications are expected to communicate with these legacy systems in addition to any extra abilities they may offer.

The mechanics of implementing RPC via SOAP aren't at all difficult. Looking to XML-RPC as a model for encoding requests, responses, and the requisite data,

---

[*] A "requirement" that many large software companies continue to overlook.

adapting this protocol to run within the realm of SOAP is a fairly direct task. Both SOAP protocol versions specifically address this issue.

There is more to providing this functionality than merely taking an XML-RPC message and wrapping SOAP envelope elements around it. The SOAP RPC capabilities aren't direct mirrors of XML-RPC. The features of SOAP (named parameters, distinct separation of message header and body) are used to full advantage in the RPC framework.

Supplying the RPC Information

To contain RPC functionality, a message has to provide the information that sets up the call and defines the result. Besides a URI to the target SOAP node, the call must provide the procedure name (referred to in some documents as the *method*) and the parameters for the call. Additionally, some information may be present that, while nor required, adds further detail and specifics to the message.

A *signature* for the procedure or method is optional rather than required. This is only from the viewpoint of the SOAP specification itself. Whether the node acting as the RPC server requires the signature is a different issue. A signature is something that defines the type information for the parameters coming in to the procedure call, as well as the return value if the procedure returns anything. Some servers require this information to provide polymorphic procedures and methods to their clients. The typing information allows the calls to be properly dispatched to the matching version of the code. It also lets a server detect badly formed calls without risking more serious runtime faults.

In addition to the optional signature, a RPC message may also provide extra information in the SOAP header. This information can't directly be part of the procedure call itself, but as will be explained in a later section, there are several types of application data that may be best suited for this method.

Putting the Call and Response in the Body

Both the request and the response in an RPC communication use the SOAP Body element. A procedure call is modeled as a SOAP structure, with each parameter to the call expressed as an accessor of the structure. The SOAP interpretation of RPC assumes that all parameters are named, just as SOAP itself does. This is a noteworthy difference from XML-RPC, in which parameters are defined by their ordinal position alone. If the call being encoded includes a signature, the order of the parameters must match the signature. The structure itself is given a name that matches the name of the method/procedure being called.

The arguments passed to and returned from the call may overlap. In the relevant sections of the SOAP specifications, the discussions of RPC refer to parameters as being one of [in], [in/out], or [out]. The parameters that are [in/out] are those present in both the request and the response. These attributes of the parameters aren't part of the call itself or the serialization; this is a notation carried forward from CORBA and SQL to further clarify the roles that procedure parameters play.

A response is also expected to be in the form of a structure, with accessors for all the parameters being passed back. These include the return value (if any) from the call, as well as any [in/out] parameters that were passed in, and any [out] parameters that were added.

> In SOAP 1.1, the specification states that the return value of the call is the first accessor in the structure for the response, with the remaining values in the order that matches the signature (if any). It also recommends, without requiring, that the structure for the response bear the same name as the request with the string Response appended.
>
> In contrast, the SOAP 1.2 specification has several changes to this model. The return value parameter is encouraged to be first, but it isn't required to be. However, it must be named result, and be namespace-qualified with a label that has been mapped to the namespace identifier, *http://www.w3.org/2002/06/soap-rpc*. In addition, it states that the return value should be present only when the value itself is a non-void (null) value. The SOAP 1.1 coverage doesn't make any reference to void or null values. Lastly, SOAP 1.2 makes no suggestion or recommendation as to the naming of the structure for the response.

For both versions, errors in the invoked procedure are handled using RPC faults, discussed later.

Use of the SOAP Header

The SOAP message header is generally less important in RPC usage. It can be used to provide transaction information, authentication credentials, as well as the usual application of routing information.

The information provided in the header can't be part of the actual method call itself. That must be fully expressed in the body.

RPC Faults

Since the framework for RPC is still SOAP itself, errors in the method or procedure execution are communicated back to the client by means of a SOAP fault structure. While general SOAP bodies don't require a Fault element be the only element within a Body, in RPC terms, a response can't signal success and failure at the same time. Because any data in the body of the response that isn't a fault constitutes success, RPC messages do have a restriction: an RPC response that contains a Fault may not contain any other elements.

RPC faults in SOAP 1.1 are simply implemented using the existing guidelines for SOAP itself. It is expected that the `faultcode` attribute would be specific to RPC application, and that the remaining attributes would be correctly utilized. SOAP 1.2 takes a more thorough look at the fault model for RPC and provides a subsection within the specification devoted to the subject.

The fault model in SOAP 1.2 uses an additional namespace identifier, which is given the label `rpc` in the specification. The URI for this namespace is *http://www.w3.org/2002/6/soap-rpc*, as used for other RPC-specific elements described earlier. The specification provides four predefined QNames for RPC-specific faults, as shown in Table 5-9. The table lists the faults in a decreasing order of precedence.

Table 5-9. RPC fault codes for SOAP 1.2

Fault code	Meaning
`env:Server`	This code is recommended for situations in which the problem is server-related, such as resource problems or a scheduled black-out period.
`env:DataEncodingUnknown`	All the elements are qualified to use the `encodingStyle` attribute provided by SOAP itself. This code is recommended for cases in which a part of the message uses an unknown encoding.
`rpc:ProcedureNotPresent`	If the requested method or procedure is unknown to the server, this fault code must be used (unless a higher-priority condition was met first).
`rpc:BadArguments`	If there is a mismatch in the arguments against a specified signature, or when the server is unable to process the arguments, this code must be used, unless a code of higher-priority has already been chosen.

Aside from these predeclared fault codes, the mechanism itself is the same as for general SOAP faults. Note that some transport bindings such as HTTP or SMTP may define additional elements or additional fault codes. If any such definitions apply, the application has a responsibility to use them as well.

In all RPC fault cases, the `detail` and `faultstring` attributes are defined on a per-implementation basis.

SOAP Transport

This section is going to briefly cover some of the different methods of transporting SOAP messages. Later chapters will go into greater depth on some of these (such as HTTP and SMTP).

Arguably the most significant difference between SOAP and XML-RPC is the fact that the designers of SOAP refrained from binding it to a specific transport protocol. While both versions of the protocol refer heavily to the application of HTTP as a method of transport, this isn't the only available option. SOAP has been demonstrated using the Simple Mail Transfer Protocol (SMTP), the Jabber wire protocol, Microsoft's .NET framework, and others. Guidelines for protocols such as the Blocks

Extensible Exchange Protocol (BEEP),* raw TCP/IP, and even FTP have been produced in various levels of maturity and acceptance.

For each protocol, one thing is common: each must define not only the way messages are physically sent, they must also define what the terms and conditions are for sending a message along that route. In most cases, the protocol definitions themselves cover the "how" element. What remains to be defined is what extra material must be added to a message to enable the transport.

Using HTTP as an example, the specification that provides the binding for SOAP over HTTP is responsible for outlining a number of elements:

- Which HTTP methods are used or supported?
- What role does the request URI play in defining the service?
- What should the Content-type header (and any other relevant headers) look like?
- How is a SOAP message encapsulated into the HTTP request?

Fortunately, the binding for HTTP is a part of the specification in both SOAP 1.1 and 1.2. Because of this, the binding is useful as both a practical application and a roadmap for defining new bindings.

In contrast, supporting SOAP over the Jabber protocol involves very little extra work on the part of the protocol. Because of the nature of Jabber itself, the protocol is already engineered for widely varied content (or *payload*). The primary concern with regards to Jabber is how to map the overall SOAP request into a Jabber payload. Matters of how to create the bridge between the SOAP functionality and the servers that receive these Jabber requests is delegated to the application developers. From the vantage point of the protocol binding, what really matters is having a clear process for getting the SOAP messages into and out of the Jabber framework. Still, the binding specification has the same responsibilities the HTTP binding has.

Another protocol of interest to developers and industry is SMTP. Often, the initial reaction to this is one of surprise because electronic mail isn't often thought of in the same request-response sense of exchange that HTTP and other, more obviously two-way protocols are. Despite this, SMTP is very capable of providing a transport binding for SOAP. The necessary element is present: SMTP provides two-way communication. It isn't often thought of in such terms because the receiver of an email message must actively choose to reply to the message, but an SMTP-based server that receives a SOAP message receives a return email address as part of it. Once the message is processed, the response can easily (and promptly) be returned to the requesting client.

---

* For more on BEEP, see *http://www.beepcore.org*.

Further Reading

As was said at the start of this chapter, this isn't a complete, exhaustive analysis of SOAP itself. There are several books written solely on the topic of SOAP, and the amount of material available on the Web is just as great, if not more so.

Appendix F contains information on SOAP books and relevant web sites, as well as mailing lists and any other resources that are applicable. We encourage you to explore these additional sources, in particular the emerging draft proposal for SOAP 1.2, which will likely reach Technical Recommendation status by the time this book is published.

CHAPTER 6
Programming SOAP

There are currently two object-oriented modules for Perl that provide support for developing SOAP client/server applications: SOAP and SOAP::Lite. This chapter introduces these two modules. By comparing and contrasting the modules, you'll learn their strengths and weaknesses.

The last part of the chapter covers other SOAP-related utility modules, which either augment the client/server SOAP modules or add SOAP-related functionality to other packages and systems. By the time you finish this chapter, you'll be able to develop basic SOAP applications with the toolkits and utility modules and make an informed choice of software to use in your SOAP projects.

A Toolkit Approach

Using a toolkit for SOAP programming is almost a requirement. The specification itself is very complex, and the XML documents are equally complex. While there is nothing preventing an application developer from coding the functionality directly, there is no reason to with the availability of toolkits for Perl.

A client is concerned with (not always in this order):

- Establishing a communication channel to the server(s)
- Constructing a valid request with the desired data
- Sending the request to the server correctly
- Retrieving and decoding the server response

The goal of a good toolkit is to abstract as much of the encoding and transport issues as possible. There are two toolkits for Perl available from CPAN. Both are discussed here, but the focus will quickly shift to the SOAP::Lite module, which is more actively maintained.

DevelopMentor's SOAP Module

The first of the modules that will be examined is the modestly named SOAP module from the engineers at DevelopMentor (*http://www.develop.com*). This module was originally engineering and written by Keith Brown, who worked in close concert with a Java engineer Don Box on a similar toolkit for Java. Their goal was to develop their tools in a side-by-side fashion, which allowed them to focus on both the feature set for the modules and on an interface that was consistent in both languages.

The primary drawback to this module is that it doesn't appear to be in active maintenance or development. The full SOAP specification isn't yet implemented in the toolkit, and likewise there is no level of support for the emerging SOAP 1.2 standard. It isn't clear what future plans there are for the module.

Example: Client to Convert a Number to Words

This script, shown in Example 6-1, connects to a public server that converts integer numbers to their text equivalents. It uses the SOAP toolkit to manage all the abstract elements such as XML encoding, the HTTP transport, and decoding the resulting XML. You can find a list of public SOAP services, including this one, at *http://www.xmethods.com*.[*]

The service uses a RPC model for its interface. The service itself is simple: it takes an integer number and returns to the client a string of English text that expresses the value in words. Our client script takes the integer as a command-line argument and prints the string it gets back from the server.

Example 6-1. num2text.pl, converting an integer to text

```
#!/usr/bin/perl

use strict;

use SOAP::EnvelopeMaker;
use SOAP::Parser;
use SOAP::Struct;
use SOAP::Transport::HTTP::Client;

my $num = shift; $num =~ /^\d+$/ or die "USAGE: $0 num\n";

my ($server, $endpoint, $soapaction, $method, $method_urn,
    $message, $envelope, $response, $parser);
$server     = 'www.tankebolaget.se';
$endpoint   = '/scripts/NumToWords.dll/soap/INumToWords';
$soapaction =
```

---

[*] While not a strictly Perl site, the range of services listed here are excellent for developing tests. They represent SOAP implementations ranging from Delphi to .Net.

Example 6-1. num2text.pl, converting an integer to text (continued)

```
                'urn:NumToWordsIntf-INumToWords#NumToWords_English';
$method      = 'NumToWords_English';
$method_urn = 'urn:NumToWordsIntf-INumToWords';

$envelope = SOAP::EnvelopeMaker->new(\$message);
$envelope->set_body($method_urn, $method, 0,
                    SOAP::Struct->new(aNumber => $num));
$response = SOAP::Transport::HTTP::Client->new( )
                ->send_receive($server, 80, $endpoint,
                               $method_urn, $method,
                               $message);
$parser = SOAP::Parser->new;
$parser->parsestring($response);
$response = $parser->get_body;
if (exists $response->{return}) {
    print "$num may be expressed as $response->{return}\n";
} else {
    print "A fault ($response->{faultcode}) occurred: " .
        "$response->{faultstring}\n";
}

exit;
```

This may appear somewhat complex, but the elements themselves are simple to understand, despite how much seems to be present in such a "simple" example.

The first few lines are common to almost all Perl SOAP clients. The block of four use statements pull in the elements of the SOAP module used within the program. For this example, we need code for the envelope, parser, construction of data structures, and the HTTP client transport layer. The next line after those simply takes the one integer argument from the command line and checks that it is, in fact, a valid integer.

The first SOAP-specific action is this line:

```
    $envelope = SOAP::EnvelopeMaker->new(\$message);
```

The $envelope object can construct and manipulate a message. In this case, the constructor is given a reference to a scalar variable, $message. When the envelope is ready to be transmitted, it's stored in this variable as one long string.

The constructor can also take a subroutine reference:

```
    $envelope = SOAP::EnvelopeMaker->new(sub { ... });
```

When the subroutine reference gets called, it is called with the envelope string and might, for example, spool the output directly to a raw TCP/IP socket.

The next line in the client script shows not only a class method for SOAP::EnvelopeMaker but also inline use of SOAP::Struct:

```
    $envelope->set_body($method_urn, $method, 0,
                        SOAP::Struct->new(aNumber => $num));
```

The set_body method can take content in three ways. You can pass in an object (as we do here with a SOAP::Struct), you can pass in a simple string to be used verbatim, or you can pass in a hash reference (which would have been serialized like a SOAP::Struct object).

The $method_urn and $method values tell the body constructor what the outer method (or containing tag) will be called, and what namespace it should be associated with. The third argument is used when the body is meant for a special-purpose use. Its value is 0 in other examples as well, for now.

The parameter is the integer value the user passed on the command line, accessed by the name aNumber. After the set_body call, the scalar variable $message now holds the XML-encoded SOAP message.

Autogenerated XML

Example 6-2 shows the XML message generated by the code in Example 6-1, with line breaks added for readability. For the sake of this example, the number given to the program was "1001."

Example 6-2. XML message for "num2text.pl 1001"

```
<s:Envelope
    xmlns:s="http://schemas.xmlsoap.org/soap/envelope/"
    xmlns:xsd="http://www.w3.org/1999/XMLSchema"
    xmlns:xsi="http://www.w3.org/1999/XMLSchema-instance"
    xmlns:n1="urn:NumToWordsIntf-INumToWords"
    s:encodingStyle=
        "http://schemas.xmlsoap.org/soap/encoding/">
  <s:Body>
    <n1:NumToWords_English id="ref-1" s:root="1">
      <aNumber>1001</aNumber>
    </n1:NumToWords_English>
  </s:Body>
</s:Envelope>
```

We won't show XML in future examples, as the toolkits successfully hide the details from you.

The XML in the example is entirely autogenerated by the classes within the SOAP module. Some things to note:

- The message is encoded as a SOAP 1.1 request (check the URN of the s namespace).
- It references earlier versions of the XML Schema.
- The URN for the method name is declared in the Envelope tag, though it could just as easily have been deferred to either the Body tag or the NumToWords_English tag itself.

- The opening tag generated for the `NumToWords_English` call goes to the trouble of defining an id attribute value and explicitly specifying that the entry is the root.

It's not unusual for autogenerated output to have abbreviated names (s as opposed to SOAP-ENV, or even soap) and unnecessary information like the attributes given in the method call's opening tag. Because the modules assume that the message isn't targeted to human reading, completeness is favored over clarity.

Though this example doesn't use it, there's also an add_header method for building the message header one entry at a time. It's documented in the manpage for the SOAP::EnvelopeMaker class, along with greater detail on the new and set_body methods.

Returning to the code, the transport code is in this block:

```
$response = SOAP::Transport::HTTP::Client->new()
                ->send_receive($server, 80, $endpoint,
                               $method_urn, $method,
                               $message);
```

The SOAP::Transport::HTTP::Client wraps a number of lower-level components such as LWP::UserAgent and the related request and response classes. In the example, there was no need to hold on to the client object, so it was used in place and discarded after the send_receive method was called. As with the other classes, the finer details of the methods and their function can be found in the documentation that comes with the package itself.

The last of the SOAP elements used in Example 6-1 are:

```
$parser = SOAP::Parser->new;
$parser->parsestring($response);
$response = $parser->get_body;
```

Upon return from the server, the value in $response should be the response message returned from the server. That message comes back in the form of an XML document, so these lines use the SOAP::Parser class to work it into a Perl-readable data structure, in this case a hash-reference.

When the SOAP elements of the application have run their course, all that is left is the if-else block, in which the body extracted from the response is checked for an element called return. This is the element a SOAP RPC implementation is supposed to use to pass back the value from a successful call. If the element isn't present, the program assumes that a fault occurred and reports a failure using the faultstring and faultcode elements of the response.

When called as in this example, with the integer value 1001, the program returns the following simple output:

```
1001 may be expressed as one thousand and one
```

Because the SOAP module doesn't appear to be currently maintained, the focus now shifts to the other Perl toolkit for SOAP.

The SOAP::Lite Module

The newer of the two SOAP modules for Perl is SOAP::Lite, the work of coauthor Pavel Kulchenko. Unlike the DevelopMentor SOAP module, SOAP::Lite provides functionality in more abstract terms. Classes are provided for client-side functionality, server implementation, data support, and a variety of other tasks. Much of the XML is hidden from the application, except where necessary (or directly relevant).

The SOAP::Lite module is also more actively maintained (keep up to date via the *soaplite.com* web site). It provides full support for SOAP 1.1, and is starting to provide support for SOAP 1.2 as well, with much of the draft specification already implemented. The module also implements XML-RPC, using the components already present in the package (parser, transport code, and the like).

Installing SOAP::Lite

The SOAP::Lite module has a thorough interactive installation process. This allows users to select which subcomponents are available, depending on whether the supporting modules are going to be installed and available. Example 6-3 shows the choices as presented when running perl Makefile.PL.

Example 6-3. Starting the SOAP::Lite installation process

```
XMLRPC::Lite, UDDI::Lite, and XML::Parser::Lite are included
by default.Installed transports can be used for both
SOAP::Lite and XMLRPC::Lite.

Client (SOAP::Transport::HTTP::Client)              [yes]
Client HTTPS/SSL support
    (SOAP::Transport::HTTP::Client, require OpenSSL)  [no]
Client SMTP/sendmail support
    (SOAP::Transport::MAILTO::Client)               [yes]
Client FTP support
    (SOAP::Transport::FTP::Client)                  [yes]
Standalone HTTP server
    (SOAP::Transport::HTTP::Daemon)                 [yes]
Apache/mod_perl server
    (SOAP::Transport::HTTP::Apache, require Apache)   [no]
FastCGI server
    (SOAP::Transport::HTTP::FCGI, require FastCGI)    [no]
POP3 server (SOAP::Transport::POP3::Server)         [yes]
IO server (SOAP::Transport::IO::Server)             [yes]
MQ transport support (SOAP::Transport::MQ)            [no]
JABBER transport support (SOAP::Transport::JABBER)    [no]
MIME messages [required for POP3, optional for HTTP]
    (SOAP::MIMEParser)                                [no]
SSL support for TCP transport (SOAP::Transport::TCP)  [no]
Compression support for HTTP transport
    (SOAP::Transport::HTTP)                           [no]

Do you want to proceed with this configuration? [yes]
```

These installation options are the defaults. The machine on which this output sample was generated had many of the optional Perl modules already available, but the installation process doesn't probe for them unless the user performing the installation enables a particular component.

If the user chooses to not accept the default, she is prompted for each option, whether to enable it with yes or disable it with no. The current values are presented as defaults, as you'd expect. After the full range of choices have been presented, the current configuration is again shown, and the user asked whether to accept and continue, or go back and make further adjustments to the configuration.

Which of the optional components to enable is a matter of taste and of what is to be expected of the applications being developed. In general, any of the components for which the needed modules are already present on the system (such as the Apache support, MIME support, or compression) might as well be enabled. Enabling secure transport support, for example, will require that the system have the Perl modules for SSL, as well as any system libraries such as OpenSSL that they require. The SSL modules, IO::Socket::SSL and Crypt::SSLeay, can be installed by CPAN as part of the installation process for SOAP::Lite itself. The configuration reports any missing modules.

Like many CPAN modules, SOAP::Lite has a fairly large suite of test scripts that will run during the make test phase of building the module. During the configuration phase, the user is given the option of skipping some of the tests, specifically those that will connect to live SOAP servers. This can be useful for systems that don't have continuous Internet access for systems behind firewalls.

Using SOAP::Lite for Clients

Because they share a common architecture and subsystem, the SOAP::Lite client developed for the number-to-string translation server looks a lot like the XMLRPC::Lite client developed in Chapter 4.

Number-to-text conversion with SOAP::Lite

Example 6-4 shows the interesting part of the client (the command-line processing code, for example, has been omitted). Take note of how much simpler this client is than the client from Example 6-1, which used the DevelopMentor SOAP toolkit.

Example 6-4. The num2name.pl script using SOAP::Lite

```
#!/usr/bin/perl

use strict;
use SOAP::Lite;

my $num = shift; $num =~ /^\d+$/ or die "USAGE: $0 num\n";
```

Example 6-4. The num2name.pl script using SOAP::Lite (continued)

```perl
my ($server, $endpoint, $soapaction, $method, $method_urn);
$server      = 'http://www.tankebolaget.se';
$endpoint    =
  "$server/scripts/NumToWords.dll/soap/INumToWords";
$soapaction =
  "urn:NumToWordsIntf-INumToWords#NumToWords_English";
$method      = 'NumToWords_English';
$method_urn = 'urn:NumToWordsIntf-INumToWords';

my $num2words = SOAP::Lite->new(uri    => $soapaction,
                                proxy => $endpoint);
my $response = $num2words
                    ->call(SOAP::Data->name($method)
                            ->attr( { xmlns => $method_urn } )
                            => # Argument(s) listed next
                            SOAP::Data->name(aNumber => $num));

if ($response->fault) {
    printf "A fault (%s) occurred: %s\n",
        $response->faultcode, $response->faultstring;
} else {
    print "$num may be expressed as " . $response->result .
          "\n";
}

exit;
```

The first area of difference comes in the inclusion of code to provide the SOAP functionality. The four use statements in the original are replaced with:

```perl
use SOAP::Lite;
```

The SOAP::Lite package loads other modules as needed.

We interact with the server via a SOAP::Lite object. Its construction is simply:

```perl
my $num2words = SOAP::Lite->new(uri    => $soapaction,
                                proxy => $endpoint);
```

The meaning of uri and proxy, and of the values in $soapaction and $endpoint, are covered later.

The remote method call is done in an extremely verbose way, for example:

```perl
my $response = $num2words->call(SOAP::Data
                                ->name($method)
                                ->attr( { xmlns =>
                                        $method_urn } )
                                => # Argument(s) listed next
                                SOAP::Data->name(aNumber =>
                                                  $num));
```

Depending on the strictness of the server, that call might be as short as:

```perl
my $response = $num2words->$method($num);
```

This syntax is covered later.*

Finally, the examination of the return value uses methods available on the returned object to test whether the response received was a fault or not. If it was, further methods (faultcode and faultstring) are used to construct an error message. Otherwise, the result is easily extracted from the response object.

The assignments to $server and $endpoint differ slightly from those in Example 6-1. In that example, $soapaction was not actually used because, by chance, its form matched what the SOAP module created internally from the values of $method and $method_urn. Here it is used when creating the SOAP::Lite handle object. The value of $endpoint ends up being the full URL, because the logic within SOAP::Transport examines the string to choose the proper transport binding. In the first example, the server's hostname and port had to be passed separately due to the way in which SOAP created the final URL.

As was mentioned earlier in the commentary, there are several places where this code could have been written more concisely. As it stands, it is roughly 10% shorter than the version which used SOAP.

Translating a use.perl.org journal stream to RSS

This next example uses the SOAP interface at the use Perl; discussion site (*http://use.perl.org*), taking the last 15 journal entries for a specified user† and creating a RSS 1.0 syndication feed from them.

The use Perl; site is built on the Slash web form code (*http://www.slashcode.org*). In addition to news and conversational forums, it provides web-log facilities to its registered users. Many well-known characters in the Perl community maintain ongoing commentary on their projects and tasks. The collection of story headlines is retrievable as a RSS feed, as is the list of most-recently updated journals. But the journal of an individual user isn't (currently) available as a RSS feed. Into this gap steps the upj2rss.pl utility in Example 6-5.

Example 6-5. upj2rss.pl, turning a journal log into RSS

```
#!/usr/bin/perl -w

use strict;

use SOAP::Lite;
use XML::RSS;

my $user = shift ||
    die "Usage: $0 userID [ usernick ]\n\nStopped";
```

---

* It isn't sufficient for this particular SOAP server, as it happens.

† Note that this SOAP interface is still very early alpha but also very useful.

Example 6-5. upj2rss.pl, turning a journal log into RSS (continued)

```
my $nick = shift || "#$user";

my $host    = 'http://use.perl.org';
my $uri     = "$host/Slash/Journal/SOAP";
my $proxy   = "$host/journal.pl";

# SOAP material starts here:
my $journal = SOAP::Lite->uri($uri)->proxy($proxy);
my $results = $journal->get_entries($user, 15)->result;
my $rss     = XML::RSS->new(version => '1.0');

$rss->channel(title => "use.perl.org journal of $nick",
              'link' => $proxy,
              description =>
              "The use.perl.org journal of $nick");
$rss->add_item(title => $_->{subject},
               'link' => $_->{url})
    for (@$results);

print STDOUT $rss->as_string;
exit;
```

Example 6-5 uses another CPAN module, XML::RSS, which is a useful tool for creating and parsing syndication feeds. Here it creates the syndication-feed version of the journal data. For this example, assume that it is a working black box that doesn't need further explanation.

Starting right after the comment that says, "SOAP material starts here," a handle object is created in much the same way as in Example 6-4. Here, rather than calling new( ) explicitly, the application lets the SOAP::Lite module do that at the time of the first method invocation (uri, in this case). Calling one of the class methods as a static method automatically triggers this behavior. The uri( ) and proxy( ) methods set the SOAPAction header and communication URL, respectively. In the previous example, these were passed as parameters to the constructor.

The next line uses this client object to invoke a method called get_entries on the server. Two arguments are passed (both integers), and the return value invokes a method called result. The return value from a method call is a reference to an object in the SOAP::SOM class. This is a class used to encapsulate the returned message body from the server. In more detailed examples later, this object will be more fully utilized. For now, it is enough to know that the result method takes the data content of the response and transforms it to a native Perl datatype. Example 6-4 returned a single string, but in this case, the data is an array reference with up to 15 journal entries (assuming there were at least that many available) for the user whose account ID on use.perl.org was the value in $user.

The rest of the script details aren't really that important. Absent here is any real checking of return values or tests for data validity. The uri and proxy methods can be safely assumed to return a valid object reference. No connections are made by calling those methods; they set only values internal to the object. The method invocation itself on the next line could have had problems, though.

Basic classes and components

These initial examples showed how few basic components are needed to accomplish tasks with the SOAP::Lite toolkit. Several classes other than SOAP::Lite came in to play, but their presence was quietly abstracted by the interface. In fact, the primary role that the SOAP::Lite class plays is to provide shortcuts to methods that are part of the classes used behind the scenes. There are methods that are actual parts of SOAP::Lite, however, as will be seen later.

What are these classes, then? Which of them should an application developer be concerned with? Table 6-1 lists the classes developers should begin with.

Table 6-1. The basic elements of the SOAP::Lite toolkit

Class	Role
SOAP::Lite	An umbrella over many of the other classes. This class provides the highest level of abstraction in the overall package.
SOAP::Transport	This is the base abstraction of the transport classes within the package. Many of the methods called on SOAP::Lite objects are filtered through to here.
SOAP::Data	This provides very simple data-encoding functionality. Through this wrapper, data objects can be associated with named accessors, specific typing, encoding, etc.
SOAP::SOM	This class is much like HTTP::Response, in the sense that applications often manipulate instance objects created from this class, without directly knowing that they are doing so. Responses from a server are passed back to a client using this class to encapsulate them.

The elements in Table 6-1 were mentioned in the discussion of the two previous examples. Two have already been explained, the other two are:

SOAP::Data
> Expect to use this class more often than may seem immediately obvious. Perl handles a wide range of datatypes in a very seamless manner, but SOAP as a general rule doesn't. If the sequence "123" is to be sent as a string, it usually has to be explicitly encoded as such. Perl would interpret it as an integer, and serialize it this way. If the server is expecting a string, an integer might not be acceptable. This is also very useful when it is necessary to control the naming of accessors for the data or when using different encodings (such as a string in a different character set).

SOAP::Transport
> The typical application rarely (if ever) directly instantiates an object of this class. However, several of the more common methods used on SOAP::Lite objects actually thread through to the instance of this class the containing object maintains. Methods such as uri, proxy, and endpoint are made available through the

abstract interface but are implemented within this class. Behind the scenes, this class manages specific protocol modules and transport bindings based on the schemes used in the URNs given to these methods.

In general, the methods from `SOAP::Lite` are considered accessor methods and as such return their current value when no arguments are passed in to the call. If arguments are passed, they return the calling object to enable the chaining of method calls. The examples thus far have used only a few of the `SOAP::Lite` methods:

new
: As would be expected, this method is the class constructor. The nature of most of the other methods in the class make this unnecessary in most cases, because the first call to another method creates the new object upon demand.

uri
: Gets or sets the URI of the remote method being accessed. This isn't the same as the web address (or other type of address) of the server itself. The URI in many cases doesn't point to an existing document. It is used as a unique identifier for the resource being used (in this case, a remote method).

: This is a confusing distinction to many people. When using SOAP over HTTP to do remote procedure calls, the messages have to have a URI that identifies the "service." This may be the same as the HTTP address, similar to it, or completely different. It is just another identifier, though, one that happens to look like a web address in most cases.

proxy
: Sets or gets the actual endpoint address to which requests will go. The string that gets passed to this method as an argument will ultimately help select the support code for the transport layer. If it is a HTTP URL, the HTTP transport module gets loaded into memory, and so forth for schemes such as Jabber or SMTP.

The latter two methods here actually act as shortcuts to the `SOAP::Transport` class, one of the several classes that `SOAP::Lite` abstracts the user from in most cases.

The `SOAP::Lite` class also has several settings that are activated when the library is imported into the application, for example:

```
use SOAP::Lite +autodispatch, +trace;
```

Many of the standard settings may also be specified here, such as uri, proxy, etc. When these are set at the import-level like this, they become the values on the global object instance that `SOAP::Lite` quietly maintains behind the scenes. It is from this object that other instances take their default values, and from this object that the on-the-fly construction of object instances happens. (Recall from the explanation following Example 6-5, that most of the methods will automatically instantiate an object of the class when they are called as static methods.)

Here are the settings that may be given to SOAP::Lite when it's imported to an application:

+autodispatch
> When this is passed, SOAP::Lite installs an AUTOLOAD mechanism in the UNIVERSAL namespace. This causes all unrecognized function names to route through this AUTOLOAD routine, which allows SOAP::Lite to attempt to manage them using the settings on the global object it maintains.

+trace, +debug
> The tracing/debugging facility is handled the same way regardless of which of the two switches are used. Both are provided if you prefer one to the other, and both are just interfaces into the SOAP::Trace class settings. The tracing facility is actually very robust and is covered in more detail later. The keyword is optionally followed by a list of events to trace. If no such list is given, all events are traced.

dispatch_from => *class name or list reference of class names*
> This facility enhances the +autodispatch functionality described earlier. The difference here is that this keyword provides one or more class names from which methods are to be auto-dispatched just as ordinary routines are auto-dispatched by the previous keyword. This option looks for only one argument following it, so specifying multiple classes requires passing them in a list reference. When this is set up, it installs the AUTOLOAD functionality only in the specified classes, not at the UNIVERSAL level. The application can still auto-dispatch without using an instance variable, but regular undefined functions in the main body will still raise errors (without attempting to contact a remote server first).

Returning to the SOAP::Trace class mentioned earlier, this is the class which encapsulates the debugging/tracing facility. This is another "behind the scenes" class, whose only visible interface is the +debug/+trace option defined earlier. As was mentioned then, the tracing class is implemented in terms of a set of events, which are listed in Table 6-2. Not all the events are relevant to both clients and servers; the table explains their roles.

Table 6-2. SOAP::Trace events and their meanings

Event	Client/server?	Meaning
transport	Client	Looks at the HTTP::Request and HTTP::Response objects during the transport cycle.
dispatch	Server	Shows the full name of the dispatched call.
result	Server	Gives the result of the method call.
parameters	Server	Shows the parameters for the method call.
headers	Server	Gives the headers of the received message.
objects	Both	Tracks calls to new and DESTROY in the classes.
method	Both	Gets the parameters to the envelope method when the first argument is the string literal, method.

Table 6-2. SOAP::Trace events and their meanings (continued)

Event	Client/server?	Meaning
fault	Both	Gets the parameters to the envelope method when creating a fault (first argument is fault).
freeform	Both	Gets the parameters to the envelope method when the argument is freeform.
trace	Both	Traces entrance into important functions.
debug	Both	Details along the stages of transport.

There is a last, pseudo-event specifier called all. Normally it isn't needed because passing +trace with no event list has the effect of enabling all events. However, you can disable an event by prefixing its name with a hyphen. Thus, the following line enables all tracing events *except* the debug events:

```
use SOAP::Lite +trace => [qw(all -debug)];
```

The default action for these events is to log the data that they get passed to STDERR. Alternately, the event given on the importing line can specify a subroutine reference or a closure, and have that called on the event instead. These trace-event callbacks receive the same information that the native ones would have received, as given in Table 6-2. An example of tracing faults might look like this:

```
use SOAP::Lite +trace => [fault => \&follow_fault];

# ...

sub follow_fault {
    warn "Fault occured:\n\t" . join("\n\t", @_) . "\n";
}
```

Dispatching methods and the object style

Recall the syntax alluded to in Example 6-4, which was used in Example 6-5. The client object called a method on the use.perl.org server in this fashion:

```
$journal->get_entries($user, 15)
```

It's no surprise that the SOAP::Lite class, which $journal holds an instance reference of, doesn't actually implement a method called get_entries. Nor would you expect a class to try to predict all the potential method names that may ever be conjured. This is a syntactical shortcut SOAP::Lite provides to client objects, one that makes the syntax of the application around that object look more comfortable and familiar.

Perl has an extremely flexible feature called *auto-loading*,[*] which is used in a variety of creative ways by other modules from both within the core of Perl and from CPAN. This is another highly creative application of that functionality.

---

[*] For more about this topic, see the perlsub manpage and the AutoLoader module's manpage.

When a client object tries to call a method that doesn't exist in the package, the class catches the call and tries to execute it remotely. The beauty of it all is that to the application using the object, it is just another method call.

With that syntax, it becomes much more familiar and comfortable to use the client object as if it were any other type of garden-variety object, containing and accessing data in local memory. The sense of abstraction has extended not just to the classes and components that implement the SOAP conversation, that abstraction has resulted in almost completely hiding the fact that there even *is* a SOAP conversation taking place.

Using the $journal object more freely, the sample program can be made to retrieve more information for each journal entry, resulting in a richer syndication:

```
my $results = $journal->get_entries($user, 15)->result;
my @results = map {
                my $entry = $journal->get_entry($_->{id})
                                    ->result;
                # Imagine this uses HTML::Parser to get
                # roughly the first paragraph
                my $desc = extract_desc($entry->{body});
                # Imagine $nick wasn't set earlier
                $nick ||= $entry->{nickname};
                # Each map-value is a hash reference:
                { 'link'       => $entry->{url},
                  description  => $desc,
                  title        => $entry->{subject} };
            } (@$results);
```

The initialization of the $rss object is the same, except that now $nick has the user's actual nickname on *use.perl.org*, instead of the script defaulting to the user ID. But then, change the lines that add the contents to the RSS channel to this:

```
$rss->add_item(%$_) for (@results);
```

Now, the resulting RSS channel has more than just the subject lines of the journal entries. The leading paragraph or so, depending on the implementation of the hypothetical extract_desc routine, has been added as the description for the RSS entry. The possibilities are limited only by the information actually provided from the call. Also, nothing in the earlier map block looks significantly different from any other object-oriented Perl usage. Only the result method being called after the get_entry method offers any clue that this might be different from a generic database or other data-store layer.

This form of method-dispatching is commonly used. However, SOAP::Lite also allows for even more-liberal dispatching, with the +autodispatch and dispatch_from options that may be set at import-time. When these are used, the functions that get automatically routed to the remote server may be any ordinary (as in *non*-method) function calls within the code. Note that in the following code fragment:

```
    use SOAP::Lite +autodispatch =>
                uri   => 'http://...' =>
                proxy => 'http://...';

not_local($arg1, $arg2);
```

both the uri and the proxy are specified at the same time as the +autodispatch setting. This provides the basis for SOAP::Lite to try and execute any "rogue" subroutines it gets handed. Assuming that the routine not_local isn't already defined somewhere else, it is handed to SOAP::Lite to try and execute remotely.

The difference made by dispatch_from is one of scoping these open-ended executions to a given class namespace:

```
    use SOAP::Lite dispatch_from => Remote =>
                uri   => 'http://...' =>
                proxy => 'http://...';

# This will fail at run-time
not_local($arg1, $arg2);
# This will not-- unless "not_local" isn't found remotely
Remote->not_local($arg1, $arg2);
```

The primary difference is that the main application namespace isn't going to trigger an attempt to run a procedure remotely. The dispatch_from functionality only hooks the auto-loading in at the level of the named classes.

The +autodispatch mechanism is very convenient but also opens the door to a lot of potential pitfalls. The most obvious of these is the danger inherent in running remote code accidentally, perhaps by way of a typo. Using the automatic dispatching can also be noisy when warnings are enabled with Perl's -w flag because of the AUTOLOAD routine SOAP::Lite installs to enable auto-dispatching. The interpreter perceives the routine as being inherited from a superclass, which is one of the warning conditions -w checks for.

Beyond the noise and potential for user error, however, is the real factor of clarity in the code, and readability to those others who may have to maintain the code long after the original author has moved on to other projects. Auto-dispatched methods that have no class qualifier at all aren't easily distinguished from actual local functions that are part of the application itself or of a local library. Consider using dispatch_from in those cases where +autodispatch seems to be the tool to use.* Leave +autodispatch for the smaller cases, one-liners, and utilities that are shorter and easier to maintain. It may seem less convenient at the time, but such compromises almost always pay dividends over the longer lifecycle of software.

---

* Another reason to use dispatch_from is the bug in UNIVERSAL::AUTOLOAD in Perl 5.8.0 that breaks +autodispatch code.

Managing data with SOAP::Data and SOAP::SOM

Recall the way data was passed to the remote method in Example 6-4. In order to maintain compliance with the server, data was constructed so that it serialized in a very strict and clean fashion. This was accomplished using the methods from the SOAP::Data class.

SOAP::Data is intended to help out the application when the default serialization of a value might be either wrong or at least incomplete. A common example is when a string appears to be a number. Because of the way Perl treats scalars, a value of 123 may be treated as an integer when it needs to be (for math operations) or a string if so needed (for concatenation as an example). Because of this flexibility, it can be hard to know for certain when such a value is meant to be a specific type. There may also be other issues beyond just the type of the data: a string may require a different encoding, or the accessor name being associated with the value may need to be given a specific namespace qualification.

Objects of the SOAP::Data class aren't generally instantiated for the long term. That is, most usage of the class is just to create an object long enough for it to be passed in a subroutine call, after which it is discarded. While there is a new method, its use is rarely seen. More often seen is this type of usage:

```
SOAP::Data->name(zipCode => 95008)->type('string')
```

This example is based on the fact that a U.S. postal Zip Code can have a four-digit extension at the end, with a hyphen separating it from the main five-digit code. Because of this, an application that accepts Zip Codes as input must take them as string data. However, the natural tendency of Perl is to treat 95008 as an integer. Because of that, such a value must be "coerced" into the correct type.

Like SOAP::Lite itself, the methods within SOAP::Data each create an object when called as static methods and return the object when called with any parameters. Any of the methods, such as value, that are called with no parameters return the current setting of the given aspect of the data. The more commonly used methods provided by this class are summarized in Table 6-3, with a complete list available in Appendix B.

Table 6-3. SOAP::Data class methods

Method	Purpose
name	The name is the accessor, or element name, by which the data is to be known in the resulting XML document.
value	This sets (or retrieves) the value of the data object.
type	This method explicitly sets a type for the data item. If this method isn't called, SOAP::Data attempts to intuit the type from an examination of the data.

Table 6-3. SOAP::Data class methods (continued)

Method	Purpose
encodingStyle	If the data item is to have an encoding different from the one that would affect it by default, the URN for that encoding is set with this method.
root	This method allows for explicitly setting the root attribute on this data item. It requires a boolean value.

Another class that is important in a "behind-the-scenes" fashion is SOAP::SOM, which was referred to in the earlier examples. This class encapsulates the returned messages from remote calls. In many cases, the class is completely transparent to the application using it. Like HTTP::Response in the LWP package, an application doesn't instantiate it. Rather, it is handed back at the completion of a remote call. Objects of this class are useful for more than simply chaining an invocation of the result method onto the end of a call. If the object itself is kept as the return value, the application can check the fault status of the call more closely.

More specifically, SOAP::SOM objects give the application full access to the deserialized envelope itself. Many of the data-retrieval methods use a syntax very much like XPath notation. Depending on the depth of data in the envelopes exchanged between a client and server, the application may only need the first few of the methods explained. There are actually a large number of methods in this class, though many don't see frequent use. The more common methods are summarized in Table 6-4.

Table 6-4. SOAP::SOM class methods

Method	Purpose
fault	Returns a boolean expression identifying whether the response is a fault or not.
faultcode	Returns the fault code, if the response is a fault.
faultstring	Returns the fault string (description), if the response is a fault.
faultactor	Return the URN of the actor involved in the fault, if the response is a fault.
faultdetail	Returns the data in the faultdetail element of the fault, if the response is a fault. Note that this element has somewhat variable definition, as discussed in the earlier chapter on SOAP.
result	For a nonfault response, this returns the result value from the remote server.
method	Returns the tag that specified the method (remote function name) that was called.
paramsout paramsall paramsin	Because server responses aren't limited to returning just one value, these methods implement management of the IN, IN/OUT, and OUT parameter styles, as discussed in Chapter 5. These parameter bindings will be discussed in greater detail in their own section.

The previous examples built on SOAP::Lite assumed that their remote calls were successful. The next example incorporates the SOAP::SOM methods to check more carefully.

Example: Automatically announcing CPAN uploads

The SOAP interface at *use.perl.org* also permits posting journal entries. At first glance, it might not be clear why a script would be used to perform a task like this, but upon closer look it becomes obvious. There are plenty of situations in which you want to automatically post some item of news to a forum, such as a developer's personal journal. This example focuses on the announcement of new CPAN uploads.

When an author uploads a new release of a package to CPAN, some automatic status messages are sent back to his registered contact address by email, signaling certain points in the submittal process. Some authors choose to then announce on one or more forums that the new code is now being mirrored across the range of servers. Because the email is an automated, reliable event that signals a successful CPAN submission, it makes an excellent herald for other types of announcements.

This sample script takes one of the two messages sent out by the PAUSE daemon (Perl Authors Upload Server) and uses some of the information within it to create the HTML body of a journal entry. The body is then posted to the user's journal at *use.perl.org*, with an appropriate subject. Not all elements of the code will be examined closely, but should be clear when looking at the script as a whole. The script will follow this explanation, as Example 6-6.

This first segment of code is the creation of the HTTP cookie data that will be part of the request. Unlike the read-only operations used in earlier examples, operations such as posting a journal entry require authentication. The *use.perl.org* SOAP service uses the same browser cookie for validation that the web server itself uses for personalization and access to individual content. This utility may not be running in an environment that has access to the user's cookie file, so it accepts credentials as a command-line argument. There are other arguments, which will all be parsed by the Getopt::Std module. The %opts hash table is a global variable that contains these options. Preparing the cookie entails the following:

```
$host = 'use.perl.org';
# Note that this path is UNIX-centric. Consider using
# File::Spec methods in most cases.
$cookie_file = "$ENV{HOME}/.netscape/cookies";

if ($opts{C}) {
    $cookie_jar = HTTP::Cookies->new;
    $cookie_jar
      ->set_cookie(0,
                   user => make_cookie(split /:/, $opts{C}),
                   '/', $host);
} elsif (-f $cookie_file) {
    $cookie_jar = HTTP::Cookies::Netscape
                    ->new(File => $cookie_file);
} else {
    die "$0: No authentication data found, cannot continue";
}
```

The `make_cookie` routine that creates the cookie from the command-line data will be shown in the final script. What is noteworthy is that the tool will give the command-line priority over an existing cookie file, and because the `HTTP::Cookies` package doesn't provide a method to check for a specific cookie, no test is made that the cookie file even provided the script with a useful cookie for this site. If it is the case that there is no valid cookie, the script will catch that at a later point.

The script next takes the mail message and extracts the data it wants from it. To make the script operate in a familiar and friendly manner, it will be designed to read the email message from the `STDIN` filehandle, like a filter. A sample message from a release of the `RPC::XML` module looks a little like this:

```
The uploaded file

    RPC-XML-0.37.tar.gz

has entered CPAN as

    file: $CPAN/authors/id/R/RJ/RJRAY/RPC-XML-0.37.tar.gz
    size: 86502 bytes
    md5: d58344bf2c80f44b95a13bf838628517

No action is required on your part
Request entered by: RJRAY (Randy J Ray)
Request entered on: Sat, 23 Mar 2002 06:37:19 GMT
Request completed:  Sat, 23 Mar 2002 06:39:00 GMT

        Virtually Yours,
        Id: paused,v 1.80 2002/03/10 06:40:03 k Exp k
```

The most relevant piece of information here is the seventh line, which starts with the sequence, `file:`. This path can be easily turned into an active CPAN URL (though the file itself is still in the process of being mirrored, and so the URL may not yet work universally). For the sake of this example, the text for the journal entry is kept to a minimum. In this case, it announces the package by the filename and provides a direct link to it using the data on line 7.

Moving to the SOAP-relevant content of the script, assume that the processing of the mail message has been done. The initial lines that set up the client to the SOAP service are generally the same as with the earlier example:

```
$host  = 'use.perl.org';
$uri   = "http://$host/Slash/Journal/SOAP";
$proxy = "http://$host/journal.pl";

$journal = SOAP::Lite
            ->uri($uri)
            ->proxy($proxy, cookie_jar => $cookie_jar);
die "$0: Error creating SOAP::Lite client, cannot continue"
    unless $journal;
```

The difference here is in the call to the proxy method, when the client object is being created. The $cookie_jar object created earlier is passed along with the URL itself. Because the URL is recognized by SOAP::Lite as a HTTP endpoint, it also recognize the cookie_jar key (and value) as relevant to the creation of a user-agent object. The jar will be incorporated into the LWP::UserAgent object that eventually handles the connections to the remote host. There are other options that can be given to the proxy method under an umbrella-option that is simply called options and which takes a hash reference as an argument. The actual options vary from one type of transport to the next. Some, such as compress_threshold, which enables compression support, require that the functionality be enabled on both ends of the conversation. These options will be dealt with in greater detail at a later point.

Making the call itself isn't that different from the earlier operation. According to the description of the service, the method used to post a journal entry is called add_entry, and it takes a sequence of key/value pairs. For now, assume that $body, $title, and $discuss were computed prior to this point:

```
$result = $journal->add_entry(subject => $title,
                              body    => $body,
                              discuss => $discuss);

if ($result->fault) {
    die "$0: Failed: " . $result->faultstring . "\n";
} else {
    printf "New entry added as %s\n", $result->result;
}
```

The result of the operation is saved in its native state as a SOAP::SOM object instance. This allows the script to test it with the expression ($result->fault) and act accordingly. If it is a fault, the application dies with the fault string as an error message. But if it succeeds, a brief message announcing success is given. It uses the result method on the object to get the new entry's ID number.

Now for the script in full. It is designed to be run from a mail-filter program such as procmail. A sample procmail "recipe" for this might look like the following:

```
:0 Wc
* Subject.*CPAN Upload
| cpan2upj.pl
```

This recipe (as procmail rules are called) matches messages whose subject line starts with CPAN Upload. The message is piped in to the script, which is called cpan2upj.pl. Example 6-6 is the complete cpan2upj.pl script.

Example 6-6. cpan2upj.pl

```
#!/usr/bin/perl -w

use strict;
use File::Basename 'basename';
use Getopt::Std;
```

Example 6-6. cpan2upj.pl (continued)

```perl
use Digest::MD5    'md5_hex';
use HTTP::Cookies;
use SOAP::Lite;

my (%opts, $user, $title, $discuss, $body, $host, $uri,
    $proxy, $file, $name, $cookie_file, $cookie_jar,
    $journal, $result);

getopts('C:c', \%opts) or die <<"USAGE";
Usage: $0 [ -c ] [ -C user:pass ]

-c              Allow comments on journal entry
-C user:pass    Provide authentication in place of (or in
                absence of) Netscape cookies. User in
                this case is UID, not nickname.
USAGE

while (defined($_ = <STDIN>)) {
    $file = $1, last if /^\s+file:\s+(\S+)/;
}
die "$0: No filename found in input, stopped" unless $file;
$name = basename $file;
$file =~ s|^\$CPAN|http://www.cpan.org|;

$user    = (getpwuid($<))[0];
$title   = "$name uploaded to PAUSE";
$discuss = $opts{c} ? 1 : 0;
$body = << "BODY";
<p>The file <tt>$name</tt> has been uploaded to CPAN, and
will soon be accessible as <a href="$file">$file</a>.
Mirroring may take up to 24 hours.</p>
<p><i>$0, on behalf of $user</i></p>
BODY

$host         = 'use.perl.org';
$uri          = "http://$host/Slash/Journal/SOAP";
$proxy        = "http://$host/journal.pl";
# Note that this path is UNIX-centric. Consider using
# File::Spec methods in most cases.
$cookie_file  = "$ENV{HOME}/.netscape/cookies";

if ($opts{C}) {
    $cookie_jar = HTTP::Cookies->new
       ->set_cookie(0,
                    user => make_cookie(split /:/, $opts{C}),
                    '/', $host);
} elsif (-f $cookie_file) {
    $cookie_jar = HTTP::Cookies::Netscape->new(File => $cookie_file);
} else {
    die "$0: No authentication data found, cannot continue";
}
```

Example 6-6. cpan2upj.pl (continued)

```
$journal = SOAP::Lite->uri($uri)
            ->proxy($proxy, cookie_jar => $cookie_jar);
die "$0: Error creating SOAP::Lite client, cannot continue"
    unless $journal;
$result = $journal->add_entry(subject => $title,
                              body    => $body,
                              discuss => $discuss);

if ($result->fault) {
    die "$0: Failed: " . $result->faultstring . "\n";
} else {
    printf "New entry added as %s\n", $result->result;
}

exit;

# Taken from the Slash codebase
sub make_cookie {
    my ($uid, $passwd) = @_;
    my $cookie = $uid . '::' . md5_hex($passwd);
    $cookie =~ s/(.)/sprintf("%%%02x", ord($1))/ge;
    $cookie =~ s/%/%25/g;
    $cookie;
}
```

Other SOAP-Related Modules

Before moving to more advanced topics like writing servers, it is worthwhile to briefly look at some other SOAP-related modules that are available on CPAN.

SOAP::payload

This package, written by Stephen Martin, is designed to aid in the encapsulation of various arbitrary types of data into SOAP payloads. The manpage offers examples geared towards relational database usage through interaction with the DBI module. It doesn't provide a transport layer or a deserialization layer. It does provide methods for working with strings and array references, as well as database handles. The URNs for things such as the SOAP namespace and the XSchema-related namespaces are configurable, too.

SOAP::Lite::SmartProxy

The SOAP::Lite::SmartProxy module is written by Daniel Yacob and is designed to extend the functionality of SOAP::Lite itself by providing "smart" proxying of services between SOAP servers in an environment where some may not be directly accessible to clients (such as firewall installations).

It installs into a similar package namespace as SOAP::Lite and provides a different URI scheme in the form of httpx to signify that the server should use the smart-proxy code. Client applications can also uses the proxy when appropriate.

Meta::Comm::Soap

Part of the Meta module by Mark Veltzer, which is a collection of some 250 or more utility classes, the Meta::Comm::Soap::Client and Meta::Comm::Soap::Server classes provide simple starting points for deriving client and server objects. They don't natively provide transport or other features; these are imported from SOAP::Lite classes. The Meta package as a whole is still alpha-level work at the time of this writing but may prove useful.

CHAPTER 7
Serving SOAP over HTTP

Whereas the previous chapter focused on developing SOAP clients, this chapter focuses on designing and developing a server. It's not that the mechanics of writing a server are complex: a server can be as simple as a client. The design of a server application can make it easy to handle requests from multiple clients, if done well. Much of this depends on whether SOAP is a part of the design and planning from the outset or whether it is an afterthought.

In this chapter we develop a sample application designed and planned with SOAP as a basic building block. The server demonstrates how easily SOAP::Lite supports HTTP development. It will also show good design of SOAP servers, including features such as authentication and code security.

Basic SOAP::Lite Servers

Clients are good examples to use when getting started with the toolkit, but without any servers out there, there would be nothing for the clients to connect to. So, what approaches and methods are there in this toolkit for designing servers? The short answer is *many*. The longer answer will span this chapter and the next.

The following snippet illustrates the elements most commonly seen in a server built using any of the SOAP::Lite server classes:

```
# Bring in the server class to be used
use SOAP::Transport::HTTP;
# Create a simple server object
my $daemon = SOAP::Transport::HTTP::Daemon
    ->new(LocalAddr => localhost => LocalPort => 9000)
    ->objects_by_reference('Example::Class')
    ->handle;
```

As the server example in this chapter is developed, then ported to other transport protocols in the next chapter, this same basic structure will recur. The server support in `SOAP::Lite` abstracts a considerable amount of detail from the developer's point of view.

No matter which server class is used by an application, it will be necessary to create a server object (at least one) and associate local (server-side) routines to be called for the incoming requests. Like the client classes described in the previous chapter, the server classes are designed so that the constructor is called automatically when needed. Explicit calls to new aren't that common (except in educational examples, of course). The `objects_by_reference` method used earlier is one of several ways servers can be associated with local subroutines. Various examples later on will show the different techniques and compare their benefits and features.

Each of the server classes has some variation of the `handle` method. In most cases, it is a loop that continues indefinitely while waiting for incoming connections. Chapter 8 which discusses the non-HTTP server classes, will show some examples that operate differently.

The rest of this chapter will proceed to design and build a simple server application. This application will not only demonstrate basic server aspects, it will also be used to illustrate the kinds of considerations that come into play when designing code to be used in a web service. It will also be the basis for the examples in Chapter 8.

The Application

The sample application maintains a "wish list," or shopping list, of books at a web-based storefront. For the sake of this chapter, the design goals are kept on the simple side. The server provides the following functionality:

- Get the current wish-list contents in an abbreviated form.
- Pull the data record for a given entry on the wish list.
- Add and remove entries from the list.
- If the user already has billing and shipping information on file, they should be able to trigger the purchase of one or more items from the list.

In the last requirement, the server doesn't handle all the issues around securely receiving a credit-card number or other confidential information. Instead, if the user's customer record indicates that they have all the needed information already on file, they are given the chance to easily make the purchases. The server also allows some operations that aren't user-specific:

- Search for books by author or title, each using substring matching.
- Retrieve a limited subset of information on a given book, less than what is given to registered users but enough to be useful to some extent.

Generally, such an application would provide much more in the way of functionality. But this simple application highlights many situations that can trouble SOAP applications of all size.

Designing the Server

What are the issues to keep in mind when designing this service? Given a known set of requirements that must be met, the design might start by taking into consideration the interface that will be made available to the outside world. That plan will shape the code that the SOAP server is eventually built upon. The SOAP server is more than just that, however. It will also have to look at the protocols by which to expose the API (which for now is just HTTP) and how to bind to those protocols.

Supporting Code

Because this is a book on web services and not on databases, the code for the underlying database layer isn't described in this chapter. It is in Appendix D with the rest of the application. For the exercise, assume that a different development group has provided the user and database code modules for integration, and that they work without any problems.[*] The interface itself is simple, and throughout the chapter the routines will be referenced by their full package, to further clarify things.

The underlying database of books is a simple DBM-derivative (using the DB_File module in the Perl core) whose content is an abbreviated O'Reilly & Associates catalog. The primary key used to track books is the ISBN number. User records are keyed by the user "nickname" and also kept in a DBM-based structure. The interface to these databases consists of just the simple, minimal operations. Because the application isn't responsible for maintaining the databases or their contents, the routines mainly cover data retrieval (except for modifying the user's wish list of books). Because they aren't the focus here, the routines are only lightly documented as they're used.

Managing the Interface

The initial temptation might be to expose the reduced database API as the SOAP service itself. This would be a bad idea for a number of reasons, the main one being that even with the limited database access this API provides, there is almost certainly going to be information in the records that shouldn't be given out, at least not without careful consideration. Instead, a composite class that encapsulates the relevant information from a user record and from book records will be used. See Figure 7-1.

---

[*] Don't laugh, it could happen.

Figure 7-1. The composite class the server will use

This midlevel class makes it easier to encapsulate the connections to the separate databases, a detail that clients of the service have no need to know. It also makes it easier to export the functionality through the server without exposing other elements in the process.

Going at this from the angle of an object-oriented design, the operations listed earlier that aren't user-specific in nature (simple searching for books by author or title and pulling a limited range of information on a specific book) might be treated as class methods, because they don't require a specific user object to invoke them.

Calling the new class `WishListCustomer`, there are three static methods to start off the implementation: `BooksByAuthor`, `BooksByTitle`, and `GetBook`. As will be shown later, that third method is combined with the normal retrieval of book information such that it decides how much information to return based on whether it is called as a static method or with a valid object instead.

These methods can be initially documented as follows:

BooksByAuthor

> Input parameter: search_for, a string.
>
> Return value: array (reference) of ISBN-based keys.
>
> Search for books whose author field contains the substring given in the author parameter.

BooksByTitle

> Input parameter: search_for, a string.
>
> Return value: array (reference) of ISBN-based keys.
>
> Search for books whose title field contains the substring given in the title parameter.

GetBook

> Input parameter: isbn, a string.

Return value: structure (reference) of book information, or undef.

Given a ISBN-based key (the ISBN minus all hyphens), return structured data pertaining to the book. As a static method, this is limited to the isbn, title, author, and url fields.

In these cases, the returned data is managed at the Perl level by references to more complex datatypes (lists and hash tables). The SOAP serialization manages their expression as proper XML Schema-based data. The code in Example 7-1 shows one of these methods, BooksByAuthor, as it appears in the WishListCustomer class.

Example 7-1. The WishListCustomer::BooksByAuthor method

```
package WishListCustomer;

sub BooksByAuthor {
    my ($class, $author) = @_;

    my $bookdb = ref($class) ? $class->{_catalog} :
                               SoapExBook::connect();
    return undef unless $bookdb;

    my @books =
        SoapExBook::get_books_by_author($bookdb, $author);
    \@books;
}
```

The code is simple, and the code for BooksByTitle will look very similar. The two could in fact be implemented as the same function as a means of choosing how to do the search, using differently named parameters and the SOAP envelope to determine if the argument was named "author" or "title." This will be revisited later, when server-side access to the SOAP envelope is discussed.

Handling the user-centric operations is a little more involved because a valid object is expected from which to derive some of the data. One operation has already been defined: GetBook. That method will be the same as an object method as it stands as a static method. The difference will be in the amount of information returned in the structure. It will also be necessary for the class to have a constructor method.

Once a client has a WishListCustomer object, it calls methods on that object to obtain the wish-list contents and add to or remove books from the wish list. There's also a method to inform the client whether or not the user can directly purchase books.

The full list of methods for the WishListCustomer class follows:

new
Input parameters: user and password, strings (optional).

Return value: A new object reference, undef if loading user failed.

This will be the constructor (using the traditional name). It creates an instance of the class, and if a user's name is given as a parameter, it preloads that user's information.

SetUser

Input parameter: named parameters in the form of key/value pairs.

Return value: object reference or an error message.

If the object isn't initialized with a user with the optional parameters to new, this method allows the client to specify the user record to load in. This allows for the client and server to negotiate more complex authentication methods. Currently supported keys are user, and either password or cookie.

Wishlist

Input parameter: none.

Return value: array (reference) of structure (reference) elements.

This retrieves the current wish-list contents as an array. Rather than just returning the ISBN-derived keys the system uses to reference books by because almost any application would need more information on the books immediately, the method returns structures that contain the ISBN, the title, and a URL link for the book. The ISBN can fetch a fuller set of information on a given book.

AddBook

Input parameter: isbn, a string.

Return value: object reference upon success, error message on failure.

This adds the book given by the ISBN-based key to the wish list. It checks that the key refers to a book in the catalog and returns a SOAP fault if it isn't.

RemoveBook

Input parameter: isbn, a string.

Return value: object reference upon success, error message on failure.

Removes the specified book from the wish list. It is silent in those cases where the passed-in ISBN isn't on the user's wish list.

CanPurchase

Input parameter: none.

Return value: boolean.

This returns a true/false value that indicates whether the user has enough information on file to be allowed to directly purchase books from their wish list. To Perl, boolean isn't as significant as it is in languages such as Java. It is areas like this that SOAP is at its best in interoperability.

PurchaseBooks

Input parameter: array (reference) of keys, or just isbn as a string.

Return value: object reference upon success, error message on failure.

As a convenience to the user (and a boon to the accounting department), this method makes it possible to buy books directly. It takes one ISBN key or an array of them, and takes care of whatever business-enterprise steps are necessary to start the process of billing the customer and shipping him the new books. The titles are removed from the wish list if the operation is a success. If it isn't, they are left in place, and a SOAP fault is returned.

Example 7-2 shows the `PurchaseBooks` method.

Example 7-2. The WishListCustomer::PurchaseBooks method

```
sub PurchaseBooks {
    my ($self, $list) = @_;

    return 'Object is missing user data'
        unless (ref($self) and my $user = $self->{_user});
    return 'User cannot make direct purchases'
        unless ($user->can_purchase);

    # Handle a single ISBN as just a one-item list
    my @books = ref($list) ? @$list : ($list);

    # Here would normally be lots of convoluted glue code to
    # interacts with enterprise systems, CRM, etc. For this
    # example, just remove the books from the wishlist and
    # update the user.
    $user->drop_book($_) for (@books);
    $user->write_user;

    $self;
}
```

This illustrates a few noteworthy elements about how the mid-level container class is handling the encapsulated data. For one thing, the method checks that it wasn't called as a static method (the `ref($self)` test on line 5). Also, note that most of the methods on the $user object are similar to ones in this class, but the local class versions aren't being used. Because each local method starts with the validity test, this means a lot of redundant testing. In the case of the `for` loop that calls the `drop_book` method, this can be quite a lot of redundancy. The disadvantage to this, however, is that it hinders future efforts to subclass this class.

This leaves only one area to be addressed: how to manage a cookie-based authentication. For the sake of simplicity, the `WishListCustomer` class uses the same MD5-based algorithm the use Perl; journal system uses, described in the previous chapter. This class copies the `make_cookie` routine from that example, and the `SetUser` method of this class is responsible for handling and testing the cookies it receives using this code. Later, when some sample clients are illustrated, some may use `WishListCustomer::make_cookie` to create authentication credentials. Simple as it may seem, this defines the interface as far as the SOAP server is concerned.

Choosing the HTTP Vehicle

Another factor to consider in designing a server like this is how exactly to bind it to a HTTP transport. The SOAP::Lite package offers a variety of ways to do this, so how does a project select the best-suited solution for the application?

Like most questions of that nature, there isn't a specific answer that fits all situations. It is because of the variety of environments and situations that such a range of choices exists. In the case of this project, part of the decision-making process is already provided in that the finished service needs to integrate with an existing system, the book database. It is often the case that web services are required to accommodate elements that are already deployed. These preexisting components naturally affect the design of the web service.

A good rule of thumb when designing these services with Perl in mind is to favor the combination of Apache and mod_perl. With these, you use the SOAP::Transport::HTTP::Apache class, either directly within a handler package for mod_perl, or through use of the Apache::SOAP wrapper that is a part of the distribution. Given the widespread acceptance of these technologies, it is a good chance that Apache, at least, is already in use. If Apache is being used, but mod_perl isn't available (and installation isn't an option), the SOAP::Transport::HTTP::CGI class is your next best option, unless the server is configured with the FastCGI protocol, in which case SOAP::Transport::HTTP::FCGI is available.

If there isn't a web server already in use on the target platform, and the web service isn't expected to endure high levels of load, then it may be enough to just use the SOAP::Transport::HTTP::Daemon class and deploy a small standalone server application that only handles the SOAP transactions and nothing more. Even in some cases where there is another web server already in use, this may prove a reasonable choice, because it frees the SOAP server from any maintenance-related issues with regards to the regular HTTP server, and vice versa.

Each of the choices has benefits and drawbacks. The Apache solution is likely to be the fastest of the bunch, but it requires mod_perl to be the most effective. As popular as that environment is, if it isn't available, the application has to evaluate other choices. Additionally, using it in that environment can expose the code to other parts of the server (through virtual hosts) that aren't meant to have access to it. The CGI approach doesn't have the performance of Apache, but it can be used under Apache::Registry as an alternative to the other model. Plus, it can be used under web servers other than Apache. The server based on the SOAP::Transport::HTTP::Daemon class would likely be the least-efficient in terms of performance and request throughput, but it has the advantage of being fully self-contained.

For this example, the initial implementation uses the standalone HTTP class. A later section adapts it with a location handler for use under Apache mod_perl.

Tying the Interface Code to SOAP

With the basic interface code designed and laid out, and the HTTP transport method chosen, it's now time to start merging the two into a functioning SOAP server. The key things to watch are how the class methods are exposed as services and how the server manages user authentication.

Starting Out

The SOAP transport class based on the `HTTP::Daemon` class of LWP is very easy to use. It looks a lot like the server snippet at the top of the chapter, in fact. What's more, you can even launch this server as a Perl one-liner!

Setting aside the one-liner approach for the moment, Example 7-3 shows the initial server in its entirety.

Example 7-3. The HTTP::Daemon-based server

```perl
#!/usr/bin/perl

use strict;

use SOAP::Transport::HTTP;
use WishListCustomer;

my $port = pop(@ARGV) || 9000;
my $host = shift(@ARGV) || 'localhost';

SOAP::Transport::HTTP::Daemon
    ->new(LocalAddr => $host, LocalPort => $port)
    ->dispatch_with({ 'urn:/WishListCustomer' =>
                      'WishListCustomer' })
    ->objects_by_reference('WishListCustomer')
    ->handle;

exit;
```

Here it is, for the sake of fun, as a one-liner:

```
perl -MSOAP::Lite -MWishListClient -e '$port = pop(@ARGV) \
    || 9000;$host = shift(@ARGV) || "localhost"; \
    SOAP::Transport::HTTP::Daemon \
      ->new(LocalAddr => $host, LocalPort => $port) \
      ->dispatch_with({ "urn:/WishListCustomer" => \
                        "WishListCustomer" }) \
      ->objects_by_reference("WishListCustomer")->handle'
```

Well, it's a one-liner except for the line breaks added to keep it readable, but this code can (and has) run as a fully functioning SOAP server.

There *is* a problem, however, with the server as it is shown. There is no access to the actual HTTP request, and thus the ability of the client to authenticate isn't there, even though the authentication code is in the underlying class. The encapsulated class (WishListCustomer) can get access to the full SOAP envelope by including the class, SOAP::Server::Parameters, in the inheritance tree. Unfortunately, that won't help in this case because the data the class needs is in the HTTP headers, not the SOAP Header block. Instead, it will be necessary to subclass both the transport and data classes. But why *both* classes?

Subclassing the Components

The reason for subclassing both classes here is simple: the subclass of SOAP::Transport::HTTP::Daemon is going to provide the request information by overloading the request method. The overloaded version of request pulls the desired information and sticks it into a global variable. Rather than reengineering the main WishListCustomer class just to fit into a SOAP server, a subclass of it intercepts the calls that are sensitive to the authentication headers and inserts the information into the list of arguments. Handling user-authentication is a tricky enough prospect by itself. It is better to not complicate the basic classes.

There are also other approaches: methods within SOAP::Server can be overloaded to insert the authentication information directly into the SOAP message's headers. If SOAP header-based authentication is already part of the server design, this might be a better solution. The Apache-related transport class has the advantage of being able to access the request object more readily from within the code. It also can take advantage of the phases of the request lifecycle under Apache that are specific to authentication.

For now, the global variable-based approach is used. Another benefit of subclassing the WishListCustomer class is that the new version can also manage the error messages directly, turning them into SOAP::Fault objects and freeing the client from the responsibility of checking the type of return value as a way of looking for success.

WishListCustomer::Daemon

The subclass for the daemon is very simple and short. Example 7-4 shows the new class in its entirety. Note that each call to this version of request clears the "global cookie jar," and that the loop over the data from the cookie headers still checks the return value from the regular expression match, rather than assuming the user-agent will never send invalid cookie data.

Example 7-4. The WishListCustomer::Daemon class

```
package WishListCustomer::Daemon;

use strict;
use vars qw(@ISA);
```

Example 7-4. The WishListCustomer::Daemon class (continued)

```
use SOAP::Transport::HTTP;
@ISA = qw(SOAP::Transport::HTTP::Daemon);

1;

sub request {
    my $self = shift;

    if (my $request = $_[0]) {
        my @cookies = $request->headers->header('cookie');
        %WishListCustomer::SOAP::COOKIES = ();
        for my $line (@cookies) {
            for (split(/; /, $line)) {
                next unless /(.*?)=(.*)/;
                $WishListCustomer::SOAP::COOKIES{$1} = $2;
            }
        }
    }

    $self->SUPER::request(@_);
}
```

Because the SOAP::Transport::HTTP classes handle everything else in a way that meets the project needs, there is nothing more for this class to do.

WishListCustomer::SOAP

In contrast, this class has more responsibility. Besides managing any authentication data sent in the request headers, there is also the basic matter of presenting the underlying functionality of WishListCustomer in a way that is more useful to a SOAP context. This should be done with as little impact on the original class as possible. Having no impact at all on the parent class is the ideal goal.

One of the things that makes this tricky is that clients using this interface with cookie-based authentication don't expect to have to call methods such as new explicitly. These clients expect to call methods such as Wishlist and AddBook immediately, without knowing what extra steps are involved.

To do this, the subclass borrows a trick from SOAP::Lite itself. The methods that aren't constructor-oriented (all but new and SetUser) get their $self value in an unusual way:

```
my $self = shift->new;
```

In turn, the version of new for this class has as the first two lines:

```
my $class = shift;
return $class if ref($class);
```

This extra bit of indirection means that the routines that require a validated user structure can still get it, if the needed information is carried in the cookie headers.

Several of the data-oriented methods need this, so they are built up using another trick from the SOAP::Lite source:

```
BEGIN {
    no strict 'refs';

    for my $method qw(GetBook BooksByAuthor BooksByTitle
                      Wishlist AddBook RemoveBook
                      PurchaseBooks) {
        *$method = sub {
            my $self = shift->new;
            die SOAP::Fault
                    ->faultcode('Server.RequestError')
                    ->faultstring('Could not get object')
                unless $self;

            my $smethod = "SUPER::$method";
            my $res = $self->$smethod(@_);
            die SOAP::Fault
                    ->faultcode('Server.ExecError')
                    ->faultstring("Execution error: $res")
                unless ref($res);

            $res;        };
    }
}
```

The three methods that can be static get this treatment as well; if the client calls them without establishing authentication, they still behave as documented. This also handles the issue of turning error reports (signaled by nonreference return values) into SOAP::Fault objects.

The CanPurchase method also needs to be defined in a similar way as the previous block, but it has an added responsibility. Perl's relaxed approach to scalar values in boolean evaluation means that there are no definitive, distinct true or false values. Perl routines simply use 1 and 0, or even undef versus anything. But for a SOAP environment, the values that CanPurchase returns must be typed as boolean; the SOAP serializer interprets the return value of WishListCustomer::CanPurchase as an integer and encodes it as such.

The overloaded version of the method handles sending a proper boolean response by explicitly typing the return value of the superclass call:

```
SOAP::Data->name('return', $self->SUPER::CanPurchase)
        ->type('xsd:boolean');
```

All that remains are the new and SetUser methods, which are shown in Example 7-5. The full version of WishListCustomer::SOAP is listed in Appendix D with the rest of the source files.

Example 7-5. The new and SetUser methods

```perl
sub new {
    my $class = shift;
    return $class if ref($class);

    my $self;
    # If there are no arguments, but available cookies, then
    # that is the signal to work the cookies into play
    if ((! @_) and (keys %COOKIES)) {
        # Start by getting the basic, bare object
        $self = $class->SUPER::new();
        # Then call SetUser. It will die with a SOAP::Fault
        # on any error
        $self->SetUser;
    } else {
        $self = $class->SUPER::new(@_);
    }

    $self;
}

sub SetUser {
    my $self = shift->new;
    my %args = @_;

    return $self->SUPER::SetUser(%args) if (%args);

    my $user;
    my $cookie = $COOKIES{user};
    return $self unless $cookie;
    ($user = $cookie) =~ s/%([0-9a-f]{2})/chr(hex($1))/ge;
    $user =~ s/%([0-9a-f]{2})/chr(hex($1))/ge;
    $user =~ s/:://.*//;

    my $res = $self->SUPER::SetUser(user   => $user,
                                    cookie => $cookie);
    die SOAP::Fault
            ->faultcode('Server.AuthError')
            ->faultstring("Authorization failed: $res")
        unless ref($res);

    $self;}
```

Note that the routines here use die to signal an error. Just returning a SOAP::Fault object isn't enough; the serializer will catch it before the server has the chance to create a proper SOAP fault response.

Revising the Daemon-Based Server

With the two new classes, it is time to revisit the server code, to see what will be needed to integrate these interfaces into the original framework. The new version of the server is shown in Example 7-6.

Example 7-6. The next-generation HTTP::Daemon-based server

```perl
#!/usr/bin/perl

use strict;

use WishListCustomer::SOAP;
use WishListCustomer::Daemon;

my $port = pop(@ARGV) || 9000;
my $host = shift(@ARGV) || 'localhost';

WishListCustomer::Daemon
    ->new(LocalAddr => $host, LocalPort => $port)
    ->dispatch_with({ 'urn:/WishListCustomer' =>
                        'WishListCustomer::SOAP' })
    ->objects_by_reference('WishListCustomer::SOAP')
    ->handle;

exit;
```

That is all there is to integrating the new code. Does that seem too easy to be true? Perl's object-oriented programming model may often be criticized by object-purists, but this is an excellent case where it helps the programmer tremendously.

Simple Access with a SOAP::Lite Client

Before moving to a further revision of the server using Apache, check out the sample client in Example 7-7. In this client, the code loads in some extra libraries to manually create a cookie with the username and password because in a more traditional environment the user would have already been in contact with the server and thus have the appropriate cookies in the browser's cookie file. Because the server is returning objects by reference, the client could use the object handle for subsequent calls. The later example with Apache shows why the client is using cookies here instead.

Example 7-7 shows the retrieval of a user's wish list, with the fuller description of books, formatted in a simple, clean display.

Example 7-7. A simple client for formatting the lists of books

```perl
#!/usr/bin/perl

use strict;

use URI;
use HTTP::Cookies;
use SOAP::Lite;
use WishListCustomer; # for make_cookie
```

Example 7-7. A simple client for formatting the lists of books (continued)

```
my ($user, $passwd) = (shift, shift);
die "USAGE: $0 username passwd [ endpoint ]\n"
    unless ($user and $passwd);

my $endpoint = shift || 'http://localhost.localdomain:9000';
my $uri = URI->new($endpoint);
my $cookie = WishListCustomer::make_cookie($user, $passwd);
my $cookie_jar = HTTP::Cookies->new();
$cookie_jar->set_cookie(0, user => $cookie, '/', $uri->host,
                        $uri->port);

my $soap = SOAP::Lite->uri('urn:/WishListCustomer')
              ->proxy($endpoint,
                      cookie_jar => $cookie_jar);

my $result = $soap->Wishlist;
if ($result->fault) {
    die "$0: Operation failed: " . $result->faultstring;
}
my $books = $result->result;

format =
@<<<<<<<<<<<<<<<<<<<<<<<<<<<<<<<<<<<<            @>>>>>
$result->{title},                              $result->{us_price}
@<<<<<<<<<<<<<<<<<<<<<<<<<<<<<<<<<<< @>>>>>>>>>>>>>>>
$result->{authors},                  $result->{isbn}

.

for (sort { $a->{title} cmp $b->{title} } @$books) {
    $result = $soap->GetBook($_->{isbn});
    # Quietly skip books that cause faults
    next if ($result->fault);
    $result = $result->result;
    write;
}
exit;
```

This example is shown in its entirety to illustrate the flexibility of the system. The same client will be used later with an Apache-based server, without any changes being made.

Improving the Code and the Service

At this stage, the code reflects a functional web service with a clearly defined interface. Now that the basic elements are written and proven, it is time to improve the server-level performance, and examine the interface and code more closely to find areas that can be improved.

Moving the Server to Apache

Example 7-7 is quite functional for a lighter-access server, but if the target deployment environment already has Apache and mod_perl available, why not use them?

There are two easily available ways to interface to Apache with the components of the SOAP::Lite toolkit. One of these uses the Apache::SOAP wrapper module included in the SOAP::Lite distribution. The other uses the Apache form of the HTTP code, SOAP::Transport::HTTP::Apache, directly within a <Perl> configuration block. This second approach is used in Example 7-8. The Apache transport is subclassed as Apache::SOAP does, with a handler method that extracts the cookie information in much the same way as the request method of WishListCustomer::Daemon.

The code in Example 7-8 bears a striking resemblance to the subclass of HTTP::Daemon shown earlier in Example 7-4. The basic task and approach are the same; what differs is when the process has the opportunity to get the request object and retrieve the cookies from it. With Apache and mod_perl, the handler method is passed an Apache-style request object, which can fetch these headers much more quickly, so the task is taken care of at this stage rather than at a later one.

Example 7-8. The WishListCustomer::Apache class

```
package WishListCustomer::Apache;

use strict;
use vars qw(@ISA);

use SOAP::Transport::HTTP;
use WishListCustomer::SOAP;
@ISA = qw(SOAP::Transport::HTTP::Apache);

1;

sub handler ($$) {
    my ($self, $request) = @_;

    my $cookies = $request->header_in('cookie');
    my @cookies = ref $cookies ? @$cookies : $cookies;
    %WishListCustomer::SOAP::COOKIES = ();
    for my $line (@cookies) {
        for (split(/; /, $line)) {
            next unless /(.*?)=(.*)/;
            $WishListCustomer::SOAP::COOKIES{$1} = $2;
        }
    }

    $self->SUPER::handler($request);
}
```

Interestingly enough, the class has no need to include any of the Apache:: classes, let alone inherit from them. Were it not for the difference in interfaces between the

Apache and daemon-based `SOAP::Transport::HTTP` classes, the same code might have been used for both.

Example 7-9 shows how Example 7-8 might be used within a `<Perl>` block of the Apache configuration file.

Example 7-9. Using the WishListCustomer::Apache handler

```
<Perl>
    use lib '/var/www/WishListCustomer';
    use WishListCustomer::Apache;

    $main::wishlist =
        WishListCustomer::Apache
            ->new
            ->dispatch_with({ 'urn:/WishListCustomer' =>
                              'WishListCustomer::SOAP' });

    $Location{'/SOAP'} = {
        PerlHandler => '$main::wishlist',
        SetHandler  => 'perl-script'
    };
</Perl>
```

Some of what is done in that example would be better done in a dedicated initialization file that manages the loading and configuration of Perl modules in a `mod_perl` environment. But what is shown in the example does work, just as well as the `HTTP::Daemon` approach (and much more quickly).[*]

Note that this version of the server doesn't use `objects_by_reference` in the configuration of the SOAP server. Managing objects by reference is much more efficient in both operational speed (as fewer objects are created and destroyed) and in the quantity of data being sent along the wire. Object references are much more compact when serialized, in most cases. It is also very useful when the nature of the object doesn't lend itself very well to full serialization. If this server had to send the object itself, instead of the method results, the serialization would probably not preserve all the underlying attributes of the user and catalog abstraction layers. And in fact, should the client see them at all? With objects that are passed back and forth by reference, the client remains shielded from these implementation details.

While the technique works for single-process approaches, such as that used with the `HTTP::Daemon` approach, it runs into a very basic problem with Apache: multiple processes. Under Apache, there is no guarantee that the server process that handled the object construction request will handle a method call request. So, if a client passes an

---

[*] For more about optimizing and managing a `mod_perl` installation, see *Writing Apache Modules with Perl and C*, by Lincoln Stein and Doug MacEachern (O'Reilly).

object handle as part of a method call, it will almost certainly be invalid to the server process that handles that call.

The server-side code addresses this by allowing all the methods to initialize an object when they go to set their localized $self variable. Because the authentication cookie will be sent with all requests, each transaction simply creates a new instance as it's needed. As a result, all operations that modify the data of an object are obligated to write such changes immediately, such as with the AddBook or PurchaseBooks method. To overcome this limitation would require adding a layer to the serialization and deserialization steps in the SOAP server that maintained object data in a shared-memory segment, or some other form of interprocess communication (IPC).

By designing the test client to use cookies from the outset, it's easier to test the Apache SOAP server with the same set of inputs that were fed to the initial server.

Revisiting the Interface

The SOAP layer as it is currently designed exactly mirrors the original class interface. Some of the operations defined by the interface seem to be redundant, however, and a SOAP interface has the option of addressing this without requiring an update of the underlying code. The SOAP interface can simply present a different API to the client.

As an example of this, the BooksByAuthor and BooksByTitle methods will be rolled into a single interface point, called FindBooks. Doing this also provides an opportunity to demonstrate accessing the SOAP envelope from within server-side code.

Designing WishListCustomer::SOAP2

The second-generation interface code replaces the two search methods with the single one suggested earlier. The WishListCustomer class will not change, but the client isn't concerned with that class. Their concern is with the interface that the SOAP server offers. The details aren't important to them.

There are two ways that the FindBooks method could discern the type of search to perform. The first would be to have a string-typed parameter passed in with the search term, and use the value of that parameter to decide whether to search by author or title. That would be the equivalent of the familiar Perl-style interface:

    $books = $obj->FindBooks(author => 'Christiansen');

However, there's no need for the extra parameter; it only adds to the overall size of the message being sent over the wire. Since SOAP provides for named parameters, why not let the name be the selector? If the input parameter is called "author," the search is by author. Similarly, the search is by title if the parameter is named "title."

This turns the nearly identical blocks that make up `BooksByAuthor` and `BooksByTitle` into the single routine (with pseudocode):

```
sub FindBooks {
    my ($class, $arg) = @_;

    my $hook = (NAME_OF_ARG($arg) eq 'author') ?
                    \&SoapExBook::get_books_by_author :
                    \&SoapExBook::get_books_by_title;
    my $bookdb = ref($class) ? $class->{_catalog} :
                               SoapExBook::connect();
    return undef unless $bookdb;

    my @books = $hook->($bookdb, $author);
    \@books;
}
```

This routine cheats slightly by not checking for invalid names but rather defaulting to a title search. In doing so, clients can get away with badly named parameters; they just end up with a title search unless they are specific about searching by author. What remains is filling in the pseudocode that allows the routine to determine the name by which the parameter was sent.

Accessing the SOAP envelope

Code that runs on a SOAP server that ultimately derives from the `SOAP::Server` class (as all the `SOAP::Transport::*` server classes do) can arrange to have the `SOAP::SOM` object that represents the deserialized request object passed along with the parameter list. With access to this object, code can retrieve the full `SOAP::Data` object that represents a given input parameter. What gets passed in the parameter list itself is just the Perl representation of the data value, and in most cases that's all that's needed. When there is a need for more information, it's available.

If the method's class inherits from `SOAP::Server::Parameters`, `SOAP::Lite` appends the `SOAP::SOM` object to the list of parameters when the method is called. Using the class methods introduced in Chapter 6, the `paramsin` method appears to be the solution to the problem, as shown in the final version of `FindBooks` in Example 7-10.

Example 7-10. Using the SOAP envelope to complete FindBooks

```
sub FindBooks {
    my ($class, $arg, $env) = @_;

    my $argname = $env->match(SOAP::SOM::paramsin)->dataof;
    my $hook = ($argname->name eq 'author') ?
                    \&SoapExBook::get_books_by_author :
                    \&SoapExBook::get_books_by_title;
    my $bookdb = ref($class) ? $class->{_catalog} :
                               SoapExBook::connect();
```

Example 7-10. Using the SOAP envelope to complete FindBooks (continued)

```
    return undef unless $bookdb;

    my @books = $hook->($bookdb, $author);
    \@books;
}
```

Initially, $argname is set to the SOAP::Data object that represents the first input parameter. The match method on the SOAP::SOM object locates this; the dataof method then retrieves that part of the structure as the SOAP::Data object. In the next line, the name method is called on the data object to get the name by which the parameter was sent.

In this simple example, it would be enough to get a reference to a hash table of the parameters by calling $env->method, which returns the contents of the "method" portion of the envelope. With only one parameter in the mix, the hash-table reference would have only one key. The method shown in Example 7-10 scales more easily for longer, more complicated argument lists.

Testing the new method

Finally, Example 7-11 shows a modified version of the earlier client that searches for books based on command-line usage.

Example 7-11. Simple client to search for books using FindBooks

```
#!/usr/bin/perl

use strict;

use SOAP::Lite;

my ($type, $string) = (shift, shift);
die "USAGE: $0 { author | title } pattern [ endpoint ]\n"
    unless ($type and $string);
my $endpoint = shift || 'http://localhost.localdomain:9000';

my $soap = SOAP::Lite->uri('urn:/WishListCustomer')
            ->proxy($endpoint);

my $result = $soap->FindBooks(SOAP::Data->name($type,
                                               $string));
if ($result->fault) {
    die "$0: Operation failed: " . $result->faultstring;
}
my $books = $result->result;

format =
@<<<<<<<<<<<<<<<<<<<<<<<<<<<<<<<<<<<<<<<< @>>>>>>>>>>>>>>>>
```

Example 7-11. Simple client to search for books using FindBooks (continued)

```
    $result->{title},                  $result->{isbn}
.

for (@$books) {
    $result = $soap->GetBook($_);
    # Quietly skip books that cause faults
    next if ($result->fault);
    $result = $result->result;
    write;
}

exit;
```

Using the `SOAP::Data` class and methods to construct the argument to the method being called, you get complete control over aspects such as `name` that let use the full features of the `FindBooks` method. Simple indeed, and scalable. Should the `FindBooks` method add other types of search keys in the future, this client can easily use them as well.

Ideas for Further Exploration

Using the code and the examples shown thus far, it should be fairly simple to further enhance or streamline the SOAP interface. Some areas that can be addressed include combining the `AddBook` and `RemoveBook` methods in a manner similar to what we saw in the last section. Alternately, a client that turns a wish list into an RSS feed can be easily developed, using Example 6-5 as a guide to the RSS module. Experimentation with different approaches to configuring the service under Apache would prove valuable should a future project appear in which the pros and cons of using objects by reference versus the performance of Apache is an issue.

Here are some ideas to consider that aren't directly related to the SOAP services themselves:

- Add a logging layer to the dispatching of requests that tracks what methods are called, with the goal of analyzing usage trends to possibly optimize client throughput.
- Explore the use of other phases of the `mod_perl` interface, such as `PerlChildInitHandler`, to optimize the configuration of SOAP servers across the death and creation of child processes.
- Consider ways to design server methods so that they can double as XML-RPC services, as well as SOAP interfaces.
- As written, the `WishListCustomer::Daemon` class and the `WishListCustomer::SOAP` class are tightly coupled due to the use of the hash table for passing the cookie

information between them. Consider better ways in which to manage the sharing of such information that are of comparable ease, but which would be more scalable to using newer interfaces such as `WishListCustomer::SOAP2`.

This all comes back to the principles that have been stressed from the outset: good design practice early on can make all the difference. Choosing to subclass the main wish-list functionality rather than modifying the original class can explore any of the previous ideas without impacting any other users of the interface. The subclass of the server class can be extended to build on other features of the request lifecycle, as needed. As Chapter 8 will show, it can also allow easy substitution of other transport protocols.

CHAPTER 8
SOAP Services Without HTTP

In previous chapters the examples of SOAP client and server applications used HTTP for transport, either explicitly, as in the case of the servers, or implicitly through the SOAP::Transport abstraction layer, in the case of the clients.

This chapter focuses on using other protocols to provide and access SOAP services. The themes and code from the previous chapter (the book buyer's wish list) still form the basis for the coding examples. In some cases, the examples will augment the HTTP services; in others, they will replace them.

As web services branch out into areas like wireless applications, other protocols are getting attention. Raw TCP/IP may be used if a platform doesn't want to implement full HTTP support. POP3 and other protocols make email more accessible from almost anywhere. Whether to use an alternate protocol is as much a design decision as choosing SOAP itself. The examples in this chapter show how the classes may be used.

Choosing a Protocol

Deciding which protocol to use is generally easy; HTTP is a de facto standard in most web-enabled environments. However, there are protocols, some older than HTTP and some newer, that can be very effective at managing SOAP traffic. Some of the protocols discussed in this chapter are a natural fit. Jabber, for example, is already based upon XML. Having a server that reads requests from an email account using POP3 lets any application that can send mail become a client.

It may also help to look at the protocols in this chapter not as replacements for HTTP but as additions to a set of solutions that include HTTP. With the spread of new devices and platforms, flexibility is more a requirement and less a luxury than it used to be.

The important factors in evaluating the alternatives presented in this chapter are how the tools can work to solve the problems you face. A server that tends to receive requests that don't require immediate response (such as a web service for managing mailing lists) can use POP3 to monitor email requests (such as subscribe and unsubscribe). The Jabber instant messaging protocol is growing in acceptance, and the design allows you to design applications other than just chat clients. There are cases in which TCP/IP is a better choice than HTTP. The goal isn't to justify each of the different protocols but rather to show how to use them if the application design calls for it.

Authentication

The non-HTTP classes share a trait that complicates the authentication layer of the WishListCustomer application. Each server class hands its requests to the SOAP::Server class directly, without processing headers like the HTTP classes do. Some classes represent cases where there is no native concept of headers (such as the TCP class); others, like the POP3 class, do have a concept of headers. However, none of these classes create HTTP::Request objects, so direct access to headers isn't inherently possible. As such, cookies can't be relied on to provide the authentication.

Server Authentication

Without cookies, the server classes must rely on the presence of authentication data in the header of the SOAP envelope. There are two ways to do this:

- Create a new version of the WishListCustomer::SOAP layer that inherits from SOAP::Server::Parameters in order to have access to the request envelope. Using the envelope, read the headers for the desired information.
- Subclass the right components on the server-class side so that at some point in the lifecycle of processing the request, the headers may be retrieved and the relevant authentication data converted to the hash table format the WishListCustomer::SOAP layer already uses.

Taking the second approach means leaving the SOAP layer untouched, which is the preferred option. This lowers the chance of a change affecting the HTTP applications and also permits their clients to continue to function without any changes.

Designing the new scheme

Because the WishListCustomer class and its SOAP layer are fairly specific about the form and function of the cookie-authentication scheme, the header implementation of the scheme is obliged to conform to this.

To do this, the scheme defines a single header element called authenticate. This element may include an attribute called name (default value: user) whose value is the name of the cookie that the HTTP code expects. The value of the element acts as the value of the cookie and should be in the format of an HTTP cookie, with all character-encoding intact.

The header doesn't set the `mustUnderstand` attribute, because servers, such as the HTTP servers, that happen to get such a header shouldn't be prevented from functioning. Instead, let the class methods create their own faults for the absence of authentication data.

A typical header looks something like this (with some formatting of the XML done for readability):

```
<wlc:authenticate xmlns:wlc="urn:/WishListCustomer"
                  name="user">
%2572%256a%2572%2561%2579%253a%253a%2532%2532%2537%2536%2534
%2564%2561%2535%2535%2535%2533%2563%2532%2530%2563%2563%2538
%2530%2563%2563%2535%2537%2539%2564%2562%2535%2562%2564%2532
%2532%2535%2537
</wlc:authenticate>
```

The server class is responsible for ensuring that any extra whitespace or newlines are removed.

Creating a generic server class

To create the server class once and once only, we will describe a *generic* server class that can be used for any transport protocol described in this chapter. The reason for this is simple: all the non-HTTP protocols need the functionality, and all use identical interfaces for server configuration. Their differences are all at the request-handling level, something that's addressed in the application anyway.

The new server class has to inherit from the basic type the server application is being built on. However, the method that is going to be overloaded to accomplish the task comes from SOAP::Server, and as such is the same for all the non-HTTP classes.

There is no reason to define a completely new class for each server protocol that follows. Instead, the class uses the special `import` method to allow the super-class to be specified at will. The new class has to provide a definition of `import` to manage the class hierarchy, and a definition of `find_target` that looks at and acts upon any relevant header blocks. Example 8-1 shows the class.

Example 8-1. The WishListCustomer::Transport class

```
package WishListCustomer::Transport;

use strict;
use vars qw(@ISA);
use subs qw(import find_target);

use SOAP::Lite;
```

Example 8-1. The WishListCustomer::Transport class (continued)

```perl
# For lack of a better default:
@ISA = qw(SOAP::Server);

1;

sub import {
    my $class = shift;
    my $new_parent = shift;

    @ISA = ($new_parent);
}

# This remains coupled to WishListCustomer::SOAP by virtue
# of the use of the %WishListCustomer::SOAP hash table.
sub find_target {
    my $self = shift;
    my $request = shift;

    %WishListCustomer::SOAP::COOKIES = ();
    my $header = $request->match(SOAP::SOM::header .
                                 '/authenticate')->dataof;
    if ($header) {
        my $key = $header->attr->{name} || 'user';
        my $value = $header->value;

        $value =~ s/\n\r\s//g;
        $WishListCustomer::SOAP::COOKIES{$key} = $value;
    }
    $self->SUPER::find_target($request);
}
```

Applications using the generic class are still responsible for loading the specific server-class code. This is easier and safer than expecting the generic class to derive from its input the proper name for a require statement. Even though the server classes in the SOAP::Lite distribution can be transformed by dropping the last element from the class name (for example, SOAP::Transport::TCP::Server yields SOAP::Transport::TCP), that convention can't be relied on.

Client Authentication

The client classes have their role to play in accommodating the envelope-based authentication as well. Unlike server applications, however, clients don't explicitly load the transport-level code, so there is no real need for a subclass that compares to WishListCustomer::Transport. What the clients do need is a convenient way to create and send headers for the credentials that requests need. Fortunately, the SOAP::Lite package provides easy support for creating header elements and passing them around.

Custom headers with SOAP::Header

The SOAP::Lite package provides a class called SOAP::Header that is an empty subclass of SOAP::Data. Recall that the SOAP::Data class encapsulates simple Perl data and adds SOAP elements such as name, type, and namespace. The purpose of SOAP::Header is to allow the serialization layer to distinguish header elements from straightforward data. By instantiating objects using this class, the serialization takes care of the rest.

Based on the design of the authentication headers presented earlier, the header has the name authenticate and has the fully encoded cookie as the content of the tag. There is no need to set the name attribute, because the default value of user is correct for any of the applications. Because the value for mustUnderstand also matches the default, it isn't specified, either.

The example clients in the following sections directly use the make_cookie method from the WishListCustomer class to create the authentication token. The basic code to create a header object is:

```
$cookie = WishListCustomer::make_cookie($user, $password);
$header = SOAP::Header->name(authenticate => $cookie)
                      ->uri('urn:/WiahListCustomer');
```

With these lines of code, the variable $header can be used as often as needed to provide the authentication in SOAP messages. Because the http clients use cookies (which are sent with every request), this allows for a similar design approach by allowing a header that is computed once and then reused between requests.

WishListCustomer::Client as a shortcut

The client applications don't need to use a generic class to simplify choosing the transport protocol. However, something that *is* very useful is a mechanism that automatically manages the authentication layer itself.

The key to the server-oriented class is finding the best point to insert a localized method that has access to the request object after serialization, but before dispatch. For the client, the trick is to find a point at which the call has been broken down into method name and arguments, but has not yet been serialized. Because the SOAP::Lite package does some creative work with AUTOLOAD to allow dispatch of remote methods to appear like local class methods, the subclass should continue to allow that to take place. In the case of SOAP::Lite, the place to insert the subclass is the call method.

The call method in SOAP::Lite starts the conversion of a method name and a list of data arguments into a remote invocation and response. It is called with the method name (a string or a SOAP::Data object) followed by zero or more parameters. All the subclass has to do is privately maintain a header object with the authentication data and then insert it into every invocation of call.

The management of the credentials is a simple method call that takes the username and password as arguments, with optional additional attribute support thrown in just to be safe. The full `WishListCustomer::Client` class is provided in Appendix D, but the overloaded `call` method is shown in Example 8-2.

Example 8-2. The WishListCustomer::Client::call method
```
sub call {
    my ($self, $method, @args) = @_;

    unshift(@args, $self->{__auth_header})
        if $self->{__auth_header};
    $self->SUPER::call($method, @args);
}
```

When no credentials have been set, nothing is added to the outgoing call.

Transports with Server and Client

Not all the transport layers examined in this chapter provide both a server and client class for application use. This section focuses on the transports that do provide both.

Using SOAP::Transport::TCP

Even with the proliferation of lightweight HTTP implementations, there are cases in which an application may need to allow for simple, direct TCP/IP communication instead of (or in addition to) HTTP. Such cases might include embedded devices with simple TCP/IP stacks, or cases in which the server just doesn't want to provide (or support) full HTTP support.

SOAP::Transport::TCP::Server

Using the `SOAP::Transport::TCP::Server` class is as easy as using the HTTP classes. The constructor method uses the `IO::Socket` class family to create and manage the sockets the object will ultimately use. Binding to a hostname and port is done in the same fashion as for the HTTP classes. Additionally, the `handle` method of the class acts as an accept loop, waiting infinitely for new connections, until interrupted.

Example 8-3 is the daemon application from the previous chapter except it includes this class in place of an HTTP variant.

Example 8-3. WishListCustomer::SOAP daemon using TCP
```
#!/usr/bin/perl

use strict;

use SOAP::Transport::TCP;
```

Example 8-3. WishListCustomer::SOAP daemon using TCP (continued)

```perl
use WishListCustomer::SOAP;
use WishListCustomer::Transport
        'SOAP::Transport::TCP::Server';

my $port = pop(@ARGV) || 9000;
my $host = shift(@ARGV) || 'localhost';

WishListCustomer::Transport
    ->new(LocalAddr => $host, LocalPort => $port,
          Listen => 5, Reuse => 1)
    ->dispatch_with({ 'urn:/WishListCustomer' =>
                      'WishListCustomer::SOAP' })
    ->objects_by_reference('WishListCustomer::SOAP')
    ->handle;

exit;
```

The flexibility of the SOAP::Lite transport layer means that a change of only a few lines switched that same basic application from one protocol to another.

SOAP::Transport::TCP::Client

Of course, the client that communicates with this server doesn't explicitly load the corresponding client class. That is handled by the SOAP::Lite module for the client.

The transport classes that provide clients also provide bindings for nonstandard protocol identifiers in the URI strings that the clients use. For the TCP transport, these strings are expected to start with the sequence, tcp://. When SOAP::Lite sees this in an endpoint, it knows to load the TCP-oriented module, just as http:// (and https://) load the HTTP code.

The client shown in Example 8-4 defaults the endpoint to a TCP binding but can just as easily use one of the other transports without changing any of the code itself.

Example 8-4. A generic, non-HTTP client application

```perl
#!/usr/bin/perl

use strict;

use WishListCustomer::Client;

my ($user, $passwd) = (shift, shift);
die "USAGE: $0 username passwd [ endpoint ]\n"
    unless ($user and $passwd);

my $endpoint = shift || 'tcp://localhost:9000';

my $soap = WishListCustomer::Client
              ->uri('urn:/WishListCustomer')
              ->proxy($endpoint);
```

Example 8-4. A generic, non-HTTP client application (continued)

```
# Set the authentication credentials
$soap->setAuth($user, $passwd);

my $result = $soap->Wishlist;
if ($result->fault) {
    die "$0: Operation failed: " . $result->faultstring;
}
my $books = $result->result;

format =
@<<<<<<<<<<<<<<<<<<<<<<<<<<<<<<<<<<<<<       @>>>>>
$result->{title},                            $result->{us_price}
@<<<<<<<<<<<<<<<<<<<<<<<<<<<<<<<<<< @>>>>>>>>>>>>>>>
$result->{authors},                 $result->{isbn}

.

for (sort { $a->{title} cmp $b->{title} } @$books) {
    $result = $soap->GetBook($_->{isbn});
    # Quietly skip books that cause faults
    next if ($result->fault);
    $result = $result->result;
    write;
}

exit;
```

The code is recognizable as the same client from the previous chapter. Gone is the code for the HTTP::Cookies class, and in its place is the SOAP::Lite subclass and a single call to a method called setAuth. The default value for $endpoint is the only indication of what protocol the client is presuming to eventually use.

Using SOAP::Transport::JABBER

The Jabber messaging protocol is a distributed messaging system that uses XML as the core means of data communication and exchange. As a topic, it is complex enough to require its own book.* Fortunately, using Jabber as a transport mechanism doesn't require an indepth understanding of the protocol itself. The SOAP::Transport::JABBER module handles the majority of the work. Jabber services can be designed to connect otherwise unrelated components (services that aren't always related to instant messaging).

Jabber can function as a bridge between disparate protocols, such as AOL Instant Messaging and Internet Relay Chat. Jabber offers store-and-forward, with servers that retain messages until an endpoint reconnects. SOAP services can be introduced

---

* See *Programming Jabber*, by D.J. Adams (O'Reilly).

into an environment like this quite easily, for tasks ranging from personal information management (calendar services, reminders) to information retrieval. As Jabber clients grow in number and proliferate, the application of SOAP as a basis for providing services as content is likely to grow as well.

To use Jabber with SOAP::Lite, you must have the CPAN module Net::Jabber installed. Because of the changes in Net::Jabber interface, the current version of SOAP::Lite (0.55) doesn't work with the latest version of Net::Jabber, so users may need to downgrade to Version 1.0021 of Net::Jabber. JABBER transport will be synchronized in a future version of SOAP::Lite. There is no need to be running a Jabber daemon on the same host providing the SOAP service via Jabber, but that host will have to be able to contact a Jabber server. Starting up a server process also requires that a Jabber profile be available for use.

Creating a Jabber-based server

The structure of the Jabber-based server isn't different from the TCP server shown earlier. The information that the server class needs to establish a connection with the Jabber server and create the proper interfaces is provided by instantiating the new object with a URI-like string that begins with the sequence, jabber://. Later, the client will use the same string to connect to the server. The server also differs in that the handle method isn't itself an endless loop like the TCP or HTTP classes provide. In Example 8-5, the daemon polls the Jabber server on a 10-second interval.

Example 8-5. The Jabber-based daemon

```
#!/usr/bin/perl

use strict;

use SOAP::Transport::JABBER;
use WishListCustomer::SOAP;
use WishListCustomer::Transport
        'SOAP::Transport::JABBER::Server';

my ($user, $passwd, $host, $port) = @ARGV;
$host = 'jabber.org' unless $host;
$port = 5222         unless $port;
my $jabber_url = "jabber://$user:$passwd\@$host:$port";

$server = WishListCustomer::Transport
    ->new($jabber_url)
    ->dispatch_with({ 'urn:/WishListCustomer' =>
                      'WishListCustomer::SOAP' })
    ->objects_by_reference('WishListCustomer::SOAP');

while (1) {
    $server->handle;
```

Example 8-5. The Jabber-based daemon (continued)

```
        sleep 10;
}

exit;
```

In the example, the command line is expected to provide the user ID, password, Jabber server, and port. Port 5222 is the current standard port for the Jabber service, and the host jabber.org is the most-used server, making it a logical default.

The Jabber-based client

Connecting to the Jabber-based SOAP server can be done with the same client used earlier for the TCP server, simply by providing a different endpoint:

```
% perl client-general rjray bad_password \
        jabber://rjray:xxx@jabber.org:5222
```

The SOAP::Transport::JABBER module hooks into the URI class, which is one of the supporting elements of LWP itself. The TCP module does this, as well. This not only provides the basis for treating jabber:// (and tcp://) with the same consideration as http:// or ftp://, it also lets the module use the methods of the URI class to extract data from the string, without having to explicitly provide the regular expressions to do so.

The architecture of the SOAP::Transport::JABBER is interesting in itself. Both client and server classes are built on the client class of the Net::Jabber package, Net::Jabber::Client. This is because even though the server class represents a SOAP server instance, it is still a client from the Jabber perspective. The client and server on the SOAP level are essentially using the Jabber server as an intermediary for their conversation. This fits with the Jabber concept of *agents*, the basic structures on which Jabber is designed. Agents handle the messages between different connections and interfaces, usually between chat clients and chat servers. But Jabber isn't limited to that, which is what SOAP takes advantage of.

Using SOAP::Transport::MQ

The MQSeries software is a commercial package from IBM that forms the communications basis for a range of applications. The software can be obtained for evaluation or purchase through IBM's web site, *http://www.ibm.com/software/ts/mqseries/*.

As with Jabber and TCP, the module registers a new type of URI scheme that can be recognized by a client request for an endpoint whose string starts with the sequence mq://. The form and content of the URI string has more in common with the Jabber form than the TCP or HTTP forms. The strings that specify the MQ connections must provide information on the queue manager, and the channels for sending and receiving messages (see Example 8-6).

Example 8-6. The MQ server daemon

```perl
#!/usr/bin/perl

use strict;

use SOAP::Transport::MQ;
use WishListCustomer::SOAP;
use WishListCustomer::Transport
        'SOAP::Transport::MQ::Server';

my ($chan, $mgr, $reqest, $reply, $host, $port) = @ARGV;
$host = 'localhost' unless $host;
$port = 9000        unless $port;
die "USAGE: $0 channel manager request_queue reply_queue " .
    '[ host port ]'
    unless ($chan and $mgr and $request and $reply);

my $mq_url = "mq://$host:$port?Channel=$chan;" .
    "QueueManager=$mgr;RequestQueue=$request;" .
    "ReplyQueue=$reply";

my $server = WishListCustomer::Transport
    ->new($mq_url)
    ->dispatch_with({ 'urn:/WishListCustomer' =>
                      'WishListCustomer::SOAP' })
    ->objects_by_reference('WishListCustomer::SOAP');

do { $server->handle } while sleep 1;

exit;
```

A client would be expected to use the same URI-style string when connecting to the server. The client from earlier in this chapter would be sufficient, if given the connection string on the command line.

Using POP3 and MAILTO

These are actually two different modules that aren't directly related or even intentionally designed to work together. However, they share a common underlying element: electronic mail. If a developer wanted to, she could develop a complete client/server model around Simple Mail Transport Protocol (SMTP), one in which communications are wrapped within ordinary email messages. A client connects to a server by sending an email to the proper address, and the client's own email address is used by the server to send back the response. Such a system can even be built using the server and client components from this section.

The examples presented in this section demonstrate one-way communications. The client class built upon the `SOAP::Transport::MAILTO` module sends requests without expecting a reply. Its concept of success is instead based on whether the message was accepted by the target SMTP server. Likewise, the server built upon SOAP::Transport::POP3 reads requests from a POP3 server and processes them, without attempting to send the results of the operations to any client.

At first glance, the usefulness of a model such as this may not be obvious. There are many types of applications, however, in which a client may not need a reply, or in which a server would not be expected to provide one. Some examples of these applications include inventory updates or position reporting from devices attached to global positioning system (GPS) gear. Operations that are generally one-sided in nature, such as periodic updates, can be written more efficiently if there is no need to wait for or receive a reply that is going to be discarded.

Some of this can be said to overlap with other, newer technologies like Jabber, which also provides a kind of "store and forward" management. Of course, the design drives the choice, and SMTP is often more readily available than Jabber.

SOAP::Transport::POP3::Server

The server shown in Example 8-7 is best associated with the Jabber server presented earlier, just as the MQ server is also a close derivative. The application requires that a host be provided, as well as a username and password for connecting to the POP3 server at the specified host.

Example 8-7. A POP3-based server

```
#!/usr/bin/perl

use strict;

use SOAP::Transport::TCP;
use WishListCustomer::SOAP;
use WishListCustomer::Transport
        'SOAP::Transport::POP3::Server';

my ($user, $passwd, $host) = @ARGV;
$host ||= 'localhost';
my $pop3_url = "pop://$user:$passwd\@$host";

WishListCustomer::Transport
    ->new($pop3_url)
    ->dispatch_with({ 'urn:/WishListCustomer' =>
                      'WishListCustomer::SOAP' })
    ->objects_by_reference('WishListCustomer::SOAP');

do { $server->handle ) while sleep 10;

exit;
```

As the Jabber and MQ modules do, the POP3 module defines `pop://` as a type of URI specification, allowing the server code to use the URI module to extract the data it needs from the string passed to the constructor. Note also that this server class must provide its own looping mechanism around the `handle` method, as Jabber and MQ do.

SOAP::Transport::MAILTO::Client

This client class is by no means the only way to send messages to the POP3-based server. Any email client can be used, or a mail-transfer agent (MTA) such as `sendmail` or `postfix`, could be used directly. As long as the client can verify a successful delivery and craft a valid SOAP message the server understands, the client can be used.

To demonstrate the `SOAP::Transport::MAILTO` module, we will create such a client. It can, in fact, be used through the same generic client presented earlier in this chapter, by specifying a suitable endpoint:

```
mailto:soap.server@soaplite.com?From=you@home.com
```

An endpoint such as this defaults to using the system's `sendmail` MTA. Additionally, it's important to point out that the default client expects to format the output from the remote method it calls, and in this case there would be no such output.

Instead, we'll make a different client. This client triggers the purchase of one or more books on the user's wish list. The script expects the user's ID and password for the SOAP server as the first two arguments, followed by the email address for the SOAP POP3 listener, and one or more ISBNs of books to purchase. The code is shown in Example 8-8.

Example 8-8. An email client using SOAP::Transport::MAILTO

```perl
#!/usr/bin/perl

use strict;

use WishListCustomer::Client;
use Sys::Hostname 'hostname';

my ($user, $passwd, $mailto) = (shift, shift, shift);
die "USAGE: $0 username passwd endpoint ISBN [ ISBN... ]\n"
    unless ($user and $passwd and $mailto and @ARGV);

my $hostname = eval { hostname };
$hostname = 'localhost' if $@;
my $endpoint = sprintf("maito:%s?From=%s&Subject=SOAP",
                      $mailto,
                      "$user\@$hostname");

my $soap = WishListCustomer::Client
            ->uri('urn:/WishListCustomer')
            ->proxy($endpoint);
$soap->setAuth($user, $passwd);
my $result = $soap->PurchaseBooks(\@ARGV);
```

Example 8-8. An email client using SOAP::Transport::MAILTO (continued)

```
if ($result->fault) {
    die "$0: Operation failed: " . $result->faultstring;
} else {
    print "Request sent\n";
}

exit;
```

As it happens, the PurchaseBooks method in the sample code doesn't actually do anything except remove the books from the list and update the user record. An actual enterprise-level application interface would have defined behaviors for cases such as keys being passed for books that aren't in the wish list, server errors in order completion, and so forth. (Not to mention the obvious: not enough room on the credit card for all the books!)

As you may have noticed, the SOAP::Transport::MAILTO module isn't explicitly loaded because the SOAP::Lite client object handles it automatically. The WishListCustomer::Client class *is* used, though, because the request still needs SOAP headers for authentication.

Standalone Protocols

Three protocols offer nontraditional ways of sending or receiving requests. SOAP::Transport::IO, for example, provides a server to read requests from a filehandle and send responses to another filehandle. SOAP::Transport::FTP::Client stores a request on the FTP server in a text file. SOAP::Transport::LOCAL::Client lets you integrate a server with your client, so SOAP requests and responses don't travel over a network at all. In this section, we look at all three modules.

SOAP::Transport::IO

The SOAP::Transport::IO module provides only a server class. It is very simple in design and potentially very flexible. A server built from SOAP::Transport::IO::Server reads a single, full request from one file handle and sends the result out on a second file handle. Each time the handle method is called, it expects to read all the data available from the input source. Depending on the type of the input source, the end of the data stream may be signaled by a literal end-of-file marker or a shutdown call on a socket. On the outgoing side, there is no assumption that the file handle should be closed or discarded after sending the response, making it more likely to be reused. Thanks to the universal nature of file handles in Perl, the code doesn't have to provide special-case handling for these different types of input sources.

The potential usefulness of this class is greater than it may appear at first glance. This class makes a good core element for an application that monitors several TCP, UDP, and Unix-domain sockets, sending all incoming requests to the same server instance. Alternately, a daemon built on this class can be responsible for monitoring areas of a filsystem, watching for requests in the form of physical files (see the FTP client in the next section).

As an example, the IO class will be used in a much simpler role, that of a Unix-style filter. The code in Example 8-9 is designed to be called from a command line, perhaps as a mail filter or part of a cron task. It reads a single request from standard-input and writes the response to standard output.

Example 8-9. The SOAP::Transport::IO::Server example

```perl
#!/usr/bin/perl

use strict;

use SOAP::Transport::IO;
use WishListCustomer::SOAP;
use WishListCustomer::Transport
        'SOAP::Transport::IO::Server';

my $server = WishListCustomer::Transport
    ->new()
    ->dispatch_with({ 'urn:/WishListCustomer' =>
                      'WishListCustomer::SOAP' })
    ->objects_by_reference('WishListCustomer::SOAP')
    ->handle;

exit;
```

Because each invocation means fresh loading and compilation of the SOAP application code, this may seem to be a less-than-optimal application, and that is true to some extent. It would be a valid application as part of a larger system, a part that manages filter-oriented or similar tasks while sharing the basic code base and architecture of a larger, more standard SOAP server on an HTTP port.

SOAP::Transport::FTP::Client

The FTP module is designed simply to upload the request as an ordinary text file on a specified server. It is similar to the SOAP::Transport::MAILTO module in that communication is one way in nature. Requests are written remotely based on the full path given in the endpoint.

Because the FTP client represents a one-way transaction, the client from the MAILTO example will be adapted to work in a more generic fashion. Rather than taking just the target POP3 host as a command-line argument, it will be adapted to require a more fully specified endpoint, in the same way the earlier generic client does.

The updated client is shown in Example 8-10. Some logic is applied to the endpoint strings before the client object gets created. A MAILTO endpoint gets a "From" address and subject added. An FTP endpoint is expected to specify only the directory portion of the path; the application creates a filename based on the user ID and a timestamp, which avoids overwriting other files on the same server.

Example 8-10. The generic version of the purchasing client

```perl
#!/usr/bin/perl

use strict;

use WishListCustomer::Client;
use Sys::Hostname 'hostname';

my ($user, $passwd, $endpoint) = (shift, shift, shift);
die "USAGE: $0 username passwd endpoint ISBN [ ISBN... ]\n"
    unless ($user and $passwd and $endpoint and @ARGV);

if (substr($endpoint, 0, 3) eq 'ftp') {
    my @time = localtime;
    my $file = sprintf("%s-%02d%02d%02d:%02d%02d.xml",
                      $user,
                      $time[5] % 100,  # year
                      $time[4] + 1,    # month
                      $time[3],        # day
                      $time[2],        # hour
                      $time[1]);       # minute
    $endpoint .= '/'
        unless (substr($endpoint, -1, 1) eq '/');
    $endpoint .= $file;
} elsif (substr($endpoint, 0, 6) eq 'mailto') {
    my $hostname = eval { hostname };
    $hostname = 'localhost' if $@;
    $endpoint = "$endpoint?From=$user\@$hostname&Subject=" .
        'SOAP';
} else {
    die "$0: endpoint only supports ftp: and mailto: ";
}

my $soap = WishListCustomer::Client
            ->uri('urn:/WishListCustomer')
            ->proxy($endpoint);
$soap->setAuth($user, $passwd);
my $result = $soap->PurchaseBooks(\@ARGV);
if ($result->fault) {
    die "$0: Operation failed: " . $result->faultstring;
} else {
    print "Request sent\n";
}

exit;
```

Again, the transparent nature of how SOAP::Lite clients load the appropriate transport module makes the application much simpler and cleaner. An FTP endpoint looks something like:

    ftp://user:pass@ftp.somewhere.com/path/to/dir

Normally, the SOAP::Transport::FTP::Client class expects the FTP endpoint to include the final element (the filename). This application provides the last piece before creating the client object. Changing the final else-clause allows the other (bidirectional) transport methods to be accepted for this application as well.

SOAP::Transport::LOCAL::Client

The last of the transport modules provided by SOAP::Lite provides a "local" mode of transport that isn't actually transport at all.

The SOAP::Transport::LOCAL module provides only a client class, but the underlying object actually encapsulates both a client and a server from within the same object. The client handles requests by passing the envelope directly to the handle method it finds in the SOAP::Server class, from which it inherits. The server part of the object is configured to look for any requested classes in the list of directories in @INC.

Using the class itself is naturally somewhat different from the other client or server classes. The main use of this class is to allow applications to test their SOAP interface code. Tests can be run using just local resources, without any real transport traffic.

These tests can be as simple as running methods to check for syntax errors. Alternatively, the code can set various levels of tracing via the trace argument when SOAP::Lite is loaded. Example 8-11 shows a simple application that searches for books by title, using a pattern provided on the command line.

Example 8-11. Using SOAP::Transport::LOCAL for simple tests

```perl
#!/usr/bin/perl

use strict;

use SOAP::Lite +trace => 'method';
use WishListCustomer::SOAP;

my $pattern = shift || 'perl';
my $soap = SOAP::Lite->uri('urn:/WishListCustomer')
                    ->proxy('local:',
                            'dispatch_with' => {
                                'urn:/WishListCustomer' => 'WishListCustomer::SOAP'
                            });

my $result = $soap->BooksByTitle($pattern);
if ($result->fault) {
    die "$0: Operation failed: " . $result->faultstring;
}
```

Example 8-11. Using SOAP::Transport::LOCAL for simple tests (continued)

```
my $books = $result->result;

format =
@<<<<<<<<<<<<<<<<<<<<<<<<<<<<<<<<<<<<<< @>>>>>>>>>>>>>>>
$result->{title},                       $result->{isbn}
.

print "Books whose title matches '$pattern':\n\n";
for (@$books) {
    $result = $soap->GetBook($_);
    # Quietly skip books that cause faults
    next if ($result->fault);
    $result = $result->result;
    write;
}

exit;
```

Calling `dispatch_with` was done a little differently in this example. While the `SOAP::Transport::LOCAL::Client` class does include `SOAP::Server` in the inheritance path, calling `dispatch_with` directly on the object triggers the auto-dispatch functionality and attempts to treat it as a remote method. By riding along on the call to proxy, we avoid this. It can also be avoided using the object returned by `$soap->transport` to call the method.

Creating New Transport Modules

Even with the wide array of transport support code offered by `SOAP::Lite`, it's possible that newer protocols or even specialized needs based on existing protocols will arise. Writing new protocol suites isn't as difficult as it might seem at first glance.

Writing a Server Transport

In effect, a new server transport was written at the start of the chapter. The `WishListCustomer::Transport` module may not initially seem like a new transport, because it only piggy-backs on an existing protocol. Despite this, it qualifies because it acts in place of any of the prepackaged server classes. And while the version as presented in the text expects the application to handle loading the "parent" class that it inherits from, it can be written to better handle automatically determining what module to load without application-level intervention.

Reasons for writing a new server class aren't limited to supporting new transport methods. The earlier example was written to handle the authentication layer. If an application wants to create transaction logs using more information than is available to the `on_dispatch` hook, the ideal approach is to subclass the desired server class and step in at the appropriate point (most likely the `handle` method). For those cases in which the actual need is to support a different protocol not yet in the core, the best approach is to look at what changes are needed from the vantage of the new and handle methods.

Specialized constructors

If the new server class is just doing things like authentication, there is probably no need to provide a specialized constructor. In cases in which a new protocol is accommodated, the chances are good that a class-specific new will have to be written.

Certain conventions have to be followed to maintain full interoperability with the rest of the SOAP::Lite suite. Unless the new class is going to completely reimplement the entire SOAP::Server interface, it should inherit from the SOAP::Server class (or from an existing subclass of it). Also, the local constructor should start out by calling the superclass new method, then making whatever local adjustments are needed to the resulting object:

```
# Assumes that $class and @args were initialized from @_
my $self = $class->SUPER::new(@args);
```

The SOAP::Server class (as well as the various subclasses in SOAP::Lite) uses a hash table reference as the basis for the object. Thus, the new class will need to design its structure around this datatype, as well. The SOAP::Lite classes all follow pretty standard data-abstraction and object-oriented methodologies. A leading underscore in the key name (_transport and _proxy, for example) indicates instance data on the hash reference.

How the new class avoids key collision is up to the developer, though choosing a clear prefix (such as the package name) generally works. And because the SOAP::Server class is designed to be subclassed, it isn't necessary to re-bless the object before returning it; it will already be blessed into the local namespace.

Writing a localized handle method

Looking at the code for the various protocol-specific modules in the SOAP::Lite distribution, it is clear that the handle method is the one most-often overloaded. This method represents the core of the server functionality, from an external interface's perspective.

How a new server class chooses to implement the handle method (if at all) is dependent on the planned nature of how the protocol views requests. Protocols such as POP3 and MQ expect requests to have been delivered to a defined location by some other means (email and a message-queue manager, respectively), whereas protocols such as HTTP and TCP expect to await notification from the operating system that incoming data is ready on a readable socket (generally by way of the accept system call). These architectural issues define how the handle method gets used in applications built using the class. The sample TCP server's `handle` method acted as an infinite loop, where the POP3 `handle` was wrapped in an explicit loop construct.

It is within the `handle` method that the server object is expected to retrieve one or more requests, using the protocol it is written to support. In many cases, once the request has been read and stored into memory, it is usually directly usable by the `handle` method of the superclass. Many of the derived server classes simply call the `SOAP::Server` handle method once they've read the request:

    my $response = $self->SUPER::handle($request);

Once the response is given back, it is then up to the new code to properly transmit it back to the client. This is assuming that a client response is part of the design; the POP3 server doesn't send a client reply because there is no client connection available to it.

Other server methods

There are other methods within SOAP::Server that may be overloaded, not to mention hooks such as `on_dispatch`. The documentation for `SOAP::Lite` and Appendix B of this book may be of help in such tasks.

Writing a Client Transport

Writing an actual new client transport module is trickier than writing a server component. The `WishListCustomer::Client` class developed earlier in this chapter isn't an actual transport class. It was a subclass of `SOAP::Lite` itself, designed to interject a consistent header element into every outgoing request.

A class intended for use as a client's transport object is very different.

Naming the client class

The name of a client class is defined by the protocol itself and the transport class it is expected to work with. All the client classes provided by `SOAP::Lite` have names that fit the following form:

    ${transport_class}::${protocol_uc}::Client

By default, `SOAP::Lite` objects have a transport object instantiated from the `SOAP::Transport` class. Using Jabber as an example, the class name becomes:

    SOAP::Transport::JABBER::Client

`SOAP::Lite` attempts to load protocol code using the transport object's class name and the uppercased protocol string. Keeping with the ongoing example, this means that when a client tries to set a proxy with a protocol specification of `jabber://`, `SOAP::Lite` (specifically, the proxy method of `SOAP::Transport`) tries to load a package called `SOAP::Transport::JABBER`, and expects a client class called `SOAP::Transport::JABBER::Client` within it.

This becomes important when choosing the name for the new client class. To work with the loading mechanism already in place, the class has to either use SOAP::Transport as the leading elements of its name or offer a different transport class that can be plugged in to the SOAP::Lite object.

Subclassing SOAP::Transport isn't difficult. The constructor isn't designed to take any arguments when called, and the only class method provided is proxy, which is responsible for either returning the current proxy object (when no arguments are passed to it) or setting a new one (when given an endpoint string as an argument). An empty subclass can provide the base elements of the class name for specifying a transport.

Constructors

A client transport class is expected to inherit from either SOAP::Client or some other subclass of it. As such, the client class may not need to overload the new method at all. As with the server class details earlier, there are plenty of cases in which a client might subclass an existing transport class just to overload a different method.

In another similarity to the server classes, a client new should build up from an object created by calling the superclass new method. These objects are also based on hash-table references, so the new client class should design for this.

When a constructor is called, it's usually called by the proxy method of a transport object. Such calls start with two parameters in the list of arguments: the string endpoint followed by the endpoint itself as passed to the proxy method. Any other arguments to the proxy method follow these two. The general design is such that arguments are expected to be name/value pairs that get converted to a hash table. The key endpoint is just one element of the hash table. If the new class constructor is expected to function in tandem with SOAP::Transport, this behavior must be supported.

The send_receive method

Just as handle is the core of a server class, the send_receive method is the core of a client-transport class. This method is called when the SOAP::Lite object has turned an ordinary method call into a serialized request.

When called, the send_receive method receives a hash table with four keys:

action
    The "action" specifier for the request, usually the SOAPAction header in an HTTP environment.

encoding
    The SOAP encoding URN, often dependent on the version of SOAP that serializes the request.

endpoint
: The URN describing the endpoint that SOAP::Lite expects the client transport object to send the request to.

envelope
: The actual XML text that comprised the request itself.

Which of these the method acts on is up to the class itself. Some of the provided transports use only the envelope.

The responsibility of the send_receive method is to get the envelope to the endpoint and return any response from the server to the caller as a SOAP::SOM object. In the case of the SOAP::Transport::MAILTO module, the response is based solely on whether the SMTP session indicated that the message was sent or whether the send failed.

In the two-way protocols, such as TCP or HTTP, the returned SOAP::SOM object is the deserialized response from the endpoint. In the SOAP::Transport::LOCAL::Client class, the send_receive method passes the envelope directly to the handle method of SOAP::Server and returns the response from that method unchanged because the value is already a SOAP::SOM object.

Other client methods

There are other client-level methods that a new class might need to overload, such as options or endpoint. The endpoint method is generally used to either fetch the current endpoint to which messages are being sent or to set a new endpoint without having to search for and load a new protocol module. A new client transport might need to do more with the value when an endpoint is changed, particularly if it involves passwords or other such data.

The SOAP::Lite documentation and Appendix B of this book cover the other methods in additional detail.

Example Transport Module

As a last example for the chapter, Example 8-12 illustrates how a transport module might look. The module provides three classes, one each for server and client, and one to act as a transport class for SOAP::Lite objects. The purpose of the package is to allow one-way applications (such as a POP3-based server and a MAILTO-based client) to use some of the block-oriented encryption modules available in Perl. This is done by overloading the proxy method to look for URN values of this format:

```
des-ftp://server.domain/path
```

The transport takes the encryption algorithm part of the protocol string, the des-ftp in the example, and removes it from the endpoint. It saves the algorithm for later reference and creates an object using the rest of the endpoint string. On the server side, the server class is designed in a very similar way to WishListCustomer::Transport from earlier in this chapter. It allows dynamic specification of what server class it should base itself on, then overloads calls to handle to decrypt the message before passing it to the parent class.

Much of the critical functionality takes place in the class called Crypt::SOAP:: Transport, which is meant to be used as a transport handler in place of the SOAP:: Transport class. It manages attribute methods for all aspects of creating objects from the Crypt::CBC class,[*] including dynamic selection of whether to treat data to hexstring treatment (in which data is converted to printable hex representation after encryption and presumed to be in such a format when being decrypted).

The classes are limited to the one-way transports due to the fact that not all the two-way packages have the same hook points in their request flow. The HTTP module can be employed because it uses clearly identified request and response methods to get and set content. By contrast, the TCP server class writes the result of the handle method directly to the client socket, with no intermediate step available for overloading.

The code is shown in Example 8-12. It isn't shown in entirety due to the length, but the full source is listed in Appendix D.

> Understand that this is meant as an illustrative example only. Not all of the block-cipher algorithms the code refers to are considered secure enough for critical data. This code should *not* used in a production setting.

Example 8-12. The abbreviated Crypt::SOAP module

```
package Crypt::SOAP;

use strict;
use vars qw(%known_cbc);

use SOAP::Lite;
use Crypt::CBC;

# A mapping table of the ciphers that can be used with the
# Crypt::CBC module. The key is the lc'd name for matching
# and the value is what must get passed to Crypt::CBC::new
%known_cbc = ( des      => 'DES',
               idea     => 'IDEA',
               blowfish => 'Blowfish',
               rc6      => 'RC6',
               rijndael => 'Rijndael' );

package Crypt::SOAP::Transport;
```

---

[*] It is available from CPAN and requires one or more cipher implementations (such as Crypt::DES, Crypt:: IDEA, Crypt::Blowfish, etc.) for operation.

Example 8-12. The abbreviated Crypt::SOAP module (continued)

```perl
@ISA = qw(SOAP::Transport);

sub proxy {
    my $self = shift->new;
    my $class = ref $self;

    return $self->{_proxy} unless @_;

    my ($cipher, $proto);
    my $endpoint = shift;
    if ($endpoint =~ /^(\w+):/) {
        ($cipher, $proto) = split(/-/, $1);
        $endpoint =~ s/^$cipher-//;
    } else {
        die "$class: No transport protocol in proxy";
    }
    if ($cipher = $Crypt::SOAP::known_cbc{lc $cipher}) {
        $self->cipher($cipher);
    } else {
        die "$class: Cipher $cipher unknown or unsupported "
            . 'in proxy';
    }

    $self->SUPER::proxy($endpoint, @_);
    $self->{_proxy} =
        Crypt::SOAP::Client->new($self, $self->{_proxy});
}

package Crypt::SOAP::Server;

sub new {
    my ($class, %args) = @_;
    return $class if ref $class;

    die "$class: Cannot create objects without a parent " .
        'class specified first'
            unless (@ISA);

    my $transport_args;
    if ($args{transport}) {
        $transport_args = $args{transport};
        delete $args{transport};
    }
    my $self = $class->SUPER::new(%args);
    $self->{_CSS_transport} =
        Crypt::SOAP::Transport->new($transport_args ?
                                    @$transport_args : ());

    $self;
}
```

Example 8-12. The abbreviated Crypt::SOAP module (continued)

```
sub handle {
    my ($self, $message) = @_;

    $message = $self->{_CSS_transport}->decrypt($message);
    $self->SUPER::handle($message);
}

package Crypt::SOAP::Client;

sub new {
    my ($class, $transport, $client) = @_;
    return $class if ref $class;

    die "$class: new() must be called with a transport " .
        'object and an existing client object'
            unless (UNIVERSAL::can($transport, 'new') &&
                    UNIVERSAL::can($client, 'new'));
    $client->{_CSC_transport} = $transport;
    @ISA = (ref $client);
    bless $client, $class;
}

sub send_receive {
    my $self = shift;
    my %args = @_;

    $args{envelope} = $self->{_CSC_transport}
                            ->encrypt($args{envelope});
    $self->SUPER::send_receive(%args);
}

1;
```

CHAPTER 9
Service Description with WSDL

WSDL provides a way for services to describe their interfaces to potential client applications. Using XML to express the inputs, operations, and messages, the description gives the would-be client all the information it needs to interact with the server. This chapter introduces the elements of WSDL and builds a description for the web service that was developed in Chapter 7.

Basic WSDL

The Web Service Definition Language (WSDL) is an XML application originally co-authored by a team of representatives from Microsoft and IBM. The current version accepted as a technical recommendation by the W3C is 1.1, which was released in March 2001. Currently, Version 1.2 of the specification is under active development under the broader scope of the W3C's working-group on web services.

WSDL is a major component behind the cross-platform nature of Microsoft's .NET platform. Many web-services platforms offer generation of WSDL descriptions as a feature of the development process, closely associating the creation of the software with formally defining the interface. On the client side, tools can generate object classes, or even whole applications, from the description as an input.

Starting Simple

To begin with, the XML document in Example 9-1 shows a very simple WSDL document, one that defines only the GetBook operation from the sample project developed in the previous chapters.

Example 9-1. Basic WSDL describing the GetBook operation
```
<?xml version="1.0"?>
<definitions name="WLC#GetBook"
    targetNamespace="urn:simple" xmlns:tns="urn:simple"
    xmlns:xsd="http://www.w3.org/2001/XMLSchema">
```

Example 9-1. Basic WSDL describing the GetBook operation (continued)

```
    xmlns:soap="http://schemas.xmlsoap.org/wsdl/soap/"
    xmlns="http://schemas.xmlsoap.org/wsdl/">
<types>
    <xsd:schema xmlns="http://www.w3.org/2001/XMLSchema"
        targetNamespace="urn:simple">
      <xsd:complexType name="BookData">
        <xsd:all>
          <xsd:element name="isbn"  type="xsd:string" />
          <xsd:element name="title" type="xsd:string" />
          <xsd:element name="url"   type="xsd:anyURI" />
        </xsd:all>
      </xsd:complexType>
    </xsd:schema>
</types>
<message name="GetBookRequest">
    <part name="isbn" type="xsd:string" />
</message>
<message name="GetBookResponse">
    <part name="return" type="tns:BookData" />
</message>
<portType name="simpleWishListExample">
    <operation name="GetBook">
      <input message="tns:GetBookRequest" />
      <output message="tns:GetBookResponse" />
    </operation>
</portType>
<binding name="GetBookBinding"
        type="tns:simpleWishListExample">
    <soap:binding style="rpc"
        transport="http://schemas.xmlsoap.org/soap/http" />
    <operation name="GetBook">
      <soap:operation soapAction="urn:/WishListCustomer">
      <input>
        <soap:body use="encoded"
            namespace="urn:/WishListCustomer" />
      </input>
      <output>
        <soap:body use="encoded"
            namespace="urn:/WishListCustomer" />
      </output>
    </operation>
</binding>
<service name="GetBookSimple">
    <port name="simpleWishListExample"
        binding="tns:GetBookBinding">
      <soap:address location="http://localhost:9000/" />
    </port>
</service>
</definitions>
```

The emphasized tags are the WSDL elements that will be explained later. This is just an example, of course. An actual WSDL specification for the service would cover all the operations, and define types, such as `BookData`, in terms of the distinction between partial and complete data retrieval.

The Parts of a WSDL Document

The basic structure of a WSDL document is shown in Figure 9-1. *Services* are made up of *ports*, which in turn are built up from *port types* and *bindings*. The `portType` and `binding` sections describe *operations*, which in turn are built from descriptions of *messages*. A message simply groups related data with specification of the type each data element conforms to.

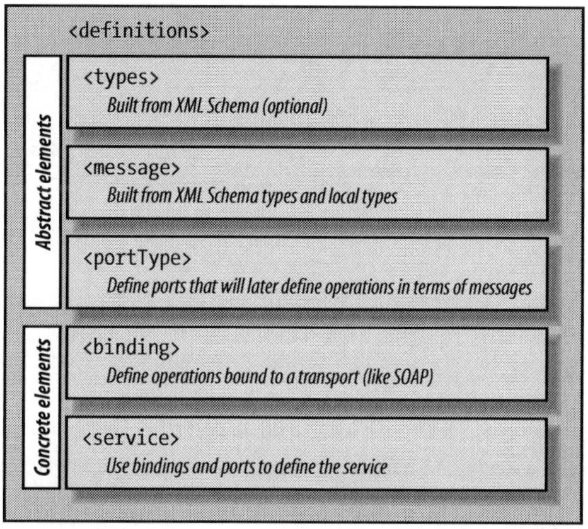

```
<definitions>
    <types>
        Built from XML Schema (optional)
    <message>
        Built from XML Schema types and local types
    <portType>
        Define ports that will later define operations in terms of messages
    <binding>
        Define operations bound to a transport (like SOAP)
    <service>
        Use bindings and ports to define the service
```

Abstract elements: `<types>`, `<message>`, `<portType>`
Concrete elements: `<binding>`, `<service>`

Figure 9-1. WSDL document structure

The first three groups of concepts in the figure are labeled *abstract elements*, while the last two are labeled *concrete elements*. Abstracts define parts of the description that are purely informational: datatypes, message content, and so on. Those factors defined as concrete define the more tangible elements: association of abstract elements to actual transport methods and the definition of the service itself in terms of communication address and protocol.

The WSDL jargon can be confusing. In WSDL terms, a port describes an operation. It's generally a given routine in the API being exposed. In general network programming language, port usually refers to a socket endpoint. The `binding` tags associate ports with transport mechanisms, such as SOAP. This concept is similar to that of binding a socket to a specific address and port in traditional network programming.

As we go through the individual elements of WSDL, we'll build a full WSDL specification for the services built in the previous two chapters.

Starting a WSDL document

A WSDL document is a set of definitions, starting from type definitions (if needed) and culminating in the service definitions. The root element for a WSDL document is the `definitions` tag. As with any other XML document, the opening tag also takes the opportunity to define relevant namespaces that will be referenced through the rest of the document.

The namespaces commonly used in WSDL are shown in Table 9-1, along with the labels that will be consistently used throughout the examples for each. In addition to providing the namespace, the opening tag may also give a *name* to the service and define the *target namespace* that covers the service as a whole.

Table 9-1. Common namespace URIs for WSDL

Namespace URI	Label	Role
http://schemas.xmlsoap.org/wsdl/	wsdl	This namespace refers to the elements of the WSDL document itself.
http://schemas.xmlsoap.org/wsdl/soap/	soap	Elements from this namespace define the properties of binding to SOAP transport.
http://schemas.xmlsoap.org/wsdl/http/	http	As earlier, defining the properties of a binding to HTTP (GET or POST).
http://schemas.xmlsoap.org/wsdl/mime/	mime	MIME binding.
Various	tns	The tns label is generally used as a shorthand for "this namespace." It refers to the namespace covering the service itself, allowing elements like new types to be localized more easily.

In addition to these namespaces, many familiar ones, such as enc (for SOAP encoding rules), xsd (XML Schema definitions), and so on, are often present.

Using this information, the outer skeleton of the WSDL for the wish-list service would look something like the XML fragment in Example 9-2.

Example 9-2. The containing tag of the WSDL

```
<?xml version="1.0"?>
<definitions name="WishListCustomer"
    targetNamespace="urn:WishListCustomer"
    xmlns:tns="urn:WishListCustomer"
    xmlns:soap="http://schemas.xmlsoap.org/wsdl/soap/"
    xmlns:enc="http://schemas.xmlsoap.org/soap/encoding/"
    xmlns:xsd="http://www.w3.org/2001/XMLSchema"
    xmlns="http://schemas.xmlsoap.org/wsdl/">

</definitions>
```

The service is given the name, `WishListService`. This name isn't actually used in constructing calls to the server, though a client may choose to use the name in creating proxy classes for operations. To avoid confusion, the same name as the main class itself from the example code is used here.

Note that the name attribute for the definitions tag is declared in the WSDL TR document as a type called NCNAME. That is defined as a name with no colon, in essence any viable name minus any ":" character. The colon is disallowed so as to avoid confusing that part of the name with a reference to a namespace.

The other attribute the tag defined is targetNamespace. This declares what the expected namespace for messages constructed using this description will be. Note that the value given for the attribute is the same URN as defined for the tns namespace on the next line. The tns label will be used later when defining types, to qualify them into the local namespace.

Documentation, types, and messages

In most cases, the first element after definitions in a WSDL document is likely to be one of types or message. There is another element that can appear at this point. The element documentation can in fact appear inside any WSDL tags. Its content is very flexible, and its purpose is to provide human-readable documentation to accompany the entities it's placed near.

A documentation element may contain other elements, and it may also contain attributes. The declaration in the WSDL schema allows for only one restriction on attributes or contained elements: that they are properly qualified and associated with a namespace, as well as being well-formed. Using a documentation tag instead of a general XML comment has the advantage of being retrievable using XPath or a Document Object Model (DOM) representation of the WSDL.

After the optional documentation, a WSDL specification may need to provide type information beyond the basic types defined by XML Schema. This is an optional section of the document because it may not be necessary if the service uses only the pre-existing types (or if the WSDL document uses the import tag to reference types from a separate file, a concept that will be discussed later in greater detail).

The types element in a WSDL file is used to contain the definitions of datatypes that are specific to the document. WSDL is defined to work with XML Schema as a means of type definition, but it isn't limited to it. The examples through the rest of the chapter will use XML Schema, however. The XML fragment in Example 9-3 shows the types block for the service being described here. It defines a type for representing the data returned on a specific book, for the data returned for books when fetching the user's wish list, and some array constructs for cases in which the return values are sets of those types.

Example 9-3. The types section of the WishListCustomer WSDL

```
<types>
  <documentation>
    This section defines the types that will be used by
    the rest of the WSDL document to describe the data
    that describes books. Only the types not already
```

Example 9-3. The types section of the WishListCustomer WSDL (continued)

```
      available from XML Schema are defined here.
  </documentation>
  <xsd:schema targetNamespace="urn:WishListCustomer">
    <xsd:complexType name="PartialBook">
      <xsd:all>
        <xsd:element name="isbn"   type="xsd:string"
                     minOccurs="1" />
        <xsd:element name="title"  type="xsd:string"
                     minOccurs="1" />
        <xsd:element name="url"    type="xsd:anyURI"
                     minOccurs="1" />
      </xsd:all>
    </xsd:complexType>
    <xsd:complexType name="Book">
      <xsd:extension base="tns:PartialBook">
        <xsd:all>
          <xsd:element name="authors" type="xsd:string" />
          <xsd:element name="us_price" type="xsd:string"/>
        </xsd:all>
      </xsd:extension>
    </xsd:complexType>
    <xsd:complexType name="ArrayOfPartialBook">
      <xsd:complexContent>
        <xsd:restriction base="enc:Array">
          <xsd:attribute ref="enc:arrayType"
              wsdl:arrayType="tns:PartialBook[]" />
        </xsd:restriction>
      </xsd:complexContent>
    </xsd:complexType>
    <xsd:complexType name="ArrayOfString">
      <xsd:complexContent>
        <xsd:restriction base="enc:Array">
          <xsd:attribute ref="enc:arrayType"
              wsdl:arrayType="xsd:string[]" />
        </xsd:restriction>
      </xsd:complexContent>
    </xsd:complexType>
  </xsd:schema>
</types>
```

Worth noting is the way `PartialBook` is defined. The `all` construct of XML Schema allows the elements to appear in arbitrary order. Were the WSDL to use sequence instead, the elements would be required to appear in the same order as the definition itself. This would require the application (or the API library, at least) to provide an extension to the serializer used by `SOAP::Lite` to ensure the ordering of the hash table keys. The downside of `all` is that the elements within are defined as appearing once or not at all. Once is fine, but these three elements are required to be present. The schema handles this by overriding the `minOccurs` attribute on the three elements.

In contrast, the Book structure is defined as an extension of PartialBook. It has the same three (mandatory) elements but adds two more. These are also defined in terms of the XML Schema all construct. However, they are allowed to not be present (remember, GetBook may return only the base three elements if the user calling it isn't validated) so that operations that are typed as returning a Book value can cooperate with the authentication layer.

The WSDL specification requires that array descriptions extend the Array type from the SOAP encoding schema. Because that schema declares the arrayType attribute as being of type QName, a type that can't be given a default in schema terms, WSDL provides its own arrayType attribute that can be given an initial value. The XML Schema attribute element declares the attribute for each of the two arrays being defined, by first referencing the attribute from the SOAP encoding schema, then providing the local version with a value based on the types just defined. Here is the first place the tns namespace label is used, to qualify the PartialBook and Book types.

The message blocks can be thought of as outlining the structure of the SOAP Body blocks (see Example 9-4). They don't define every element that will eventually go into a SOAP request, but they do define the set of parts (parameters) that eventually get used in creating such requests. For the operations defined later, the input to and output from the operation will be specified in terms of the messages defined by these blocks.

Example 9-4. The message blocks for WishListCustomer

```
<message name="BookRequest">
  <part name="user" type="xsd:string" />
  <part name="isbn" type="xsd:string" />
</message>

<message name="BookResponse">
  <part name="return" type="tns:Book" />
</message>

<message name="ISBNListResponse">
  <part name="return" type="tns:ArrayOfString" />
</message>

<message name="BooksByAuthorRequest">
  <part name="user" type="xsd:string" />
  <part name="author" type="xsd:string" />
</message>

<message name="BooksByTitleRequest">
  <part name="user" type="xsd:string" />
  <part name="title" type="xsd:string" />
</message>

<message name="SimpleRequest">
  <part name="user" type="xsd:string" />
</message>
```

Example 9-4. The message blocks for WishListCustomer (continued)

```
<message name="SimpleResponse">
  <part name="return" type="xsd:anyType" />
</message>

<message name="BookListResponse">
  <part name="return" type="tns:ArrayOfPartialBook" />
</message>

<message name="BooleanResponse">
  <part name="result" type="xsd:boolean" />
</message>

<message name="PurchaseBooksRequest">
  <part name="user" type="xsd:string" />
  <part name="list" type="tns:ArrayOfString" />
</message>
```

The naming of the messages is arbitrary, but in this example the messages are suffixed with either Request or Response based on which role they will be used in. Some of the responses that don't actually return data (just the object instance, such as AddBook) are set to the special XML Schema type, anyType. This saves defining the structure of the class objects in the types section. After all, depending on whether the server is configured to return objects by reference or not, the structure of the type can be significantly different.

The message elements are built from sequences of part elements. Each part is given a name attribute and references either a type or an element, using attributes of the respective names. In the example, the schema in the types section defines only types, no elements. Had the schema declared any elements, they could be referenced by one or more of the part tags here.

All the request messages defined in the example fragment define an element in the request portion of the message named user. This element corresponds to the authentication layer that was defined for the service in the two previous chapters. Message declarations are abstract specifications, and the elements they define aren't limited to appearing just in a SOAP Body tag, for example. At this point in the sample description, SOAP isn't yet a part of the picture. There is nothing that binds specific message elements to specific transport models.

This also defines another part of the service strategy. Even though the server code can operate on an objects-by-reference basis, the WSDL is being constructed for a simple RPC-style interface. This makes for a cleaner, more easily followed example. It also means that the new and SetUser methods don't need to be exposed via the WSDL document. Operations such as AddBook or PurchaseBooks signal their success simply by not returning faults.

At this point, the emerging WSDL document has declarations for the types that are used and the structure of the input and output messages for the various operations. Defining those operations is the next step.

Operations and portType

When defining a service, related operations are grouped under an umbrella called the portType. A WSDL description isn't limited to defining only one such block, though in most simple cases, one occurrence of the portType tag is sufficient.

A portType block gathers the various operation definitions into one unit. Each operation is defined using an element called operation. Operations are named structures, and the names must be unique for each operation within a portType, just as multiple portType blocks must have unique names within their enclosing definitions block. An operation may be specified more than once, however, if the document is defining an overloaded operation. In that case, the name attributes of the input and/or output tags within the separate operations must be distinct, so that processors of the WSDL can see the differences. In these cases, the different blocks are still effectively defining just one operation. They are specifying the different signatures (to use an XML-RPC term) the API function itself offers. Overloading will be discussed in greater detail later.

To help illustrate this, Example 9-5 shows the single portType block for the sample WSDL being built for this chapter, with some of the operation blocks contained within.

Example 9-5. The portType declaration for WishListCustomer

```
<portType name="WishListCustomerPort">

  <operation name="GetBook">
    <input message="tns:BookRequest" />
    <output message="tns:BookResponse" />
  </operation>

  <operation name="BooksByAuthor">
    <input message="tns:BooksByAuthorRequest" />
    <output message="tns:ISBNListResponse" />
  </operation>

  <operation name="AddBook">
    <input message="tns:BookRequest" />
    <output message="tns:SimpleResponse" />
  </operation>

  <operation name="CanPurchase">
    <input message="tns:SimpleRequest" />
    <output message="tns:BooleanResponse" />
```

Example 9-5. The portType declaration for WishListCustomer (continued)

```
  </operation>

</portType>
```

Not all the operation declarations are shown because they are all very similar in their structure. Because of the simple nature of this service, there is little diversity at this point.

All the operations defined in this `portType` block conform to what the WSDL specification calls the *request-response* model. The endpoint receives a request and issues a response to the data contained in the request, even if that data is limited to just the name of the operation. The WSDL specification also defines three other models: *one-way*, *solicit-response*, and *notification*.

Operations that follow the one-way model are those that only send a message from the client to the endpoint. The `SOAP::Transport::MAILTO` package provides a client class that sends messages that are treated as one-way. Likewise, the server class of the POP3 transport module also operates in a one-way model. At the other end of the spectrum, notification operations are those in which the endpoint sends a message to the client without having received any prior input, much like a RSS feed service.

The solicit-response model is similar to request-response, except that the endpoint sends a message first, and the client sends a response to that message. Both solicit-response and request-response have optional third message types in their declaration: fault.

WSDL derives the model of an operation by the types and order of the messages that are declared within the `operation` block. The models themselves are abstract representations that have no direct bearing on how the rest of the WSDL document is treated. Example 9-6 shows how the different models would appear. The snippets shown are adapted from the WSDL specification itself (for more information on the specification, see *http://www.w3.org/TR/wsdl*).

Example 9-6. Operation models in WSDL

```
<portType name="examples">
  <!-- One-way operation -->
  <operation name="one_way">
    <input message="..." />
  </operation>

  <!-- Notification operation -->
  <operation name="notification">
    <output message="..." />
  </operation>
```

Example 9-6. Operation models in WSDL (continued)

```
  <!-- Request-response operation -->
  <operation name="request_response">
    <input message="..." />
    <output message="..." />
    <fault name="..." message="..." />
  </operation>

  <!-- Solicit-response operation -->
  <operation name="request_response">
    <output message="..." />
    <input message="..." />
    <fault name="..." message="..." />
  </operation>
</portType>
```

The fault element is optional in the two-way models. It refers to a message declaration that describes the informative part of a fault, if one occurs. How this is mapped to an actual message is dependent on the transport model used in the actual binding of operations to transports. In the case of SOAP, for example, the message a `fault` element refers to becomes the content of the `detail` component of the SOAP fault construct.

The input and output elements may also have name attributes. The names must be unique within the scope of the enclosing `portType` tag. More accurately, all of the input and output elements do have names, but WSDL defines default values for the names to make writing WSDL documents easier. Any of these elements that don't have name attributes are assigned names based on the model and the name of the enclosing operation. Table 9-2 shows the set of rules for deriving the names based on circumstance. For one-way and notification operations, the name from the `operation` is applied to the input or output tag, as appropriate. For request-response and solicit-response, the operation name is appended with one of `Request`, `Solicit`, or `Response`, as applies.

Table 9-2. Input/output naming rules for operations

Operation model (operation name is "example")	Default input name	Default output name
One-way	Example	No output
Notification	No input	Example
Request-response	ExampleRequest	ExampleResponse
Solicit-response	ExampleResponse (see note in text)	ExampleSolicit

For the solicit-response names, remember that the input tag refers to the response that the client sends back to the endpoint, hence the name ending in `Response`. In the sample operation blocks in Example 9-5, all the input and output elements will fall back on these defaults.

When fault components are specified in either of the two-way models, the `fault` tags must have `name` attributes present. This is because an `operation` may specify more than one `fault` that could possibly result from the operation itself. The values of the fault name attributes are required to be unique only within the scope of the `operation` element, not the enclosing `portType`. This is different from the `input` and `output` elements.

Bindings

It's through the binding of the defined port types to actual transport specifications that services are built up. The abstractions built from the `portType` elements and the `message` elements that went into them contribute to the definition of the concrete half of WSDL that is `binding` and `service`.

The `binding` tag acts as a container much like the `portType` element from the previous section. A `binding` has a correlation to a `portType`, though it isn't limited to a one-to-one mapping; there may be multiple `binding` blocks that reference the same `portType` definition. A single `binding` block must define bindings for exactly one protocol, so cases in which the WSDL is expected to describe multiple access methods will have multiple bindings. A binding doesn't, however, specify address information. That is handled later, in the `service` declaration.

The WSDL specification provides the basis for three varieties of binding, which are shown in Table 9-3 along with the URN identifiers for their XML namespaces.

Table 9-3. WSDL binding declarations

Protocol	URN	Description
SOAP	http://schemas.xmlsoap.org/wsdl/soap/	Element and attribute definitions for binding a port to SOAP as a transport and encoding.
HTTP	http://schemas.xmlsoap.org/wsdl/http/	Elements and attributes for HTTP support, both POST and GET methods, for HTTP transport and some degree of encoding.
MIME	http://schemas.xmlsoap.org/wsdl/mime/	Elements and attributes for MIME encoding of messages, used with HTTP and/or SOAP to specify transport.

Recall from Table 9-1 that the URN given for the SOAP binding is one of the namespace declarations commonly found in WSDL documents, often labeled with the identifier soap. The other bindings are generally labeled http and mime when they are referenced in examples in the W3C specification (and also later in this chapter). The sample `definitions` tag in Example 9-2 has already declared the soap namespace identifier and mapped it to the appropriate URN from Table 9-3.

Returning to the task of writing the bindings for the `portType` defined in Example 9-5 (`WishListCustomerPort`), Example 9-7 shows the binding element and its contents for one operation, the `GetBook` call. Because the example is fairly simple, all the operations have the same structure in the `binding` block.

Example 9-7. The SOAP binding for GetBook

```
<binding name="SOAP" type="tns:WishListCustomerPort">
  <soap:binding style="rpc"
      transport="http://schemas.xmlsoap.org/soap/http" />
  <operation name="GetBook">
    <soap:operation soapAction="urn:WishListCustomer" />
    <input>
      <soap:body use="encoded" parts="isbn"
          namespace="urn:WishListCustomer"
          encodingStyle=
          "http://schemas.xmlsoap.org/soap/encoding/" />
      <soap:header use="encoded" part="user"
          message="tns:BookRequest" wsdl:required="0"
          namespace="urn:WishListCustomer"
          encodingStyle=
          "http://schemas.xmlsoap.org/soap/encoding/" />
    </input>
    <output>
      <soap:body use="encoded"
          namespace="urn:WishListCustomer"
          encodingStyle=
          "http://schemas.xmlsoap.org/soap/encoding/" />
    </output>
  </operation>
</binding>
```

Starting with the opening `binding` tag itself, there are two attributes present: `name` and `type`. As with other places in which `name` occurs as an attribute, its presence here is to uniquely identify this set of bindings from others that may occur within the WSDL document. The `type` attribute refers back to a previously defined `portType`. Because there is just the one in this sample document, the relation here is pretty clear.

Immediately within the `binding` tag provided by the WSDL schema is the `soap:binding` element. This element is the first indication that the bindings being presented are going to be specifically for SOAP. There are two possible attributes for this element: `style` and `transport`. The `style` attribute tells whether the messages will be in `rpc` or `document` style. The differences will be discussed later, but for now know that this example uses the `rpc` style. This attribute is optional, but the default value is `document`, which isn't the desired value in this case. The `transport` attribute is required and points to the URI that identifies the transport by which SOAP will send and receive the messages. In this case, it indicates the HTTP transport. This is in fact the same URN that specifies HTTP as a binding model, but in this role it serves only to specify how the user should expect the actual endpoint addressing to appear.

As with the `portType` container element earlier, the `operation` tag delineates the various functions that the binding will present to clients. The `name` attribute of the `operation` tag refers specifically to an `operation` tag within the `portType` block having the same name. Just as there may have been multiple `operation` tags for a given function there, they can appear here, as well, if the WSDL is describing an overloaded function.

The `soap:operation` tag introduces the SOAP-specific information for the operation. The element allows two attributes, only one of which is used here: `soapAction`. If that seems familiar, it's because its role is to specify what goes into the `SOAPAction` header when using HTTP as a transport. It shouldn't be present if the `soap:binding` element didn't specify a URI indicating HTTP as the transport. The second allowable attribute in this element is the same `style` setting that `soap:binding` supports. It's only needed at this level if the specific operation wished to override the value of the earlier setting.

The critical parts of these blocks lay in the `input` and `output` tags, and the `fault` tags if present. These sections ultimately define what the bodies of the messages will look like. Recall the input block from Example 9-7:

```
<input>
  <soap:body use="encoded" parts="isbn"
      namespace="urn:WishListCustomer"
      encodingStyle=
      "http://schemas.xmlsoap.org/soap/encoding/" />
  <soap:header use="encoded" part="user"
      message="tns:BookRequest" wsdl:required="0"
      namespace="urn:WishListCustomer"
      encodingStyle=
      "http://schemas.xmlsoap.org/soap/encoding/" />
</input>
```

When the abstract operation for `GetBook` was defined, input was declared in the form of a message called `BookRequest`, which specified two parts: `isbn` and `user`, referring to the ISBN of the desired book and the (optional) registered-user information. This specification for operation is stating that the `isbn` value will be sent within the SOAP body, while the user data will come as a header.

The `soap:body` element controls what eventually appears in the `Body` tag of the SOAP message. It's an obvious relationship, but there is a lot of information being given by this element. The `part` or `parts` attributes define which element from the `message` (as defined by the `part` tags) will be present in the body (`part` may only refer to one element, `parts` may refer to any number, space-separated if more than one). If neither `part` nor `parts` is present, the body is assumed to contain all the parts defined in the message. The `use` attribute is required, and must be one of `literal` or `encoded`. A value of encoded, the most common, means that the content of the parameters is encoded according to the style given in the `encodingStyle` attribute, which is identical in nature to the same attribute as defined for SOAP messages. If `use` is set to `literal`, it means that the SOAP message will be constructed exactly according to the abstract definitions in the types section of the WSDL. The `namespace` attribute provides the target namespace for the `Body` itself.

The use of soap:header is a little bit different. It also understands the use, namespace, and encodingStyle attributes as they apply to soap:body. The part attribute has the same role but is required in this case. It also requires a message attribute that names the abstract message definition it's using, in which the element from part must exist. If the header is declared with use set to literal, the schema definition for the element that part specifies may include definitions for the soap:actor and soap:mustUnderstand attributes. If use is set to encoded, these aren't permitted. A soap:header may refer to a part from a different message than the soap:body element refers to. Because the user-authentication information isn't explicitly required by the GetBook operation, this header uses the required attribute from WSDL to tell any application reading the description that the header may not be present. When required is set to a true value, the element must be present in the message. The soap:body element, for example, has an implied wsdl:required value of true (or 1) because the SOAP specification requires that the Body tag be present.

The relationship between soap:body and soap:header is very close. Between the name attributes of the operation and input (or output) tags, the exact message specification is chosen from the portType. That abstract specification details the parts that are supposed to be present in the body, and the parts are divided between the soap:body and any soap:header elements declared. In some cases, a multipart MIME encoding may lead to some parts appearing in different places within the whole message, rather than having them all enclosed within the Body tag of a SOAP message. The same default naming rules for the input and output tags apply to the binding sections as to the portType section.

Faults are handled in the specification of bindings using the soap:fault element, or soap:headerfault element for faults that occur in headers. The examples given earlier did not include these definitions because these tags provide the structure of the detail element of the SOAP Fault structure, and the example application's faults only use the faultcode and faultstring elements. The soap:fault element uses the same name, use, encodingStyle, and namespace attributes that have been defined earlier. Because the fault declaration in portType is required to have a name, so is soap:fault. The value of name refers back to the name of the corresponding fault from the portType block. Faults are declared outside of input or output tags.

The soap:headerfault specification is given within a soap:header element to signify a possible fault at the header level. It uses the same attributes as soap:header does, including the mandatory name and message attributes. As with soap:header, it may refer to a part in a message different from the one on which the soap:body tag is based.

Service definitions

The last part of the WSDL puzzle is the service element, which defines the actual service as it's to be presented to clients. In contrast to the complexity that can creep into the binding declarations, the service block is generally very simple. The block for the sample specification is shown in Example 9-8.

Example 9-8. The service block for WishListCustomer
```
<service name="WishListCustomer">
  <port name="WishListCustomerPort" binding="tns:SOAP">
    <soap:address location="http://localhost:9000" />
  </port>
</service>
```

The service tag has only one attribute and one possible child element. The name attribute gives the service a unique name (among other service blocks). Naming allows for several services to be defined by one WSDL document.

The only child element of service is port, which has two attributes but no child elements defined within the WSDL schema. The attributes that are permitted are name and binding. The function of name should be clear, and the value must be unique within the enclosing service tag. The binding attribute refers to a binding block defined elsewhere in the WSDL document. In the case of this example, there is only the one binding defined, named SOAP. A WSDL specification can define multiple bindings, and in turn a service can define multiple port elements. If there are multiple ports, there are three rules from the W3C specification to keep in mind:

- Ports don't communicate with each other. One port's output can't be specified as another port's input.
- When a service has multiple ports that share the same port type but use different bindings, this is intended to present alternatives, allowing clients to select which port to communicate with, based on whatever criteria they choose, such as protocol, etc.
- Examining a service's ports illustrates the port types the server offers. The extension elements within the port tags provide a relationship back to a specific type of binding, thereby informing potential clients.

Because the WSDL schema defines no child elements for port, the only elements that can appear there come from the SOAP, HTTP, or MIME extensions (or any future extensions that may be developed). In Example 9-8, the soap:address element provides the URI clients use to contact the server. In keeping with the transport attribute of the soap:binding tag earlier, the URI refers to an HTTP endpoint. The URI is provided by the attribute called location.

The final version of the WSDL is listed in Appendix E. With annotation in the form of numerous documentation elements, the file is in excess of 400 lines.

HTTP and MIME Binding in WSDL

Thus far, the WSDL sample document has focused on the SOAP binding methodology. But the WSDL specification defines two other binding methods, HTTP and MIME. These can work together, separately, or with the SOAP bindings previously described.

Extending WSDL with HTTP

The HTTP bindings for WSDL aren't very different in structure or meaning from the SOAP bindings. The most significant difference is the need to specify which operation (or *verb*, in HTTP terminology) will perform the operation, and how the arguments are to be transformed into the HTTP request.

Unlike SOAP, there's little inherent structure to HTTP requests. Whether using POST or GET, the basic model of requests is to provide the parameters as sequences of *name=value* pairs. The specific syntax and encoding of the data is determined by the verb, but there is little else that differs. Expressing complex data is difficult due to the flat nature of the encoding.

The HTTP binding extensions for WSDL consist of the five elements described in Table 9-4. Refer back to Table 9-3 for the namespace URN that references the binding schema. In most published examples, the URN is assigned to the label http.

Table 9-4. HTTP binding elements

Element	Role
http:address	Used in the service element, this provides the physical address for the service as a URL in an attribute called location. Similar to the soap:address element.
http:binding	This is used in the binding element, to specify that the binding will be based on the HTTP layer. It has one attribute, verb, that is one of GET or POST. The attribute is required.
http:operation	Operations for the HTTP binding are specified by providing a relative URI within this element, as a value for an attribute called location. The URI must be relative because it's appended to the URI in http:address.
http:urlEncoded http:(urlReplacement)	One of these two is present in the input element when the http:binding element specifies GET as the value of verb. They indicate how the values being passed are to be transformed into parts of the HTTP request line.

The WSDL fragment in Example 9-9 shows practical application of the HTTP extension elements to the binding and service elements of the WSDL description that has been the running example this chapter.

Example 9-9. HTTP binding, first draft

```
<binding name="HTTP" type="tns:WishListCustomerPort">
  <http:binding verb="GET"/>
  <operation name="GetBook">
    <http:operation location="GetBook" />
```

Example 9-9. HTTP binding, first draft (continued)

```
    <input>
      <http:urlEncoded />
    </input>
    <output>
      <mime:mimeXml part="return" />
    </output>
  </operation>
</binding>

<service name="WishListCustomer">
  <port name="WishListCustomerHTTP" binding="tns:HTTP">
    <http:address location="http://localhost:9001" />
  </port>
</service>
```

In this example, the `http:urlEncoded` tag is used in the `input` element. This tells the client that requests to the service should have their input parameters encoded into the URL using the standard rules for parameter encoding. Because the GetBook operation uses parameters named user and isbn, this looks like (with the full URL):

```
http://localhost:9001/GetBook?user=...&isbn=...
```

Note how the URL itself is built by concatenating the `location` values from the `http:address` and `http:operation` elements. The values of the parameters must also be encoded, in order to escape characters, such as spaces, ampersands, and percent signs.

Another thing to note is that the output is built using the MIME extension elements, described later. The HTTP extensions don't describe any output encoding methods. Instead, output is described using either the SOAP encoding elements from the SOAP extension or the MIME elements as in this example. HTTP and MIME are often used together in this context.

Example 9-10 shows a second draft of the same operation under an HTTP binding. Only the operation section is shown to illustrate the way `http:urlReplacement` works.

Example 9-10. HTTP binding, second draft

```
<operation name="GetBook">
  <http:operation location="GetBook/(user)/isbn=(isbn)" />
  <input>
    <http:urlReplacement />
  </input>
  <output>
    <mime:mimeXml part="return" />
  </output>
</operation>
```

When using the `http:urlReplacement` method, the value of the `location` attribute is examined for patterns that match an input part name within parentheses. In the case of GetBook, the parts are simple. The user element is meant to be inserted between two slashes, with no other labeling. This can imply that another mechanism, such as the Apache web server's request lifecycle-based authentication, may be handling that part of the process. The isbn parameter is encoded with a label, similar to URL encoding. Using this approach gives a greater degree of control over the format and placement of the parameters to the call.

When http:urlReplacement is performed, it's performed only against the location part of the corresponding http:operation tag. It happens before this value is appended to the location part of the soap:address. All matching is done before any values are substituted, so content in a value being pasted in can't trigger a later match.

When using the POST verb for HTTP, URL encoding is no longer an issue, but content-encoding becomes an issue instead. Fortunately, encoding of parameters for POST requests is quite standard, with a well-defined MIME content type. Example 9-11 shows the third draft of the HTTP binding, this time centered around POST.

Example 9-11. HTTP binding, third draft

```
<binding name="HTTP" type="tns:WishListCustomerPort">
  <http:binding verb="POST">
  <operation name="GetBook">
    <http:operation location="GetBook" />
    <input>
      <mime:content
          type="application/x-www-form-urlencoded" />
    </input>
    <output>
      <mime:mimeXml part="return" />
    </output>
  </operation>
</binding>
```

This again shows the close relationship between the HTTP and MIME extensions.

Using the MIME extension elements

In the case of the HTTP bindings, it was shown that the extension didn't provide any elements for expressing output, relying instead on the MIME or SOAP extensions to handle that. Likewise, the MIME extensions don't define any elements for the transport elements of bindings, only for describing content. The MIME extension elements are described in Table 9-5. Refer to Table 9-3 for the namespace URN that is used to reference these extensions.

Table 9-5. The MIME extension elements for bindings

Element	Role
mime:content	This element is provided in order to avoid defining a new element for every MIME format. When the only information that needs to be conveyed is the content type (and possibly the part name), this element may be used with the attributes type and part, respectively.
mime:multipartRelated mime:part	These elements work together to specify data as a collection of related MIME parts. The first element declares the content as being of the multipart/related MIME content-type, while the mime:part elements define the individual parts.
mime:mimeXml	To define a message part that is XML but isn't a compliant SOAP message (doesn't conform to the SOAP schema), use this element. It has one attribute, part, that refers to a message component. The content for this part of the message will be the data, serialized but not fully SOAP-encoded.

In addition to the typing rules defined in Table 9-5, when using the MIME extensions with the SOAP extensions, a soap:body element may be specified as a content element. It's equivalent to specifying a mime:content element in which the type attribute is text/xml and the content is expected to be contained within a SOAP envelope.

Example 9-12 illustrates how the different elements of the MIME extension work together. Because the operations from the sample WSDL don't exercise the full flexibility MIME offers, this example isn't related to the previous ones.

Example 9-12. Simple MIME extensions demonstration

```
<definitions name="MIMEsample"
    targetNamespace="urn:MimeSample"
    xmlns="http://schemas.xmlsoap.org/wsdl/"
    xmlns:tns="urn:MimeSample"
    xmlns:wsdl="http://schemas.xmlsoap.org/wsdl/"
    xmlns:soap="http://schemas.xmlsoap.org/wsdl/soap/"
    xmlns:mime="http://schemas.xmlsoap.org/wsdl/mime/"
    xmlns:xsd="http://www.w3.org/2001/XMLSchema">

  <message name="in">
    <part name="fractal" type="xsd:string" />
    <part name="xrange" type="tns:float-range" />
    <part name="yrange" type="tns:float-range" />
    <part name="resolution" type="tns:resolution" />
  </message>
  <message name="out">
    <part name="return" type="xsd:binary" />
    <part name="graph" type="tns:graph-detail" />
  </message>

  <portType name="GenerateFractal">
    <operation name="MakeFractal">
      <input message="in" />
      <output message="out" />
```

Example 9-12. Simple MIME extensions demonstration (continued)

```
    </operation>
  </portType>

  <binding name="fractal" type="tns:GenerateFractal">
    <soap:operation soapAction="urn:MakeFractal" />
    <input>
      <soap:body use="literal" />
    </input>
    <output>
      <mime:multipartRelated>
        <mime:part>
          <mime:content part="return" type="image/png" />
        </mime:part>
        <mime:part>
          <soap:body part="graph" use="literal" />
        </mime:part>
      </mime:multipartRelated>
    </output>
  </binding>

  <service name="FractalMaker">
    <port name="FractalPort" binding="fractal">
      <soap:address location="http://fractal.com/SOAP" />
    </port>
  </service>
</definitions>
```

While a much longer example, it shows the MIME extensions working side by side with the SOAP extension elements. The WSDL describes a hypothetical fractal calculation engine, in which the input is a SOAP message with information such as the type of fractal to compute, the ranges of calculation on some of the axes, and the resolution of the desired image to return. Rather than try to manage the image into a SOAP data element, the return model uses MIME multipart/related to handle the data that gets sent back to the client. The highlighted section shows how the image is specified using mime:content with a type of image/png. Following that part of the message, the graph element, presumably an XML structure describing the specifics of the fractal space being modeled, is returned as a soap:body content element. The end result is that the graph portion of the message comes across in an easily parsed SOAP envelope, while the image comes in a separate MIME container.

Overloading Operations in WSDL

The overloading of operations is a delicate subject within web-services discussion circles. Different people have different points of view, placing varying support or importance on the concept and its useful application to web services in general, and WSDL in particular. Regardless, it's available using the syntax WSDL provides, and thus may prove a useful addition to the web-services toolbox.

Specifying an overloaded operation requires coordinated definitions in both the declaration of the abstract operations and the binding of the abstract messages to concrete communication models.

Overloading when declaring operations

To demonstrate how to express overloaded operations in WSDL, the examples will leave the WishListCustomer application briefly, going back to the *use.perl.org* journal system—specifically, to the add_entry operation defined in that interface.

For the sake of the example, we will alter the interface slightly. As written, the interface doesn't suit itself to WSDL expression. The add_entry call may be called in one of two ways:

- Exactly two arguments, the journal entry subject and body, respectively.
- A list of key/value pairs, with up to five pairs. The allowed keys are subject, body, posttype, discuss, and tid.

The second calling convention doesn't impose an order on the arguments, which is a problem to represent in WSDL. To accommodate this, the second convention is changed to a single array-of-string type. Example 9-13 shows the first part of the WSDL, the opening definitions tag, the single type-declaration for the array, and the messages the operation will need.

Example 9-13. Initial elements of the WSDL for add_entry

```
<definitions name="UsePerlJournal"
    targetNamespace="http://use.perl.org/Slash/Journal/SOAP"
    xmlns="http://schemas.xmlsoap.org/wsdl/"
    xmlns:tns="http://use.perl.org/Slash/Journal/SOAP"
    xmlns:wsdl="http://schemas.xmlsoap.org/wsdl/"
    xmlns:soap="http://schemas.xmlsoap.org/wsdl/soap/"
    xmlns:enc="http://schemas.xmlsoap.org/soap/encoding/"
    xmlns:xsd="http://www.w3.org/2001/XMLSchema">
  <types>
    <xsd:schema targetNamespace=
                "http://use.perl.org/Slash/Journal/SOAP">
      <xsd:complexType name="ArrayOfString">
        <xsd:complexContent>
          <xsd:restriction base="enc:Array">
            <xsd:attribute ref="enc:arrayType"
                wsdl:arrayType="xsd:string[]" />
          </xsd:restriction>
        </xsd:complexContent>
      </xsd:complexType>
    </xsd:schema>
  </types>
  <message name="TwoElementInput">
    <part name="subject" type="xsd:string" />
    <part name="body" type="xsd:string" />
  </message>
```

Example 9-13. Initial elements of the WSDL for add_entry (continued)

```
<message name="ListInput">
  <part name="list" type="tns:ArrayOfString" />
</message>
<message name="AddEntryResult">
  <part name="return" type="xsd:int" />
</message>
```

Thus far, there is nothing different about this WSDL than was seen in the previous examples. The difference becomes visible in Example 9-14, when the portType is defined for the journal system.

Example 9-14. The portType declaration for the journal

```
<portType name="UsePerlJournalPort">
  <operation name="add_entry">
    <input name="TwoElementCall"
           message="tns:TwoElementInput" />
    <output name="TwoElementReturn"
           message="tns:AddEntryResult" />
  </operation>
  <operation name="add_entry">
    <input name="ListCall" message="tns:ListInput" />
    <output name="ListReturn"
           message="tns:AddEntryResult" />
  </operation>
</portType>
```

In this block, the operation element appears twice, both times naming add_entry as the operation being defined. The blocks differ in their nature from the previous examples in that the input and output elements are given explicit names, rather than relying on the defaults. Because the return types are identical for both calls, naming the output part isn't necessary but is done to avoid confusion. The combinations of operation name and input/output names uniquely identify the ways in which add_entry may be called.

Implementing overloaded operations within bindings

With the abstract definitions in place, the responsibility for exposing the multiinterface add_entry call falls to the binding and service elements. These are shown in Example 9-15.

Example 9-15. The binding and service elements for add_entry

```
<binding name="UsePerlJournalSOAP"
         type="tns:UsePerlJournalPort">
  <soap:binding style="rpc"
                transport=
                "http://schemas.xmlsoap.org/soap/http" />
  <operation name="add_entry">
    <soap:operation
```

Basic WSDL | 207

Example 9-15. The binding and service elements for add_entry (continued)

```
            soapAction=
            "http://use.perl.org/Slash/Journal/SOAP" />
    <input name="TwoElementCall">
      <soap:body use="encoded"
          namespace=
          "http://use.perl.org/Slash/Journal/SOAP"
          encodingStyle=
          "http://schemas.xmlsoap.org/soap/encoding/" />
    </input>
    <output name="TwoElementResult">
      <soap:body use="encoded"
          namespace=
          "http://use.perl.org/Slash/Journal/SOAP"
          encodingStyle=
          "http://schemas.xmlsoap.org/soap/encoding/" />
    </output>
  </operation>
  <operation name="add_entry">
    <soap:operation
        soapAction=
        "http://use.perl.org/Slash/Journal/SOAP" />
    <input name="ListCall">
      <soap:body use="encoded"
          namespace=
          "http://use.perl.org/Slash/Journal/SOAP"
          encodingStyle=
          "http://schemas.xmlsoap.org/soap/encoding/" />
    </input>
    <output name="ListResult">
      <soap:body use="encoded"
          namespace=
          "http://use.perl.org/Slash/Journal/SOAP"
          encodingStyle=
          "http://schemas.xmlsoap.org/soap/encoding/" />
    </output>
  </operation>
</binding>
<service name="UsePerlJournal">
  <port name="UsePerlJournalPort"
        binding="tns:UsePerlJournalSOAP">
    <soap:address location=
                  "http://use.perl.org/soap.pl" />
  </port>
</service>
```

Aside from the specific naming of the input and output elements, these bindings look like the previous examples. But the presence of the names tells the client using this WSDL which of the two abstract models should be paired with the actual operational binding. Fortunately, the rest of the specification for the operations is standard. However, if there was a need to break parts up between soap:body and soap:header elements, or through parts in the MIME extension elements, it would be more important for an application processing the WSDL to know exactly which parts were expected to be present.

These examples have addressed only one part of the *use.perl.org* interface because that was all that was relevant to the concepts here. To be thorough, a full WSDL description (with `documentation` elements) is provided in Appendix E, along with the WSDL from the previous examples. Note that the WSDL doesn't address the cookie-based authentication means that the journal interface uses. Neither the SOAP nor the HTTP extension elements to WSDL provide a way to describe HTTP cookie content in messages.

Why bother with overloading in Perl?

While these examples show how to express overloaded operations in WSDL, the question still remains as to why this should be needed when Perl is so flexible and accommodating in what it can accept in a parameter list.

The answer lies in the fact that the goal of web services is to avoid any language-specific dependencies or issues. Even if a service is written in Perl, it's a plain fact that it will likely be accessed by languages other than Perl. The sample script from Chapter 6, which posted journal entries to *use.perl.org*, sprang from a comment about writing such a utility directly in Emacs Lisp. The Perl solution was designed as a filter—less to promote Perl than to prevent coupling the solution to just Emacs.

Not all languages have the luxury of subroutines that can examine their argument lists in the fashion Perl can. Conversely, a common oversight in developing Perl clients to connect to non-Perl services is to overlook matters such as the naming and formal typing of parameters to service calls. It's in bridging these gaps that WSDL truly proves its worth.

Other WSDL Elements

The examples built through the course of the last few sections didn't cover all the elements and bindings offered by WSDL. There are attributes that provide hints related to parameter order within RPC-like calls, and there is the issue of document-style message encoding, as opposed to RPC. There is also the support for modular document development with the `import` element of WSDL.

Controlling arguments with parameterOrder

When creating bindings for rpc-style encoded messages, it's possible to define the order in which the parameters will appear in the message. The attribute called `parameterOrder` specifies a list of one or more parameter names (`part` elements from the `message` definitions), separated by spaces. It's present in the `operation` tag, and serves as a hint only. It can be safely ignored by readers of the WSDL who aren't concerned with RPC signatures.

When the `parameterOrder` attribute is used, it follows a certain set of rules, according to the W3C WSDL specification:

- The parts order in the attribute reflects the signature of the RPC operation.
- The return parameter for the `output` block isn't included in the list. Its presence is already assumed.
- Parts in the list that appear in both the `input` and `output` blocks are considered *in/out parameters*.
- Parts that appear only in the `input` block are *in parameters*, while those that appear only in the `output` block are *out parameters*.

The `parameterOrder` attribute has no affect on non-RPC document styles.

Document-style message encoding

In the example WSDL, the `soap:binding` element included an attribute called `style`, which was set to the value `rpc`. The default style under WSDL is called `document`. When an operation is describing document-style messages, the name of the operation doesn't get incorporated into the resulting message body, as it does with the `rpc` style.

The document style is meant to indicate that the operation is sending and receiving full documents that have no further need for manipulation. In the case of `rpc` messages, the assumption is that the message describes the parameters of an operation. To indicate this, the message body is made up using the operation name as a containing element. In all the examples so far, the RPC style has been the norm.

The `message` elements used in document-style operation blocks describe the actual message bodies themselves, completely. No additional wrapping is done. The role of the `use` attribute becomes more important in document-styled messages. Message parts that reference elements instead of a schema type have the element wrapping the data, acting as a child of the containing element (Body when the use attribute applies to the `soap:body` tag, and so forth).

Modular WSDL with the import element

One feature of WSDL not yet addressed is the ability to use external sources from within a WSDL specification through the `import` element.

The `import` element in WSDL establishes a link between a location and a namespace. Whether or not the processing of `import` results in the loading of the additional document is dependent on the application. What is required is that the elements and types from the referenced file are available via the namespace used.

A common use of `import` is to allow the XML Schema declarations of types to be kept in a separate file, usable by other schema-driven application besides WSDL. Imagine that the XML Schema declarations from Example 9-3 were kept in a file called wishlisttypes.xsd, the URI for which was based on the service address: *http://localhost:9000/wishlisttypes.xsd*. In place of the types tag in the sample WSDL, the following line can provide access to the type declarations through the rest of the WSDL description:

```
<import namespace="urn:WishListCustomer"
    location="http://localhost:9000/wishlisttypes.xsd" />
```

The value of the namespace attribute in this case is the namespace that covers the description itself. Another namespace can be used, providing there's a way to use it when referencing the types (the label tns has already been set up for the namespace).

The import element may be used multiple times, to pull in definitions from different files or even to associate the same set of definitions with multiple namespaces. It isn't unusual to see a document use import in place of the types element.

WSDL Programming

Because of the relatively young age of WSDL as an accepted technology, the modules and tools available to develop Perl applications with it or based on it are still somewhat scarce. However, its acceptance in other arenas is growing in strength. Most noteworthy is Microsoft's .NET framework, which automatically creates WSDL for a published service and makes it available at a URL related to the address of the base service. Because of this, tools and applications need to be WSDL-aware.

WSDL Schema Support in SOAP::Lite

The SOAP::Lite package currently offers a certain degree of support for basic WSDL specifications. If a schema is provided as either a local file or an accessible resource (such as a HTTP URI), it can create stub routines for a class definition that provides transparent access to the service.

The basic intent of the SOAP::Schema class within SOAP::Lite is to provide transparent support for schemas in a fairly generic manner. At present, it supports only WSDL with limited support for complex types and objects. Unlike the .NET service from Microsoft, there is nothing within SOAP::Lite that provides on-demand generation of WSDL from a published service. A service developer must still produce the description by some other means.

SOAP::Lite client support for WSDL

A SOAP::Lite client can load a service description using the service method on the object, usually at creation-time or during the compilation stage. The following code fragments show different approaches to using the method. The first loads the service description at compile time, when the SOAP::Lite package is being used:

```
use SOAP::Lite service => 'http://localhost/wishlist.wsdl';
```

> ## On-Demand WSDL: The WSDL::Generator Module
>
> A recent addition to the CPAN is the `WSDL::Generator` package from Pierre Denis at Fotango, Ltd. Although still in an alpha stage, the package offers great promise.
>
> Using another alpha-level module by the same author called `Class::Hook`, the generator catches all calls to class methods in the running application. It works using Perl's auto-loading control to intercept calls to unknown routines in unknown packages. `Class::Hook` takes care of transparently locating the code for the requested class and loading it. At the beginning of a call to a method, the hooks record information on the name and class of the method being called, as well as on the nature of the input arguments. Upon return from the method, the returned value is noted and examined. After a thorough run of an application, `WSDL::Generator` should be able to fashion a reasonable WSDL description for the service.
>
> Because of the way `Class::Hook` manipulates calls, using this package directly with `SOAP::Lite` is probably not recommended. However, assuming that the server has a reasonably comprehensive testing application (which of course was part of the project planning, right?) that exercises all the service's features, adding in WSDL generation can be as simple as loading the module and adding a few lines to the test script.

In this case, the service is specified as a HTTP URL, which is fetched by the `SOAP::Schema` class using classes from the LWP package. The service may also be a file on a local filesystem. An alternative to loading the service at the outset is to specify it when creating the client object. This is more flexible because there is less need for compile-time versus runtime issues to be taken into account. The schema source may be a command-line argument or a value computed from external sources:

```
my $schema = shift || 'file:./wishlist.wsdl';
my $soap = SOAP::Lite->service($schema);
```

When a client object uses a service description, there is no need to specify the `uri` or `proxy` values, as most previous client examples did. Those values are contained within the WSDL, in the form of the `targetNamespace` attribute of the `definitions` element and the `location` attribute of the `soap:address` element.

When the `service` method is used, the object created by the `SOAP::Lite` constructor gets blessed into a different class than usual. The name for the class is taken from the `name` attribute of the `service` element itself, and all the methods are derived from the `operation` elements in the `binding` used by the `port` element that defines the SOAP binding. The `service` method can also accept optional `service` name and `portType` name parameters; they can be useful when the WSDL file has multiple `portType` or `service` names.

Calls to the methods made available by the service description return native Perl data types rather than `SOAP::SOM` objects. There's no need to call the `result` method, but the trade-off is that the additional information from a SOAP::SOM object isn't available directly. The self and call methods can access the SOAP::SOM object in this case:

```
my $som = $soap->self->call; # AFTER the call
```

Code-generation based on WSDL

Another way in which the SOAP::Lite package provides support for WSDL is through a tool that comes with the package called stubmaker.pl.

The stubmaker.pl tool is a handy utility that both demonstrates the WSDL support in SOAP::Lite and produces a useful result. When run against a WSDL file or URL that refers to a WSDL resource, it generates a loadable Perl module from the services defined by the WSDL. The resulting file's name is based on the class name that would be selected if the service were loaded directly by a SOAP::Lite client object. The WSDL for the WSDL describing the WishList service would yield a file called WishListCustomer.pm (which would be very different from the file by that name in the software project), while the WSDL for the *use.perl.org* journal system would yield UsePerlJournal.pm. Calling the tool is simple enough:

```
perl stubmaker.pl file:./useperlorg.wsdl
```

Once the stub file has been generated, it can then be used in a client in place of explicitly configuring the client settings:

```
perl -MUsePerlJournal -e 'get_entries(shift, shift)' 1 15
```

The WSDL samples in Appendix E can be fed to the utility to see examples of the code it generates.

SOAP::Schema shortcomings

The schema support code in SOAP::Lite as of version 0.55 is still under development. Support is limited to WSDL alone, and it doesn't support all the more detailed facets of WSDL. It doesn't handle complex types and XML Schema type declarations. Parameters that are declared as belonging in the SOAP header are treated in the parameter list as thought they are meant to be in the body. When applied to the wishlist.wsdl file, the user parameter is consistently passed in the SOAP body, making the resulting stubs unusable when authentication is required.

For simpler schemas, such as the *use.perl.org* journal in which authentication is handled separately through HTTP cookies, the SOAP::Lite support is very effective and useful. It can be presumed that the support will continue to undergo development and enhancement along with the rest of the package.

CHAPTER 10
Service Advertising and Discovery with UDDI

The Universal Description, Discovery, and Integration (UDDI) specifications represent a step beyond simply describing web services. They outline methods by which services can take the initiative to seek out and identify other services with which they want to interact. Relationships ranging from the simply functional to the complete business lifecycle can be established and implemented.

This chapter introduces the basic concepts behind UDDI. The topic is complex enough to warrant its own book, so we encourage you to take the information presented here and use it as a basis for further research.

> Unlike the XML, XML Schema, SOAP, and WSDL protocols described previously, the UDDI protocols are potentially hindered by intellectual property issues. While the final words on IP claims have yet to be written, you should be aware that such claims exist. The technologies described in this chapter aren't under consideration as potential Technical Recommendations by the W3C, at least partly for reasons of possible IP encumberment.

Defining UDDI

UDDI, was initially developed in a partnership between IBM and Microsoft. As more companies have begun adopting the technology, the list of contributors to the design and specification has likewise grown. Where the programmer's reference for Version 1 of the specification listed five authors (two each from IBM and Microsoft, and one author from Ariba, Inc.), the Version 2 programmer's reference drew upon the input of 26 authors working under the direction of 3 editors. The Version 3 specification has 37 authors, working group contributors, and advisory group contributors.

UDDI doesn't define unique encoding or transport protocols. It is designed to be used with XML (as a means of expressing information) and SOAP (as the vehicle by which information is exchanged). Building on these readily available components simplifies the overall design of UDDI and makes developing tools for it that much easier.

Basic UDDI Data Structures

UDDI represents the functionality of a given business entity in terms of a set of data structures. The structures are represented in XML when messages are being exchanged, whether between registries and client applications or between registries themselves. UDDI Version 1 defines four such structures, while the Version 2 specification adds a fifth to the mix.

businessEntity
: The businessEntity structure is the usually the encapsulating element for a UDDI document that describes a business. Within it are informational elements such as name and description, as well as nested instances of businessService.

businessService
: The role of the businessService structure is to describe a single web service provided by the business entity containing it. One or more of these may be contained within a wrapping businessServices element inside the top-level document structure. One instance of this type will have information such as name and description, and just as this is generally contained within an entity description, it nests instances of bindingTemplate.

bindingTemplate
: The bindingTemplate structure is where the technical descriptions of web services begin to take form. Within this structure will be contained references to tModel structures, as well as the first element directly recognizable as being related to a web service: the accessPoint element, which will contain attributes defining the means of access to the service itself (URL, email address, etc.).

tModel
: The usage of the tModel element within a UDDI document is a little different than the other elements. Where the other elements are considered unique to the document by virtue of their hierarchical placement, the tModel is mostly present by reference rather than directly contained within the document itself. The tModel structure describes and references abstract data, ranging from business tax codes to categorical identifiers, to just about anything a tModel can be set up for. Many useful tModel definitions already exist within UDDI registries.

publisherAssertion
: This element is added in UDDI Version 2. It asserts a relationship between two business entities described by their respective UDDI records. The reasoning behind this is to allow large companies or enterprises to publish UDDI for their various subentities, while still being able to show the inherent relationship between the various units. The same relationships can be defined for entities that aren't part of the same larger company but interact together in some other well-defined fashion.

Figure 10-1 shows the relationship between these different structures. While the basic outline shows businessEntity containing businessService and so forth, most of the structures are allowed as sole content in a message. For example, the publishing API that will be described later has calls that create or update just businessService or bindingTemple records. In such cases, a full businessEntity description isn't needed (or accepted).

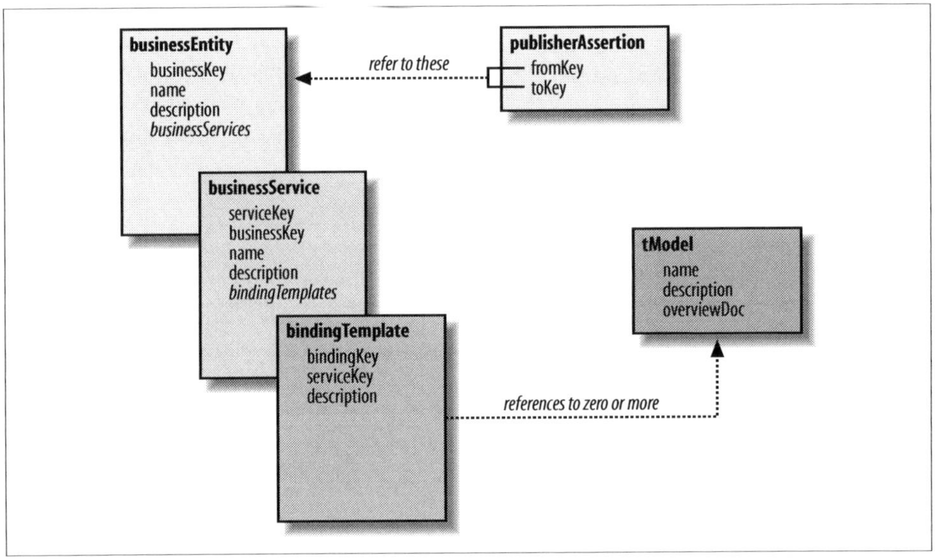

Figure 10-1. The relationship between the UDDI data structures

Special data and source considerations

Before going into the details of the XML structure behind the core UDDI datatypes, it will help to first understand a few basic elements.

Each core type represent data that is kept in a persistent state by the UDDI registries. Because of this, each includes in its schema declaration a unique key as part of the overall structure itself. The keys themselves are simple string data, but they are provided by the registries. These are called Universally Unique Identifiers (UUIDs), and applications are expected to determine them by examining the data structures returned from queries. When publishing new information, the UUID-based attributes are omitted, which tells the registry server to obtain new ones for the new data. Generally, the new UUID values are part of the data returned from a successful call. The strings themselves are long and obfuscated, but fortunately developers aren't expected to construct them explicitly.

Many of the structures contain or reference data values from several established, standardized sources. These are the classifications used to categorize a company's business services when adding data to the registry. These are also the terms used to craft queries to find businesses and business services that provide a particular, desired bit of functionality. The supported codings include North American Industry Code Standard (NAICS), United Nations/Standard Products and Services Classification (UN/SPC), and Dun & Bradstreet D-U-N-S numbers, to name a few.

Details of businessEntity and publisherAssertion

This section will start with `businessEntity`. Because this is the outermost layer of a full business/provider descriptive, it carries the responsibility of describing the business itself. This description ranges from name and contact information to possibly even the "brick and mortar" address.

Example 10-1 shows a sample `businessEntity` structure. For the example itself, the `businessKey` attribute (which holds an instance of the previously mentioned UUID) is much shorter and simpler than real values would be.

Example 10-1. A typical businessEntity

```
<businessEntity businessKey="uuid:3425-1010-321"
                operator="http://www.ibm.com"
                authorizedName="Joe Uddi">
  <discoveryURLs>
    <discoveryURL useType="businessEntity">
      http://soap.ora.com/?uddi
    </discoveryURL>
  </discoveryURLs>
  <name>ORA, Inc.</name>
  <description>
    The #1 provider of books on Open Source and technology
  </description>
  <contacts>
    <contact useType="Account Information">
      <description>
        For account creation and support
      </description>
      <personName>John Q. Perl</personName>
      <email>jqperl@ora.com</email>
    </contact>
  </contacts>
  <businessServices>
    <!-- Here, you would see businessService elements -->
  </businessServices>
  <identifierBag>
    <!-- The data present here will be explained below -->
  </identifierBag>
  <categoryBag>
    <!-- Again, the data here will be explained later -->
  </categoryBag>
</businessEntity>
```

All the optional elements allowed within a businessEntity are shown here (though not all the subelements are present). Some content that is normally present is deferred until later, when other structures are presented.

The opening element here bears the three attributes specific to the element: businessKey, operator and authorizedName. These are explained in Table 10-1.

Table 10-1. Attributes for businessEntity

Attribute	Type	Meaning
authorizedName	String	This is the name of the person who registered the businessEntity structure with the registry site. When publishing data via the publish-side of the API, this shouldn't be included.
businessKey	UUID	The UUID for this record. When creating the business entity's record initially, this shouldn't be in the publishing API call. Later, when this record is used to make updates, this attribute acts as the needed key for the operation.
operator	String	This indicates the registry hosting this record and is usually given as a URL (though it isn't required to be). As with authorizedName, this is filled in on the registry side and shouldn't be present when using the API's publish functions.

The first element present here is the discoveryURLs container. This is an optional element that provides alternate sources for the current document in the form of one or more discoveryURL elements. When the business data structures are saved, the registry generates URLs for them and appends them (when necessary) to the list that gets used for this element. This allows fetching specific instances of a businessEntity structure. The useType attribute determines the type of structure pointed to by the URL: a businessEntity or businessEntityExt (covered later).

The other initial tags of the structure are those that provide the description information on the business itself. The name and description elements are fairly obvious in their role, and name is required. The contacts container is also very simple in nature, it contains one or more instances of a contact record.

The role of the contact record is to provide information on a single point of contact within the company. This contact may be an email address, a phone number, or even a postal address. The nature of the structure is flexible. First, the contact tag has an optional attribute useType that's free form in its content; it indicates to the reader what the type of contact information is. In this example, it reads Account Information, but the content can also be simple abbreviations following an agreed-upon syntax for machine processing. Of the subelements of contact, only personName is required. It should indicate the person to whom the contact record is referring. The description, phone (not shown), and email elements are all free-form string data as well, and all are optional. The last optional element for a contact record is address, which presents general address information such as for postal mailing. A contact structure may have more than one address structure within it.

The details of the address structure are slightly different between the two versions of UDDI. In UDDI 1, the structure is simple: the address tag has two optional attributes, useType and sortCode. The useType attribute is purely informational, as with contact itself. The sortCode attribute is open-ended in nature, intended to help sort multiple addresses for human-readable presentation. It can be numeric, alphabetic, or an indicator of which of the addressLine records should be used for sorting. UDDI doesn't define a specific behavior. Contained within the address tag is a sequence of one or more addressLine elements that contain simple text information. Each element may also have useType and sortCode attributes, which have the same meaning within the scope of the lines for a given address. Because UDDI defines no specifics for sorting or using sortCode, it treats the ordering of the addressLine elements as significant, and they are guaranteed to be preserved within a registry. In UDDI 1, addressLine elements have a suggested line-length limit of 40 characters.

The type and content of data in a UDDI 2 address structure is very similar to what was just described but has some extensions and difference. First, both the useType and sortCode attributes are present with the same meaning as in UDDI 1. In addition, though, there may be a tModelKey attribute present, that refers to a previously defined tModel structure. These are defined later, but for now it is enough to know that such a referenced structure makes all the data fields in the tModel available to the address structure. This leads to the changes to addressLine in UDDI 2; it no longer uses useType and sortCode as attributes. Instead, keyName and keyValue may be used. The contents of the addressLine elements are still treated in the same way, and their order is still preserved by the UDDI registry when the data record is saved. Additionally, rather than having a suggested 40-character limit to the lines, they have a mandatory 80-character limit. When the opening address tag bears a tModelKey attribute, the keyValue and keyName attributes are combined with that value to create a keyed reference (explained later, in the section on the tModel structure). When no tModelKey is present, the attributes are free form.

Moving from the informational elements, the businessServices tag is a container for zero or more of the businessService structures detailed in the next section. No attributes are present here.

Finally, the identifierBag and categoryBag elements allow a businessEntity to refer to identifying structures or categorizations that may be used in queries to find the business. More on these will be explained later, when tModel structures and references are covered.

While businessEntity has the widest range of elements, publisherAssertion is generally the smallest of the structures. This structure will have three elements, called fromKey, toKey, and keyedReference. Both fromKey and toKey refer to specific entity records and contain the UUID that identifies them. The keyedReference is an empty element that must have three attributes: tModelKey, keyName, and keyValue. Together, the three values reference a tModel structure that describes the nature of the relationship between the two business entities referred to by the previous elements.

A publisherAssertion record is considered validated only when both business entities publish the same relationship assertion, with the appropriate UUIDs in the fromKey and toKey elements. In some cases, the same owner may control both entity records, such as when there are diverse service offerings from the same company. The publisherAssertion can associate these, and in such cases, the registry recognizes that the same company owns both businessEntity records and requires only the one assertion.

Details of businessService

The businessService structure presents a web service (possibly one of many) provided by the business entity it's associated with. Contained within a businessService structure is information on the type of web service, binding information for the service, categories it belongs to, and so forth. Example 10-2 shows a businessService structure.

Example 10-2. The businessService structure

```
<businessService serviceKey="uuid:1800-2655-328"
                 businessKey="uuid:3425-1010-321">
  <name>WishList Book Service</name>
  <description>
    Manage and even order the books you really want!
  </description>
  <bindingTemplates>
    <!-- Here will be bindingTemplate instances -->
  </bindingTemplates>
  <categoryBag>
    <!-- Similar to the role in businessEntity, above -->
  </categoryBag>
</businessService>
```

The first thing to note is that the businessService structure itself is much simpler than the businessEntity structure. Working from the bottom to the top this time, the categoryBag as seen here is of the same structure as for Example 10-1 and will be deferred until referencing is discussed. The bindingTemplates element is a container for the bindingTemplate structure covered in the next section. The name and description elements are similar in their role to the entity structure, and name is also a required element here.

The attributes that are specific to this element are shown in Table 10-2.

Table 10-2. Attributes for businessService

Name	Type	Description
serviceKey	UUID	This is a required attribute and contains the UUID that uniquely refers to this service record. When creating a service record with the publishing API routines, the attribute should be empty.
businessKey	UUID	When a service record is being viewed independent of the entity record it belongs to, this attribute maintains the connection back to the owning entity.

The `businessKey` attribute is needed only when the `businessService` record is the whole of the message. Each service must be associated with the correct entity record. When the top-most element is `businessEntity`, there is an implicit ownership relation, and the key isn't needed. When just fetching or updating a service record, it is needed to indicate the owning entity record.

Details of bindingTemplate

It is with the `bindingTemplate` structures that the web-services aspect of things begins to take shape. Within this element may be found the address of the server, and perhaps pointers to a description such as a WSDL resource for the service. In addition, by referencing and parameterizing `tModel` structures, a wider variety of information may also be made available. Example 10-3 shows a `bindingTemplate` structure.

Example 10-3. The bindingTemplate

```
<bindingTemplate bindingKey="uuid:uuid:3425-1010-220"
                 serviceKey="uuid:1800-2655-328">
  <description>Wishlist SOAP Binding</description>
  <accessPoint URLType="http">
    http://localhost:9000
  </accessPoint>
  <tModelInstanceDetails>
    <tModelInstanceInfo tModelKey="uuid:FEEB-1E">
      <description>
        One tModel instance reference
      </description>
      <instanceDetails>
        <description></description>
        <overviewDoc>
          <description>Point to the WSDL</description>
          <overviewURL>
            http://localhost/wishlist.wsdl
          </overviewURL>
        </overviewDoc>
        <instanceParms>
          <!-- Many different things could go here -->
        </instanceParms>
      </instanceDetails>
    </tModelInstanceInfo>
  </tModelInstanceDetails>
</bindingTemplate>
```

Starting with the similarities, the bindingKey and serviceKey should be intuitive. While bindingKey serves to uniquely identify the binding record itself, the serviceKey attribute is used only when the template is in a document by itself, and thus needs to specify what businessService structure it belongs to. This is the same role played by the businessKey attribute in the service structure in the previous section.

The optional description element is also present, but for this structure there is no naming element. The description element is ubiquitous throughout UDDI as has been shown, and will continue to appear in other structures.

Following the description, the user has a choice of two elements: accessPoint or hostingRedirector. This example uses the accessPoint element to provide a HTTP URL. The URLType attribute informs the reader what the content of the element represents. Besides the http value, it can also be mailto, https, ftp, fax, phone, or other. UDDI is meant to be flexible enough to provide information even on nonelectronic forms of contact.

The hostingRedirector element is used when a template means to simply refer to another one, one that provides a service that matches the current criteria but is indexed and stored under other headings. If this element is used instead of accessPoint, it is an empty element with a single attribute, bindingKey. The attribute contains a UUID value that points to a different bindingTemplate. The new template should be retrieved and used in place of the current one.

With the tModelInstanceDetails container, the template can reference any number of tModel records. While this element is required to be present, it can be empty. If it has content, that content must be one or more tModelInstanceInfo structures. The example provides a hint at what these look like, but they will be described in greater detail in the next section.

tModel, tModelInstanceInfo, and referencing

The tModel is the hardest-working UDDI data structure and the one least documented. When researching UDDI, most references to the nature and role of the tModel read nearly identically, in many cases simply quoting the specification and leaving the explanation at that. But there is a clear and intuitive way to regard the tModel, what it is and what role it plays in UDDI as a whole.

Example 10-4 shows a tModel structure. Note that this example isn't as relevant as the others were for their sections, because a tModel is defined more by the context in which it gets referred to than by the actual data stored in the UDDI registry.

Example 10-4. A tModel structure

```
<tModel tModelKey="uuid:FEEB-1E"
        operator="http://www.ibm.com"
        authorizedName="tModel tModerator">
   <name>tModel Sample</name>
```

Example 10-4. A tModel structure (continued)

```
    <description>A sample tModel with no meaning</description>
    <overviewDoc>
      <description>Point to the definition</description>
      <overviewURL>http://localhost</overviewURL>
    </overviewDoc>
    <identifierBag />
    <categoryBag />
</tModel>
```

Let's discuss the attributes first. The tModelKey is a UUID that identifies the structure itself. The operator and authorizedName attributes have the same function they did in businessEntity and are optional. However, a tModel structure doesn't belong to a specific entity or service description, so there is no referencing key to a parent structure here. A tModel structure doesn't ever appear directly in one of the previous structures; it's referred only by reference (except when it is being published or updated, of course).

The required name and optional description elements are present here as well, with the same role they play in other structures. Also present are the identifierBag and categoryBag container elements. Because tModel instances are searchable as well as any other types, these allow for further refinement of how a given tModel may be found in a client's search. Those two will be revisited shortly.

The overviewDoc element is where the actual description of the data model is provided, if so desired by the record's author. Another opportunity for description, and then an overviewURL element that may point to almost anything: a WSDL description if the tModel is describing a type of service, or perhaps a XML Schema document if it is describing content structure. The overviewDoc element may contain just the description, or it may not be present at all.

In fact, a tModel is more like a *type* specification than a structured part of something in particular. The actual relevance and meaning behind a given tModel is dependent on the context its reference appears in. In an entity structure, the models referenced in the identifier and category bags are used to associate the business and its services with one or more well-defined classifications. In contrast, the binding templates that accompany a service description use models to describe details such as the protocol and address of the service or how the service's API (such as a WSDL description) may be obtained. It wouldn't be fair to compare a tModel to a class, but without type information all information, in an applications memory is just binary data. It is the application of typing that tells an integer from a string pointer, and a tModel works in a similar fashion. Take the following snippet, for example:

```
    <keyedReference tModelKey="uuid:EA8-69-C0C5"
                    keyName="D-U-N-S"
                    keyValue="18002255288" />
```

The keyedReference element is the datatype that appears within identiferBag and catagoryBag elements. The example is a hypothetical (both the UUID and value are fictional) specification of a Dun & Bradstreet D-U-N-S classification number. The model pointed to by tModelKey is expected to explain what the keyValue attribute actually means. The keyName is like a variable name; it's there as an identifier rather than an active part. The actual tModel record for a D-U-N-S number would explain, probably with a pointer to a relevant web site, what numbers indicate what business types. Without that explanation, the meaning of the 11-digit value can be anything from a database key to a phone number.

Referencing of tModel structures is present at almost all levels of UDDI. Recall the identifierBag and categoryBag elements that were documented with the entity and service structures (and are also allowed in a tModel structure as well). These are used to contain instances of the keyedReference element shown earlier. As the snippet illustrates, this is an empty element with three attributes: tModelKey,* keyName, and keyValue. The name and value keys tell what the "parameter" is called, and what value it holds.

> Some of the examples so far have shown empty identifierBag and/or categoryBag elements. This is allowable in UDDI Version 1, but it's disallowed in Version 2 of UDDI.

In Version 2 of UDDI, the keyedReference element is also used inside a publisherAssertion structure to reference a tModel that has been set up to define the relationship between the business entities. While all three attributes in the reference element are required, the keyName and keyValue may be empty if they aren't needed in a particular case.

The other place in which referencing of tModel structures is found is in the tModelInstanceInfo structure. This structure appears in the container element called tModelInstanceDetails, which is part of the binding structure. The instance structure is different from a straight reference in that it references the abstract concept, as opposed to using the abstract to lend meaning to a specific value. Example 10-5 shows this concept applied to providing a reference to a WSDL description.

Example 10-5. Referencing the tModel for WSDL description

```
<tModelInstanceInfo tModelKey="uuid:486466966884">
  <instanceDetails>
    <overviewDoc>
      <description>
        This example references the description of how
```

---

* The tModelKey attribute is actually optional, because this element can also be used to express more generic key/value pairs.

Example 10-5. Referencing the tModel for WSDL description (continued)

```
        a WSDL service definition is provided to the
        client. The tModel referenced should have been
        created already, with the URI of the WSDL file.
      </description>
      <overviewURL>
        http://localhost/wishlist.wsdl
      </overviewURL>
    </overviewDoc>
    <instanceParms>
      http://localhost/parms.txt
    </instanceParms>
  </instanceDetails>
</tModelInstanceInfo>
```

In this example, the instance info structure refers to a tModel that defines the interface by referring to a URI where the WSDL file can be retrieved. There's no need to define a key/value pair just to refer to the existing model structure so that clients of the service can find the description. The only thing that must appear is the tModelKey attribute, which refers to the tModel by its UUID. There is allowance for an optional description element (not shown in this example) followed by the instanceDetails element. This element contains information mainly for end users more than for automated clients. It allows the publisher of the record to make notes about what he is referring to and why. The overviewDoc block allows a description and a URL to be provided.

Following the overview information is the instanceParms element. This element is very badly documented in the UDDI specifications. In Version 1, the content is defined as either a URL or an XML string, which is to be namespace-qualified into a namespace other than that of UDDI itself. But the XML Schema that describes the structure of the UDDI elements forbids embedded XML. This was noted and corrected in the Version 2 specification. Here, a simple URL is shown as an example. The role and content aren't defined by UDDI; they are negotiated between clients and providers. The URI may be line-delimited key/value pairs, an XML Schema, etc.

Publish and Query Interfaces

UDDI uses SOAP as the actual communications-level protocol for managing requests and responses between clients and servers. This is helpful because it keeps end users from having to learn yet another protocol for their applications.

The programming interface is roughly divided into two sections: the routines that publish data to a registry and those that query a registry for information. We limit coverage here to basic details because of the complex nature of the elements involved. For greater depth, refer to the Programmer API documents on the UDDI home page at *http://www.uddi.org*.

The querying routines

The API routines that make up the querying interface are designed to enable applications that generally follow one of three models: browse, drill-down, and invocation. The routines themselves are summarized in Table 10-3 (with a note for those that are only in UDDI Version 2).

Table 10-3. The UDDI query routines

Name	Description
find_binding	Looks for bindingTemplate records based on a serviceKey passed with the request. The matching records are contained within a bindingDetails element.
find_business	Finds business entity records based on the given search criteria and returns a list structure (under the element businessList) upon success. The contents reference the matched records and summarize their service entries as well.
find_relatedBusinesses (UDDI 2 only)	Finds business records based on mutual relationships, as given by publisherAssertion records.
find_service	Finds service records for a given businessKey value. Returns results in a container fashion similar to the previous calls.
find_tModel	Locates a list of tModel entries that match a given criteria.
get_bindingDetail	Finds and returns specific bindingDetail structures based on UUIDs specified in a bindingKey argument. Multiple keys may be specified.
get_businessDetail	Finds and returns businessEntity records based on businessKey as an argument.
get_businessDetailExt	Finds and returns extended entity data for businesses. Generally returns the same data as the previous call but may add extra data if the source of the record supports it.
get_serviceDetail	Finds and returns businessService records, as with previous API calls.
get_tModelDetail	Retrieves tModel records based on requested UUIDs, as per previous calls.

Each name represents a SOAP call, and can be managed and deployed using the basic classes from SOAP::Lite. Fortunately, as will be covered in a later section, the SOAP::Lite package provides some classes specifically geared towards UDDI.

The set of query routines fall into two categories: those that search based on criteria, and those that pull specific records based on known UUIDs. The find_* names all perform searches; the get_* names fetch specific data. The former group is used mainly for locating data based on a set of parameters, while the latter set is generally used for checking registry data against internal caches to catch updates. It doesn't make good design sense to repeat searches over and over, but it may be necessary to check if the owner of a record has recently updated it.

Using findQualifiers in calls

When using the find_* routines, applications can manage the sorting and the nature of the searching itself using one or more *search qualifiers*, which are managed using the findQualifiers element, an optional parameter to the find_* set. If present, it must be the first element in the call structure (appearing before any of the call-specific parameters). The contents are zero or more `findQualifier` elements, each of which contain one qualifier from the set detailed in Table 10-4.

Table 10-4. The set of findQualifier values

Name	Function
`exactNameMatch`	The default when matching names is to match loosely on the leftmost word in the name fields (up to the first whitespace character). This qualifier instructs the operation to match the name exactly.
`caseSensitiveMatch`	The default behavior of name-matching is case-insensitive. This qualifier instructs the operation to consider word case when matching.
`sortByNameAsc`	When there is more than one record in the set of results, the list is sorted based on the sort qualifiers. This qualifier specifies that the records should be sorted by name, in ascending order. This is only applicable when all records have a name element at their top level. This is the default when all records have name elements.
`sortByNameDesc`	Sorts the records by name, but in descending order. Applicable only when all records have name elements.
`sortByDateAsc`	Sorts the records in ascending order of the date on which they were last updated. This is the default when name sorting isn't applicable, and is also the secondary-sort criteria within records with identical names.
`sortByDateDesc`	Date-sorts the records in descending order.

Multiple qualifiers may be given for a find operation. Their order of precedence is simple: the *Match qualifiers (which may be logically combined) have the highest precedence. Following those are the name-sort qualifiers, which are mutually exclusive (but have the same precedence). Last are the date-sort qualifiers; these are also mutually exclusive but share the same precedence level.

The UDDI Version 2 specification added five more qualifiers,[*] shown in Table 10-5. These interact with the search keys that are specified in category and identifier bags (via `keyedReference`) that may be passed in some of the find_* calls. By default, all such keys are treated as part of a logical AND evaluation; that is, all must be true (matched) in order for the search to select the record.

Table 10-5. findQualifier values added in UDDI 2

Name	Function
`orLikeKeys`	Keys that are considered similar to those that reference the same `tModel` in the reference element. This qualifier causes all similar keys to be logically OR'd together, allowing for a choice of one from a set of like keys. Keys (or sets of keys) that reference other `tModel` definitions are AND'd with the result from the set.

---

[*] Initially, there were six new qualifiers, but the sixth (soundex, to use the Soundex algorithm to match strings) was dropped in the third errata to the v2 specification.

Table 10-5. findQualifier values added in UDDI 2 (continued)

Name	Function
orAllKeys	This qualifier is the opposite of the default behavior. It instructs the search to use a logical OR operation on all the search keys in place of the AND. This differs from the previous qualifier in that similarity in groups doesn't come into play.
combineCategoryBags	Used only in a call to find_business, this qualifier tells the search operation to combine all the categoryBag groups for a entity, including those contained within its subelements. This means a search key matches if there is a match in a service record owned by the entity.
serviceSubset	This is also limited to the find_business call. In this case, the category search keys are compared only to the categoryBag elements in the service structures. Any category data at the entity level isn't considered.
andAllKeys	Describes the default behavior; included in the set for completeness.

The orLikeKeys qualifier applies the grouping to all sets of keys that reference a common tModel. This enables queries that search for any one of several from one type-model, and any one of several from a second type model, and so on. The second set of qualifiers expands the application's control over the search itself. The set from UDDI 1 offered only a small amount of control, focusing more on presentation.

The orAllKeys, orLikeKeys, and andAllKeys qualifiers are mutually exclusive and share the same precedence as the *Match qualifiers from the first set. The combineCategoryBags and serviceSubset (which are also mutually exclusive) are orthogonal to the rest of the qualifiers, making their actual precedence unimportant.

Publishing and editing business information

In addition to making queries against a UDDI registry, the interface also allows for publishing information about a business and editing (or deleting) information already published.

The routines in this part of the API fall (roughly) into three categories: those for creating and updating data, those for deleting existing data, and those for security and general purposes. Table 10-6 shows the general-purpose calls.

Table 10-6. Security-related and general API calls

Name	Description
discard_authToken	Informs the registry server that the authToken (obtained using get_authToken) is no longer needed.
get_authToken	All operations in the publishing API require an authentication token, or authToken. This call obtains one such token, using the user ID and credentials the registry server requires.
get_registeredInfo	Gets an abbreviated list of all the businessEntity and tModel keys the authenticated user controls.

Table 10-6. Security-related and general API calls (continued)

Name	Description
get_assertionStatusReport (UDDI 2 only)	Gets a status report on publisher assertions controlled by the authenticated user. Used to manage both the established and the tentative (awaiting both parties) assertions.
get_publisherAssertions	(UDDI 2 only) Returns a list of all publisherAssertion records controlled by the authenticated user.

The main purpose of this group of functions is to manage authentication tokens. These two API calls are provided in the specification for the sake of registry servers that don't provide their own, more specialized authentication interface. The API itself requires only that the rest of the publishing-oriented routines have an authentication token of some sort. The exact nature of obtaining such a token is up to the server implementation. A server may use HTTP headers or even place authentication credentials in SOAP headers (as demonstrated in the Chapter 8 examples).

The routines that save UDDI data are listed in Table 10-7. These can create new data and make changes to existing data. The structures passed in to these calls signify which behavior (create or update) should be done by the presence or absence of the appropriate key attribute.

Table 10-7. The UDDI creation API routines

Name	Description
add_publisherAssertions (UDDI 2 only)	Adds one or more assertions to the list of those controlled by the publisher.
save_binding	Saves a new bindingTemplate or updates an existing one, depending on the presence (or absence) of the bindingKey attribute.
save_business	Saves or updates a businessEntity record.
save_service	Saves or updates a businessService record.
save_tModel	Saves or updates a tModel record.
set_publisherAssertions (UDDI 2 only)	Saves a complete set of assertions for a publisher account. Any existing assertions in the list are replaced, and any existing assertions that aren't in the list are deleted from the registry.

Each save_* function behaves in an essentially identical fashion. All require an authInfo element as the first parameter, containing the token given to the application by the server. Following this element is one or more of the appropriate structure. If the structure is being created by the operation, the key attribute for the type must be empty. Note that those structures that are themselves tied to other containers (the relationship between binding and service, or service and entity) must have the correct key for their parent structure present. This must be present whether creating or updating. A structure can be moved from one container to another by specifying a new value in the parent key.

When multiple structures are passed to a single save_* call, their processing order isn't actually defined, though in most cases they are processed in the order in which they appear.

The add_publisherAssertions and set_publisherAssertions calls are used for managing the assertions of the given user. Adding assertions is similar to the saving routines covered earlier. After a first parameter of authInfo, the call provides one or more publisherAssertion structures. Each is added to the publisher's set of assertions but aren't made public until the owner of the second entity publishes a corresponding assertion (an error results from the call if neither of the referenced businessEntity structures is owned by the publisher making the call). Such tentative assertions are visible through the get_assertionStatusReport routine from the previous table. The set_publisherAssertions call is slightly different in that it makes potentially sweeping changes to the publisher's collection of assertions. In one call it is possible to add, update, and delete assertions. All assertions provided in the call (after the initial authInfo element) are added if they don't exist, or updated if they match (by the combination of fromKey and toKey) an existing assertion. Any existing assertions that aren't in the provided list are deleted.

The last group of functions are listed in Table 10-8. These calls remove data from a registry.

Table 10-8. The deletion API routines for UDDI

Name	Description
delete_binding	Removes the bindingTemplate structures specified (by their keys) from the registry.
delete_business	Removes businessEntity structures.
delete_publisherAssertions (UDDI 2 only)	Removes one or more assertions from the table that exists for the publisher. This requires the full assertion structure because there is no associated key.
delete_service	Removes businessService structures.
delete_tModel	Effectively deletes tModel structures by hiding them from the find_tModel search routine. tModel structures aren't actually deleted because references to them may still exist. Even after "deletion," a get_tModelDetail call can be made on the UUID and get the details of the "deleted" tModel.

As you'd expect, all deletion routines also require the authInfo element as their first parameter. All but the deletion of assertions use only the keys (UUIDs) of the records to be deleted.

Further reading

In addition to providing greater detail about the API routines, the formal specification documents from the UDDI web site also include detailed explanations of the types of errors that can occur from various operations, as well as definitions for the SOAP-level faults an application can expect to see in the event of such errors.

The documents are downloadable in both PDF and Microsoft Word formats, except for XML Schema documents, which are plain text. For UDDI Version 2, the set of documents includes errata to the Data Structures document and the Programmer's API document. Even with a good programming toolkit available, it is worthwhile to have these documents handy for reference.

Programming with UDDI::Lite

If the explanation of UDDI thus far has seemed short on examples, it's simply because there is no need to handcode UDDI applications. The SOAP::Lite module provides UDDI support in the form of the UDDI::Lite class and supporting elements. Because UDDI itself uses ordinary SOAP methods for communication, working with the toolkit elements will be as familiar and comfortable as the previous SOAP::Lite examples. The classes and their methods are also present in the reference presented in Appendix C.

At present (as of SOAP::Lite Version 0.55), UDDI support is primarily limited to version 1, with no available hooks to the new API routines in Version 2.

The UDDI::Lite Family

The classes in the UDDI support set all inherit from their SOAP::Lite counterparts, which means that their interfaces are very similar. Most of the application-level work is done through objects instantiated from the UDDI::Lite class. The new method, the constructor, takes the same style of arguments as the constructor for SOAP::Lite. Like that class, most methods return the object reference upon success, to enable chaining of method calls.

The UDDI::SOM and UDDI::Data classes are made available for managing the response objects and the encoding of input parameters, respectively. The UDDI::Data class also manages an object-oriented interface to the UDDI structures that are returned from calls. This object model is covered in greater detail later on.

The UDDI support extends to two more classes, UDDI::Serializer and UDDI::Deserializer. These classes inherit from and extend the functionality of their SOAP::Lite counterparts with UDDI-specific considerations. As with the SOAP classes, these are rarely needed for use within an application. They are instantiated by the UDDI::Lite object behind the scenes.

Connecting through UDDI::Lite

Using the UDDI::Lite class for connections is very like using SOAP::Lite. The simple application in Example 10-6 shows the basic steps of connection to and communicating with a UDDI registry. It simply calls find_business with an initial letter 26 times (from A to Z), printing the number of businesses under each initial, and listing them. (Note that running this application may produce considerable output.)

Example 10-6. A simple UDDI application

```perl
#!/usr/bin/perl

use strict;
use UDDI::Lite;

my $uddi =
    UDDI::Lite->proxy('http://uddi.microsoft.com/inquire');

for my $letter ('A' .. 'Z') {
    my $results = $uddi->find_business(name => $letter)
                       ->result;
    my @list = $result->businessInfos->businessInfo;
    printf "%c: (%d)\n", $letter, scalar @list;
    printf "\t%s\n", $_->name for (@list);
}

exit;
```

In this example, the object-model that UDDI::Data implements is first illustrated. The variable $results is assigned the data from the deserialized message returned by the registry. When calling find_business, the return message is an outer businessInfos container tag, within which will be zero or more businessInfo elements with abbreviated content from the businessEntity record. Regardless of the type of message, the model is the same: the reference returned by the UDDI::SOM::result method is blessed into the UDDI::Data package, and from that reference the element names may be called as methods.

Getting and reading data from UDDI::Data

The following XML fragment is the basic structure returned by the find_business call from Example 10-6:

```xml
<businessList generic="1.0" xmlns="urn:uddi-org:api">
  <businessInfos>
    <businessInfo>
      <name>...</name>
      ...
    </businessInfo>
    <businessInfo>
      ...
    </businessInfo>
  </businessInfos>
</businessList>
```

When the application got the UDDI::Data object that resulted from the deserialization of that structure, the only element at the top level was businessList. At this level, the $results variable is primarily useful for referencing the first level of XML tags, businessInfos itself. If the attributes are needed, they can be accessed at this point with the attr method.

However, the object that $results->businessInfos returns is much more useful. For one thing, if the element is a leaf tag (one containing no subelements), the value method returns the content. If there are any attributes present, the attr method returns a hash reference containing them and their values. Each call to such a tag method returns a UDDI::Data object. In the example, rather than save the intermediate object, the application just uses the new reference to call a tag method for the next level, the one that returns the data associated with the businessInfo elements contained within the outer element.

As with the data-manipulation methods in SOAP::Lite, those in this instance are sensitive to being called in a list or scalar context. In the example, the call to the businessInfo method is done in a list context, ensuring that all such subelements of businessInfos are gathered into the array variable @list. One element present in the structure at this level is the name, which contains the business name as presented in its entity record within the registry. For the simple application, that's all that's interesting. To print, the for loop iterates over the collected objects in @list and calls the name method on each.

Another thing this section's example brings to light is the fact that the structures returned from the find_* routines don't always closely resemble the basic data structures. Table 10-9 lists the container tags and their contents for the various find_*routines.

Table 10-9. Structure of messages from UDDI calls

Call	Returns
find_binding	bindingDetail container with zero or more bindingTemplate structures.
find_business	businessList container, which holds one businessInfos container. Within that are zero or more businessInfo elements, each of which contains name, description, and a serviceInfos container. The container holds zero or more serviceInfo elements, which have serviceKey attributes and contain name elements for the service structures associated with the entity record.
find_relatedBusinesses (UDDI 2 only)	relatedBusinessesList container, with one relatedBusinessesInfos container within it. This holds zero or more relatedBusinessInfo structure. These contain name, description, businessKey (as an element rather than an attribute), and up to two sharedRelationships elements. These reference the business relationship through keyedReference record.
find_service	serviceList container element with one serviceInfos container. This holds zero or more serviceInfo structures as detailed previously.
find_tModel	tModelList containing a single tModelInfos container. This holds zero or more tModelInfo elements, which have tModelKey attributes and contain name elements for the tModel structures they refer to.

Fortunately, the returned values from the get_* routines are much clearer. Each returns basic UDDI data structures, the number of which depends on how many keys were passed in the request and how many keys were found in the registry.

Showing More Detail for a Business

This section presents a more in-depth sample application that uses UDDI::Lite to display a greater amount of detail on one or more business, based on command-line arguments. The application itself is too long to list here, but the full code (with annotations) is provided in Appendix E.

The idea

The premise for this sample application is simple: given a business name (or partial name), dump the more relevant information from the UDDI registry in a human-readable format. The goal is to become familiar with both the structures of UDDI, and the use of the UDDI::Lite toolkit itself.

While the application can peer down as deeply as the tModel structures themselves, it goes only as deep as the bindings for now. You should take the script and experiment with it, adding the additional functionality as desired. Another useful facet of the example is to run it with full tracing on (using the trace interface defined in Chapter 6). Because the UDDI::Lite class directly inherits from SOAP::Lite, it may also use the SOAP::Trace facility with the same interface. A script can be run with tracing without having to modify the script; it can simply be passed as an argument to the Perl command itself:

```
perl -MUDDI::Lite=trace,debug application [ arguments ]
```

Recalling the debug tracing level from Chapter 6, it's especially useful because it shows the SOAP envelopes for messages, which can help you understand the structure of data being returned by the registry.

Using UDDI::Lite with auto-dispatch

This application takes advantage of the auto-dispatch capabilities of the SOAP::Lite toolkit. It also chooses to import some handy utility functionality (such as data-building routines name and findQualifiers) from UDDI::Data. Let's examine some lines from the first part of the application:

```
use Text::Wrap qw(wrap $columns);
use Getopt::Long 'GetOptions';
use UDDI::Lite +autodispatch =>
            proxy => 'http://uddi.microsoft.com/inquire',
            import => 'UDDI::Data';

GetOptions(\%opts, qw(case exact showkeys)) and
    $name = shift or
```

```
            die "USAGE: $0 [ --case ] [ --exact ] [ --showkeys ] " .
                "name\n";
```

The application not only uses the UDDI::Lite classes, but it also uses Getopt::Long for command-line parsing and Text::Wrap for simple text formatting. Here are the options it recognizes:

--case

Tells the application to make the name lookup case-sensitive. The default in UDDI is case-insensitive.

--exact

By default, the UDDI registry takes the name given as an argument and matches it as a partial string to records in their database. This option forces the match to be exact.

--showkeys

Because the UUID keys have no real human-readable meaning, the application doesn't display them by default. This option requests that the keys be printed along with the other data.

The options (except for --showkeys) can create a set of findQualifier elements for the eventual call to find_business. This segment creates the parameters for the call:

```
@qualifiers = ('sortByNameAsc');
push(@qualifiers, 'exactNameMatch')        if ($opts{exact});
push(@qualifiers, 'caseSensitiveMatch') if ($opts{case});
push(@params,
     findQualifiers(findQualifier(@qualifiers)),
     name($name));
```

This is simple logic: the routines findQualifiers, findQualifier, and name are imported from UDDI::Data. In fact, the sortByNameAsc qualifier isn't actually needed, because it's the default behavior. However, it simplifies the logic to have it here and keeps the application from passing an empty list of qualifiers to the call.

Making the call itself and iterating over the list of businesses returned by the registry are equally as simple:

```
my $result = find_business(@params);
dump_business($_)
    for ($result->businessInfos->businessInfo);
```

Note that because auto-dispatching is used, the return value from find_business is already converted to a UDDI::Data object. As with the earlier example, the interim businessInfos containment structure is quietly skipped over, with the application going directly for the list of businessInfo structures. The actual processing of most of the information is simple. While the dump_business routine isn't very special, it calls a routine named dump_service that deserves some attention.

Recalling Table 10-9, the structures returned from find_business aren't complete businessEntity records. For this application, they return enough business-level information to suit the purpose (the name and description fields). They also provide limited information on the services, but in this case it isn't enough for the application's purpose. Consequently, the dump_service routine must take what information it does get and use that to retrieve the full structure:

```
sub dump_service {
    my $svc = shift;

    my ($key, $service);

    $key = $svc->serviceKey;
    return unless
        $service = get_serviceDetail($key);
    $service = $service->businessService;
    print '   Service: ', $service->name, "\n";
    print '      uuid:', $service->serviceKey, "\n"
        if $SHOWKEYS;
    if (my $description = $service->description) {
        $columns = 64;
        print wrap("\t    ", "\t    ", $description), "\n";
    }
    print "\n";
    dump_template($_)
        for ($service->bindingTemplates->bindingTemplate);
}
```

The emphasized lines in this segment show where the incoming data, which is a UDDI::Data object that describes a serviceInfo structure, is turned into the key through which the businessService record is retrieved. As a fortunate turn, this structure contains the bindingTemplate records in full, so the dump_template routine won't have to go to the same lengths.

The full application is listed in Appendix E, under the name show_biz.* The code is documented (the comments removed from the previous snippets for brevity), and will hopefully provide a good starting point for further exploration of UDDI. Because the publishing routines (both for creation and deletion) require registration and overhead for tasks such as authentication, there aren't any examples here that use them. There are some demonstrations of the routines in the UDDI test suite in the SOAP::Lite package, and the UDDI::Lite classes and methods are documented in Appendix C, along with the rest of the SOAP::Lite interface.

---

* It shows business information, after all, so the pun was too tempting to pass up.

CHAPTER 11
REST: Representational State Transfer

Until now our focus has been XML-RPC and SOAP-based web services. However, recent developments in this field show that these methods don't cover all available web services. One alternative is Representational State Transfer, or REST. Despite the long history (in Internet time) and large number of applications that run the Internet, this approach for developing distributed applications wasn't popular until recently. Some of the more vocal proponents of the REST style include Roy Fielding, Mark Baker, Jeff Bone, Paul Prescod, and Roger Costello. The information presented in this chapter is based largely on their ideas.

Think of a distributed system[*] in which every resource has a standard way to reference it (URI), uses a standard method of access (HTTP), has well-defined document structure of its metadata and representation (XML), supports multiple formats (through content negotiation and transformations), refers to other related resources in which the client can dig for more information (XLink, XPointer), has a standard way to describe how resources can be accessed (WSDL, WRDL), advertises its presence in a standard manner (UDDI, WS-Inspection), and uses a common mechanism for authentication and authorization. It isn't expected that all the pieces will be in place at once; this vision can be implemented incrementally. What's more, it can be done for little additional cost if the simple principles described in this chapter are followed.

Defining REST

REST stands for Representational State Transfer, a term coined by Roy Fielding in his doctoral dissertation. (Check it out at *http://www.ics.uci.edu/~fielding/pubs/dissertation/top.htm.*) The author introduces the REST architectural style, developed

---

[*] This is a restatement of Phillip J. Windley's vision outlined in *http://www.das.state.ut.us/cc/aug2002/ciomessage.html.*

as an abstract model of the web architecture to guide the redesign and definition of the HTTP and URIs.

> REST encompasses a simple philosophy for modeling problem domains: "give a URI to everything that can be manipulated by a limited set of operations and let the client software determine the usage metaphor." This pattern is ubiquitous: a small number of methods applied to diverse kinds of data.

The main questions that motivated the development of the REST architectural style were: how to introduce a new set of functionality to an architecture that is already widely deployed and how to ensure that its introduction doesn't adversely impact, or even destroy, the architectural properties that have enabled the Web to succeed. This chapter discusses one possible answer to that question. Some examples will be provided, although the main focus of the discussion is on architecture and design of applications in accordance with REST's principles; examples are added purely for illustrative purposes and will provide you some guidelines.

The Scientific Definition

If you aren't comfortable with definitions derived from Ph.D. dissertations, you can skip this section (it will be kept short).

The REST style is an abstraction of the architectural elements within a distributed system. The key aspects of REST are the nature and state of data elements (compare this approach to the distributed object style, in which the key aspect is the encapsulation of all data within the processing components). REST identifies six data elements: a resource, resource identifier, resource metadata, representation, representation metadata, and control data, shown in Table 11-1.

Table 11-1. REST data elements

Data element	Examples
Resource	The intended conceptual target; "the home page of the O'Reilly web site," "the latest version of the SOAP::Lite toolkit"
resource identifier	Name, URI; http://soaplite.com/download/SOAP-Lite-latest.zip
resource metadata	Vary
Representation	Sequence of bytes, HTML document, archive document, image document
representation metadata	Last-Modified, media type; text/xml
control data	If-Modified-Since, If-Match

The key abstraction of information in REST is a *resource*. Any information that can be *named* can be a resource: a document, a home page of a weblog, or a search result. A resource is a conceptual object that has identity, state, and behavior. A *resource identifier* (in the form of a URI) identifies the particular resource that might be observable via its *representations*. A representation (for example, a web page or a document) is something that you get from a resource and not the resource itself. Some resources are static; their representations don't change. When queried, they always correspond to the same sequence of bytes. Other resources are dynamic: their value changes over time, but the semantics stay the same. The semantics are unique (one concept, one identity) and distinguish one resource from another.

Representation metadata describes the representation and *resource metadata* describes the resource. *Control data* defines the purpose of a message between components, such as the action being requested. If the value set of a resource consists of multiple representations, content negotiation may be used to select the appropriate representation depending on the message control data.

The Practical Definition

The Web is full of resources that are named by URLs and have different representations. For example, CPAN (the Comprehensive Perl Archive Network) defines a resource that may be described as "Distribution of SOAP::Lite module v0.55." Clients may access this resource using this URL:

http://search.cpan.org/author/KULCHENKO/SOAP-Lite-0.55/

A representation of the resource is returned. This might be a HTML page that provides information about the module. This representation places the client application in a *state* (another representation, for example a XML document, may place the client in a different state). The client traverses the returned representation and accesses another resource using a link in the document:

http://search.cpan.org/src/KULCHENKO/SOAP-Lite-0.55/Changes

The client application changes the state based on the returned representation. As a result, the transfer of state occurs with each resource representation; hence Representational State Transfer.

REST is an architecture style that separates a server's implementation from a client's perception of resources. It enables transfer of data in streams of unlimited size and type, supports intermediaries as data transformation and caching components, and concentrates the application state within the user agent components. It leverages HTTP and the URI namespace for all types of applications and allows for independent evolution of clients, servers, and intermediaries. In the future it may allow accessing individual data objects as resources.

Figure 11-1 gives a summary of REST in one diagram.

All these services that have been used in past years—search engines (Google), book ordering services (Amazon), CPAN—are services created according to REST principles.

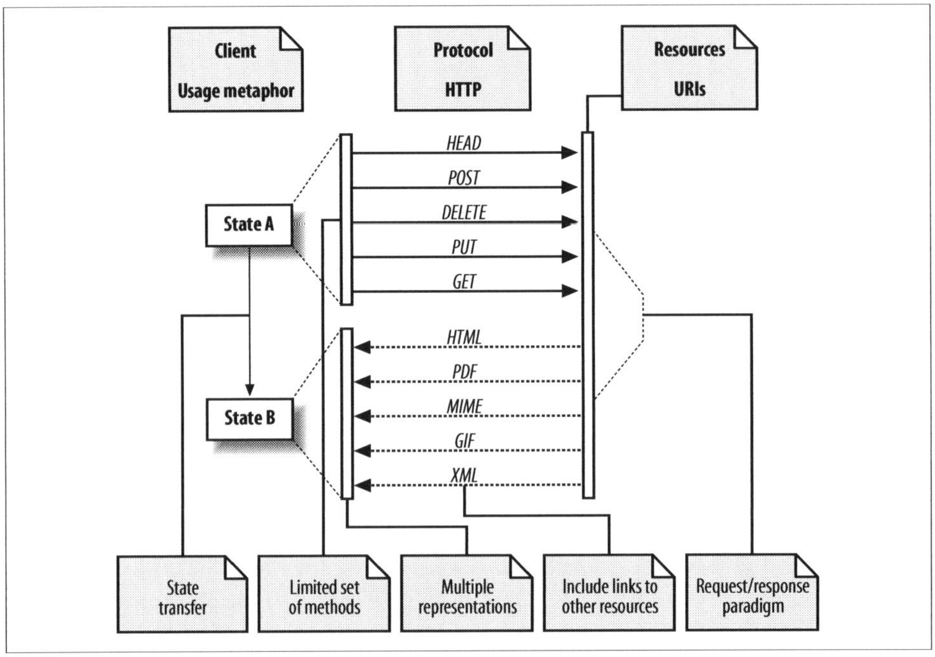

Figure 11-1. REST definition

REST Principles

There are 12 principles, shown in Table 11-2. Most are either self-explanatory or will be covered later in this chapter.

Table 11-2. REST principles

Group	Principle
Resources	(1) A resource is anything that has identity.
	(2) Every resource has a URI.
	(3) A URI is "opaque," exposes no details of its implementation.
Protocol	(4) GET operations are "idempotent," free of side effects.
	(5) Any request that doesn't have side effects should use GET.
	(6) All interactions are stateless.
Representations	(7) Data and metadata formats are documented.
	(8) Data is available in multiple flavors.
	(9) Representations include links to other resources.
Style	(10) Document and advertise your service API.
	(11) Use available standards and technology.
	(12) Refine and extend architecture, standards and tools.

The first group of principles relates to standardized addressing (URI), which describes how to address resources. The second group of principles relates to standard application protocol (HTTP), which describes what operations can be applied to the resources. Stateless interaction in this context means that each request from client to server must contain all the information necessary to execute the request, and can't take advantage of any stored context on the server. The third group of principles relates to standard resource representation (HTML, GIF, JPG, XML-based vocabularies), which describes what data is passed to resources or accepted from them. Standardization of all these key elements of the REST approach allows for the achievement of widespread interoperability, and an ability to rapidly and independently evolve clients, servers and systems as a whole.

Aesthetics of URI Design

Uniform resource locators (URLs), like uniform resource names (URNs), are a subset of the general class of uniform resource identifiers (URIs). The distinction between URIs, URLs, URNs, and the rest of resource identifiers is often more confusing than useful.[*] In this chapter, the term "URI" refers to all of them.

URI syntax

Before going into detail about resource modeling, let's first review and elaborate on URIs as discussed in Chapter 2. An absolute URI reference consists of three parts: a *scheme*, a *scheme-specific* part, and a *fragment identifier*. Some schemes are hierarchical, allowing for both relative and absolute URIs (http:) and some aren't, allowing only absolute URIs (such as mailto:). For hierarchical namespaces, a scheme-specific part is broken down into *authority*, *path*, and *query* components. Relative URI references can be created by omitting the scheme and authority components (they are implied by the context of the URI reference). These forms of URI reference syntax are summarized as follows:

```
<scheme>:<scheme-specific-part>#<fragment>
<scheme>://<authority><path>?<query>#<fragment>
<path>?<query>#<fragment>
```

Resource modeling

The strength and flexibility of REST comes from the pervasive use of URIs. REST is about exposing resources through URIs, not services through messaging interfaces. On this view, URIs are acted on by HTTP methods, and the result of those actions is to transfer representations of some resource from the origin server to the client that

---

[*] If you're interested, the paper "URIs, URLs, and URNs: Clarifications and Recommendations" describes the relationship among the concepts and the reason for the confusion. Check it out at *http://www.w3.org/TR/2001/NOTE-uri-clarification-20010921/*.

initiated the request. Some REST advocates call the process of bringing an application into this model "resource modeling," i.e., how to model a given problem domain as a set of resources. Each component of the URI should be a resource for which operations make sense. One guiding principle is to ask "does it make sense to use GET, PUT, POST, or DELETE operations on this named resource?"

Most URIs are opaque to client software most of the time. In other words, a public API shouldn't depend on the structure of the URIs; the structure of the URI is irrelevant to client software. URI opacity opens the door to new URI schemas and different interpretations of URI spaces. It isn't possible to satisfy opacity requirements in all cases: URIs that include fragment identifiers aren't opaque to the client because the fragment identifier is evaluated on the client. For HTML, the fragment ID is an ID of an element within the HTML object (anchor). For XML, if it is just a word, it is the XML ID of an element in the document.

Putting any kind of method name, action, or process in a URI is typically considered poor style in REST (because resources are objects rather than processes or services, URI parts should be named for nouns rather than verbs). Using a name to identify a process is RPC-like; using a name to identify a processor is REST-like. The difference is important, because a processor can conceivably have its own state. It would seem that this is an academic debate about naming styles and conventions, but it is actually more important than that: at its core, this debate is about what a resource is or can be, and what underlying models and design processes should be, to achieve REST-fullness. Decomposing a problem domain into a set of resource representations with a generic interface isn't the same as decomposing the same domain into a set of objects and type-specific operations on those objects. There is a mismatch between REST and current process of modeling problem domains as system of objects.

Imagine a description of a simple model with two domain entities: mailbox and message. Even when the model is restricted to representation as a hierarchical collection of resources, there are still a number of options to explore (*pavelkulchenko* is the name of mailbox and 567 is the unique number of the message in the mailbox):

/mailbox=pavelkulchenko/message=567
/pavelkulchenko/567
/mailboxes/pavelkulchenko/messages/567
/mail?mailbox=pavelkulchenko;message=567

Even though the choice may not be immediately clear, for a number of reasons that will be covered later, this approach is the favored one:

/mailboxes/<mailboxId>/messages/<msgId>/

Using it, you can model resources. The following part refers to a collection of mailboxes:

/mailboxes/

This part refers to an instance, i.e., a particular mailbox:

/mailboxes/<mailboxId>/

This refers to a collection of messages:

/mailboxes/<mailboxId>/messages/

This refers to an instance, i.e., a particular message:

/mailboxes/<mailboxId>/messages/<msgId>/

Extending into the message themselves, you'd use the following to refer to a fragment of the message:

/mailboxes/<mailboxId>/messages/<msgId>/#from

This refers to a set of messages filtered from a collection:

/mailboxes/<mailboxId>/messages/<msgId>/?after=20020831

You can continue and include *parts/<partId>* to address MIME parts of the message or include *first/last* instead of *<msgId>* to address the first or last messages in a mailbox.

The reason that the slashes have been instituted as the common universal syntax for a hierarchical boundary is their familiarity. Hierarchical schemes are common, and the relative naming within hierarchical space has many advantages. Relative naming allows small groups of documents that are located closely within a tree to refer to each other without being aware of their absolute position within any absolute tree.

It's easy to say that URIs change because of the lack of forethought (and it's probably true in many cases), but it is important to realize that many properties of URIs are social rather than technical in nature. Creating URIs that can be used in one year or ten from now requires thought, organization, and commitment on the part of authorities assigning URIs.

There is nothing about HTTP that makes URIs unstable. URIs change when there is some information in them that changes—authors' names, status, corporate structure, database design, and project name are all things that can change over the course of time and thus change a URI. We're in the bind that we need information in the URI to access the resource it identifies, but the very act of putting information in the URI makes it fragile. The only way out of the bind is to include the minimum information that is enough to identify a resource.

It is important to emphasize that a URI points to a resource as a concept, rather than a document. Don't expose the mechanism of how a server runs (cgi-bin, servlet, or mod_perl URIs). Make a change to the mechanism (even though the content stays the same), and all the URIs change. It's highly unlikely that, if you follow these principles, you'll come up with a URL such as *http://www.foo.org/cgi-bin/articles.pl?newsid=1234567*. Instead, it is more likely that if you follow REST principles you'll get something more like *http://www.foo.org/articles/1234567*.

This much space has been devoted to URIs because it's extremely important to properly understand and implement resource names.

Methods

The HTTP specification provides a number of generic methods (the HEAD, GET, and POST methods were discussed in Chapter 2), but only five are relevant to this discussion: GET, HEAD, POST, PUT, and DELETE. Table 11-3 recalls the operations from Chapter 2 and defines the new ones.

Table 11-3. REST methods

Method	Meaning
GET	Retrieves a resource
HEAD	Retrieves representation and resource metadata
POST	Inserts, updates, or extends a resource; may change the state of other resources
PUT	Creates, updates, or replaces a resource
DELETE	Deletes a resource

Unifying the method vocabulary provides tremendous opportunities for simplifying interactions. It is precisely because HTTP has few methods that HTTP clients and servers can grow and be extended independently without confusing each other. Essentially, what are needed are methods that correspond to the "CRUD" concept: Create, Retrieve, Update, and Delete. In HTTP they are called GET, POST, DELETE, and PUT.

GET method

To get a representation from a resource, a client uses the HTTP method GET. This operation is *idempotent*, which means that a client may use the result of a previous operation instead of repeating it; the state of the server shouldn't be changed in ways that are visible to the client. GET is restricted to a single URL line, which enforces one of the design principles: everything interesting should be URL-addressable. Wanting to create a system in which resources aren't URL-addressable means needing to justify that decision.

POST method

Modifying a resource uses the POST operation. This meaning of POST can be ambiguous. It can mean append, create, remove, or modify a portion of resource, or something else entirely. This ambiguity leads to a number of misuses. For example, in violation of one of the REST principles, it can be used for data queries without side effects.

A web-based address book from a well-known vendor illustrates this point. Users can submit the query with an arbitrary string using the POST method and submit the query with a predefined unique identifier using the GET method. If a client wants to link to the address book using the name of a given person, it isn't directly possible (a client can use a scripting language to submit the form, but this isn't always feasible). This is an example of design that violates REST Principle 5: any request that doesn't have side effects should use GET.

Here's a good test of REST-fulness: can an application do a GET on the same URLs it POSTs to, and if so, does it get something that in some way represents the state of what it has been building with the POST operations?

DELETE method

To delete a resource, use the DELETE method on a valid URL.[*]

PUT method

To change the representation of a resource, a client uses the PUT method. There is a subtle different between the POST and PUT methods. To distinguish between the two, consider a simple example that will be described in greater detail later in this chapter. To get an image of a cover page, a technical editor may use a service that creates the image from a template based on a number of parameters (such as title, cover, or animal); whereas a graphical designer may create the same image in a program such as Photoshop and submit it.

The editor uses POST to submit parameters; the server application modifies a resource based on the submitted parameters and returns the URL of the modified resource (which might be different from the URL the request was submitted to). The designer uses PUT to submit the image; the server modifies the representation. Both can update a resource or create a resource if there is none, but the difference is that PUT (and DELETE) operates on a representation as a whole, where POST submits information that causes a server to modify, create, or delete the resource (or multiple resources), often with a URL that is different from that submitted.

A PUT request may also include a Content-Range header to request modification of only a portion of the entity. It may also include the If-Match and If-None-Match headers to indicate which various entity versions to modify. Thus, including a header, If-None-Match: *, in a PUT request allows a new entity to be created only if it doesn't already exist.

---

[*] You may note that the DELETE method is supposed to be used to delete the resource. However, the POST method can delete resources too. Consider a situation in which a mailbox has to be deleted along with all messages. That operation would be executed using POST, rather than DELETE, because more than one resource is involved. At the same time, it is possible to DELETE a resource that has multiple representations. For instance, a DELETE /image operation may delete GIF, PNG, and JPG representations of the resource.

Security

REST greatly simplifies security and benefits it in a sociological manner. Where RPC protocols try as hard as possible to make the network look as if it isn't there (such as the SOAP::Lite module's support of the autodispatch mode, which tries to make remote calls look local), REST requires that the software developer design a network interface in terms of methods and resources. Whereas RPC interfaces encourage clients to view incoming messages as method parameters to be passed directly and automatically to programs, REST requires a certain disconnect between the interface (which is REST-oriented) and the implementation (which is usually object-oriented).

Resource-centric web services are inherently firewall-friendly: only four main operations are permitted (not counting HEAD). Server configurations can apply the four basic permissions to each data object (GET, POST, PUT, and DELETE), and they mean what they say: GET means get, and DELETE means delete. Many REST proponents believe that it will be impossible to securely and widely deploy a protocol across administrative boundaries without knowing the precise meaning of the methods. Using the hierarchical nature of the resource URI, servers may allow or disallow specific operations on subresources.

HTTP authentication and authorization are topics that most web developers are already familiar with. It's easy to assume that a service can't hide on the Internet, but the sole fact of making a resource addressable doesn't make it accessible. For instance, servers can create cryptographically unguessable URIs or associate unguessable signatures with each URI to insure that the resource gets accessed only from a legitimate source. Unguessable URIs are essentially a form of security mechanism known as a *capability*. Capability security is simple, but it requires software and end-users to adhere to a discipline that sharing a URI is equivalent to sharing the resource (a widely used service that employs this method is QuickTopic, available at *http://quicktopic.com/*).

Programming REST

You may notice the absence of code examples in this section. Why doesn't the REST programming section include any code? It is largely because REST is more about a mindset rather than code, more about design than implementation.

It may look simple (because it is), but there are some important points to keep in mind while developing applications in the REST style. This section describes them briefly and links them back to the REST principles (see Table 11-2). The section that follows this scrutinizes some of the points and provides code examples.

Think about the business problem in terms of resource manipulation rather than API design. Enabling web services requires making data available for use by applications without knowing ahead of time exactly how that data will be used. Start by modeling the persistent resources that is to be exposed. Follow the DRY (Don't Repeat Yourself) principle: every piece of knowledge must have a single, unambiguous, authoritative identity within a system (yet may have multiple representations) [Principles 1, 2, and 8]. The key is to identify all the conceptual entities that the system exposes as resources and to assign a unique URL to each of them. Be careful with names even if you plan to use them only as a temporary resource; an old saying goes: nothing is more permanent than "temporary."

Sort publicly exposed resources into those that are immutable by the client (retrieved by the GET method), and those that are mutable (modified by the PUT, POST or DELETE methods) [Principles 4 and 5]. Develop a habit of PUTing and DELETEing resources when appropriate. Implement methods that will allow both sender and receiver to make the absolute minimum of assumptions as to the other's state [Principle 6]. Multiple requests should not be required to implement a single logical operation.

Document the format that the application expects, accepts, and returns [Principle 7]. Provide an XML representation for each resource when possible [Principle 8]. Specify the representational schema of both mutable and immutable resources with a formal mechanism (for example, XML Schema, DTD, Schematron, or RelaxNG). Describe and document how the resources can be accessed [Principle 10].

Use a "gradual unfolding methodology" to expose data for clients. Include links to other related resources in (almost) every representation to enable clients to drill down for more information [Principle 9]. Otherwise, the retrieved representation (while valuable by itself) will be the end of story (the decision about the next step to take will have to be made out of hand).

Know and use the software. Set up a server to do content negotiation, authentication, authorization, compression, caching, vacuuming, and house cleaning [Principles 11 and 12].

Invest in abstractions today and in implementations tomorrow. Abstractions can survive the storm of changes from different implementations and new technologies. Realize that things believed in strongly today will get abstracted away in the future.

REST Primer

The REST architectural style is best explained with an example. Therefore, the rest of this section will present a hypothetical example that depicts O'Reilly deploying services using the REST architectural style.

O'Reilly plans to deploy several web services to enable its customers to:

- Get a list of books
- Get detailed information about a particular book
- Get detailed information about authors

- Submit a purchase order
- Update or cancel a purchase order

O'Reilly also wants to enable their authors to:

- Add and update author biographical information

For internal purposes, O'Reilly also wants to enable their editors and designers to:

- Create or update a cover for the book

The next step is to consider how these services can be implemented in a REST style.

Modeling Resources

Before you can model resources, you must create a domain model, which describes entities and their relationships and provides the information necessary for resource modelling (see Figure 11-2).

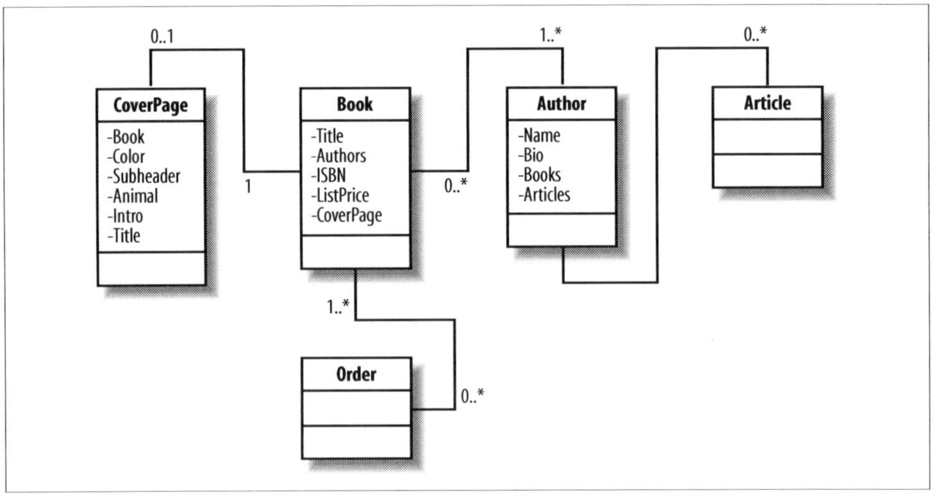

Figure 11-2. Book service domain model

Based on this domain model, it is possible to model the resources and design URIs to access them. The web service makes available a specific URL to represent a books list resource, for example, */books/*.

The absolute URL for this resource may look like *http://www.oreilly.com/books/*, but because the hostname and protocol will not change, there is no need to include them in the examples.

Note that the process the web service uses to generate the response is completely transparent to the client. A list of books may be available as a physical document or may be created by the server side application at run-time. All the client has to do is submit a request, and a document containing the book list is returned.

The XML document that a client receives may look like this:

```
<?xml version="1.0"?>
<Books xmlns="http://schema.oreilly.com/book"
       xmlns:xlink="http://www.w3.org/1999/xlink">
  <Book id="progwebsoap" xlink:href="progwebsoap/">
    <Title>Programming Web Services with SOAP</Title>
    <Authors xlink:href="progwebsoap/authors/"/>
    <ISBN>0596000952</ISBN>
    <ListPrice>34.95</ListPrice>
  </Book>
  <Book id="progxmlrpc" xlink:href="progxmlrpc/">
    <Title>Programming Web Services with XML-RPC</Title>
    <Authors xlink:href="progxmlrpc/authors/"/>
    <ISBN>0596001193</ISBN>
    <ListPrice>34.95</ListPrice>
  </Book>
</Books>
```

There are several important things to notice. XML is only one of the possible representations that a client may receive as a result of content negotiation (which will be discussed later). The example also includes xlink:href attributes that point to the resources that contain related information (book and author details in this case). This is a key feature of REST. A client changes its state by accessing the alternative resources addressed by URLs in response document.

> An xlink:href attribute is described in XLink specification that defines an attribute-based syntax for attaching links to XML documents. The most current version of the XLink specification can be found at *http://www.w3.org/TR/xlink/*.

Note that, even though the server can make these URLs absolute (*/books/progwebsoap/* or even *http://www.oreilly.com/books/progwebsoap/*), for now it is kept relative. The benefit of doing this will be clearer when discussing the "cover page" service. The model can use the ISBN (as Amazon does, for example) instead of using unique book identifier (as O'Reilly does), but it wouldn't change anything in this design and implementation.

It is important to decide what information to include in this representation and what to keep for subsequent requests. It was decided to present Title, ISBN, and ListPrice elements and provide links to other resources. While it is possible to include all relevant information, it's not always feasible or practical. For example, book information may include a cover page; author information may include the author's bio and pictures as well as links to articles. There is no reason to include all this information in the book list, so the line must be drawn somewhere.

At this stage, the server has implemented a service that returns a list of books. Work can now focus on the service that returns specific information about a particular book. This service will be available through the URL */books/progwebsoap/*.

The XML that the client receives (only as one of several representations) may look like this:

```
<?xml version="1.0"?>
<Book id="progwebsoap"
      xmlns="http://schema.oreilly.com/book"
      xmlns:xlink="http://www.w3.org/1999/xlink">
  <Title>Programming Web Services with SOAP</Title>
  <Authors xlink:href="authors/">
    <Author id="jamessnell" xlink:href="authors/jamessnell/">
      <Name>James Snell</Name>
    </Author>
    <Author id="dougtidwell" xlink:href="authors/dougtidwell/">
      <Name>Doug Tidwell</Name>
    </Author>
    <Author id="pavelkulchenko" xlink:href="authors/pavelkulchenko/">
      <Name>Pavel Kulchenko</Name>
    </Author>
  </Authors>
  <ISBN id="isbn">0596000952</ISBN>
  <ListPrice>34.95</ListPrice>
  <CoverPage xlink:href="coverpage"/>
</Book>
```

Again, observe how information in this document is linked to other resources: list of authors, detailed information about each of the authors, and the cover page. It allows the client to drill down to get more detailed information.

Now look at what happens when a client follows a link. Relative URLs that are being used have only a locally different part of the URI in them (*authors/pavelkulchenko/* in this example). The application that follows the link combines it with the absolute URI of the resource that the application has remembered (perhaps something like *http://www.oreilly.com/books/progwebsoap/*) and generates a new absolute URL of the resource, *http://www.oreilly.com/books/progwebsoap/authors/pavelkulchenko/*.

In response to this request, a client may receive this document:

```
<?xml version="1.0"?>
<Author id="pavelkulchenko"
        xmlns="http://schema.oreilly.com/book"
        xmlns:xlink="http://www.w3.org/1999/xlink">
  <Name>Pavel Kulchenko</Name>
  <Bio xlink:href="bio"/>
  <Books xlink:href="books/"/>
  <Articles xlink:href="articles/"/>
</Author>
```

Here's a good place to step back and take a look at what has been done thus far. The design has modeled four resources and created four services (and the list of authors for a particular book was the bonus service; it wasn't in the initial list). These are shown in Table 11-4.

Table 11-4. *The resources and services thus far*

Resource	Service
/books/	A list of books
/books/progwebsoap/	Information about a particular book
/books/progwebsoap/authors/	A list of authors for a particular book
/books/progwebsoap/authors/pavelkulchenko/	Information about a particular author

Now it is easy to model other URLs, shown in Table 11-5.

Table 11-5. *Other resources using the model*

Resource	Service
/authors/	List of authors
/authors/pavelkulchenko/	Information about a particular author
/authors/pavelkulchenko/books/	Books by a particular author
/authors/pavelkulchenko/articles/	Articles by a particular author
/authors/pavelkulchenko/bio	The author's bio

The */authors/* resource represents the list of all O'Reilly authors, while the resource */authors/pavelkulchenko/* represents information about a particular author (which is the same as */books/progwebsoap/authors/pavelkulchenko/*). The resource represented by the sequence, */authors/pavelkulchenko/books/*, represents the list of books written by a particular author and in this case, */authors/pavelkulchenko/books/progwebsoap/* links to the same resource as */books/progwebsoap/*.

Note that structure of the URI is irrelevant to client software: it always operates on a URI as a whole. Even when relative URIs are used, they are processed according to the algorithm described in the URI specification, without an application knowing anything about their internal structure.

Creating Multiple Representations

Only one representation has been dealt with for now (XML), but in a real world environment, it will definitely be a good idea to provide a broad range of representations to satisfy the needs of different clients. Imagine that the service makes the */books/* resource available in RSS format; a user can then subscribe (using one of the many available RSS readers) to that feed and see when new books come out. In a similar fashion, a RSS representation for the */books/progwebsoap/* resource may return news about a book, and for */authors/*, may return information about new authors. Following that line of reasoning, a representation for */authors/pavelkulchenko/* may return a news feed about the particular author (books, articles and everything related). Some of these resources may even be requested in PDF format.

All this variety of formats and representations brings up an interesting question: how does the server know what format to return for a particular request?

It was easier in the good old days. Most available resources were documents, so there was no need for a server to choose what format to use (most resources had only one representation). Even in the case of Common Gateway Interface (CGI) scripts, it was the rare situation when one resource had multiple formats, and yet it was mostly the client's responsibility to figure out what to do with the response based on the Content-Type or other representation metadata. As a result, browsers (which represented the vast majority of client software) became greedy: "give me everything; I am smart enough to figure out how to deal with it." In many cases that was true, but now servers want to accommodate nonbrowser clients and keep the compatibility with browser-based clients when possible.

There are three primary ways to convey desired format information:

- File extensions ("GET /image.gif")
- Query string ("GET /image?type=gif")
- "Accept" header ("GET /image" with "Accept: image/gif")

File extensions are bad for several reasons: they circumvent the content negotiation, they trick client software into thinking that a file extension has something to do with the content type, and they don't work with resources that are collections of other resources (A */books.rss/* resource would be clumsy at best). Imagine a server using the URL */images/camel.gif* and needing to upgrade it to */images/camel.png* for some reason. This is a problem, because of the need to update all links that point to that resource (note that only the representation of the resource has changed; the meaning of it stays the same). Using */images/camel* as a link, the client and server can do a content negotiation based on values of Accept, Accept-Encoding, Accept-Language, and UserAgent headers, customer preferences, or even legal obligations, without affecting other resources or client software. For example, a PDF version of a purchase order can be returned in different languages based on client preferences. However, file extensions aren't easy to avoid: many resources mirror local filesystems, and extensions are used on the server side to provide a hint to the web server about the content type it should return.

Query strings are only slightly better and still share the main weakness: a server always returns the format a client asks for without leaving a room for negotiation.

A more appropriate role for the query string is to carry additional information that may change the representation of a resource or collection of resources without changing semantics. For instance, it can filter or sort entities in a collection:

    .../books/?number=10;orderby=date
    .../books/?status=outofprint

The Accept header solution is better for a number of reasons. It allows a generic resource to exist and support multiple dimensions (formats, languages, client requirements, preferences, etc.) that may result in many different representations. It releases the technology from the constraint of being tied to a particular data format and allows independent evolution on client and server sides: a server may add a new format without a client even knowing it, and a client may request specific formats from a server, allowing resolution with minimum round trips.

The major drawback of this approach is that the client application has to know not only about URLs to get a proper format, but also about headers; there is client software in use that doesn't have this capability. Another issue with this approach is that it doesn't work well for different formats that share the same content type (which might be important for XML-based documents). Although it may be possible to specify this information in parameters on the Accept header, this approach isn't standardized.

Doing this also means designing and developing server software in a way that will allow content negotiation and make it aware of content negotiation headers and related responsibilities. If done right, a client can request PDF representation using a Accept: application/pdf header, XML representation using Accept: text/xml, application/xml, and SOAP representation using Accept: application/soap+xml. Multiple preferences and different weights can be assigned.

Developing REST Applications

Returning to the client side, Example 11-1 is a sample application from the client's perspective. It traverses the list of books searching for a particular book, gets the list of authors, and then gets the resource that describes an individual author. Finally, it prints the bio for each author.

Example 11-1. A REST-style client using SOAP::Lite deserialization

```perl
#!perl -w

use strict;

my $startURL = 'http://www.soaplite.com/oreilly/books/';

# get list of O'Reilly books
foreach my $book (parse(get($startURL))->Book) {

  # look for Programming web services with SOAP
  next unless $book->ISBN eq '0596000952';
  print $book->Title, "\n";

  # get link to Authors for the book
  my $authorsURL = absurl(href($book->Authors), $startURL);
  foreach my $author (parse(get($authorsURL))->Author) {
    print $author->Name, "\n";
```

Example 11-1. A REST-style client using SOAP::Lite deserialization (continued)

```
    # get link to particular Author
    my $authorURL = absurl(href($author), $authorsURL);
    my $bio = parse(get($authorURL))->Bio;

    # get link to Author's bio
    my $bioURL = absurl(href($bio), $authorURL);
    print parse(get($bioURL)), "\n";
  }
}

sub href {
  return shift->attr->{'{http://www.w3.org/1999/xlink}href'};
}

sub get {
  use LWP::UserAgent;
  my $url = shift;
  my $req = HTTP::Request->new(GET => $url, HTTP::Headers->new);
  $req->header(Accept => 'text/xml');
  my $res = LWP::UserAgent->new->request($req);
  die $res->status_line unless $res->is_success;
  return $res->content;
}

sub parse {
  use SOAP::Lite;
  return SOAP::Custom::XML::Deserializer->deserialize(shift)->root;
}

sub absurl {
  use URI;
  my($url, $baseurl) = @_;
  return $url unless $baseurl;
  URI->new_abs($url, $baseurl)->as_string;
}
```

There is one little detail that is worth mentioning: when modeling the URI for a resource that points to a collection of other resources (such as */books/* or */authors/*), be careful to end the URI with a slash character (/). It serves as a visual aid for users and developers (resources that point to collections have a slash at the end, and resources that point to instance documents don't). More importantly, the algorithm that converts a relative URL into an absolute one is written in such a way that it produces */books/authors/jamessnell/* from the pair */books/progwebsoap* (no trailing slash) and *authors/jamessnell/*. The expected result from this production would be */books/progwebsoap/authors/jamessnell*. Using a final slash (as in */books/progwebsoap/*) brings the expected result.

This code used the custom deserializer that is included with the SOAP::Lite package, but applications are free to use any other code for parsing XML documents. For example, you can use the simple code in Example 11-2 (based on the XML::Parser module).

Example 11-2. A simple XML parsing using XML::Parser

```perl
#!/usr/bin/perl -w

use strict;
use XML::Parser;

sub parse {
  XML::Parser->new(
    Namespaces => 1, Handlers => {Start => \&start},
  )->parse(shift);
}

sub start {
  my($xp, $el) = (shift, shift);

  while (@_) {
    my($nm, $v) = (shift, shift);
    my $ns = $xp->namespace($nm) || '';
    print $el, " => ", $v, "\n"
      if $nm eq 'href' &&
         $ns eq 'http://www.w3.org/1999/xlink';
  }
}

use LWP::Simple;

parse(get('http://www.soaplite.com/oreilly/progwebsoap/'));
```

Using this to process the XML document that was returned in the response for accessing the */books/progwebsoap/* resource, yields this output:

```
Authors => authors/
Author  => authors/jamessnell/
Author  => authors/dougtidwell/
Author  => authors/pavelkulchenko/
CoverPage => coverpage
```

Working with POST, PUT, and DELETE Methods

That was probably the easiest part: four resources, one method (GET), and a fairly simple XML payload. Let's now extend the services, and model and implement other operations.

The first step is to implement the service that allows authors to add or update their bio information. This example will be using a simple format and only one operation, PUT. The choice between the POST and PUT methods isn't always obviously clear. The rationale here is that the URL of the resource (*/authors/pavelkulchenko/bio*) is already

known, no other resource is modified, and operation is on the resource as a whole
(though it is possible and perfectly legal to update only part of the resource using a
Content-Range header).

The dialog between client and server may look like the following. Here's the request:

```
PUT /authors/pavelkulchenko/bio
Content-Type: text/xml
Content Length: NNN

<Bio xmlns="http://schema.oreilly.com/book">....</Bio>
```

Here's the response:

```
201 Created
```

The client code that posts the bio using LWP::UserAgent module is given in
Example 11-3.

Example 11-3. A REST-style PUT request using LWP::UserAgent

```
use LWP::UserAgent;

my $url = 'http://not-real-url.oreilly.com/authors/pavelkulchenko/bio';
my $bio = '<Bio xmlns="http://schema.oreilly.com/book">....</Bio>';
my $req = HTTP::Request->new(PUT => $url, HTTP::Headers->new, $bio);
$req->content_type('text/xml');
$req->content_length(length $bio);

my $res = LWP::UserAgent->new->request($req);

print $res->status_line;
```

What if the design is extended to accept plain text messages and convert them to
XML? It is easy to change the content type from *text/xml* to *text/plain* and submit the
text version of a bio, but can a client still use the PUT method? For purists, the answer
is probably "no," because the PUT method would be used for a transformation of the
representation. If transformations are allowed, it isn't clear what to do with requests
that modify only part of the resource. For the practical implementation the answer is
probably "yes," because requiring POST in this case means that the operation on the
resource depends on the implementation and violates one of the REST principles:
details on how to store information on the server side must be irrelevant to the client.

Implementing a Purchase Order Service

The next example is more complex. It allows customers to submit, update, or cancel
purchase orders. The design uses */books/orders/* as the resource for purchase order
submission. This URL works as a factory of orders, creating URLs for particular
orders. Again, there are a number of choices:

- POST the purchase order to that resource and get back a URI for the order (when accepted).
- Send a GET request asking for an order number, then PUT the order there.

Two disadvantages of using the POST method

POST has a reliability problem if a client loses its contact with the server after POSTing a purchase order. The order might have been accepted, and the reply was lost, but then again the order might have been lost and should be resent. There's no way for the client to know what happened. POST can also be confusing here; a client could use POST to submit an initial order, but then PUT to update it.

Two disadvantages of the GET and PUT combination

The first disadvantage of using the GET method is that the */orders/* resource is already taken. The system may want it to do something different, for instance to return a list of orders for particular customer. Because of this, a different resource (for example, */orders/new*) is needed that will respond to GET requests and return a URL in which the order can be submitted (the only real disadvantage is that two roundtrips are required). The second disadvantage is that now the server has a potential race condition to address (if it doesn't keep the generated order numbers on the server side, it can generate the same order number for more than one customer), and the PUT request has to be smart enough to deal with that.

Choosing the implementation

Because the reliability problem seems to be the more interesting issue to address, the example will implement the GET and PUT combination.* For now, the actual XML documents for purchase orders will be skipped over (you can design these as an exercise), and the text will describe the interactions only to highlight the important aspects.

First, a client receives the information about the resource where the URL and number for a new order can be obtained (*/books/progwebsoap/orders/new* in this example). This information may be included as part of the book list (the */books/ representation*), or it may be published somewhere.

Following this, the client sends a GET request to the URL and receives back a new URL where the order should be submitted.

Here's the request:

```
GET /books/progwebsoap/orders/new
```

---

* Though the network may go down during the PUT request, it is safe for a client to resubmit the message when in doubt, because an order with the same number will be treated as the same order, whereas resending the order with the POST message may result in duplicate orders.

Here's the response:

```
200 OK
Location: http://www.oreilly.com/books/orders/987654321

<Order xmlns="http://schema.oreilly.com/book"
       xmlns:xlink="http://www.w3.org/1999/xlink"
       id="987654321" xlink:href="../987654321"/>
```

Finally, the client uses the new URL (from the `Location` header or the `href` attribute of the `Order` element) to submit the order using the `PUT` method. The client will also include in the request the header `If-None-Match: *`, to indicate that it wants the order to be accepted only if it doesn't already exist. The server returns a fault if someone has already submitted an order with that number.

Here's the request:

```
PUT /books/orders/987654321
Content-Type: text/xml
Content-Length: NNN
If-None-Match: *

<Order xmlns="http://schema.oreilly.com/book">....</Order>
```

The response for this request will be `201 Created` or `412 Precondition Failed`, depending on the existence of the resource.

For subsequent requests that update the resource, the client may want to include the `If-Match` header instead of `If-None-Match`, to require the presence of the resource:

```
PUT /books/orders/987654321
Content-Type: text/xml
Content-Length: NNN
If-Match: *

<Order xmlns="http://schema.oreilly.com/book">....</Order>
```

The `DELETE` request (which will mean the cancellation of the order) can be implemented in a similar fashion. Similarly, the `GET` request for this resource (*/books/orders/987654321*) may return different representations (XML, HTML, or PDF) in keeping with the role of `GET` in this kind of system.

Implementing Cover Page Service

The last example briefly describes the design that implements the cover page service. The reason for including it is that the resource in this example accepts both `POST` and `PUT` requests and shows the important difference between them. First of all, it makes sense to allow updates to a cover page only when the book is in the preproduction stage. Starting with a decision to put all related resources under a URL */preproduction/*, the server will also restrict access to it. From this, the resource */preproduction/books/* now returns the list of all books in preproduction status. Because the system is using relative URLs, there is no need to change the way XML documents are created. The service allows two different requests because the cover page can be generated in two different ways: by the technical editor, providing color, subheader, animal, color and title and using the POST method to submit this information; and by a graphical designer, providing the image of the cover page using the PUT method to submit it. A GET method to that resource may return PNG, GIF, PDF, or some other representation depending on request properties.

Documenting Service API

Making services available may not be enough to make them popular unless the API is documented with a widely understood format. Two specifications that look promising for documenting the APIs of REST services (besides plain text or HTML formats) are Web Services Description Language (WSDL) and Web Resource Description Language (WRDL).

Here's a quote from the WRDL specification (which can be found at *http://www.prescod.net/rest/wrdl/wrdl.html*):

> REST is defined by four interface constraints: identification of resources, manipulation of resources through representations, self-descriptive messages, and hypermedia as the engine of application state.
>
> These four things are addressed in this specification through:
> - the association of URIs with resourceTypes
> - the association of resourceTypes with representationTypes
> - the recognition of representationTypes through XPaths
> - the built-in support for navigation through hyperlinks

Still, there's no instant winner: the WSDL specification isn't well suited to describe REST services (e.g., even though both QUERY STRING and PATH can be parameterized (see the section "HTTP and MIME Binding in WSDL" in Chapter 9 for more information, specifically Example 9-10), it isn't possible using the current specification to specify the value of the HTTP headers to select the representation), and the WRDL specification is new and not endorsed by any standards body (which may be seen as advantage, depending on your point of view).

What Makes REST Hard

REST is simple in details and (mostly) easy to understand, but it can be hard to execute. Despite its advantages, HTTP-based, URI-centric resource modeling isn't the usual way you think about networking issues, and REST-based web services aren't very common. Applying REST style requires you to resolve problems by manipulating addressable resources instead of method calls to components. The APIs communicated to clients should be in terms of HTTP manipulations on XML documents addressed by URIs instead of familiar method calls with parameters. REST is about imposing a programming discipline of many URIs and few methods. Here are several things that have been found difficult about REST:

It's flexible
> This one of its main strengths *and* weaknesses. Its flexibility allows resources to be used in ways that can't be envisioned now, at little additional cost. Even though REST consists of a set of architectural constraints, there is still enough space for abuse. It's generally good to make choices that preclude the least number of future alternatives.

It's hard to come up with the right URI
> The significance of identity for a given URI is determined by who owns the URI. The Web relies on the author choosing a resource identifier that best fits the nature of the concept being identified.

It's hard to refactor
> As soon as a service publishes its resource, it can't take it back without breaking client applications. It can't rely on a client to follow the sequence of links before coming to the resource. One of the things that can be done is to make client applications take note of redirects.

It's hard to come up with the right fault handling model
> The currently available fault handling model, while robust and simple, may not be suitable for all applications. For those occasions where it isn't, a designed fault handling system will either duplicate or circumvent one available in the protocol.

It's hard to make and keep developers aware of the architectural style
> Currently available tools make it possible to do The Wrong Thing as easily as The Right Thing. Designing for REST requires an abstraction skill and mindset different from those developed practicing object-oriented analysis and design. Learning and practicing the REST style can allow designers and developers to do The Right Thing more often. The full value of REST will not come until all the practices are in place.

It's hard to get the full tool support when developing application in the REST style
> Any REST proponent will point out that REST has the most widely deployed and useful tool support, which is absolutely true; however, it is important to realize that these tools support the current usage patterns, which may not be exactly of the same style as that which has been described. Take this URI:
>
> */books/progwebsoap#isbn*
>
> The significance of the fragment identifier is a function of the MIME type of the object, and application behavior depends on the MIME types of returned representation. Imagine that the representation is XML, and *isbn* is an XML ID of the ISBN element in that document (or maybe even written in full notation as xpointer(id("isbn"))). After many years, there is still very little code to properly deal with fragments like these in resource identifiers.

REST and SOAP

Lengthy and passionate discussion between REST and SOAP proponents resulted in the WebMethod feature being added to the current draft (Version 1.2) of the SOAP specification. The specification can be found at:

http://www.w3.org/TR/soap12-part2/#webmethodstatemachine

Here's a quote from the specification:

> Applications SHOULD use GET as the value of webmeth:Method in conjunction with the §6.3 SOAP Response Message Exchange Pattern to support information retrievals which are safe, and for which no parameters other than a URI are required: i.e., when performing retrievals which are idempotent, known to be free of side effects, for which no SOAP request headers are required, and for which security considerations don't conflict with the possibility that cached results would be used.

In addition to that, the SOAP 1.2 Working Group has proposed a new SOAP media type (application/soap+xml) that allows SOAP processors to accept GET requests (POST was the only method previously allowed) and to return a SOAP message as the resource representation in response to a GET request. That was allowed from the REST perspective earlier; it was just standardized from the SOAP perspective, so that a larger number of clients can access SOAP endpoints.

REST is based on resources, a limited but diverse set of operations, and a well-defined document format. Both camps agree that much of the value of provided services is in the precise description of the structure expected in requests and responses. Given the document/literal encoding and combination of the described WebMethod feature and Message Exchange Pattern defined in the SOAP 1.2 specification, SOAP and REST web services can be much closer to each other than the heated debates make them seem.

We'll leave comparing SOAP and REST interfaces to you. There are only a handful of services available through REST and SOAP/XML-RPC interfaces; Amazon (SOAP and REST), Google (SOAP and REST, though the REST interface that returns XML isn't publicly available), and Meerkat (XML-RPC and REST) are among the best known.

Whether working on world-facing web services now or in two years, the biggest challenge will be not in describing the interfaces or deciding what method to run, but in aligning business documents and processes with those of others. The technology used to move data from place to place isn't important, but the business-specific document and process modeling is (fortunately, that's the part where SOAP and REST proponents seem to agree). Given the proper format (for instance, RDF), a client application developed REST-style may be able to dynamically learn the meaning of the representation. Given links to the next state built within each response, a client application may be able to deduce dynamically which link to traverse. Dynamic learning of the representation combined with dynamic determination of link traversals would create an adaptive engine. Does this sound like the next generation of the web services?

CHAPTER 12
Advanced Web Services Topics

Technologies covered so far in this book provide the basic functionality required to build loosely coupled, platform-neutral distributed systems. Even though they work fairly well, none of these core web service specifications were designed to provide by themselves the mechanisms for describing or implementing complex interactions, particularly those run by businesses. It's generally agreed that the set of functionality that describes a full web services stack includes the following:

Message routing
> Allows rich message exchange patterns and intermediaries

Reliable messaging
> Implements guaranteed message delivery, sessions, and events

Packaging
> Establishes standards for packaging messages with attachments, indexing, and compression

Security
> Provides authentication, authorization, confidentiality, nonrepudiation, privacy, and integrity of the information

Transactions
> Allows the execution of distributed transactions

Workflow and orchestration
> Describes and combines services into sophisticated end-to-end business processes

Choreography and conversations
> Documents message exchange and defines protocols each party has to comply with

Negotiation
> Describes the protocol for negotiation of terms and conditions of contracts

Extended service description
    Includes behavioral elements such as quality of service, preconditions and constraints and others

Service management
    Audits, monitors, and prioritizes version services usage; also provides fail over, load balancing and service level agreement compliance

There isn't yet a full set of specifications to address all of these aspects. This chapter describes some of the techniques and specifications that aimed to fill the gaps in the web services architecture.

Message Routing

As discussed in Chapter 5, SOAP is a lightweight wire protocol that defines a processing model but doesn't describe a message path. Using the simplicity of the protocol and extensibility through modularity, it's possible to construct rich messaging semantics; actor (defined as role in the SOAP 1.2 specification) and mustUnderstand attributes provide necessary mechanisms for describing nodes targeted for specific processing (intermediaries or ultimate destination). Intermediaries are nodes that lie between initial sender and ultimate receiver and act as both sender and receiver of SOAP messages; they are central to SOAP. The SOAP message model provides a distributed processing mechanism in which the SOAP actor attribute can indicate which part of a message is intended for a given SOAP receiver.

Web Services Routing Protocol (WS-Routing)

The Web Services Routing Protocol specification can be found at:

    http://msdn.microsoft.com/library/en-us/dnglobspec/html/ws-routing.asp

It describes a simple, stateless, SOAP-based protocol for routing SOAP messages in an asynchronous manner over a variety of transports, including HTTP and TCP. The WS-Routing specification was developed by Microsoft and supersedes SOAP Routing Protocol (SOAP-RP) specification.

In addition to the processing model defined by the SOAP specification ("when message gets to node A do this, and when it gets to node B do that"), WS-Routing defines a message path ("to get to node A, message must travel through nodes C and D").

To express routing information, WS-Routing defines a single header element path and several subelements within that header:

- A to element for ultimate recipient of the message
- A fwd element for forward path specification

- A rev element for reverse path specification
- id and relatesTo elements for optional message correlation

The communication model described in WS-Routing is very simple: the sender of the message (specified by an optional from element) indicates the ultimate receiver of the message (using the to element) and forward path through zero or more intermediaries (using a fwd element). Even though intermediaries may insert additional nodes in the forward message path, they must not modify the to element. Here is a simple example that includes to and fwd elements:

```
<m:path xmlns:m="http://schemas.xmlsoap.org/rp/">
  <m:to>http://www.oreilly.com/books</m:to>
  <m:fwd>
    <m:via>http://www.oreilly.com/logger</m:via>
  </m:fwd>
  <m:id>uuid:12345678-9999-0000-aaaa-5b760641c1d6</m:id>
</m:path>
```

The via element indicates an intermediate receiver of the message and can be either empty or an absolute URI.

It's important to emphasize that while the value of to and fwd (or more precisely via) elements are URIs, they represent only a role name (an intermediary, which is a SOAP node, can act in one or more roles), and there are no routing or message exchange semantics associated with the role name. In other words, a message addressed to *http://www.oreilly.com/books* can be processed by any node that thinks it should act in this role (and may have nothing to do with the physical location expressed by the same URI).

So, how does the sender learn the physical address where the message has to be sent? Because WS-Routing allows dynamic modification of the message path, there is no requirement that the complete message path has to be known when the message leaves the initial sender. All the sender has to know is the ultimate destination and the SOAP node next to itself in the message path (perhaps a SOAP router, which is a special kind of intermediary that knows how and where to send the message next). All the intermediary has to know is the next SOAP processor in the message path. As a result, it decouples the SOAP-based framework not only from the physical structure of the network, but also from the transport protocols that deliver the message.

Optionally, the reverse path of the message can be specified by the rev element. The reverse path is built dynamically as a message flows in the forward direction, but only when the initial sender inserts a rev element in the header. The purpose of the reverse path is to indicate a possible path that can send the message back to the initial sender; there's no requirement that the reverse path actually be used.

The capability to identify the message and to correlate that message with other messages is essential to the ability to establish a rich message exchange pattern. It might be used to correlate between request and response messages, between fault and faulty messages or between any other somehow related messages. The value of the `id` element is a unique identifier that identifies the message and the `relatesTo` element can be used to refer to that message. Note that the `relatesTo` element doesn't describe how messages are related, it merely states the fact of the relationship; semantics of the relationship are expected to be defined somewhere in the message or transferred out of band.

Being self-describing (all routing information is carried entirely within a message itself), WS-Routing is relatively transport-independent and defines bindings to several transport protocols: HTTP, TCP, UDP, and DIME.

All this functionality allows implementation of three key scenarios: message forwarding through known intermediaries, message resolution using dynamic modification of forward path, and reverse path routing through building a reverse path.

Web Services Referral Protocol (WS-Referral)

The Web Services Referral Protocol specification can be found at:

http://msdn.microsoft.com/library/en-us/dnglobspec/html/ws-referral.asp

It describes a SOAP-based, stateless protocol for inserting, deleting, and querying routing entries in a SOAP router.

Why the need for one more specification that describes message routing? WS-Routing specification defines a message path and allows sender or intermediary to specify how a message will travel, but it doesn't answer how a SOAP router gets this information. WS-Referral answers that question by introducing a simple model of a SOAP router being able to delegate a URI space or a part thereof to another SOAP router by manipulating its routing entries. Varying the amount of information known by the router, it's possible to support various scenarios:

- Dynamic configuration of SOAP routers and allowing them to learn about SOAP intermediaries
- Outsourcing of URI space and load balancing
- Progressive discovery of resources

The WS-Referral's basic unit is the referral statement (defined as a `ref` element), which includes five elements:

- A `for` element to indicate the actor or role for which the referral is intended.
- An `if` element to specify a set of conditions that the recipient of the referral must understand in order to use it. Only two mandatory `if` conditions are defined in the specification: `invalidates` to cancel previously registered referrals and `ttl` to set a time-to-live limit on the validity of a referral.
- A `go` element to specify one or more SOAP routers where the message has to be sent when `for` and `if` conditions are satisfied.

- A desc element to include additional information the recipient may use, but doesn't need to understand in order to use the referral. For example, it can be used to carry a hint of which router to choose when the go element specifies more than one.
- A refId element to uniquely identify the referral, so that SOAP routers can refer to a specific representation of a referral statement, for example, in operations that invalidate the referral.

This pseudocode describes the possible interpretation of a referral statement:

    for actor or role name matching any of the names listed in the for element
    if the set of conditions listed in the if element is satisfied
    go via one of the SOAP routers listed in the go element

Here's an example that uses exact and prefix matching of an actor or role and specifies what one SOAP router may look like this:

```
<r:ref xmlns:r="http://schemas.xmlsoap.org/ws/2001/10/referral">
  <r:for>
    <r:exact>http://www.oreilly.com/books/authors</r:exact>
    <r:prefix>http://www.oreilly.com/books/orders</r:prefix>
  </r:for>
  <r:if/>
  <r:go>
    <r:via>http://www.oreilly.com/mirror</r:via>
  </r:go>
  <r:refId>uuid:11111111-2222-3333-4444-5567895432d6</r:refId>
</r:ref>
```

The WS-Referral specification describes not only the structure of the referral statement but also the mechanism by which messages are exchanged. There are three referral messages:

Register referral messages
    Instructs the SOAP router to insert or delete the enclosed referral statement. It provides a "push" method of router configuration.

Query referral message
    Queries the SOAP router for referrals. It provides a "pull" method that allows router and intermediaries to learn about existent message path.

Referral header messages
    Can be any SOAP message that carries a referral header and includes one or more ref elements that carry referral statements. It allows a message to piggyback referrals on an existing message exchange path.

Note that despite the references to WS-Routing, WS-Routing and WS-Referral specifications to provide orthogonal services allowing WS-Referral to be used with other message path models if so desired. In a similar fashion, WS-Routing can be used with configuration mechanisms other than WS-Referral. Here is how they all work together:

- SOAP enables distributed processing but doesn't specify a message path.
- WS-Routing enables messaging via a message path but doesn't include a configuration.
- WS-Referral provides a configuration; it tells how to navigate through the path provided by WS-Routing.

Packaging

Packaging is about support for documents composed of possible several entities that may include both structural and binary data. It may seem strange that after all these years of hard work on XML-related specifications, there is no final answer about the packaging mechanism, and new specifications keep coming up to specifically address this subject.

Probably the easiest way to package information isn't to package it at all. Even though an HTML page doesn't include images, it's still possible for an application to traverse links and access and present them, as well as any additional information. Equally, resources can be accessed using another communication channel and referenced from within the XML document using XML Linking Language (XLink, *http://www.w3.org/TR/xlink/*) or similar specification. However, this isn't always feasible for security, performance, or infrastructure requirements reasons.

XML looks like an obvious choice when considering a packaging mechanism. It's simple, and it's extensible. Still, to no surprise, there are several problems with XML (which all grow from the text nature of the XML format).

First, it has to be extended to allow true binary data. XML is defined as a character stream, and there is no way to embed raw binary data directly within an XML document; all binary data must be encoded as characters. There are several possible encodings; for example, the XML Schema specification defines usage of Base64 or hexadecimal digits for including arbitrary data, but they aren't very efficient.

Second, XML as a format is ill-suited for random access. Whitespace flexibility, entity expansion, and the expectation that document is serially scanned from beginning to end work against random access. It's suboptimal to have to receive and parse the entire document when only a fragment of it is required for further processing. XML Fragment Interchange specification (*http://www.w3.org/TR/xml-fragment*) was especially designed to address this problem.

Third, the XML format isn't recursive. It's often difficult to embed an XML document within another XML document, even though "there is more than one way (to try) to do it." It's possible to:

Provide a link to an external source
    In this case, an application is responsible for resolving those links.

Include reference to an external source using XML Inclusions specification
   The difference from the previous option is that XML Inclusions describes a media-specific transformation that generally occurs at a low level, so an application doesn't need to worry about it. You can find more information on the XML Inclusions specification at:
   http://www.w3.org/TR/xinclude/

Include it as an XML fragment
   This obvious alternative doesn't work for arbitrary XML documents because they may include XML declaration and processing instructions, have different encoding, or not be a well-formed XML document, which renders invalid the entire document.

Include it as an escaped string
   An XML fragment can be escaped or wrapped into CDATA element, but this doesn't solve the problem with different encodings and doesn't allow simple access to escaped data without parsing the entire XML document.

Include it as a binary fragment
   Forget that included data is XML document and include it as any other binary data would be included.

Because XML isn't the most concise representation, the format produced by one of the compression algorithms is the next option to consider. While compression can be used at the transport level, and it's quite possible that it will be introduced in a way similar to XML Encryption (discussed later in this chapter) to allow selective compression of elements in XML document, it's highly unlikely that it will be used as a packaging format.

The Multipurpose Internet Mail Extensions (MIME, *http://www.ietf.org/rfc/rfc2045.txt*) is a well-known and widely used format. Even though it can combine groups of files or documents into one package for transmission, it isn't without flaws:

- The MIME format doesn't require length fields, which can impact its suitability for random access. Even if positions of parts are calculated and included with the message, it's possible that some parts of the MIME message will be (re-)encoded in transmission, introducing errors in already calculated positions.

- It isn't an XML application and doesn't work well with filters and streaming transformations (there is no XSLT analogue for MIME).

One new option is the Direct Internet Message Encapsulation (DIME, *http://www.ietf.org/internet-drafts/draft-nielsen-dime-02.txt*) specification proposed by Microsoft jointly with IBM. DIME gets its strength from a short and focused requirement list and provides simple structure, performance benefits, and media-type definition decentralization (although, it doesn't have the extensibility MIME provides).

MIME and SOAP with Attachments

The MIME specification defines a message container (called an *entity*) that contains one or more entities (an entity that is packed inside another entity is called a body part); each entity includes an entity body and entity header. Messages that have more than one part are described in terms of `multipart` MIME types (such as `Multipart/Related` or `Multipart/Alternative`) and define the boundary of the contained body parts. The boundary is simply a unique text string that isn't present in any body part.

The SOAP Messages with Attachments (SwA, *http://www.w3.org/TR/SOAP-attachments*) specification describes the simple way of encapsulating entities related to SOAP messages using the MIME multipart mechanism. The rules are very simple:

- The SOAP message must be carried as the root body part of the MIME `Multipart/Related` structure.
- All other MIME parts must contain either a `Content-ID` or `Content-Location` header and can be referenced from the SOAP message using the `href` attribute.

The message structure produced according to these rules is illustrated in Example 12-1.

Example 12-1. A message created according to the SwA specification

```
MIME-Version: 1.0
Content-Type: Multipart/Related; boundary=MIME_boundary; type="text/xml"

--MIME_boundary
Content-Type: text/xml; charset=UTF-8
Content-Transfer-Encoding: 8bit

<?xml version='1.0' ?>
<SOAP-ENV:Envelope xmlns:SOAP-ENV="http://schemas.xmlsoap.org/soap/envelope/">
<SOAP-ENV:Body>
   <image xmlns="http://whatever.com/" href="cid:image"/>
</SOAP-ENV:Body>
</SOAP-ENV:Envelope>

--MIME_boundary
Content-Type: image/tiff
Content-Transfer-Encoding: binary
Content-ID: <image>

...binary TIFF image...
--MIME_boundary--
```

There's only one thing to notice. The attached part includes a `Content-ID` header (`<image>` in this example); an element in the SOAP envelope refers to that part using a `href` attribute (`cid:image` in this example; the `cid` scheme refers to a specific part of a message).

The SOAP::Lite module provides transparent access to data packaged this way (there is nothing to do on the client or server side to accept MIME-encoded messages; the value of the image element in this example will be the picture itself when accessed using SOAP::Lite), however, the current version (0.55) doesn't help to create messages with attachments. The SOAP::MIME package (created by Byrne Reese and available from CPAN) extends support for parsing MIME messages providing direct access to the attachments and also allows composing messages with attachments. Its interface is simple:

```
use SOAP::Lite;
use SOAP::MIME;
use MIME::Entity;

my $cid = "bar";
my $ent = build MIME::Entity
    Type         => "image/gif",
    Encoding     => "base64",
    Path         => "image.gif",
    'Content-Id' => "<$cid>",
    Disposition  => "attachment";

my $som = SOAP::Lite
    ->uri("...")
    ->proxy("...")
    ->parts($ent)
    ->send_image(SOAP::Data->name("foo")->attr({href => "cid:$cid"}));
```

It's quite possible that this functionality will be included in a future version of the SOAP::Lite module.

DIME and WS-Attachments

The structure of DIME message is somewhat similar to the structure of MIME messages (yet it uses a different terminology). Parts are called *records* and they consist of a header and a payload, which can be either a complete object or a chunk of an object. Similar to the MIME format, DIME uses headers to carry metadata about an object encoded in a payload.

There are several important differences between the DIME and MIME formats. First, MIME identifies the structure of content stored in the body by a type specified in a Content-Type header, whereas DIME indicates the type of the payload in two ways. The first way is identical to the usage of MIME media type as type identifier; the second (optional) method defines the type through the use of the URI. The second difference between the formats is that even though DIME records are 32-bit word aligned variable length records, each record includes a fixed length binary array with flags and lengths of four elements that follow: OPTIONS, TYPE, ID, and DATA. As a result, the length of the record is always known, and it's easy to implement random access.

The DIME specification defines a mechanism to create chunked records; it allows the sender to split up an entity into multiple records to minimize memory requirements. A complete DIME or MIME message can be nested within a DIME (or MIME) message.

The confusingly named WS-Attachments specification can be found at:

   http://www.ibm.com/developerworks/webservices/library/ws-attach.html

It's from Microsoft and IBM and defines a mechanism for encapsulating a SOAP message and zero or more attachments in a DIME message. The rules are pretty straightforward:

- The primary SOAP message part must be carried as the first payload of the DIME message. (DIME doesn't have a mechanism similar to the start parameter used in MIME to point to the root body part.)
- Any other part should include payload identifier so that it's possible to refer to the part from the SOAP message.

Because DIME is a binary format, it isn't easy to provide an example of the message. Some of the tracing tools (e.g., YATT, *http://www.pocketsoap.com/yatt/*, written by Simon Fell) support a hexadecimal view mode, which simplifies the debugging.

The DIME specification is still fairly new, and it remains to be seen what role DIME will play in the web-services infrastructure and how well it will be supported by other vendors.

Security

Security has always been one of the most important and complex issues in information technologies because it's vital in the business world to protect the data, to ensure the integrity of messages and transactions, and to maintain confidentiality of the information. It was easy in earlier days when the main focus was physical security: all the computers were locked in a room with restricted access and accessed only locally by limited number of people. Internet and web-based environments have changed all that.

Security issues can be addressed at three primary levels: transport level, message or protocol level, and application level. It can be difficult to draw the line between them; for example, HTTP, which is an application protocol on top of TCP, is considered to be the transport level for web services protocols that use it. This section discusses the transport and message levels. Application-level security would be something like the addition of user credentials to the application data that gets transferred and isn't covered here.

Key Concepts

Security means different things to different people, so we generally try to be as specific as possible. For example, is a "secure service" one in which no one but the intended recipients can read the messages? Is it one in which no one but the recipients know they're even exchanging messages? Is it the one in which a hostile third party can't fake messages? Is it all or none of the above? Here are the key concepts:

Security
   A system's ability to resist unauthorized attempts at usage or behavior modification, while still providing service to legitimate users.

Identification
   The process of presenting an identifier to a system, so that the system can recognize a party and distinguish it from other parties.

Authentication
   The process of verifying an identity claimed by or for a party. It's usually executed as validation of the party's credentials that can be as simple as a password or as complex as a X.509 certificate or Kerberos ticket. The more secure the method of authentication, the more confident you can be that parties who interact with the system are who they claim to be.

Authorization
   The process of determining whether an authenticated identity is allowed to access the resource or perform a requested action, such as approving the loan, sending a purchase order or viewing the page. The two most widely used methods of access control are based on access control lists (ACL) or roles.

Integrity
   The process by which it's ensured that information is intact and not changed by accident or due to malicious intent. The data integrity is protected by applying cryptographic technologies; in most cases, hash functions are used.

Confidentiality
   The process of making information unreadable by third parties. It ensures that content may be accessed only by authorized parties, even when an intruder overcomes or bypasses other control mechanisms. In most cases confidentiality is achieved by applying encryption technologies, but other approaches are also possible, ranging from hiding links to the resource (*security by obscurity*) to hiding the existence of information in otherwise accessible content (*steganography* and *digital watermarking*) to hiding the information in intentionally added junk messages (*chaffing*).

Nonrepudiation
   The ability of a party involved in a transaction to enforce the terms of the agreement against the other party. In other words, no party involved in a transaction can successfully deny it had involvement in the completion of the transaction.

> ## Hash Functions and Digital Signatures
>
> A *cryptographic* hash function is an algorithm that produces a fixed-length hash from a variable-length message and for which it's computationally infeasible to find either (a) message that maps to a predefined hash result or (b) several messages that map to the same hash result. The idea is that if one party computes the hash, and any bytes in the message change, the recomputed hash will change, and it becomes possible to detect tampering. Examples of cryptographic hash functions are MD2, MD4, MD5, SHA, SHA1, MDC2, and RIPEMD-160. MD5, Digest, or SSLeay modules from CPAN can be used to apply these algorithms.
>
> A *keyed* hash is a cryptographic hash in which the mapping is varied by a second parameter (the first is the message itself) that is a cryptographic key. It makes such a hash more secure, because when the message changes, a new hash result can't be calculated without knowledge of the secret hey. Examples of the algorithms that produce keyed hashes are HMAC-MD5, HMAC-SHA, and HMAC-RIPEMD-160. The Digest::HMAC module from CPAN can be used to apply these algorithms.
>
> A *digital signature* is a value computed with a cryptographic algorithm and attached to the message, in a way that allows the recipient of the message to verify the message's origin and integrity. Usually, a cryptographic hash function is applied to the message to get a hash result, which then is transformed using a private key from the signer. The signature value is the protected hash, because the algorithm used to create a hash ensures that if the message changes, the digital signature will no longer match it.

Privacy
: The state of being free from unauthorized access to personally identifiable information. Encryption technology may be used to achieve confidentiality but can't prevent inappropriate sharing of protected information. Privacy relates to control over what is done with this information and whether it's made available to other parties without the owner's concern; it's usually accomplished by a combination of technical and legal means.

Auditing
: The process of maintaining a trail of all actions acted upon the system. Audit trails generally serve two purposes: they can spot attacks on the system (even though it may be too late to stop it), and they also can check for unacceptable behavior.

Digital rights management
: The process of ensuring that content is used according to license agreement. Normally, access rules are incorporated with the content, and the client is responsible for enforcing constraints.

Transport Level Security

Basic authentication is commonly used on the Internet and unfortunately it provides very weak security protection. With basic authentication, username and password travel as clear text and are only weakly protected through a Base64 encoding. Moreover, because of the stateless nature of the HTTP protocol, the requestor must authenticate itself every time it accesses the protected resource, giving network sniffers many chances to intercept passwords.

It's easy to create code that provides basic authentication using the LWP::UserAgent module:

```perl
#!perl -w

use LWP::UserAgent;

my $url = shift
   || 'http://soaplite:authtest@services.soaplite.com/auth/examples.cgi';
my $rsp = LWP::UserAgent->new->request(new HTTP::Request GET => $url);
print $rsp->is_success ? $rsp->content : $rsp->status_line;
```

In a similar fashion, SOAP resources protected by basic authentication can be accessed using the SOAP::Lite module (note that this example shows how to provide username and password using the get_basic_credentials method, instead of embedding them in URI directly):

```perl
#!perl -w

use SOAP::Lite;

sub SOAP::Transport::HTTP::Client::get_basic_credentials {
  return 'soaplite' => 'authtest'; # username => password
}

print SOAP::Lite
  -> uri('http://www.soaplite.com/My/Examples')
  -> proxy('http://services.soaplite.com/auth/examples.cgi')
  -> getStateName(21)
  -> result;
```

Digest authentication was introduced in 1997 with HTTP 1.1 to address problems with basic authentication. While it still carries all the risks of any password-based authentication scheme that's dependent on the quality of the password, it uses a challenge/response technique to confirm that the requestor knows the proper name and password without actually transmitting the password information across the network. The LWP::UserAgent module also supports this method of authentication.

NTLM challenge/response authentication is a proprietary authentication scheme designed and implemented by Microsoft. It's similar to digest authentication, but unfortunately, uses a different challenge/response mechanism, and so the two are incompatible. Even though NTLM authentication is officially supported only for

Microsoft products, there are several modules available on CPAN that work with this method: Apache::AuthenNTLM provides server-side support for Apache servers, and the NTLM and Authen-NTLM packages provide client-side support.

The Secure Sockets Layer (SSL) provides transport layer security. It is also known as Transport Layer Security (TLS) protocol defined by the Internet standard RFC 2246, which can be found at *http://www.ietf.org/rfc/rfc2246.txt*. SSL/TLS offers several security features including authentication (through client and server certificates), data integrity, and data confidentiality. The protocol known as HTTPS is really HTTP over SSL/TLS. Because HTTP's integration with SSL is transparent for the implementation of HTTP services (although it comes with some hit on performance), it can readily be used with any implementation that sits on top of an HTTPS-aware infrastructure. A web service over HTTPS with basic authentication is probably the most common way to implement transport security.

IP Security Protocol (IPSec) is another standard for transport security. Similar to SSL/TLS, it also provides secure sessions with host authentication, data integrity, and confidentiality. It also serves a larger issue of transport beyond one particular protocol: it's the base of most modern Virtual Private Networks (VPN).

Secured/Multipurpose Internet Mail Extensions (S/MIME) is a specification for encoding any content into ASCII character representation. It provides message integrity and allows for authentication. Because S/MIME uses client-side certificates, it suffers from the problems typical for those certificates: they have to be installed on the client side, they are difficult to revoke and invalidate, and they don't allow delegation of trust to allow other agents to act on someone else's behalf.

There is one more aspect that hasn't been discussed yet but is a hot topic for many security experts who talk about web services and transport security: firewalls. Most web services calls use HTTP as a transport and hence go through port 80, bypassing the firewall security or requiring some additional steps to filter the XML traffic.

As discussed earlier, the current version of the SOAP specification (1.1) includes a SOAPAction header. This header lets the transport infrastructure know it's a SOAP request, so that the infrastructure may act accordingly. However, this header is made optional in the current draft of the new SOAP specification (1.2) and likely will go away. People tend to agree that even if it may seem like a hole in the firewall security, sending an RPC request isn't very different from sending a document that triggers some action on a server side (those differences will be discussed later in this chapter) and as such, it should bear similar security constraints.

XML Security

XML security standards provide a set of technical specifications to meet security requirements of XML-based systems and applications. This section covers the general XML security standards; their integration with web services will be outlined in the "Web Services Security" section that follows.

There are five core security standards:

- XML Signature Syntax and Processing (XML Signature): for integrity
- XML Encryption: for confidentiality
- XML Key Management (XKMS): for key management
- Security Assertion Markup Language (SAML): for authentication and authorization assertions
- XML Access Control Markup Language (XACML): for stating authorization rules

There are also other specifications, such as Extensible Rights Markup Language (XrML) for digital rights management and Platform for Privacy Preferences (P3P) for expressing privacy preferences and policies, but they aren't detailed here.

These standards leverage and extend existing XML and security technologies as follows:

- The XML security standards reuse existing cryptographic and security technologies, and leverage existing XML standards to support current XML efforts. For example, several crytographic algorithms are used by XML security specifications by associating unique URIs with them. XPath expressions are used by the XML Signature specification to refer to fragments of XML for processing.
- The XML security standards define a shared meaning for the XML vocabularies that represent security information. One example is the `KeyInfo` element defined in XML Signature recommendation and used in other specifications, such as XML Encryption and WS-Security (all are discussed later in this chapter).
- XML security technologies allow security techniques to be applied to the entire XML document, to fragments of the XML document, to XML elements and element content, as well as to binary documents.
- The XML security standards allow implementation of end-to-end security, which is especially important when the message is routed through a number of intermediaries. Being associated with the content, rather than with a transport, persistent security also allows documents to be stored preserving the security context. Still, transport level security can be applied when necessary.

The XML Signature, XML Encryption, and XML Key Management specifications are produced by the World Wide Web Consortium (W3C), whereas Security Assertion Markup Language and XML Access Control Markup Language are specifications developed by the Organization for the Advancement of Structured Information Standards (OASIS). Even though the specifications developed by the two standards bodies complement each other, they go through different processes. Companies are becoming increasingly concerned about the complexity and speed of the W3C standardization process, and the recent submission of the WS-Security specification to OASIS rather than to W3C highlights that.

W3C Standardization Process

W3C is a consortium founded by Tim Berners-Lee in 1994. The goal was to create an international body to further develop the Web, which was rapidly taking off at that time.

The main products of the W3C are the specifications it produces. The highest status a specification can get inside the W3C is Recommendation. Before becoming a Recommendation, a specification undergoes several steps:

1. A specification begins as a Working Draft (WD). Working drafts are written by Working Groups (WG) and generally represent work in progress and a commitment by the W3C to pursue work in a particular area. For example, working drafts of the SOAP Version 1.2 specification[a] were prepared by XML Protocol Working Group.[b]
2. Last Call Working Draft is a special public instance of a Working Draft for which the Working Group seeks technical review form other groups, W3C members, and the public.
3. When the review period is completed, a specification becomes a Candidate Recommendation (CR). At this period the specification is on active trial for a period of time to see if implementations succeed in conforming to it and become interoperable.
4. As soon as a specification is believed to meet all the relevant requirements of the Working Group and any accompanying requirements document, it becomes a Proposed Recommendation (PR).
5. Finally, the specification becomes a Recommendation.

Some specifications start with a request by one or more members or working groups, while others start as a concrete proposal to the W3C, in the form of a submission. Those submissions are published by the W3C as nonnormative Notes. For example, the XSL, SOAP, and XKMS specifications started as Notes.

---

a. *http://www.w3.org/TR/soap12*
b. *http://www.w3.org/2000/xp/Group/*

XML Signature Syntax and Processing (XML Signature)

The XML Signature Syntax and Processing specification can be found at:

http://www.w3.org/TR/xmldsig-core/

It defines mechanisms for creating and representing digital signatures.

An XML Signature can be applied to arbitrary digital content (the actual binary data being operated on by an application). The specification also defines techniques that address the variations allowed in XML, such as whitespaces, encoding, or attributes order. The reason for the concern is that cryptographic algorithms don't distinguish between markup and content and always operate on exact text, while XML allows some flexibility in physical representation for logically equivalent XML documents. The process of generating the common physical representation is called *canonicalization* (defined in XML Canonicalization specification, *http://www.w3.org/TR/xml-c14n*) and has to be applied before a digital signature is generated and validated.

Symmetric and Asymmetric Cryptography

Symmetric cryptography (also called secret-key or private-key cryptography) is a set of algorithms that employ the same key for encryption and decryption, or signature creation and verification. Both parties share the same key they must keep secret (hence the name secret-key cryptography). Examples of these algorithms are DES, DES-EDE3, IDEA, RC2, RC4, RC5, Blowfish, and CAST. Crypt-DES, Crypt-DES_EDE3, Crypt-IDEA, Crypt-RC4, Crypt-RC5, and Crypt-Blowfish modules from CPAN can be used to apply these algorithms.

Asymmetric cryptography (also called public-key cryptography) is a set of algorithms that use a pair of keys (a public key and a private key. The public key is for verification of signature and encryption, and the private key is for creating a digital signature and decryption. Examples of these algorithms are Diffie-Hellman, DSA, RSA, El Gamal, and Rijndael. Crypt-DH, Crypt-DSA, Crypt-RSA, Crypt-IDEA, and Crypt-Rijndael modules from CPAN can be used to apply these algorithms.

An XML Signature can be applied to the content of one or more resources in different ways, depending on the desired application. The result of the processing is the Signature element that includes created signature and related information. Depending on the location of the signature and signed content, three types of signatures can be generated.

An *enveloped* signature is included in the signed element, as in this example (note that the definition for PurchaseOrder element has to allow this kind of enclosure):

```
<PurchaseOrder Id="1234567">
  ....
  <Signature xmlns="http://www.w3.org/2000/09/xmldsig#">
    <SignedInfo>
      <CanonicalizationMethod
         Algorithm="http://www.w3.org/TR/2001/REC-xml-c14n-20010315"/>
      <SignatureMethod Algorithm="http://www.w3.org/2000/09/xmldsig#dsa-sha1"/>
      <Reference URI="#1234567">...</Reference>
    </SignedInfo>
```

```
        <SignatureValue>...</SignatureValue>
    </Signature>
</PurchaseOrder>
```

An *enveloping* signature includes content being signed in the signature, within an `Object` element:

```
<Signature xmlns="http://www.w3.org/2000/09/xmldsig#">
    <SignedInfo>
        <CanonicalizationMethod
            Algorithm="http://www.w3.org/TR/2001/REC-xml-c14n-20010315"/>
        <SignatureMethod Algorithm="http://www.w3.org/2000/09/xmldsig#dsa-sha1"/>
        <Reference URI="#1234567">...</Reference>
    </SignedInfo>
    <SignatureValue>...</SignatureValue>
    <Object>
        <PurchaseOrder Id="1234567">...</PurchaseOrder>
    </Object>
</Signature>
```

A *detached* signature is created over data external to the signature element. It usually applies to separate data objects but can also refer to data objects that reside within the same XML document but are sibling elements.

```
<Signature xmlns="http://www.w3.org/2000/09/xmldsig#">
    <SignedInfo>
        <CanonicalizationMethod
            Algorithm="http://www.w3.org/TR/2001/REC-xml-c14n-20010315"/>
        <SignatureMethod Algorithm="http://www.w3.org/2000/09/xmldsig#dsa-sha1"/>
        <Reference URI="http://www.foo.org/purchaseOrder.xml">...</Reference>
    </SignedInfo>
    <SignatureValue>MC0C...</SignatureValue>
</Signature>
```

Signature attributes (these are properties of a signature and have no relationship to XML attributes), such as time of signing, can be optionally signed by identifying them from within a `Reference` element.

The XML Signature specification supports the application of multiple signature to an XML document or sections of the document. The `Transform` mechanism allows doing that by permitting you to sign data derived from processing of the content. For example, an application that wishes to sign a form but permit users to modify limited field data without invalidating a previous signature might use XPath to exclude those portions that the user needs to change. Transforms are a very powerful mechanism and can include operations such as canonicalization, encoding/decoding (including compression/inflation), XSLT, XPath, or XML Schema validation.

XML Encryption

The XML Encryption specification can be found at:

http://www.w3.org/TR/xmlenc-core/

It defines a process for encrypting data and representing the result in XML.

Similar to XML Signature specification, XML Encryption can be applied at a fine level of granularity to XML content: to arbitrary data (including an XML document), to an XML element, or to XML element content. The result of the processing is the `EncryptedData` element that replaces the element or content in the encrypted version of the XML document.

In addition to the fine granularity of the encryption process, the specification also allows for the super-encryption of data (in other words, encrypting of XML in which some elements are already encrypted) and provides a separation of encryption information from encrypted data. The specification defines a simple encryption mechanism (yet it supports the variety of encryption algorithms and techniques) and doesn't address authentication, authorization, access control and trust issues.

The flexibility of the specification allows implementation of the end-to-end protection that protects not only data in transit, but also in storage, and allows part of the information to be revealed to intermediaries (if necessary). Consider this fictitious `PurchaseOrder` element:

```
<PurchaseOrder>
  <Number>...</Number>
  <Date>...</Date>
  <Details>...</Details>
</PurchaseOrder>
```

While it's possible to apply the encryption to the whole element, it's also possible to allow intermediaries to access the `Number` and `Date` but not the `Details` element. The `PurchaseOrder` element is encrypted:

```
<EncryptedData xmlns='http://www.w3.org/2001/04/xmlenc#' MimeType='text/xml'>
  <CipherData>
    <CipherValue>MC0C...</CipherValue>
  </CipherData>
</EncryptedData>
```

Here, only the `Details` element is encrypted:

```
<PurchaseOrder>
  <PurchaseOrderNumber>...</PurchaseOrderNumber>
  <OrderDate>...</OrderDate>
  <EncryptedData Type='http://www.w3.org/2001/04/xmlenc#Element'
     xmlns='http://www.w3.org/2001/04/xmlenc#'>
    <CipherData>
      <CipherValue>AD0A...</CipherValue>
    </CipherData>
  </EncryptedData>
</PurchaseOrder>
```

Because the document can be not only encrypted but also signed, it brings an interesting question: how is the order of the processing determined? It's important to know, because if an element is signed and then encrypted, it has to be decrypted first, otherwise the signature won't match. The XML Decryption Transform specification, (found at *http://www.w3.org/TR/xmlenc-decrypt)*, defines a resolution to the decryption/verification ordering issue.

Note the ability to sign the content that includes markup may pose additional security risks, particularly those that are associated with a known plaintext attack. Knowledge about particular text that was encrypted can make it easier to break the encryption and the availability of schema definition for a particular document makes plaintext attacks more likely.

XML Key Management (XKMS)

The XML Key Management specification can be found at:

http://www.w3.org/TR/xkms/

It specifies protocols for distributing and registering public keys, suitable for use in combination with XML Signature and XML Encryption specifications.

The XKMS specification comprises two parts—the XML Key Information Service Specification (X-KISS) and the XML Key Registration Service Specification (X-KRSS). The X-KRSS specification defines a protocol for a web service that accepts registration of public key information. Once registered, the public key may be used in conjunction with other web services including X-KISS. The X-KISS specification defines a protocol for a trust service that resolves public key information contained in XML Signature elements. The entire process of registering, obtaining, and revoking keys can be delegated to the trust service, freeing the application from part or all of the tasks required to process key information. As a result, an application can be abstracted from the implementation details of the underlying Public Key Infrastructure (PKI) used to establish and carry on trust relationships.

The protocol defined by the X-KISS specification allows location and validation of the information required for signature verification or encryption. In both cases, public key information is returned. However there is one important difference: the locate service doesn't validate or report the revocation status and trustworthiness of used certificate.

The protocol defined by the X-KRSS specification allows registration, revocation, and key recovery. Note that the XKMS specification doesn't define how key management is secured. Implementations are responsible for protecting the confidentiality and integrity of the exchanged information.

Even though the message syntax presented in both specifications is designed to allow use of SOAP and WSDL specifications, it's possible to express the messages in a syntax other than XML and over protocols other than SOAP.

Security Assertion Markup Language (SAML)

The XML Security Assertion Markup Language specification can be found at:

http://www.oasis-open.org/committees/security/

It defines an XML vocabulary for sharing authentication and authorization assertions, enabling third-party management of these functions. Assertions convey information about authentication acts performed by subjects, and authorized decisions about whether subjects are allowed to access certain resources.

An *assertion* is a declaration of facts about subject. SAML allows an issuer to make three different kinds of assertion statements:

Authentication
   The specified subject is authenticated by a particular means at a particular time. SAML allows assertions to specify which type of authentication mechanism is used and supports several such mechanisms. Note that this assertion describes only the fact of authentication that happened previously and doesn't verify or revoke credentials this authentication is established on.

Attribute
   The specified subject is associated with the provided attribute, which has a particular value.

Authorization decision
   The request to allow the specified subject to access a particular resource if the specified evidence has been granted or denied.

Even though SAML assertions may be generated and exchanged using a variety of protocols, SAML also specifies a message exchange protocol that defines how the issuer can be queried for available assertion statements. Three types of queries are defined:

Authentication
   "What authentication assertions are available for this subject?" A successful response includes assertions containing authentication elements.

Attribute
   "What is the value of the requested attribute for this subject?" A successful response includes assertions containing attribute assertions.

Authorization decision
   "Is this subject allowed to access this resource in the specified manner, given the specified evidence?" A successful response includes assertions containing authorization decision statements.

SAML defines an XML-based protocol by which clients can request assertions from SAML authorities. It also defines one SOAP binding (mapping of SAML request/ response message exchanges into standard communication protocol) and two Web

Browser Single Sign-On profiles (sets of rules describing how to embed and extract SAML into a framework or protocol).

XML Access Control Markup Language (XACML)

The XML Access Control Markup Language specification can be found at:

http://www.oasis-open.org/committees/xacml/

It defines an XML vocabulary for expressing access-control techniques in the form of policy statements for a variety of information systems and devices. This can then provide a consolidated view of the policy in effect across many systems and devices, which in turn aids in the enforcement of such policies.

XACML defines not only a vocabulary for expressing authorization rules but also a vocabulary for expressing a variety of conditions to be used to create rules. The specification defines rules as targets, effects, and conditions. A target defines the set of resources, subjects, and actions. XACML is designed to be used in combination with SAML; for example, XACML uses the SAML definitions for subjects and actions. An effect indicates the intended consequence of an evaluation for the rule and may have a value of either "permit" or "deny."

An important aspect of the specification is that it allows rules to be combined and describes how this is done. In addition to the simple combination of rules, they can also be collected into policy statements that include a target, rule-combining algorithm, a set of rules, and obligations. The target of a policy statement determines whether a policy is applicable and may be declared either explicitly (by the policy writer) or implicitly (derived from targets of component rules). An obligation is an action that is performed once the authorization decision is made (one of the examples included in the specification sends a notification email each time a patient's medical record is accessed).

Web Services Security

The XML security standards described in the previous section form the basis for providing security to other XML-related initiatives, such as web services. The Web Services Security specifications link together web services protocols (such as SOAP) and security specification (such as XML Signature and XML Encryption). Knowledge that data can be securely transmitted, processed, and stored is essential to the future of web services.

Web Services Security Language (WS-Security)

The Web Services Security Language specification can be found at:

http://www.ibm.com/developerworks/library/ws-secure/

Released by Microsoft and IBM, it subsumes and expands upon earlier specifications in this field (namely SOAP Security Extensions, WS-License, and older versions of WS-Security), and aims to describe a unified, flexible, and extensible security framework for web services.

WS-Security defines a SOAP extension to provide end-to-end message integrity, confidentiality, and single message authentication. It specifies how to associate security tokens with messages and is designed to be extensible and allow support for multiple security token formats, including but not limited to Kerberos tickets and X.509 certificates.

The WS-Security specification defines a Security element to be used in the SOAP message headers as a container for all other elements defined in the specification. For instance, the code in the following example shows how a SOAP request with simple UsernameToken may look:

```
<s:Envelope xmlns:s="http://www.w3.org/2001/12/soap-envelope"
            xmlns:wsse="http://schemas.xmlsoap.org/ws/2002/04/secext">
    <s:Header>
        ...
        <wsse:Security>
            <wsse:UsernameToken>
                <wsse:Username>PaulK</wsse:Username>
                <wsse:Password>GooReria</wsse:Password>
            </wsse:UsernameToken>
        </wsse:Security>
        ...
    </s:Header>
    ...
</s:Envelope>
```

To generate this header using the SOAP::Lite module, use the following code:

```
use SOAP::Lite maptype => {};

my $wsse = "http://schemas.xmlsoap.org/ws/2002/04/secext";
my $securityHeader = SOAP::Header->name(Security => {
  UsernameToken => {
    Username => SOAP::Data->type('' => 'PaulK'),
    Password => SOAP::Data->type('' => 'GooReria'),
  }
})->uri($wsse)->prefix('');

my $result = SOAP::Lite
  # include header as an additional parameter
  ->securedMethod(@parameters, $securityHeader);
  ...
```

A BinarySecurityToken element might be used instead of the UsernameToken element to allow binary or other non-XML formats to be included in the message:

```
<wsse:BinarySecurityToken
  xmlns:wsse="http://schemas.xmlsoap.org/ws/2002/04/secext"
```

```
        ValueType="wsse:X509v3"
        EncodingType="wsse:Base64Binary">
        AOCD...
</wsse:BinarySecurityToken>
```

In this example, `ValueType` identifies the type of the security token (X.509v3 certificate), and `EncodingType` describes the method used to encode the data: Base64 or hex.

Integrity of the header and body elements may be provided using the XML Signature specification. As covered in the previous section, the `Signature` element can be used to carry on signature information. Confidentiality of the information in the message may be protected by means of XML Encryption. As already discussed in the section on XML Encryption, the encrypted element is replaced by an `EncryptedData` element; for every portion of SOAP message that is encrypted, one subelement has to be added to the `Security` header block. It can be a `ReferenceList` or `EncryptedKey` element that refers to encrypted fragment, or an `EncryptedData` element when non-XML attachments are encrypted.

When the message contains an invalid signature, invalid or unsupported type of security token, or produces a decryption failure, it has to be rejected, and an error may be reported using SOAP's fault mechanism. All errors are grouped in two classes: unsupported and failure.

The WS-Security specification cooperates well with the other XML security standards and defines two profiles for XML-based tokens: one for SAML and another for XrML. For more information, check out *http://msdn.microsoft.com/library/en-us/ dnglobspec/html/ws-security-xml-tokens.asp*.

Using WS-Security, SAML assertions can be attached to SOAP messages by placing them inside the Security header element:

```
<s:Envelope xmlns:s="...">
    <s:Header>
        <wsse:Security xmlns:wsse="...">
            <saml:Assertion xmlns:saml="..." ...>
                ...
            </saml:Assertion>
            ...
        </wsse:Security>
    </s:Header>
    <s:Body>
        ...
    </s:Body>
</s:Envelope>
```

In a similar fashion, XrML licenses can be attached to SOAP messages by placing the license element inside the `Security` header element:

```
<s:Envelope xmlns:s="...">
    <s:Header>
        <wsse:Security xmlns:wsse="...">
```

```
            <xrml:license xmlns:xrml="...">
                ...
            </xrml:license>
            ...
        </wsse:Security>
    </s:Header>
    <s:Body>
        ...
    </s:Body>
</s:Envelope>
```

Given all that, WS-Security provides a flexible way for the message sender to claim the security properties by associating security tokens with the message.

WS-Policy, WS-Trust, WS-Privacy, WS-SecureConversations, WS-Federation, and WS-Authorization

The Web Services Security architecture and roadmap document can be found at:

http://www.ibm.com/developerworks/webservices/library/ws-secmap/

It indicates plans for other specifications, which are still only plans at the time of writing:

WS-Policy
    Describes the security capabilities, constraints and policies on intermediaries and endpoints (e.g., required security tokens, supported encryption algorithms, privacy rules)

WS-Trust
    Describes a security trust model that enables web services to securely interoperate across multiple trust domains

WS-Privacy
    Describes a model for web services clients and services to state and enforce privacy preferences and organizational privacy practice statements

Follow-up specifications are layered on top of the previous specifications and include WS-SecureConversations, WS-Federation, and WS-Authorization:

WS-SecureConversations
    Describes how to establish message exchanges between parties including security context exchange across trust domains using key exchange

WS-Federation
    Describes how to manage identities in a heterogeneous federated environment

WS-Authorization
    Describes how to manage authorization data and policies in a web services environment

Some of the proposed and existing security standards have considerable overlap and the relationships between WS-* specifications and XKMS, SAML, and XACML specifications aren't immediately clear.

Services Discovery

The Universal Description Discovery and Integration (UDDI) specification described in Chapter 10 provides the way to advertise and discover web services; however, it doesn't support all possible patterns of discovery. It's often compared with Yellow Pages, but people don't always use the Yellow Pages to find services they need: they may already know about the service existence, but don't know the details; they may get the new service from the service provider they already use; or they get referral from people they know. While it's possible to implement these patterns using UDDI, it isn't the best tool for the job. The Web Services Inspection Language was proposed to fill the niche.

Web Services Inspection Language (WS-Inspection or WSIL)

The Web Services Inspection Language specification can be found at:

http://www.ibm.com/developerworks/webservices/library/ws-wsilspec.html

Released by IBM and Microsoft, it consolidates concepts that can be found in ADS and DISCO specifications. It also provides an XML format for specifying rules for aggregating references to existing services and assisting in the inspection for available services.

The structure of WS-Inspection document is succinctly simple. The inspection element is the root element of the document and contains only three types of elements: zero or more abstract, zero or more service, and zero or more link elements. The abstract element can be used for documentary purposes to provide a location for small textual description of the service. The service element can provide links to service descriptions and may have zero or more abstract elements (try to guess what those are for) and zero or more name elements. It must have at least one description element. The link element can provide a link to other inspection documents and related aggregation information sources. The name element can associate a name with the service and is intended only for human consumption. The structure of a simple WS-Inspection document is shown in the Example 12-2.

Example 12-2. A simple WS-Inspection document
```
<?xml version="1.0"?>
<inspection xmlns="http://schemas.xmlsoap.org/ws/2001/10/inspection/">
  <abstract>O'Reilly book service </abstract>
  <service>
    <description referencedNamespace="http://schemas.xmlsoap.org/wsdl/"
                 location="http://oreilly.com/books.wsdl"/>
```

Example 12-2. A simple WS-Inspection document (continued)

```
  </service>
  <service>
    <description referencedNamespace="http://schemas.xmlsoap.org/wsdl/"
                 location="http://oreilly.com/authors.wsdl "/>
  </service>
  <link referencedNamespace="http://schemas.xmlsoap.org/ws/2001/10/inspection/"
        location="http://oreilly.com/partners.wsil"/>
</inspection>
```

The description element provides the most useful information in the inspection document. It provides pointers to service description documents of various formats (all of which may describe the same service), allowing consumers to pick one they find most useful. The referencedNamespace attribute identifies the namespace to which the referenced document belongs, thus unambiguously describing the type of the service description. The optional location attribute may point to the actual reference of the description. The location attribute is optional because the description element may contain the extensibility element that provides all necessary location information, in which case the location attribute isn't needed.

The WS-Inspection specification defines WSDL and UDDI bindings that provide additional information about a described service. For example, a WSDL binding may provide hints about the presence of endpoint information in a WSDL document (<reference endpointPresent="false"/>), and the UDDI binding may provide references to UDDI businessEntity or businessService entries. Developing additional bindings is also covered by the specification.

Inspection documents will be of low value if there is no easy way to locate and access these documents. The WS-Inspection specification describes several ways to discover a WS-Inspection document. First, the inspection document may be discovered by traversing other inspection documents and following links provided in link elements. Second, an inspection document may be stored in an inspection.wsil file and placed where the most common entry points to web sites or applications are located. Third, the inspection document can be linked from within HTML documents using a META tag:

```
<!DOCTYPE HTML PUBLIC "-//W3C//DTD HTML 4.0 Transitional//EN">
<HTML>
  <HEAD>
    <META name="serviceInspection" content="localservices.wsil">
    <META name="serviceInspection" content="http://www.oreilly.com/services.wsil">
  </HEAD>
  <BODY>...</BODY>
</HTML>
```

Be warned that wide open exposing of the services and service descriptions may pose a security risk. Also, because the specification permits inspection documents in different locations, it may be wise to separate descriptions for public and private services and protect not only the service itself, but also a service description, for example, using basic authentication for HTTP protocol.

UDDI and WS-Inspection specifications should be viewed as complimentary technologies that support each other and can be used separately or together depending on the situation. For example, search engines may access links to WS-Inspection descriptions linked via META elements in HTML documents, and store retrieved information in a UDDI repository. Alternatively, the UDDI repository can be discovered through the links in WS-Inspection documents.

Reliable Messaging

Reliable messaging is a simple concept that refers to the ability of a sender to deliver a message once and only once to its intended recipient and is a necessary building block for many cross-application communications (when someone sends a payment, it's reasonable to expect the payment will be received, and it's received only once). The most primitive method of doing this is to keep sending the message to the destination until the recipient acknowledges receipt of the message. While the description of this task takes just a couple of lines, it's surprisingly difficult to implement and the complete implementation may easily have thousands of lines of the code (okay, hundreds if done in Perl but still it's pretty significant difference) when all the possible failure scenarios have to be addressed. Here are the requirements:

- The message has to be saved in persistent storage, so it can be delivered even when the sending application crashes.
- The message has to contain a unique identifier, so the receiver can discard any duplicates it receives.
- The state of the conversation has to be saved in persistent storage, so that an acknowledgement can be delivered even when the receiving application crashes.
- The acknowledgement has to include a correlation identifier, so that the sender can match the acknowledgement with the message it acknowledges.
- When the message can't be delivered (for instance, network is down) the sending application has to be notified about the situation and reason for failure.

When implementing reliable messaging, it's important to decide what layer will support it. One possibility that was already discussed in Chapter 11 is to put it in the application. Another possibility is to do that in a transport layer. Reliable HTTP specification takes the later approach.

HTTPR

HTTPR is a protocol for the reliable transport layered on top of HTTP (HTTP 1.1 to be precise) that was designed by IBM. Even though there are other products that support reliable messaging (IBM WebSphere/MQSeries, Microsoft Message

Queuing, and SonicMQ have supported it for years), it's mostly done via proprietary protocols. IBM's HTTPR is an attempt to provide a vendor-neutral protocol for this purpose.

HTTPR specification defines commands, message structure (how metadata and application messages are encapsulated within the payload) and simple protocol rules (making it possible to ensure that each message is delivered to its destination application exactly once or is reliably reported as undeliverable).

There are five HTTPR commands defined by the specification:

PUSH
> Sends one or more messages to the server. The response indicates whether messages have been received.

PULL
> Invites the server to return any messages waiting for delivery. The response may include one or more messages or be "empty" if there are no messages ready for delivery.

EXCHANGE
> Sends and receives messages (it's a combination of PUSH and PULL commands). When the server process responds quickly enough it can get a response message delivered in a single command flow; however, despite the request/response notion of HTTP, HTTPR isn't aware of the request/reply relationship.

REPORT
> Reports which batches of messages has been received by client (request) and server (response).

GET-RESPONDER-INFO
> Begins a session to do the capability negotiation and to determine the responder identity.

Each HTTPR command is encoded as the body of an HTTP POST request with a simple structure:

```
POST /foo HTTP/1.1                        ; HTTP POST
Content-Length: NNN                       ; all other HTTP headers
                            ; CRLF        ; end of the HTTP header
NNN                         ; 1*HEX CRLF  ; size of 1st HTTP chunk
request: PUSH 1.0           ; Request     ; HTTPR request
transactionid: 0000000000000001 ;         ; all other HTTPR headers
                            ; CRLF        ; end of the HTTPR header
Bar                         ; *Payload    ; HTTPR payload
payload-disposition: last   ; Terminator  ; last part of the body
0                           ; 0 CRLF      ; last chunk
                            ; CRLF        ; end of the message
```

The HTTPR specification also defines and describes such capabilities as unit of work, sessions, message ordering, batches, and pipelining (several outstanding requests).

Look for more information on HTTPR at:

http://www.ibm.com/developerworks/webservices/library/ws-httprspec/

Business Process Management

Businesses are changing rapidly and becoming increasingly complex with even less clear boundaries between (and inside) companies. Most of the business interactions are complex in structure, transactional, stateful, and asynchronous; some of them are long-lived, with complex relationships between their participants.

While this section is called "business process management," there are several terms that are often used in the same context but still have slightly different meaning: orchestration, choreography, conversation, composition, coordination, collaboration, workflow, and business process management. A few are defined here to minimize the confusion:

Orchestration (also *composition* and *workflow*)
: Defines a composition of smaller services into a larger service. It describes how services get called including specific order of interaction, and addresses the possible dependencies between those services.

Choreography
: Defines an interaction script—a message exchange between different services. Even though it may indicate the sequence of messages and identify trading partners and their roles in the interactions, it isn't an executable logic; it's a contract all participants are compliant with.

Coordination
: Defines a contract for distributed synchronization.

Collaboration
: Defines a contract or agreement over the technical aspects of the relationship.

Before diving into the conversation about specifications that describe some of these aspects of business process management, two important topics have to be discussed: document style and distributed transactions.

Document and RPC Styles

Most of the discussions so far were focused on the RPC style of method execution and the document style was only briefly discussed in a previous chapter. Here is a quick remainder for those who skipped some of them: document (also called messaging) style means that an XML document is sent as the payload of the SOAP message. For many people, RPC and document styles are like two different sides of a coin: RPC style is associated with the message signature and data types, whereas document style is associated with the document structure and XML processing. The reality is that the wire representation doesn't dictate a programming model. It's one of the things people frequently confuse when comparing document and RPC styles. Two others are granularity of interfaces and synchronous versus asynchronous messaging models.

The representation on wire and a programming model are orthogonal to each other; both RPC and a document style can be programmed using object-oriented and XML approaches. Although there are some differences, they are minimal: RPC style tends to provide more methods and work with simpler data, whereas document style operates mostly on rich data using no methods at all (it's also possible to look at it as if it's using only one method, send). The diagram in Figure 12-1 illustrates this.

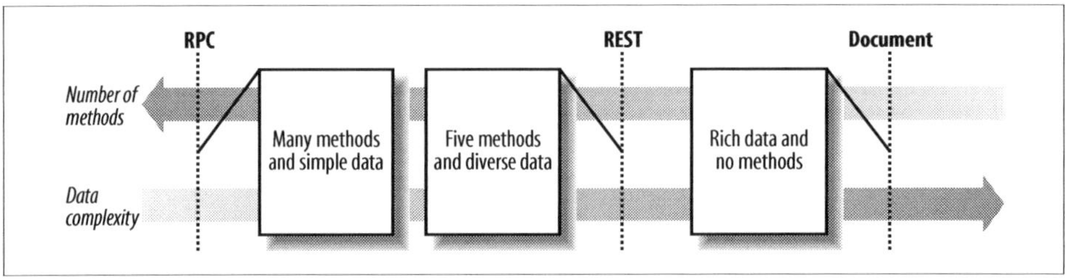

Figure 12-1. RPC, REST, and document styles

Granularity of interface generally refers to the level of detail provided by the interface. Fine-grained (also called chatty) interfaces provide high level of details, whereas coarse-grained (or chunky) interfaces provide low level of details. RPC methods are often associated with fine-grained interfaces and document style with coarse-grained interfaces, but as with programming models, in reality they are orthogonal; messages implemented using both RPC and document styles can be coarse- or fine-grained. Examples of fine-grained RPC request include getAccountBallance and getInterestRate, which return the account balance and interest rate, respectively. Coarse-grained getAccountSummary requests return the account balance, current interest rate, and five last transactions. Object-oriented style encourages fine-grained interfaces with better flexibility and maintainability; the very nature of distributed applications prescribes coarse-grained interfaces.

The difference between asynchronous and synchronous messages is a different story. It has to be emphasized that in most cases when people make the distinction, they are talking about real-time and deferrable interactions. The difference between these two is clearer: if a real-time message can't be sent immediately, this is an error and the client has to be notified. This is a business-oriented rather than a technical distinction. Both real-time and deferrable interactions can be implemented using synchronous (request/response) or asynchronous paradigm; for example, clients may send a POST request, get back a 202 Accepted code with a new URI included in the Location header, and then come back later to send a GET request to that URI to get a response.

The point of the discussion is that even though RPC-style messages tend to be real-time, fine-granular requests mapped to object-oriented methods for execution, they could be something else too. In the same sense, document-style messages tend to be deferrable, coarse-grained messages, associated with document processing but could be something else.

The interesting question to consider is: how does the receiver know what to do when the document style is used; in many cases there is no action included with the message, only data. The answer is that there are always some semantics associated with the message; in some cases this knowledge is transferred out of band. Semantics is the understanding of the intent of a thing or a concept. When an application receives a "purchase order" or "request for comment," it knows what to do with it (if not, a fault message is returned or there is a problem with the application). If two different responses are returned for the same data, there are two different semantics associated with that data. Even when the REST style is used semantics are present; for example, the DELETE request for the order resource can mean "cancel the order."

Distributed Transactions

A business transaction is an interaction in the real world, usually between a business and an individual or another business, where the state of one of the object changes. Transactions have four critical properties (also known as ACID properties):

Atomicity
> The transaction executes completely or not at all (all-or-nothing execution). The successful completion of a transaction is called *commit* and the failure of a transactions is called abort (or *rollback*). Atomic transaction implementations typically hold data resources (e.g., locking) and physical resources (e.g., connections, threads, memory) and assume short time duration and high trust.

Consistency
> Internal consistency of the affected resource (for example, database) is preserved (unaffected properties don't change).

Isolation
> The transaction executes as if it were running alone, with no other transactions. Effects of the execution aren't visible until the transaction commits; as the result, transactions appear to be executed serially (one by one), even if they are performed concurrently.

Durability
> All changes caused by the transaction execution are stored in persistent storage, and results will not be lost in the failure.

When a transaction updates data on two or more systems in a distributed environment, atomicity of a transaction still has to be ensured. This may pose a significant challenge, because, as was discussed in the section on reliable messaging, a system may fail for different reasons, and multiple systems may fail and recover independently. One solution that deals with such problems is the *two-phase commit* (2PC) protocol. All actions taken prior to commit or abort aren't visible to other activities and are stored in persistent storage; they get committed as soon as participants vote to complete successful execution.

Commit is an irrevocable action: a transaction can't be aborted once it's committed. However, it's possible that, for whatever reason, a transaction has to be reversed even after it's already committed. The transaction that reverses the action of some previous transaction is called a *compensating* transaction. The example of the compensating transaction would be the delivery of the luggage to the right address after it was mistakenly routed to the wrong airport (it isn't always possible to cancel or roll back that activity). In some cases, the compensating transaction is simply a recording of the fact that something wrong happened.

Transactions and Coordination

This section describes protocols that describe managing the business interactions in a loosely coupled, asynchronous environment. These include WS-Coordination and WS-Transaction, jointly developed by Microsoft, IBM, and BEA; and Business Transaction Protocol developed by OASIS.

Web Services Coordination (WS-Coordination)

The Web Services Coordination specification can be found at:

http://www.ibm.com/developerworks/library/ws-coor/

It defines an extensible framework for coordinating activities that defines a set of coordination protocols and enables participants to reach consistent agreement on the outcome of distributed activities. The coordination protocols that can be defined in this framework can accommodate a variety of activities, including protocols for simple short-lived operations and protocols for complex long-lived business activities.

The framework is described by defining a coordination service that consists of the following elements:

An activation service
    Defines a CreateCoordinationContext operation that enables an application to create a coordination instance or context. The activation service isn't required to be supported; the exact semantics are defined in the additional specification.

A registration service
    Defines a Register operation that enables an application to register for coordination protocols. The registration service must be supported by a coordination service.

A coordination type
> Describes specific set of coordination protocols; one coordination type may have multiple coordination protocols that define the coordination behavior and the message exchange between the participants. The definition of coordination protocols are provided in an additional specification (for example, WS-Transaction specification discussed next).

Because of the simplicity of WS-Coordination specification, it's quite reasonable to expect that its functionality will be used not only by WS-Transaction but also by other specifications to establish context for business interactions.

Web Services Transaction (WS-Transaction)

The Web Services Transaction specification can be found at:

> *http://www.ibm.com/developerworks/library/ws-transpec/*

It leverages WS-Coordination specification by using it to define two coordination types to support atomic transactions (AT) and business activities (BA). It does this by defining the behavior and messages required by the respective coordination protocols.

The WS-Coordination protocols are used for transactions to create a new atomic transaction context, to propagate that context in messages between web services, and to register for participation in coordination protocols, depending on the participant's role in the activity. Each protocol is one of the coordination protocols of the atomic transaction coordination type defined in the specification. These protocols include Completion, CompletionWithAck (completion with optional notification), 2PC (two-phase commit), PhaseZero (notification that is sent before the 2PC protocol started), and OutcomeNotification (notification on completion of a transaction).

While atomic transactions are important building blocks, they aren't sufficient for the overall coordination. Responding to a request may take a very long time. Human approval, assembly, manufacturing, or delivery may have to take place before a response can be sent. Business activities require resources to be shared prior to completion.

The Business Activity protocols handle long-lived activities and compensating transactions (business logic to handle business exceptions). There are only two coordination protocols for business activities defined by WS-Transaction specification: BusinessAgreement and BusinessAgreementWithComplete.

Note that even though it isn't stated by the specification, reliable messaging is required to deliver messages "at least once" (or better "exactly once").

Overall, even though are WS-Transaction specification lacks some features presented in other transaction protocols (like BTP, which will be briefly covered next) it looks simpler than its predecessors. This makes it easier to implement and lowers barriers for adoption.

Business Transaction Protocol (BTP)

The Business Transaction Protocol specification can be found at:

http://www.oasis-open.org/business-transaction/

Developed by OASIS, it defines an XML-based protocol that supports business transactions constituting units of work across multiple loosely coupled, distributed parties. There are several types of transactions defined in the specification:

- *Atomic* transactions produce the atomic outcome, such that all of the participants will either confirm or cancel.
- *Cohesive* transactions, as defined by the specification, relax the isolation property ("effects of the transaction aren't visible until the transaction commits"). Cohesive interactions are allowed to be externally visible before the interaction is committed. In addition, a cohesion may deliver different termination outcomes to its participants such that some will confirm, and the rest will cancel; it allows the initiator to select a final subset of participants to commit. Finally, consistency is determined by agreement and interaction between the participants.
- *Compound* transactions are simply defined as a combination of atomic and cohesive transactions (they can be compounded or nested) to support more complicated scenarios such as supply chain and intermediaries.

BTP also provides a great deal of flexibility by including the concept of "conditional commitment" that allows the participant application to associate a timeout value with the "prepared" response. On the whole, it enables sophisticated workflows, including reliable aggregation of multiple steps into a single unit of work. The specification defines XML messages that can be exchanged over many carriers, but it also provides binding to SOAP 1.1, thus allowing transaction coordination for web services.

Business Process Specifications

There are several standards in the general area of business process management:

- Business Processing Execution Language for Web Services (BPEL4WS), developed by Microsoft, IBM, and BEA
- Business Process Modeling Language (BPML), developed by the Business Process Management Initiative
- Web Service Choreography Interface (WSCI), developed by BEA, Intalio, SAP, and Sun
- Business Process Specification Schema (BPSS), proposed by the UN/CEFACT Business Transition Working Group as part of the ebXML specification
- Enterprise Distributed Object Computing (EDOC), proposed by the Object Management Group

- XML Processing Description Language (XPDL), proposed by the Workflow Management Coalition

Because there is no single standard that the majority of vendors agree to support, it isn't clear at this moment what specification will dominate the web-services field. The latest development in this area is BPEL4WS (or shortly BPEL) specification covered in this section.

One reason for covering BPEL is its relative simplicity compared to other specifications. History suggests that large and complex "once-and-for-all" standards, such as ebXML, even if better in some aspects, eventually lose out to simpler standards such as the growing web services protocol stack. Simple standards have a huge advantage over the complex ones: they are simple. While XML Schema, UDDI, and BPEL specifications aren't recommended as a bed-time reading, most other standards and specifications covered in this book are pretty simple. A specification has to pass a one-man test (one person can comprehend, explain, and implement the specification if needed) or it's unlikely that it will have a bright future ("deep pockets" can marginally compensate the one-man test failure for some specifications).

Business Process Execution Language (BPEL)

The Business Process Execution Language specification can be found at:

http://www.ibm.com/developerworks/webservices/library/ws-bpel/

Codeveloped by IBM, Microsoft and BEA, it's a long-awaited result that converges two previously competing standards: Web Services Flow Language (WSFL) from IBM, and Microsoft's XLANG, used as a XML business process language in BizTalk Server.

The BPEL specification provides a standard programming language businesses can use to define how to combine web services to accomplish tasks and relies on other specifications (like WS-Coordination, WS-Transaction, WS-Security, and the rest) to support it. The WS-Coordination specification describes how the individual web services interact within that task. The WS-Transaction specification ensures that all the transactions are either successfully completed or fail as a group. The WS-Security specification can provide the message integrity and protect semantically significant headers (like a message timestamp) and the message body.

The specification describes two approaches:

The executable process
Defines the process model that reflects the actual behavior.

The abstract process
Specifies the message exchange resulting from the process model. The business protocols that comprise abstract processes don't reveal the internal behaviors and process maps of a particular model.

BPEL documents are executable scripts that can be interpreted by business process engines to implement the described process, which makes them portable across environments that support BPEL (in a way similar to XSLT scripts, which can be executed in Perl, Java, C#, or other environments).

The specification defines a process as a combination of activity, a number of partners and containers, with specific correlation sets, fault handlers, and compensation handlers attached.

The control flow is defined as a mix of block structured and state transition control flow definitions, which use links to connect a source and a target activity (if an activity has incoming links associated with it, then it doesn't start until the status of all those links has been determined). There are sequence, switch, while, pick, flow, assign, throw, compensate, terminate, wait, and empty activities. When a fault occurs, normal processing is terminated, and control is transferred to the correspondent fault handler. The specification also supports the compensating actions through the compensation handlers. Both fault handling and compensating are supported recursively by introducing the notion of scope, which is an execution context for each activity, with the fault handlers and a compensation handler associated with it.

The message flow is implemented using receive, reply, and invoke activities; when executed in the same business context these activities can be correlated using properties combined in the correlation sets. Input messages are consumed by the receive activity, and output messages are produced by the reply activity (always in response for a request previously accepted through a receive activity). Consequently, the invoke activity is used within the process that produces the synchronous request or asynchronous response (the original requester will use a receive activity to consume the delivered response).

The data is passed between the different activities in an implicit way through the sharing of globally visible data containers. Containers represent data that is important for the correct execution of the business process and exchange specific data elements via the use of assign statements.

The interesting aspect of BPEL implementation is that trust becomes even more important as the interdependencies between participants grow: companies not only expose their interfaces but also share their process models with one another (even though distinction between private and public processes can be made); that poses new security risks and make companies not only more flexible in their interactions and adaptable in their processes but also more vulnerable.

Implementation Considerations

Two big concerns face the Perl programmer implementing web services: Unicode and performance. Perl 5.8 has solid Unicode support, required for XML processing, but most programmers have never needed to use it. Perl has traditionally been slammed for performance, but it's possible to write blazing web services in Perl. This section addresses both issues.

Internationalization

XML performs all character processing in terms of the Universal Character Set (UCS) specification. Look for more information on UCS at:

http://www.unicode.org/unicode/uni2book/u2.html

Many specifications that use XML speak about the character set or charset of a string or a document, which denotes both the character repertoire and the encoding form (or simply, encoding) used to represent sequences of characters as sequences of bytes. The XML specification requires all XML processors to support both the UTF-8 and UTF-16 encodings of UCS.

UTF-8, the most common encoding, is the Unicode Transformation Standard (defined in UCS specification) that serializes a Unicode character as a sequence of one to four bytes. The advantages of UTF-8 encoding are well-known: it's compact compared with other encoding forms, it uses one byte to encode ACSII characters, and every XML parser must know how to deal with it. UTF-16 encoding is slightly more complex; it requires a minimum of two bytes, and the XML specification requires usage of a Byte Order Mark (BOM) with this encoding. Per UCS specification, a BOM signature is allowed to be used for all the encoding forms (UCS-4, UCS-2, UTF-32, UTF-16, and UTF-8) to correct an erroneous byte order (for all messages that use a byte ordering other than big-endian). It isn't intended to specify the byte order; rather it gives a strong hint about which encoding form is used (yet the XML specification requires it to be used with UTF-16).

You may be lucky and never have to deal with the sending or receiving of non-English characters. If you do have to, there are several questions to ask: what encoding to use, how to convert data into that encoding, and how to specify the encoding for messages on the wire.

If you send characters that don't require a specific code table (such as Chinese, Japanese, or Korean languages), it's best to stay with UTF-8 or ISO 8859-1 encodings. To convert between ISO 8859-1 and UTF-8 encodings using Perl 5.6 and later, the following code may be used:

```
my $utf8 = pack('U*', unpack('C*', 'привет'));
```

Those who need to work with other encodings may use Unicode::Map8, Unicode::String, or Encode modules. Also, the Unicode support supplied with Perl 5.8 is much more complete and allows the easy conversion between different encodings using the Encode module from Perl's standard library:

```
use Encode;

$utf8 = decode('iso-8859-1', $data);
# this code will make $utf8 consist of completely valid UTF-8 string
# AND turn utf8 flag on (unless $data is in ASCII/EBCDIC only)
```

To specify the encoding on wire using the SOAP::Lite module encoding method may be used:

```
use SOAP::Lite;

# specify type explicitly so it won't be encoded as base64
my $string = SOAP::Data->type(string => 'привет');
my $result = SOAP::Lite
  -> proxy ("...")
  -> uri ("...")
  -> encoding('iso-8859-1') # specify encoding, because default is UTF-8
  -> hello($string)
  -> result;
```

Nothing needs to be done on the server side. The XML::Parser module that is used by default in SOAP::Lite always returns data using UTF-8 encoding. There is one thing to watch for: returned strings are always encoded as UTF-8, but they may not be recognized as UTF-8 strings by Perl, which might be important in some cases.

The XML::Parser module (Version 2.28 and later) tags generated strings as UTF-8 in Perl 5.6 and beyond. For all other occasions (for example, you're running an old version of XML::Parser), something similar to the following code can be used in Perl 5.7 and beyond:

```
$result = pack 'U0A*', $result;
```

Simon Cozen's "Perl and Unicode" tutorial (*http://www.netthink.co.uk/downloads/unicode.pdf*) and Grant McLean's "Perl-XML Frequently Asked Questions" (*http://perl-xml.sourceforge.net/faq/*) provide extensive coverage on this topic.

Besides the character set and encoding considerations, there is one more aspect of internationalization that people who work with XML need to be aware of. Text encapsulated in XML can be represented in many different human languages, and applications often need to process them differently (e.g., as the result of content negotiation, one or the other value has to be presented). The XML specification defines a special attribute, xml:lang, which specifies the language that represents the data in an element. For instance, xml:lang="en" can be used to mark elements in language-dependent context.

Performance and Optimization

The first thing that comes to mind when performance and optimization for web-based applications are discussed is the switch from CGI application on the server side to something more persistent, like mod_perl, FastCGI, or PerlEx from ActiveState.

The usage of `mod_perl` or a daemon server instead of CGI for `SOAP::Lite` implementation may improve the performance tenfold in some situations; however, there are some cases when you want to get better results.

Even though the `SOAP::Lite` module isn't the best performer in a web-services world, the modular structure lets you swap out components to get implementations that address your specific requirements, such as the ability to send big documents or do streaming processing.

Because parsing XML messages is involved in the processing of an every request, the first natural step is to change the default `XML::Parser` module to some other module that provides better performance (`XML::LibXML::SAX::Parser` module looks promising, even though it can be more expensive memory-wise). Another reason for changing the parser would be the ability to do the SOAP processing on platforms where `XML::Parser` isn't available (like WinCE, this situation may change before this book gets published). Even though `SOAP::Lite` package includes the lightweight regexp-based parser (`XML::Parser::Lite`) that works anywhere where Perl works, it doesn't provide the full XML parser support. Matt Sergeant's `XML::SAX::PurePerl` parser is the better choice. Note that you may need to use additional module to convert SAX callbacks into Expat callbacks currently used in `SOAP::Lite`; a future version of `SOAP::Lite` may include direct support for SAX interface. The code to register a new parser looks simple:

```
use SOAP::Lite;

BEGIN {
  package MyParser;
  use base qw(SOAP::Parser);

  # parser code here
}

my $soap = SOAP::Lite
  ->proxy("...")
  ->uri("...");
# register new parser
$soap->deserializer->parser(MyParser->new);
```

In most cases the change of the parser doesn't provide the significant performance boost: most of the time, deserializer spends doing memory management and memory management is still the most time-consuming operation in many computing processes. Serializer and deserializer can be replaced in a similar fashion (both on client and server side), thus allowing new functionality to be implemented (such as streaming processing) and still reusing the rest of the components:

```
my $soap = SOAP::Lite
  ->proxy("...")
  ->uri("...")
  ->deserializer(MyDeserializer->new)
  ->serializer(MySerializer->new);
```

The last thing to mention in this section is that XML parsing isn't the only option available to parse and process XML messages. Because Perl is so good at dealing with the text, and XML messages are all text, it's possible to implement regexp-based parsing to extract the parameters and other information required to execute the method call. Although the logic that generates that regular expression can be quite complex, it's possible to generate the pattern once, store it, and match the incoming requests against stored patterns. While this solution has limited scope, it can be used for simple requests (having regular processing for all other requests), and preliminary tests show that this approach can reduce the response time in a factor of 10.

WS-Next

There's no doubt that web services are still in a nascent stage. However, looking around, it's easy to find many live working systems that use web services to solve real problems for people and businesses. Most of the implemented systems work either inside the enterprise, or across multiple enterprises, and mostly operate with simple concepts and already available vocabularies.

In development are more than 20 specifications in the web-services field that address aspects such as routing, security, packaging, service description, advertising and discovery, transactions, and business process workflow. However, it's important to realize that most describe *how* to do things, rather than *what* to do. In most cases "what" is overlooked and as the result, there is no shared understanding of concepts, metadata, and semantics. The huge amounts of work that have been done by many standards bodies to somehow address this problem and define common vocabularies wasn't as fruitful as many people hoped. This is due to a couple of reasons. First, defining vocabularies is a difficult and time-consuming task. Second, even when standards are defined, people don't always follow them and if they do, standards don't adapt well to the constantly changing business requirements and environment.

Most problems companies experience in this field are social rather than technical. Different cultures, points of view, historic roots, and business processes create different semantics and disjoint vocabularies. A complete solution that would be a functional, adaptable, flexible, and maintainable system will include not only a sophisticated loosely coupled physical infrastructure (web services) but also an information infrastructure with similar properties (shared understanding of semantics and concepts) and perhaps even a human infrastructure (right people do the right things in terms of process, planning, and architecture).

Web services are only the first step in the right direction.

APPENDIX A
XML-RPC Toolkit Programming Reference

This appendix provides a reference to the three XML-RPC toolkits discussed in Chapter 4. Its material is presented in the same order in which the toolkits themselves were presented in that chapter. This is meant to augment the manpages the classes provide, so you should also be familiar with those materials.

RPC::XMLSimple

This is the lightest-weight of the three toolkits. It relies on the presence of the LWP and XML::Parser modules from CPAN.

The following is based on Release 1.0 of RPC::XMLSimple.

RPC::XMLSimple

This class is rarely loaded directly into an application. Usually, the application uses one of the client or server classes, each of which load this module. The class provides the following methods:

new(*optional key/value pairs*)
: The constructor that returns new object instances of the encoder object, which is the object class this package provides. The options are passed as key/value pairs (not a hash reference). Recognized options are:

    encoding
    : Provides a specific encoding for the documents that are created. If this isn't given, the default encoding for XML (UTF-8) is assumed.

    use_objects
    : If this is passed with a value that is non-zero, the encoder returns data from parsed documents only as objects, rather than native Perl values. See the explanation of the data object classes later in this section.

encode_call(*method, optional list of arguments*)
: Using the method name in the first argument and any additional arguments, creates the XML fragment for the methodCall portion of a request message and returns it.

encode_response(*result value*)
: Creates a methodResponse XML fragment, using the return value passed as the argument.

encode_fault(*code, message string*)
: Creates a methodResponse XML fragment using the passed code and string as the values for an XML-RPC fault.

serve(*request message, method table*)
: Decodes the first argument as a XML-RPC request message, and attempts to look up the named method in the hash-table reference passed as the second argument. The hash reference should map method names to subroutine references. If the name is found in the table, the code reference is invoked with the arguments extracted from the request message. The return value of the routed call is returned by this method. If the named method isn't found, or if a fatal error occurs in the dispatched subroutine, a fatal exception is thrown in the form of die.

decode(*message*)
: This method converts a XML-RPC message to a Perl structure that represents it in terms of native Perl data. The return value is a hash reference with three keys:

    method_name
    : This field has data only when the decoded message was a request. In such a case, the value is the name of the method being called.

    type
    : One of call, fault, or response. This field identifies the type of message that was decoded.

    value
    : An array reference of the values in the message. When the message is a response or a fault, the array has only one element (in the case of faults, the element is always a hash reference with keys faultCode and faultString). When the message is a request, the array contains all the parameters to the call (which also means it may be empty).

base64, boolean, double, int, string, date_time
: Each method returns a new data object containing the value passed in as an argument. The corresponding data classes are listed next. The return value is an object reference that can call a method named value to retrieve the underlying Perl value encapsulated within.

Here are the data classes RPC::XMLSimple manages:

```
RPC::XMLSimple::Base64
RPC::XMLSimple::Boolean
RPC::XMLSimple::Double
RPC::XMLSimple::Integer
RPC::XMLSimple::String
RPC::XMLSimple::DateTime::ISO8601
```

The correlation between the classes and the shortcut methods earlier should be clear. Each class implements the following two methods:

new(*value*)
> Creates a new object of the class, with the given value.

value
> Returns the value encapsulated by the object.

In practice, the convenience methods provided by the basic class as well as the client class should be sufficient. Direct use of these classes shouldn't be necessary. Note that the classes don't cover the array and structure types; these are identified by their reference status (as either array or hash references).

RPC::XMLSimple::Client

This class is used for developing client applications with the toolkit. The following methods set up the object and enable it to communicate transparently with a remote server.

new(*optional key/value pairs*)
> This is the class constructor, returning a new instance object. The arguments are passed key/value pairs (not a hash reference). Here are the recognized arguments:
>
> url
>> This argument is required. It specifies the remote address of the server the client is going to connect to.
>
> proxy
>> If given, specifies a URL through which connections to the server are proxied.
>
> encoding
>> Specifies a character encoding to use for outgoing messages. If not given, the XML default (UTF-8) remains.
>
> use_objects
>> If passed with a non-zero value, all values from remote calls are returned to the application as data objects rather than native Perl values.
>
> debug
>> If set to a non-zero value, causes the serialized XML request and response to be sent to the terminal.

call(*method name, arguments list*)
: Attempts to call the named method with the given list of arguments on the remote server that was specified at object creation time. The return value from the request becomes the return value of this method. The data will be a Perl data, unless use_objects was set when the client object was created. In that case, the return value will be one of the data classes detailed earlier (or one of an array or hash reference).

base64, boolean, double, int, string, date_time
: These are convenience methods to make the data-wrapper classes available at the client level without instantiating an object of the RPC::XMLSimple class. Their function is identical to that of the earlier methods by the same name.

RPC::XMLSimple::Daemon

Server objects are created from this class. It provides only the constructor shown here, which goes immediately into the socket's listen-accept loop after procession the input arguments.

new(*optional key/value pairs*)
: Creates a new object of the class, and drops into the accept-loop for the underlying IO::Socket::INET object. Like the previous classes, the arguments are passed as ordinary key/value pairs, not a hash reference. All the arguments are passed to the IO::Socket::INET super-class constructor unchanged. The only option recognized locally by the class is the following:

    methods
    : This parameter takes a hash reference as the value. The hash reference maps RPC method names to subroutines references (which may also be anonymous subroutines or closures). The keys in the hash table are the names by which the routines will be called by remote clients. The values are used for indirect function calls, with all request arguments passed in their native Perl form. No other special processing is done.

Any arguments valid for IO::Socket::INET may be used here, such as LocalPort, ReuseAddr, etc.

XMLRPC::Lite

The XMLRPC::Lite package and related classes are part of the larger SOAP::Lite package, which is described in greater detail in Appendix B. The coverage will focus on only the XML-RPC aspects. Many classes described here inherit from SOAP::Lite counterparts. In these cases a basic definition is provided, leaving the main definitions to accompany their classes in Appendix B.

The following is based on Release 0.55 of SOAP::Lite.

XMLRPC::Lite

The following classes are all made available by loading the `XMLRPC::Lite` module. There are also some behind-the-scenes classes that aren't documented here, because they aren't intended to be replaced or extended.

XMLRPC::Lite

Inherits from: `SOAP::Lite`.

This class is used for creating client objects that in turn communicate with remote servers. There are more methods available to this class than are listed here, because it inherits directly from `SOAP::Lite`. Many methods in that class aren't relevant to implementing XML-RPC, so the object attributes they manipulate are ignored by the serializer.

One noteworthy feature that `XMLRPC::Lite` inherits from its parent class is the automatic creation of object as needed, when methods are called as class methods. In most applications, an explicit creation of the client object with `new` is generally not needed. Some of the methods may also be used at compile-time to influence global behavior. This will be explained after the method listing. All methods return the object reference on success unless otherwise specified. Errors trigger either the fault handler or a call to `die`.

new(*optional argument list*)
: This is the class constructor, which creates new objects. It requires no arguments itself, and treats any arguments passed in as key/value pairs in which the key is one of the following method names, and the value is the argument to pass in when calling that method (if a method requires two or more parameters, the value would be an array reference). All methods are invoked after the new object has been allocated and blessed into the appropriate class.

proxy(*URL*)
: Set or retrieve the current value of the address the client is to connect to. The value may also be changed with the next method, but `proxy` must be called first because it handles the loading of the appropriate support for the transport scheme (HTTP, etc.). Returns the current value if called with no argument.

endpoint(*URL*)
: Change the address the client connects to, without reloading the transport code. The new address must use the same scheme as the previous value. Returns the current endpoint if called with no argument.

call(*method name, optional parameters*)
: Call a remote method by name, optionally with the parameters specified in the rest of the parameter list. `XMLRPC::Lite` objects can call remote methods as if they are local methods on the object itself, but some method names may contain characters Perl doesn't permit in a subroutine name.

serializer(*optional value*)
: Sets (or returns, if called with no argument) the serializer object used by this object for turning requests into XML. Applications should rarely need to change this value, but retrieving the object makes it possible to call the methods detailed later under XMLRPC::Serializer.

deserializer(*optional value*)
: Like serializer but operates on the deserialization object, which turns incoming XML into Perl data for handling by the rest of the application.

readable(*boolean*)
: A shortcut for $obj->serializer->readable($boolean). If set to true, the serializer puts extra line breaks and space in the XML to make it visually appealing.

on_fault(*optional value*)
: Sets or returns (when called with no parameter) the value of the code reference used when a fault happens. The subroutine reference (if set) is invoked with a single parameter, the XMLRPC::SOM object that contains the fault. If no on_fault handler is set, the default action is to call die with the text of the fault.

XMLRPC::Data

Inherits from: SOAP::Data.

The XMLRPC::Data class is made available to aid in serializing Perl data that is ambiguous enough that the serializer can't always automatically identify the type. Unlike SOAP, data in XML-RPC is relatively free of metadata, so using this class is much simpler and clearer than its parent class.

Objects need only be created when the value in question needs explicit typing. Once an object is created, the type and value may be manipulated with these methods:

new(*arguments*)
: Creates a new data object. If there is only one argument, it is taken as the value to encapsulate, and the type is inferred from the appearance. If the argument is a series of key/value pairs, the keys must correspond to available XMLRPC::Data class methods, and the values are arguments. The keys may be either of type or value, though there are some methods that are ignored by XML-RPC (but will not cause a runtime error if present).

type(*new type, optional value*)
: Sets the type for the data object or gets the current value if no arguments are passed. The type should be one of: int, i4, double, string, dateTime, or base64. If a second value is included, it is assumed to be a new value for the object and replaces any current value.

value(*new value*)
: Sets the value for the object, or if called with no arguments, returns the current value.

XMLRPC::Data objects may be passed as parameters when using the `call` method on a XMLRPC::Lite object (or when using the indirect or autodispatch approaches).

XMLRPC::SOM

Inherits from: SOAP::SOM.

All values returned from calls made by a client object are instances of this class. While this class has access to all the methods from SOAP::SOM, the convenience methods listed here are recommended rather than using `match` and `valueof` with various arguments.

match(*path*)
: Matches the expression passed in, returning a new XMLRPC::SOM object for the node that is matched. The path syntax is based on XPath. Refer to the documentation for this method under SOAP::SOM for more information.

valueof(*node*)
: Retrieves the data contained within the node passed in as an argument. The node value should be a XPath-like expression and is evaluated in the context of the node value calling the method. More detail is available under the SOAP::SOM section in Appendix B.

The following are the supported convenience methods that return data in Perl format rather than serialized or object-encapsulated format.

envelope
: Returns the "envelope" of the message, which in the case of XML-RPC means a hash reference with one key. The key will be either `methodCall` or `methodResponse`, depending on the nature of the message. However, because this is most likely used on the client side, `methodResponse` will be more common. The value associated with the key will be a hash reference representing the rest of the message.

method
: Returns the method name in a request message. Specifically, it is the data of the `methodName` element.

fault
: If the message encapsulates a XML-RPC fault, this method returns a hash reference with two keys, `faultCode` and `faultString`. If the message contained no fault, undef is returned.

faultcode, faultstring
: These methods are shortcuts to the two elements of a fault, without having to retrieve the fault first (using the previous method). If there is no fault, the return value from either of these is undef.

result
: For an object that represents the result of a remote call, this method returns the actual result value (as Perl data). If the message is a fault, this method returns undef.

The following two methods provide access to the parameter lists of XMLRPC::SOM objects. They are defined here because they behave slightly differently from the inherited methods by the same name in SOAP::SOM.

paramsin
: Returns a XMLRPC::SOM object containing all parameters to a methodCall message. Returns nothing if called on a response message.

paramsall
: Returns a XMLRPC::SOM object encapsulating the return parameter from a response message. Returns nothing (undef) if called on a request message.

XMLRPC::Deserializer and XMLRPC::Serializer

Inherits from: SOAP::Deserializer and SOAP::Serializer, respectively.

The deserialization object is used by both client and server objects to transform XML messages into Perl data, while the serialization object transforms requests and responses from Perl data to XML messages. XML-RPC is much more stringent than SOAP because there are no permitted alternatives for encoding; for this reason, application developers shouldn't need to subclass or otherwise alter these objects. However, if such a need arises, you use the same set of methods as their SOAP::Lite counterparts, with some overridden for XML-RPC application.

XMLRPC::Server

Inherits from: SOAP::Server.

This class derives from the SOAP::Lite equivalent and overrides the initialization code to provide functionality geared towards XML-RPC. It isn't meant to be used directly by application developers but rather allows the server classes that are defined later a common initialization method that can be shared.

XMLRPC::Server::Parameters

Inherits from: SOAP::Server::Parameters.

This is an empty class for use when writing code for deployment through a server based on the XMLRPC::Server class. It inherits two methods from the parent class, but the primary purpose is to be a superclass to code written for a XML-RPC server. When a server derived from the server classes (that are detailed later) dispatches an incoming request, it checks to see if the class to which the receiving method belongs inherits from this class. If so, the XMLRPC::SOM object that represents the message's envelope is added at the end of the list of parameters to the local subroutine call.

XMLRPC::Transport::HTTP

This module provides the implementation of HTTP transport for servers. Clients don't use modules from the XMLRPC::Transport::* hierarchy because they can use the same transport code SOAP::Lite does.

This module provides three different server classes to use either directly or as parent classes for new code. All three classes inherit from their SOAP::Lite counterparts. None define any new methods of their own; methods should be taken from the class listings in Appendix B. In particular, the methods of note for the classes used for XML-RPC serving are new, dispatch_to, and handle.

XMLRPC::Transport::HTTP::CGI

Inherits from: SOAP::Transport::HTTP::CGI.

This class is designed for use in standard CGI environments.

XMLRPC::Transport::HTTP::Daemon

Inherits from: SOAP::Transport::HTTP::Daemon.

The implementation of this class uses an object of the HTTP::Daemon class, from the LWP module, to provide the actual server functionality.

XMLRPC::Transport::HTTP::Apache

Inherits from: SOAP::Transport::HTTP::Apache.

This class is designed to work as a basis for an Apache/mod_perl content handler that serves XML-RPC requests. It doesn't operate in quite the same way as the daemon-based server described earlier; it expects the traditional server loop functionality to be handled by Apache rather than within the class.

XMLRPC::Transport::POP3

This module provides just the XMLRPC::Transport::POP3::Server class, which inherits from SOAP::Transport::POP3::Server. It implements a XML-RPC server that reads the incoming messages from a POP3 mailbox. XML-RPC clients may use the mailto: scheme to send such requests.

XMLRPC::Transport::TCP

This module provides just a `XMLRPC::Transport::TCP::Server` class, which inherits from `SOAP::Transport::TCP::Server` in this case. This implements a server that uses straight TCP/IP rather than HTTP for communication. Clients may also use a scheme of `tcp:` to communicate with such servers.

RPC::XML

The `RPC::XML` package is the newest player in the Perl/XML-RPC field. The classes described here cover data encoding, client and server functionality, and features geared specifically towards the Apache/mod_perl environment.

The following is based on Release 0.44 of `RPC::XML`.

RPC::XML

The actual `RPC::XML` module itself is an umbrella for all the data-oriented classes that support the client and server classes described here. In general, it isn't necessary to load this package directly because the client and all the server classes do so themselves.

The first group defined include the data classes. These encapsulate Perl data prior to serialization into an XML-RPC message. The data classes are:

```
RPC::XML::int
RPC::XML::i4
RPC::XML::double
RPC::XML::string
RPC::XML::boolean
RPC::XML::datetime_iso8601
RPC::XML::base64
RPC::XML::array
RPC::XML::struct
RPC::XML::fault
```

The methods common to all these classes are:

new(*value*)

> Creates a new object that encapsulates the given Perl value. In most cases, the input value is a simple scalar. The main purpose of the data classes is to allow forced-typing of data that doesn't match the automatic typing (such as using the value 10 as a string instead of an integer). However, the following exceptions exist:

- The `RPC::XML::boolean` class may take any of the values: yes, true, or 1 for a true value; no, false, or 0 for a false value.
- If `RPC::XML::datetime_iso8601` is passed a value with only digits, it is assumed to be the value from the time built-in function and is converted to an ISO 8601 representation in Universal Coordinated Time.
- `RPC::XML::array` may take an array reference or a list of values. Any leading array reference causes the rest of the list to be ignored. The list reference will be expanded when creating the object.
- The `RPC::XML::struct` class may take a hash reference as a single argument or a set of key/value pairs. `RPC::XML::fault` is a subclass of the struct class and may take either an existing `RPC::XML::struct` object (from which values are copied), exactly two arguments (the code and string, in that order), or two key/value pairs with the requisite keys of faultCode and faultString.
- The `RPC::XML::base64` class takes the (presumably binary) data chunk as a first argument and an optional second argument. If the second argument evaluates to non-null, it signifies that the chunk of data is already Base64 encoded. Otherwise, it is assumed to be clear text.

value
: Returns the value encapsulated within the object. Both the `RPC::XML::array` and `RPC::XML::struct` classes accept an optional argument to this method. If that argument is non-null, the values returned are *shallow* copies. This means that any data objects contained as values (either within the array or as values in the hash) aren't recursively expanded but instead returned as references to the original.

type
: Returns the object's type, as defined in the XML-RPC specification. In most classes, this is the same as the last element in the class name. The `RPC::XML::datetime_iso8601` class actually returns the string dateTime.iso8601.

as_string
: Generates and returns the XML fragment to represent the object's value within a XML-RPC message.

is_fault
: In all classes except `RPC::XML::fault`, this returns false (0). In the fault class, it returns true (1). This allows simple testing of return values from remote calls for fault status without having to explicitly check the type.

In addition to the previous data classes, there are two message classes provided by this module:

RPC::XML::request
RPC::XML::response

Both support the following methods:

new(*parameters*)
> Creates new objects and returns them. The response class takes only a single argument, the value to be returned to the caller. The request class requires at least one argument. The first parameter is taken to be the name of the remote method to be called. Any additional arguments are encoded as parameters to the call.

as_string
> Returns the XML representation of the message as a complete valid XML document.

In addition to these methods, RPC::XML::request supports:

name
> Returns the method name that the request is coded to call.

args
> Returns the list of arguments to be passed to in the method call as a list reference. If there are no arguments, a reference to an empty list is returned.

The RPC::XML::response class supports:

value
> Returns the data object that contains the return value from the response.

is_fault
> Returns a true/false value that indicates whether the response contains a fault.

The package exports some convenience functions, if requested. In the following list of functions in the RPC::XML namespace, each indicates which tag an application may use to import the symbol. Symbols may be directly imported, as well.

time2iso8601(*optional time, optional time zone*)
> Takes the time value passed in as seconds (presumably from the built-in time function) and converts it to an ISO 8601 string in UTC. If the second parameter is passed, it is assumed to be an offset in hours from UTC that the value should represent. If no parameters are given, the value from time is used directly. This may be imported with the tag :all, as well as being directly imported.

smart_encode(*one or more values*)
> Takes one or more Perl values and attempts to "smartly" convert them to data objects. This routine is used by the RPC::XML::array and RPC::XML::struct constructors to handle their values. Any passed-in values that are already data objects are returned unchanged. This too may be imported with the :all tag.

RPC_BOOLEAN, RPC_STRING, RPC_I4, RPC_INT, RPC_DOUBLE, RPC_DATETIME_ISO8601, RPC_BASE64
> These encoding functions may be used as shortcuts rather than explicitly creating an object of the appropriate data class with new. All are imported with the tag

:types, as well as being included in the :all tag. Each takes a single Perl value as an argument and returns an object of the appropriate data-type class as a result. Note that most constructors make no effort to validate their data, so it is up to the application to send correct data for classes such as RPC::XML::double or RPC::XML::datetime_iso8601. Also note that the two-argument form of the RPC::XML::base64 constructor isn't available via this function.

RPC::XML::Client

The client class provides all the functionality needed to initiate remote connects, make requests and obtain the responses from them. It's a container class, encapsulating a LWP::UserAgent object, a HTTP::Request object, and a RPC::XML::Parser object. The first two are from the LWP package, while the last is a part of the RPC::XML package (it isn't documented in this chapter because currently it can't be manipulated at the application level). The LWP::UserAgent object manages all communications for the client object, while the HTTP::Request object is prepopulated with all the headers needed for XML-RPC compliance. This keeps the client from having to create a new request object for every remote call.

The client class recognizes the following methods:

new(*URL, optional key/value pairs*)
: Creates new objects of the class. It requires at least one parameter, the URL of the server that requests will be sent to. Any additional arguments are treated as key/value pairs. The known parameters are listed here and any not in the list are copied onto the object unchanged (allowing for subclasses to have their own instance values). Here are the known parameters:

    error_handler, fault_handler, combined_handler
    : These set the error and/or fault handlers to a code reference given as the value of the pair. combined_handler sets both handlers to the same reference. It is applied first, so also passing one of the others overrides the combined handler setting.

url(*optional new URL*)
: Returns the current URL that the client is connecting to for requests. If a new value is passed as an argument, it sets that as the URL. The old value is returned in the latter case should the application wish to restore it at some point.

useragent
: Returns the LWP::UserAgent object that the client encapsulates. This allows the application to call methods on that object directly, such as setting proxy information, etc.

request
: Returns the HTTP::Request object contained within the client, allowing the application to call methods on the object directly.

simple_request(*argument list*)
: Makes a request to the remote server and returns the response as a native Perl value. Faults will be returned as hash references, and internal errors will result in undef being returned, and the error message stored in the global scalar, $RPC::XML::ERROR. This is a wrapper around the send_request method to ease short applications by returning Perl data rather than data objects. Any configured error or fault handlers will be triggered if so needed.

  The arguments to the method may take one of two forms: either a method name (an ordinary Perl string) followed by zero or more arguments or an object of the RPC::XML::request class. In the former case, any arguments already in object form aren't converted; those that aren't pass to smart_encode (defined earlier).

send_request(*argument list*)
: Also sends requests to the remote server, but the return value is a data object or a nonreference value if an error occurred. The argument type and disposition are the same as for the previous method. Any fault response from the server triggers the fault handler, if set. Any error in transport triggers the error handler, if that is set. Should either handler throw an exception by using die, the method never returns.

credentials(*realm, user name, password*)
: Sets the credentials used for Basic Authentication, for requests against a URL that uses this form of authentication. This is a proxy into the credentials method of LWP::UserAgent, and is more convenient than retrieving the user-agent object and calling the same method.

compress_requests(*optional boolean*)
: The client objects attempt to use content compression if the Compress::Zlib module from CPAN is available, and if the server supports it. Because the client can't know in advance if a server supports compression, this method allows an application to force the use of compression if it's known for certain that the server supports it. If no argument is passed, it returns the current setting. This method doesn't preserve the old setting as other methods in the class do.

compress_thresh(*optional new value*)
: Gets (and optionally sets) the threshold value when compression is applied to an outgoing message. The default value is 4096 (4K), meaning that any XML message body greater than number of bytes in length is compressed. When setting the value, the old value is returned in case the application intends to restore it at a later point.

error_handler, fault_handler, combined_handler(*optional code references*)
: These methods retrieve and set the handlers for errors and faults. Each returns the current handler (error or fault) when called, with the combined_handler method returning a two-item list. If called with an argument, the argument must be a code reference. It is set as the new handler of the given type, and the old value(s) returned.

RPC::XML::Server

The basic server class provides the core functionality for serving XML-RPC requests. It is subclassed by the Apache server code (covered later). The XML::RPC::Server class is also a container, holding an instance of the HTTP::Response class and possibly an instance of the HTTP::Daemon class as well. As with the client class's use of the HTTP::Request object, the HTTP::Response object here is created and prepopulated with the headers required for XML-RPC compliance, allowing the server to avoid creating and seeding a new response object for every incoming request. The class creates and stores an instance of HTTP::Daemon by default, but this can be prevented with arguments to the constructor. The server object may use the Net::Server module from CPAN (if available) to handle the communications, or in the case of the Apache::RPC::Server subclassing, it doesn't need a HTTP listener at all.

Here are the methods in this class:

new(*optional key/value pairs*)
> This is the class constructor. It creates and returns a new object, using any of the following options. Options are passed as key/value pairs, not as a hash reference.
>
> no_http
>> If passed with a non-false value, this inhibits the creation of the HTTP::Daemon object within the server object being built. This is used directly by the Apache::RPC::Server constructor and may be used by application developers intended to use Net::Server in place of HTTP::Daemon. This doesn't trigger loading of Net::Server; see server_loop.
>
> no_default
>> If passed with a non-false value, prevents the loading of the default server methods that are a part of the RPC::XML package. These are described later. The Apache server module uses this option, then later uses add_default_methods (also described later) to control the actual methods that are loaded.
>
> path, host, port, queue
>> These four values control the settings on the underlying HTTP::Daemon object, or possibly the Net::Server object. The host and port values specify the host name (or IP address) and port to bind the listening socket to. The queue value specifies the size of the listening queue for the socket. The path value indicates what URL path components should be added to the URL string the server advertises in the url method (defined later).
>>
>> Depending on how server_loop is called when Net::Server is being used, any of these values may be overridden.
>
> xpl_path
>> Server objects can load their methods from specially formatted files. By default, the server object has a limited list of directories it searches for these files. This option provides an array reference as a value, and if passed the contents of the array reference, are added to the list of directories to search.

timeout
: When HTTP::Daemon is reading an incoming request on a socket, it uses this value as the time-out value. The connection is dropped if the client doesn't get the full request to the server before the given amount of time has elapsed. The value is expressed in seconds, and the default value is 10.

auto_methods
: If passed with a non-false value, this tells the server to search for a method when a request comes in for an unknown name. The list of directories for XPL files are searched for a file whose name (minus the .xpl extension) matches the requested name. Note that this feature is a potential security issue.

auto_updates
: When a method is loaded from an XPL file, the server records the modification time of the file. If this option is passed with a non-false value, each call to the given method checks its file to see if it has been updated, and if so rereads the file before dispatching the method. Note that this also presents a security risk.

version

Returns the version number of the package in use. Should be overridden in subclasses.

product_tokens

Returns the name of the class followed by the version number, in a style similar to other HTTP servers: NAME/VERSION. Useful for constructing Server: headers in outgoing messages.

url

Returns the URL address that is used to contact the server.

requests

Returns the number of requests the server has handled thus far.

response

Like the client object methods, this returns the HTTP::Response object that the server contains, so that methods may be called on it if needed.

started(*optional boolean*)

When called with a non-null value, this method calls the built-in time function and notes the time that the server (presumably) started waiting for requests. When called with no argument, the stored value is returned, which may then be used as a sort of "server up-time" meter.

add_method(*method argument*)

This is the primary way to add published methods to a server object. The argument may take one of three forms: the name of a XPL file, a precreated code object (see the section "Server-Side Code Classes"), or an ordinary hash reference. Both the XPL file and object forms are self-contained. The hash reference will be examined for the following keys:

name
> (Required) This parameter gives the name of the new method, as it will be presented to clients.

code
> (Required) The value of this parameter must be a code reference (symbolic references can't be used). It is stored as the actual Perl code to be invoked when the server dispatches a call to the particular method.

signature
> (Usually required) The value for this parameter is an array reference containing the signatures that the method offers. Signatures provide information about the types and order of arguments, and the type of the return value a given call produces. The function type of code object doesn't use signatures, so this parameter is optional for that type; it's required for the others.

help
> This key provides the help text for the method, which is used by the introspection API, particularly the system.methodHelp call.

type
> This tells add_method whether the hash reference is defining a method, procedure, or function object. The difference between these types is explained later. The default value is method.

version
> If passed, the value of this key is stored as the version of the method encapsulated by the underlying object. This value isn't used anywhere internally, but it is used in the Apache status module, described later.

hidden
> If passed with a non-false value, this marks the new code object to be hidden from the provided introspection API.

add_default_methods(*optional detail arguments*)
> Adds the server-side methods that are provided with the RPC::XML package; these implement the client/server introspection interface discussed in Chapters 3 and 4. The list of arguments can limit the list loaded by specifying filenames that are specifically looked for in the directory in which the XPL files are kept (if the *.xpl* extension is missing from a name, it is silently added). If the list of names contains the string except (or -except), all names following that token are excluded from the list of methods to be loaded. These particular methods are searched for only in the directory in which the RPC::XML::Server module itself resides.

add_methods_in_dir(*directory, optional detail arguments*)
> Similar in functionality to the previous, except that the first argument in the list is taken to be a specific directory to search, rather than defaulting to the

module's installation directory. The nature of the rest of the parameters is the same as in add_default_methods.

delete_method(*name*)
: Deletes the method whose external (published) name matches the input parameter. Returns the server object on success or an error message on failure.

get_method(*name*)
: Retrieves the object that encapsulates the server method whose published name matches the input parameter. The return value is an object, not a hash reference. See the section "Server-Side Code Classes."

list_methods
: Returns a list of the published methods that the object has associated with it. The list is returned with names, not the underlying objects.

share_methods(*server, list of names*), copy_methods(*server, list of names*)
: These two methods enable mingling of server-side method objects between two server instances. The share_methods call puts references to the same code objects into the calling server object. The copy_methods approach differs in that each target code object is cloned, creating a new object that points to the same underlying code reference. New code objects are then installed on the calling server object, but the compiled Perl code is still shared.

    The first argument is a server object to get the code objects from. The list of names must be one or more published names of server-side code on the target object. Any of the values in the list of names may be a Regex object (created using qr// in Perl). If any of these are detected, the regular expression is evaluated against all the code object's names on the target server object, and all matching objects are added to the list. For example:

        ($S2->share_methods($S1, qr/^meerkat/)

    results in all methods on $S1 whose published names start with meerkat are shared onto $S2.

    Note that using either of these methods on a code object that contain closures (code references with binding to lexically scoped values) means that each server object shares the same lexically bound values.

server_loop(*optional key/value pairs*)
: Enters the loop in which the socket is monitored for connections. When a HTTP::Daemon object is present, the only argument recognized in the parameters list is signal. This parameter, if passed, specifies a signal name (or an array reference containing several names) that should be set up as the monitored interrupt signal for the server loop. A signal handler is attached to the specified signal(s) to terminate the otherwise infinite loop and return to the caller.

    If no HTTP listener is created (no_http was set in the constructor), it attempts to load the Net::Server module. If successful, the class's @ISA hierarchy is changed to include Net::Server, and the run method of that class is entered with all the arguments passed in from the original call. See the documentation for that module for more on the range and meaning of the parameters to run.

dispatch(*request*)

A server object uses this method to actually turn a request into a server-side method call and result. The argument may be either an XML document, a scalar reference to the XML (to reduce the memory used in duplicating strings on the stack), or a RPC::XML::request object. If the argument is XML (or the scalar reference to XML), it is first converted to object form. The method then looks up the requested method and fashions the call to that method. The return value from this is an object of the RPC::XML::response class.

xpl_path(*optional array reference*)

Gets the search path for XPL files as an array reference. If passed with an array reference as an argument, it sets a new search path for XPL files. This completely replaces the existing list, so to augment a list, the application must first retrieve the current list and include it in the new one. The old path is returned as an array reference when setting a new path.

Server-Side Code Classes

Server-side code can behave as ordinary subroutines or as class methods, depending on the way the code is hooked into the server. The RPC::XML package uses a set of different code object classes to maintain the difference between the types.

Details of the XPL file format are provided in the module documentation and won't be covered here.

Each class supports the following methods:

new(*arguments*)

This is the constructor for the class. The arguments may be either a filename (if there is exactly one argument that isn't a reference), a hash reference, or a list of key/value pairs. The file is assumed to be a XPL file and the constructor will attempt to load it. The hash reference is assumed to be contain some subset of the keys listed here and will be copied to a new reference which is then blessed into the correct package. If the arguments are a series of key/value pairs, the following keys are recognized:

name

The name by which the code object is published on a server.

code

A code reference to the Perl subroutine/closure that is actually executed for requests. Symbolic references aren't accepted.

signature

This key may appear more than once. Each time, it specifies a signature that the new code object can accept. The signature may be a string or an array reference of types. If the argument to new was a hash reference, this key must point to an array reference whose items are also array references.

help
Provides the help text for the method, used by the introspection interface.

version
Provides a version string for the code being encapsulated, but it is used only in status reporting, not in any calls.

hidden
The value for this should be a boolean that tells whether the code object should be excluded from any listings generated by the introspection API.

clone
Creates a clone of the calling object and returns it. In the clone, everything is a copy of the original (including the array reference of signatures) except for the code reference, which is the same as in the original object.

name, code(*optional code reference*), signature(*optional array reference*),
help(*optional string*), hidden(*optional boolean*), version(*optional string*)
These are accessors for the data within the object. The name field can't be changed, but the others may take a single argument that replaces the existing value for the given attribute. Unlike the accessors for the server and client classes, these always return the current value, even when setting it. To preserve old values, they must be retrieved before the new value is set.

is_valid
Returns a boolean value indicating whether the object has enough information to be added to a server object. Checks primarily for a valid name, code reference, and signature list (if signatures are used).

add_signature(*list of new*)
Adds one or more new signatures to the internal table. Each argument in the list of new signatures may be a string or an array reference. Strings must be space-separated type identifiers. The array references should contain one type identifier per element. If any of the new signature creates a conflict with an existing signature (cases in which the same set of input types is expected to yield a different return type), all changes are abandoned, and an error message is returned. The object reference is returned on success.

delete_signature(*list to delete*)
Removes the signatures specified in the list of arguments. The syntax of the arguments is the same as for add_signature. All signatures are deleted (nonexistent ones are silently ignored). An error message is returned if the resulting signature table is invalid (in this case, if it is now empty), otherwise the object reference is returned.

match_signature(*signature*)
> Attempts to match a signature to the object's signature table. If found, the expected return type is passed back. If it isn't found, a false value is returned.

call(*server object, parameters*)
> Calls the underlying Perl code, with the parameters passed in the arguments list. The first argument to call must be an object that derives from RPC::XML::Server. The server object is the initial parameter in the list when calling code that is supposed to behave like a class method. The return value is a data object of the type that matches the signature of the arguments passed in.

reload
> Tells the object to reload the XPL file it was originally created from. If it isn't loaded from an XPL file, the method silently returns without doing anything.

RPC::XML::Method

Code objects created in the RPC::XML::Method class call their encapsulated code references in a fashion that emulates a method call. The server object is passed as the first parameter in the list to the Perl subroutine. Using this object reference, the code may interact with the server to get information about how it was called (by what name, and by what signature) or to call other routines on the server by their published interface, rather than requiring internal knowledge.

RPC::XML::Method derives from RPC::XML::Procedure.

RPC::XML::Procedure

The RPC::XML::Procedure class of code objects calls its encapsulated subroutines with an ordinary argument list. The server object isn't available to the code being invoked.

RPC::XML::Function

This class of code objects doesn't use signatures. It is designed for quick and simple creation of XML-RPC wrappers around existing code and libraries. Calls to the underlying Perl subroutine are done the same way as with the XML::RPC::Procedure class. As such, these routines don't have access to the server object.

RPC::XML::Function derives from XML::RPC::Procedure.

Apache::RPC::Server

The Apache::RPC::Server class is a subclass of XML::RPC::Server that is engineered especially for use as an Apache/mod_perl location handler. The following methods are unique to this package or significantly different from the parent class:

handler
: This method is defined so that mod_perl can use the class directly as a location handler. It's prototyped as a method handler in mod_perl terms, allowing applications to subclass it if desired. It's called as a method (meaning that an object reference or package name is the first parameter passed in) with the Apache object (the request) as a parameter.

init_handler
: This method is provided as a possible handler for the mod_perl PerlChildInitHandler phase. As implemented, it calls the child_started method only on each XML-RPC server object within the internal table Apache::RPC:: Server maintains. It is also prototyped as a method handler, so it too may be overridden in a subclass.

new(*key/value pairs*)
: The constructor for this class is a little different from its parent. It calls the parent constructor to create the actual object, and most of the parameters are passed through directly to the parent (along with setting no_http). It also attempts to configure itself as much as possible from the Apache environment and then adds itself to an internal table that the class maintains, before returning the new object reference. Here are the parameters directly used by this constructor (not passed to the parent):

    apache
    : A reference to an Apache object reference, which is used to access location configuration information and other needed internals.

    server_id
    : The server ID is just a string that distinguishes XML-RPC servers within a single Apache server. Because multiple servers may be set up from Apache configuration blocks alone, this offers an alternative to using <Perl> blocks to set up such situations. If not passed, the URL location that Apache has the handler mapped to is used.

    prefix
    : Provides a prefix that is applied to all the directory-level configuration options new attempts to locate and use. Overrides any value that might be set by the Apache configuration for the option prefix.

    Configuration of the Apache::RPC::Server objects using directory configuration values is covered in detail in the manpage for this class.

child_started(*optional boolean*)
: Similar to the started method in the parent class, but it keeps a separate value from the start time. Under mod_perl, the server objects may be created during initialization and passed to child processes when Apache creates them. This value notes when the given child started, versus when the server object itself may have started.

version
: Identical to the parent method of the same name, except that it instead returns the version string for this package.

list_servers
: Returns a list of the server objects by their server ID. May be called as a static method.

get_server(*server ID*)
: Retrieves a server object by the unique server ID. Also may be called as a static method.

The manpage for the class contains examples for directly creating objects and assigning them as location handlers within `<Perl>` blocks in the Apache configuration. When the handlers are set up in this fashion, the `handler` method gets the server object rather than the class name in its argument list, which makes for faster handling of requests.

Apache::RPC::Status

This class isn't used within applications but deserves some attention here. It implements a status monitor similar to the `Apache::Status` package, for monitoring the XML-RPC servers on a given Apache installation. Like the `Apache::RPC::Server` class, the handlers are prototyped as method handlers, to allow for subclassing this package if desired. Installation of this monitor is covered in the manpage for the class. Here are the methods that a new derivative may wish to override or extend:

new(*parameter list*)
: Creates a new object to handle requests for a location. The package maintains a default object internally if the status monitor is set up with just Apache configuration directives. The only recognized parameter is `serverclass`, which defaults to `Apache::RPC::Server`. This is needed because the status monitor has to call some static methods from the class in order to get the server objects, etc.

handler
: The main location handler provided by this class handles generating all HTML pages, based on the CGI-style parameters passed in the URL.

init_handler
: At present, this does nothing except check for a directory-configuration value called `ServerClass`, which has the same function as the `serverclass` parameter to `new`. Included to facilitate subclassing.

make_url(*request, optional flag*)
: Creates a URL for generating hyperlinks. The first parameter must be either the Apache request object originally passed to `handler` or a `CGI` object (from the `CGI` class in the Perl core). The optional flag, if set to a true value, requests that the

URL be suitable for use when Apache::RPC::Status is configured to be connected to the Apache::Status module.

apache_status_attach

Attempts to attach the XML-RPC status monitor to the main screen of the Apache::Status package.

More detail about the information the monitor provides is detailed in the manpage for the class. This includes guides for extending the monitoring capabilities themselves.

APPENDIX B
SOAP::Lite Programming Reference

In this appendix, the classes within the SOAP::Lite toolkit are treated to a per-method overview, as a supplement to the manpages from the toolkit itself, as well as the material in the earlier chapters of the book.

SOAP::Lite

The classes documented in this section are all available when an application loads the SOAP::Lite module via use or require. The order in which the classes are presented is based on general usage patterns; those which are directly used more often are presented first. Not all the classes within this file are present here; those which are meant only to be support elements are omitted.

SOAP::Lite

The first group of methods presented are the constructor and the accessor methods. All accessor methods share the trait of returning the current appropriate value when called with no arguments, while returning the object reference itself when called with a new value for the field in question. This allows the set-attribute calls to be chained together.

new(*optional key/value pairs*) $client = SOAP::Lite->new(proxy => $endpoint)
> This is the constructor of the class. Many of the accessor methods defined here may be initialized at creation by providing their name as a key, followed by the desired value. The example provides the value for the proxy element of the client.

transport(*optional transport object*) $transp = $client->transport();
> Provides access to the transport object that the client has allocated to manage the communication layer operations. You can set this by passing a new object that derives from SOAP::Transport, but this is generally not needed or recommended. Several of the following methods are shortcuts to this object's accessors.

serializer(*optional serializer object*)   `$serial = $client->serializer()`

Provides access to the `SOAP::Serialization` object that the client uses to transform the elements and data of a request into an XML document for the sake of transport. As with `transport`, this may be set by providing a new object reference, but it is generally not needed.

proxy(*endpoint, optional extra arguments*)   `$client->proxy('http://soap.xml.info/endPoint');`

The *proxy* is the server or endpoint to which the client is going to connect. It shouldn't be confused with the `uri` method discussed later, which refers to a different element of the conversation. This method allows the setting of the endpoint, along with any extra information that the transport object may need when communicating the request. Indeed, this method is actually an alias to the proxy method of `SOAP::Transport`. It is the same as typing:

    $client->transport()->proxy(...arguments);

When extra information is needed, it is also passed in the call to this method. Connecting to a server that uses browser cookies for authentication can be done by creating an instance of the `HTTP::Cookies` class (from the `LWP` package) and passing it as the value following a key of `cookie_jar`. The value for socket-timeouts may also be set this way. The full range of options vary by transport method. One common theme is that the endpoint string is always the first argument, with all additional arguments following it.

endpoint(*optional new endpoint address*)   `$client->endpoint('http://soap.xml.info/newPoint')`

It may be preferable to set a new endpoint without the additional work of examining the new address for protocol information and checking to ensure the support code is loaded and available. This method allows the caller to change the endpoint that the client is currently set to connect to, without reloading the relevant transport code. Note that the `proxy` method must have already been called before this method is used.

service(*service URL*)   `$client->service('http://svc.perl.org/Svc.wsdl');`

`SOAP::Lite` offers some support for creating method stubs from service descriptions. At present, only WSDL support is in place. This method loads the specified WSDL schema and uses it as the basis for generating stubs.

outputxml(*boolean*)   `$client->outputxml('true');`

Controls whether the returned information from a remote method call is the raw XML from the server. The default is to process the data from the server and present it to the caller as an object of the `SOAP::SOM` class. If the application prefers to use a different parser or do something else entirely with the results, this method may be used to inhibit the parsing of the returned information.

autotype(*boolean*)   `$client->autotype(0);`

This method is a shortcut for:

    $client->serializer->autotype(boolean);

By default, the serializer tries to automatically deduce types for the data being sent in a message. Setting a false value with this method disables the behavior.

readable(*boolean*)   `$client->readable(1);`

This method is a shortcut for:

`$client->serializer->readable(boolean);`

When this is used to set a true value for this property, the generated XML sent to the endpoint has extra characters (spaces and new lines) added in to make the XML itself more readable to human eyes (presumably for debugging). The default is to not send any additional characters.

soapversion(*optional value*)   `$client->soapversion('1.2');`

If no parameter is given, returns the current version of SOAP that is being used by the client object to encode requests. If a parameter is given, the method attempts to set that as the version of SOAP being used. The value should be either 1.1 or 1.2.

envprefix(*QName*)   `$client->envprefix('env');`

This method is a shortcut for:

`$client->serializer->envprefix(QName);`

The namespace label used for the main SOAP namespace elements (such as Envelope, Body, and the attributes) defaults to SOAP-ENV. As has been discussed in earlier chapters, the label itself isn't important. But applications that wish to explicitly choose a different one (such as env to denote a SOAP 1.2 message) may do so with this method.

encprefix(*QName*)   `$client->encprefix('enc');`

This method is a shortcut for:

`$client->serializer->encprefix(QName);`

As with the `envprefix` method, this gets or sets the label used for the namespace of the encoding rules. The default value is SOAP-ENC, as is generally used in SOAP 1.1 messages, though the label itself has no actual meaning.

While it may seem to be an unnecessary operation to set a value that isn't relevant to the message, such as the namespace labels for the envelope and encoding URNs, the ability to set these labels explicitly can prove to be a great aid in distinguishing and debugging messages on the server side of operations.

encoding(*encoding URN*)   `$client->encoding($soap_12_encoding_URN);`

This method is a shortcut for:

`$client->serializer->encoding(args);`

Where the earlier method dealt with the label used for the attributes related to the SOAP encoding scheme, this method actually sets the URN to be specified as the encoding scheme for the message. The default is to specify the encoding for SOAP 1.1, so this is handy for applications that need to encode according to SOAP 1.2 rules.

typelookup   `$client->typelookup;`

This method is a shortcut for:

    $client->serializer->typelookup;

Gives the application access to the type-lookup table from the serializer object. See the section on `SOAP::Serializer`.

uri(*service specifier*)   `$client->uri($service_uri);`

This method is a shortcut for:

    $client->serializer->uri(*service*);

The URI associated with this accessor on a client object is the service-specifier for the request, often encoded for HTTP-based requests as the `SOAPAction` header. While the names may seem confusing, this method doesn't specify the endpoint itself. Often times, the value may look like a valid URL. Despite this, it doesn't have to point to an existing resource (and often doesn't). This method sets and retrieves this value from the object. Note that no transport code is triggered by this because it has no direct effect on the transport of the object.

multirefinplace(*boolean*)   `$client->multirefinplace(1);`

This method is a shortcut for:

    $client->serializer->multirefinplace(*boolean*);

Controls how the serializer handles values that have multiple references to them. Recall from previous SOAP chapters that a value may be tagged with an identifier, then referred to in several places.

When this is the case for a value, the serializer defaults to putting the data element towards the top of the message, right after the opening tag of the method-specification. It is serialized as a standalone entity with an ID that is then referenced at the relevant places later on. If this method is used to set a true value, the behavior is different.

When the `multirefinplace` attribute is true, the data is serialized at the first place that references it, rather than as a separate element higher up in the body. This is more compact but may be harder to read or trace in a debugging environment.

self   `$ref = SOAP::Lite->self;`

Returns an object reference to the default global object the `SOAP::Lite` package maintains. This is the object that processes many of the arguments when provided on the use line.

The following method isn't an accessor style of method but neither does it fit with the group that immediately follows it:

call(*arguments*)   `$client->call($method => @arguments);`

As has been illustrated in previous chapters, the `SOAP::Lite` client objects can manage remote calls with auto-dispatching using some of Perl's more elaborate features. call is used when the application wants a greater degree of control over the details of the call itself. The method may be built up from a SOAP::Data object, so as to allow full control over the namespace associated with the tag, as well as other attributes like encoding. This is also important for calling methods that contain characters not allowable in Perl function names, such as A.B.C.

The next four methods used in the SOAP::Lite class are geared towards handling the types of events than can occur during the message lifecycle. Each of these sets up a *callback* for the event in question:

on_action(*callback*) $client->on_action(sub { qq("$_[0]") });
: Triggered when the transport object sets up the SOAPAction header for an HTTP-based call. The default is to set the header to the string, *uri#method*, in which URI is the value set by the uri method described earlier, and method is the name of the method being called. When called, the routine referenced (or the closure, if specified as in the example) is given two arguments, uri and method, in that order.

on_fault(*callback*) $client->on_fault(sub { popup_dialog($_[1]) });
: Triggered when a method call results in a fault response from the server. When it is called, the argument list is first the client object itself, followed by the object that encapsulates the fault. In the example, the fault object is passed (without the client object) to a hypothetical GUI function that presents an error dialog with the text of fault extracted from the object (which is covered shortly under the SOAP::SOM methods).

on_nonserialized(*callback*) $client->on_nonserialized(sub { die "$_[0]?!?" });
: Occasionally, the serializer may be given data it can't turn into SOAP-savvy XML; for example, if a program bug results in a code reference or something similar being passed in as a parameter to method call. When that happens, this callback is activated, with one argument. That argument is the data item that could not be understood. It will be the only argument. If the routine returns, the return value is pasted into the message as the serialization. Generally, an error is in order, and this callback allows for control over signaling that error.

on_debug(*callback*) $client->on_debug(sub { print @_ });
: This is kept for backwards-compatibility with earlier versions of the toolkit. Each method has a trace step built in, which is called at routine entry. This specifies a callback to be used when these trace statements are reached.

    Because this is deprecated, it is recommended that applications use the +debug and +trace facilities described later under SOAP::Trace. Note also that debugging isn't handled on a per-object basis; if this method is used on a given object, it sets debugging behavior for all objects of the class.

SOAP::Data

The SOAP::Data class provides the means by which to explicitly manipulate and control all aspects of the way in which Perl data gets expressed as SOAP data entities. Most of the methods are accessors, which like those in SOAP::Lite are designed to return the current value if no new one is passed, while returning the object reference otherwise (allowing for chained method calls). Note that most accessors (except value) accept a new value for the data object as a second argument.

new(*optional key/value pairs*)   `$obj = SOAP::Data->new(name => 'idx', value => 5);`
> This is the class constructor. Almost all of the attributes related to the class may be passed to the constructor as key/value pairs. This method isn't often used directly because SOAP::Data objects are generally created for temporary use. It is available for those situations that require it.

name(*new name, optional value*)   `$obj->name('index');`
> Gets or sets the current value of the name, as the object regards it. The name is what the serializer will use for the tag when generating the XML for this object. It is what will become the accessor for the data element. Optionally, the object's value may be updated if passed as a second argument.

type(*new type, optional value*)   `$obj->type('int');`
> Gets or sets the type associated with the current value in the object. This is useful for those cases where the SOAP::Data object is used to explicitly specify the type of data that would otherwise be interpreted as a different type completely (such as perceiving the string 123 as an integer, instead). Allows the setting of the object's value, if passed as a second argument to the method.

uri(*new uri, optional value*)   `$obj->uri('http://www.perl.com/SOAP');`
> Gets or sets the URI that will be used as the namespace for the resulting XML entity, if one is desired. This doesn't set the label for the namespace. If one isn't provided by means of the prefix method, one is generated automatically when needed. Also allows the setting of the object's value, if passed as a second argument to the method.

prefix(*new prefix, optional value*)   `$obj->prefix('perl');`
> Provides the prefix, or label, for use when associating the data object with a specific namespace. Also allows the setting of the object's value, if passed as a second argument to the method.

attr(*hash reference of attributes, optional value*)   `$obj->attr({ attr1 => 'value' });`
> Allows for the setting of arbitrary attributes on the data object. Keep in mind the requirement that any attributes not natively known to SOAP must be namespace-qualified. Also allows the setting of the object's value, if passed as a second argument to the method.

value(*new value*)   `$obj->value(10);`
> Fetches the current value encapsulated by the object, or explicitly sets it.

The last four methods are convenience shortcuts for the attributes that SOAP itself supports. Each also permits inclusion of a new value, as an optional second argument.

actor(*new actor, optional value*) `$obj->actor($new_actor_name);`
> Gets or sets the value of the actor attribute; useful only when the object generates an entity for the message header.

mustUnderstand(*boolean, optional value*) `$obj->mustUnderstand(0);`
> Manipulates the mustUnderstand attribute, which tells the SOAP processor whether it is required to understand the entity in question.

encodingStyle(*new encoding URN, optional value*) `$obj->encodingStyle($soap_11_encoding);`
> This method is most likely to be used in places outside the header creation. Sets encodingStyle, which specifies an encoding that differs from the one that would otherwise be defaulted to.

root(*boolean, optional value*) `$obj->root(1);`
> When the application must explicitly specify which data element is to be regarded as the root element for the sake of generating the object model, this method provides the access to the root attribute.

SOAP::SOM

Objects from the SOAP::SOM class aren't generally instantiated directly by an application. Rather, they are handed back by the deserialization of a message.

new(*message*) `$som = SOAP::SOM->new($message_as_xml);`
> As said, the need to actually create an object of this class should be very rare. However, if the need arises, the syntax must be followed. The single argument to new must be a valid XML document the parser will understand as a SOAP response.

The following group of methods provide general data retrieval from the SOAP::SOM object. The model for this is an abbreviated form of XPath. Following this group are methods that are geared towards specific retrieval of commonly requested elements.

match(*path*) `$som->match('/Envelope/Body/[1]');`
> This method sets the internal pointers within the data structure so that the retrieval methods that follow will have access to the desired data. In the example path, the match is being made against the method entity, which is the first child tag of the body in a SOAP response. The enumeration of container children starts at 1 in this syntax, not 0.
>
> The returned value is dependent on the context of the call. If the call is made in a boolean context (such as if ($som->match($path))), the return value is a boolean indicating whether the requested path matched at all. Otherwise, an object reference is returned. The returned object is also a SOAP::SOM instance but is smaller, containing the subset of the document tree matched by the expression.

valueof(*node*)   `$res = $som->valueof('[1]');`

When the SOAP::SOM object has matched a path internally with the match method, this method allows retrieval of the data within any of the matched nodes. The data comes back as native Perl data, not a class instance (see dataof). In a scalar context, this method returns just the first element from a matched node set. In an array context, all elements are returned. Assuming that the earlier call happens after the earlier call to match, it retrieves the result entity from the method response that is contained in $som, as this is the first child element in a method-response tag.

dataof(*node*)   `$resobj = $som->dataof('[1]');`

Performs the same operation as the earlier valueof method, except that the data is left in its SOAP::Data form, rather than being deserialized. This allows full access to all the attributes that were serialized along with the data, such as namespace and encoding.

headerof(*node*)   `$resobj = $som->headerof('[1]');`

Acts much like dataof, except that it returns an object of the SOAP::Header class (covered later in this chapter), rather than SOAP::Data. This is the preferred interface for manipulating the header entities in a message.

namespaceuriof(*node*)   `$ns = $som->namespaceof('[1]');`

Retrieves the namespace URI that governs the requested node. Note that namespaces are inherited, so this method will return the relevant value, even if it derives from a parent or other ancestor node.

The following methods provide more direct access to the message envelope. All these methods return some form of a Perl value, most often a hash reference, when called. Context is also relevant: in a scalar context only the first matching node is returned, while in an array context, all matching nodes are. When called as a static method or as a regular function (such as SOAP::SOM::envelope), any of the following methods returns the XPath string that is used with the match method to retrieve the data.

root   `$root = $som->root;`

Returns the value of the root element as a hash reference. It behaves exactly as $som->valueof('/') does.

envelope   `$envelope = $som->envelope;`

Retrieves the "Envelope" element of the message, returning it and its data as a hash reference. Keys in the hash will be Header and Body (plus any optional elements that may be present in a SOAP 1.1 envelope), whose values will be the serialized header and body, respectively.

header   `$header = $som->header;`

Retrieves the header portion of the envelope as a hash reference. All data within it will have been deserialized. If the attributes of the header are desired, the static form of the method can be combined with match to fetch the header as a SOAP::Data object:

```
$header = $som->match(SOAP::SOM::header)->dataof;
```

headers   `@hdrs = $som->headers;`

Retrieves the node set of values with deserialized headers from within the Header container. This is different from the earlier header method in that it returns the whole header as a single structure, and this returns the child elements as an array. In other words, the following expressions yield the same data structure:

```
$header = ($som->headers)[0];
$header = $som->valueof(SOAP::SOM::header.'/[1]');
```

body   `$body = $som->body;`

Retrieves the message body as a hash reference. The entity tags act as keys, with their deserialized content providing the values.

fault   `if ($som->fault) { die $som->fault->faultstring }`

Acts both as a boolean test whether a fault occurred, and as a way to retrieve the Fault entity itself from the message body as a hash reference. If the message contains a fault, the next four methods (faultcode, faultstring, faultactor, and faultdetail) may be used to retrieve the respective parts of the fault (which are also available on the hash reference as keys). If fault in a boolean context is true, the result, paramsin, paramsout, and method methods all return undef.

faultcode   `$code = $som->faultcode;`

Returns the faultcode element of the fault if there is a fault; undef otherwise.

faultstring   `$string = $som->faultstring;`

Returns the faultstring element of the fault if there is a fault; undef otherwise.

faultactor   `$actor = $som->faultactor;`

Returns the faultactor element of the fault, if there is a fault and if the actor was specified within it. The faultactor element is optional in the serialization of a fault, so it may not always be present. This element is usually a string.

faultdetail   `$detail = $som->faultdetail;`

Returns the content of the detail element of the fault, if there is a fault and if the detail element was provided. Note that the name of the element isn't the same as the method, due to the possibility for confusion had the method been called simply, detail. As with the faultactor element, this isn't always a required component of a fault, so it isn't guaranteed to be present. The specification for the detail portion of a fault calls for it to contain a series of element tags, so the application may expect a hash reference as a return value when detail information is available (and undef otherwise).

method   `$method = $som->method`

Retrieves the "method" element of the message, as a hash reference. This includes all input parameters when called on a request message or all result/

output parameters when called on a response message. If there is a fault present in the message, it returns undef.

result $value = $som->result;
Returns the value that is the result of a SOAP response. The value will be already deserialized into a native Perl datatype.

paramsin @list = $som->paramsin;
Retrieves the parameters being passed in on a SOAP request. If called in a scalar context, the first parameter is returned. When called in a list context, the full list of all parameters is returned. Each parameter is a hash reference, following the established structure for such return values.

paramsout @list = $som->paramsout;
Returns the output parameters from a SOAP response. These are the named parameters that are returned in addition to the explicit response entity itself. It shares the same scalar/list context behavior as the paramsin method.

paramsall @list = $som->paramsall;
Returns all parameters from a SOAP response, including the result entity itself, as one array.

SOAP::Fault

This class encapsulates SOAP faults prior to their serialization or after their deserialization. The methods available are a constructor and four accessors. Each accessor creates an object on demand, just as the other classes do, when called as a static method. Like other accessors in the SOAP::Lite package, they return the object itself when setting the attribute.

new(*optional data*) $fault = SOAP::Fault->new(faultcode => 'Server');
Explicitly creates a new SOAP::Fault object. Any of the four attributes represented next by accessor methods may be passed in the argument list with values immediately following their attribute name.

faultcode(*optional value*) $fault->faultcode('MethodUnknown');
Returns the current fault code or sets it if a value is given.

faultstring(*optional value*) $fault->faultstring("There is no $method here");
Returns or sets the fault string.

faultactor(*optional value*) $fault->faultcode($header->actor);
Returns or sets the fault-actor element. Note that the actor isn't always required in a SOAP fault.

faultdetail(*optional value*) $fault->faultcode(bless { proxy => $ip }, 'Err');
Returns or sets the fault's detail element. Like the actor, this isn't always a required element (refer back to the chapter on SOAP structure for discussion of these fault elements). Note that fault detail content in a message is represented

as tag blocks. Thus, the values passed to this accessor when setting the value are either SOAP::Data objects, or more general blessed hash references.

In addition to these methods, the SOAP::Fault package also provides detail as an alias for faultdetail. The former is the actual name of the element with SOAP faults, but the latter name is less ambiguous when regarded with the rest of the SOAP::Lite package. Objects of this class also have a special stringification enabled. If an object is printed or otherwise stringified, the value produced is faultcode: faultstring, with the attribute values of the object.

SOAP::Transport

Objects of the SOAP::Transport class manage two roles: they manage both the parameters related to transport as set through the containing SOAP::Lite object, and they abstract the selection and loading of an appropriate transport module. This is done with an AUTOLOAD function within the class that intercepts all methods beyond the two defined next and reroutes them to the underlying transport implementation code.

new $trans = SOAP::Transport->new;
This is the constructor, which isn't usually called by an application directly. An application can use this to create a fresh new SOAP::Transport object, which may be installed using the SOAP::Lite->transport method defined earlier. No arguments are recognized.

proxy(*optional URL string*) $trans->proxy('http://www.blackperl.com/SOAP');
Gets or sets the proxy (endpoint). This method must be called before any other methods are called. The proper transport code is loaded based on the scheme specified by the URL itself (http, jabber, etc.). Until this method is called the first time with a URL string, the underlying code has yet to be loaded, and the methods aren't available. When getting the current proxy (calling with no parameters), the returned value is a reference to the client object created from the protocol class that matched the endpoint, not the endpoint itself.

For the other methods that become available after proxy is called, see the later section on the SOAP transport modules.

SOAP::Serializer

The SOAP::Serializer class is the means by which the toolkit manages the expression of data as XML. The object that a SOAP::Lite instance uses by default is generally enough for the task, with no need for the application to create its own. The main purpose of this class is to provide a place for applications to extend the serializer by defining additional methods for handling new datatypes. The methods available through this class are:

new(*optional key/value pairs*)   `$serialize = SOAP::Serializer->new();`

This is the constructor method for the class. In addition to creating a basic object and initializing it with default values, the constructor can also take names and values for most of the accessor methods that the class supports.

envelope(*method, data arguments*)   `$serialize->envelope(fault => $fault_obj);`

Provides the core purpose for the `SOAP::Serializer` class. It creates the full SOAP envelope based on the input passed in to it. The data arguments passed in the list of parameters to the method are divided into two sublists: any parameters that are `SOAP::Header` objects or derivatives of go into one list, while the remainder go into the other. The nonheader objects are used as the content for the message body, with the body itself being largely dependent on the value of the first argument in the list. This argument is expected to be a string and should be one of the following:

method
: The envelope is being created to encapsulate a RPC-style method call.

response
: The message being created is that of a response stemming from a RPC-style method call.

fault
: For this specifier, the envelope being created is to transmit a fault.

freeform
: This identifier is used as a general-case encoding style for messages that don't fit into any of the previous cases. The arguments are encoded into the envelope's Body tag without any sort of context sensitivity.

Any value other than these four results in an error.

envprefix(*optional value*)   `$serialize->envprefix('env');`

Gets or sets the prefix that labels the SOAP envelope namespace. This defaults to SOAP-ENV.

encprefix(*optional value*)   `$serialize->envprefix('enc');`

Gets or sets the prefix that labels the SOAP encoding namespace. Defaults to SOAP-ENC.

soapversion(*optional value*)   `$serial->soapversion('1.2');`

If no parameter is given, returns the current version of SOAP that is being used as the basis for serializing messages. If a parameter is given, attempts to set that as the version of SOAP being used. The value should be either 1.1 or 1.2. When the SOAP version is being set, the package selects new URNs for envelope and encoding spaces and also calls the xmlschema method to set the appropriate schema definition.

xmlschema(*optional value*) $serial->xmlschema($xml_schema_1999);

Gets or sets the URN for the schema being used to express the structure of the XML generated by the serializer. If setting the value, the input must be the full URN for the new schema and is checked against the list of known SOAP schemas.

SOAP::Header

Objects instantiated from the SOAP::Header class are functionally the same as SOAP::Data objects, and as such share all the methods from that class. The distinction may be cosmetic, but it is present so that applications may more easily distinguish header blocks from more generic data elements.

SOAP::Constants

A number of "constant" values are provided by means of this namespace. The values aren't constants in the strictest sense; the purpose of the values detailed here is to allow the application to change them if it desires to alter the specific behavior governed.

$DO_NOT_USE_XML_PARSER

The SOAP::Lite package attempts to locate and use the XML::Parser package, falling back on an internal, pure-Perl parser in its absence. This package is a fast parser, based on the Expat parser developed by James Clark. If the application sets this value to 1, there will be no attempt to locate or use XML::Parser.

There are several reasons you might choose to do this. If the package will never be made available, there is no reason to perform the test. Setting this parameter is less time-consuming than the test for the package would be. Also, the XML::Parser code links against the Expat libraries for the C language. In some environments, this could cause a problem when mixed with other applications that may be linked against a different version of the same libraries. This was once the case with certain combinations of Apache, mod_perl and XML::Parser.

$DO_NOT_USE_CHARSET

Unless this parameter is set to 1, outgoing Content-Type headers will include specification of the character set used in encoding the message itself. Not all endpoints (client or server) may be able to properly deal with that data on the content header, however. If dealing with an endpoint that expects to do a more literal examination of the header as whole (as opposed to fully parsing it), this parameter may prove useful.

$DO_NOT_CHECK_CONTENT_TYPE

The content-type itself for a SOAP message is rather clearly defined, and in most cases, an application would have no reason to disable the testing of that header. This having been said, the content-type for SOAP 1.2 is still only a recommended draft, and badly coded endpoints might send valid messages with invalid Content-Type headers. While the "right" thing to do would be to reject such messages, that isn't always an option. Setting this parameter to 1 allows the toolkit to skip the content-type test.

SOAP::Schema

This class provides an umbrella for the way in which SOAP::Lite manages service description schemas. Currently, the only support present is for the Web Services Description Language (WSDL) (see the next section). This is another of the classes not generally designed to be directly instantiated by an application, though it can be if so desired.

new(*optional key/value pairs*) `$schema = SOAP::Schema->new(parse => $schema_uri);`
This is the class constructor. With no arguments, it creates a blank object of the class. Any arguments that are passed are treated as key/value pairs in which the key represents one of the methods described here, and the value is what gets passed when the method itself gets invoked.

parse(*service description URI*) `$schema->parse('http://schemas.w3.org/soap.wsdl');`
Parses the internal representation of the service description prior to the generation of stub routines to provide method-like access to the remote services.

access(*service description URI*) `$schema->access('http://soap.org/service.wsdl');`
Loads the specified service description from the given URL, using the current value of the schema accessor if none is provided. The full content of the URL is returned on success, or an exception is thrown (via die) on error.

load `$schema->load;`
Takes the internal representation of the service and generates code stubs for the remote methods, allowing them to be called as local object methods. Stubs are generated for all the functions declared in the WSDL description with this call because it's enough of a class framework to allow for basic object creation for use as handles.

schema `$current_schema = $schema->schema;`
Gets (or sets) the current schema representation to be used by this object. The value to be passed when setting this is just the URI of the schema. This gets passed to other methods such as access for loading the actual content.

services `$hashref = $schema->services;`
Gets or sets the services currently stored on the object. The services are kept as a hash reference, whose keys and values are the list of returned values from the WSDL parser. Keys represent the names of the services themselves (names have been normalized into Perl-compatible identifiers), with values that are also hash references to the internal representation of the service itself.

SOAP::Schema::WSDL

At present, the SOAP::Lite toolkit supports only loading of service descriptions in the WSDL syntax. This class manages the parsing and storing of these service specifications. As a general rule, this class should be even less likely to be used directly by an application because its presence should be completely abstracted by the previous class (SOAP::Schema). None of the methods are defined here; the class is only mentioned for sake of reference.

SOAP::Client

The SOAP::Client class exists purely as a superclass for client classes declared by the various transport modules detailed here. The methods it provides are all simple accessors; they return the current value when called with no arguments or set the attribute value and return the object reference when called with an argument. These attributes include:

code, message, status
: Stores the response code, message, and status from the most-recent send attempt. For some protocols, such as FTP, the same value is used for all three because of the lack of finer-grained detail (the default is to ensure that all three attributes contain data, even if redundant). Other protocols (such as HTTP) have distinct values in each.

endpoint
: Identifies the current endpoint to which messages are being sent. This should match the value of the transport method from the SOAP::Transport class, but setting this doesn't propagate to the transport object. It is better to use the transport object (or the shortcut via the SOAP::Lite object itself) when setting this.

is_success
: The success or failure of the most-recent transmission is noted here as a boolean value.

options
: The options attribute keeps a hash-table reference of additional options and their values. At present, only one option is used by any of the transport modules:

    compress_threshold
    : The value of this option should be a numerical value. If set, and if the Compress::Zlib library is available, messages whose size in bytes exceeds this value will be compressed before sending. Both ends of the conversation must have it enabled.

    Other options may be defined using this mechanism. Note that setting the options using this accessor requires a full hash reference be passed. To set just one or a few values, consider retrieving the current reference value and using it to set the key(s).

SOAP::Server

The SOAP::Server class provides the basic framework for the transport-specific server classes to build upon. Note that in none of the code examples provided with SOAP::Lite nor in any of the book examples, is this class used directly. Instead, it is designed to be a superclass within more specific implementation classes. The methods provided by SOAP::Server itself are:

new(*optional key/value pairs*)   `$server = SOAP::Server->new(%options);`
  Creates a new object of the class. Various default instance values are set up, and like many of the constructors in this module, most of the class methods described here may be passed in the construction call by giving the name followed by the parameter (or an array reference if there are multiple parameters).

action(*optional new value*)   `$action = $server->action`
  Retrieves or sets the value of the action attribute on the server object. This attribute is used when mapping the request to an appropriate namespace or routine. For example, the HTTP library sets the attribute to the value of the SOAPAction header when processing of the request begins, so that the find_target method described later may retrieve the value to match it against the server's configuration. Returns the object itself when setting the attribute.

myuri(*optional new value*)   `$server->myuri("http://localhost:9000/SOAP");`
  Gets or sets the myuri attribute. This specifies the specific URI that the server is answering requests to (which may be different from the value specified in action or in the SOAPAction header).

serializer(*optional new value*)   `$serializer = $server->serializer;`
deserializer(*optional new value*)   `$server->deserializer($new_deser_obj);`
  As with the client objects, these methods provide direct access to the serialization and deserialization objects the server object uses to transform input and output from and to XML. There is generally little or no need to explicitly set these to new values.

options(*optional new value*)   `$server->options({compress_threshold => 10000});`
  Sets (or retrieves) the current server options as a hash-table reference. At present, only one option is used within the SOAP::Lite libraries themselves:

  compress_threshold
    The value of this option is expected to be a numerical value. If set, and if the Compress::Zlib library is available to use, messages whose size in bytes exceeds this value are compressed for transmission. Both ends of the conversation have to support this and have it enabled.

Other options may be defined and passed around using this mechanism. Note that setting the options using this accessor requires a full hash reference be passed. To set just one or a few values, retrieve the current reference value and use it to set the key(s).

dispatch_with(*optional new value*)   `$server->dispatch_with($new_table);`

Represents one of two ways in which a SOAP::Server (or derived) object may specify mappings of incoming requests to server-side subroutines or namespaces. The value of the attribute is a hash-table reference. To set the attribute, you must pass a new hash reference. The hash table's keys are URI strings (literal URIs or the potential values of the SOAPAction header), and the corresponding values are one of a class name or an object reference. Requests that come in for a URI found in the table are routed to the specified class or through the specified object.

dispatch_to(*optional list of new values*)   `$server->dispatch_to($dir, 'Module', 'Mod::meth');`

This is the more traditional way to specify modules and packages for routing requests. This is also an accessor, but it returns a list of values when called with no arguments (rather than a single one). Each item in the list of values passed to this method is expected to be one of four things:

Directory path
    If the value is a directory path, all modules located in that path are available for remote use.

Package name
    When the value is a package name (without including a specific method name), all routines within the package are available remotely.

Fully qualified method name
    Alternately, when the value is a package-qualified name of a subroutine or method, that specific routine is made available. This allows the server to make selected methods available without opening the entire package.

Object reference
    If the value is an object reference, the object itself routes the request.

The list of values held by the dispatch_to table are compared only after the URI mapping table from the dispatch_with attribute has been consulted. If the request's URI or SOAPAction header don't map to a specific configuration, the path specified by the action header (or in absence, the URI) is converted to a package name and compared against this set of values.

objects_by_reference(*optional list of new values*)   `$server->objects_by_reference(qw(My::Class));`

This also returns a list of values when retrieving the current attribute value, as opposed to a single value.

This method doesn't directly specify classes for request routing so much as it modifies the behavior of the routing for the specified classes. The classes that are given as arguments to this method are marked to be treated as producing persistent objects. The client is given an object representation that contains just a handle on a local object with a default persistence of 600 idle seconds. Each operation on the object resets the idle timer to zero. This facility is considered experimental in the current version of SOAP::Lite.

on_action(*optional new value*) $server->on_action(sub { ...*new code* });

Gets or sets the reference to a subroutine that is used for executing the on_action hook. Where the client code uses this hook to construct the action-request data (such as for a SOAPAction header), the server uses the on_action hook to do any last-minute tests on the request itself, before it gets routed to a final destination. When called, the hook routine is passed three arguments:

action
: The action URI itself, retrieved from the action method described earlier.

method_uri
: The URI of the XML namespace the method name is labeled with.

method_name
: The name of the method being called by the request.

on_dispatch(*optional new value*)   ($uri, $name) = $server->on_dispatch->($request);

Gets or sets the subroutine reference used for the on_dispatch hook. This hook is called at the start of the request-routing phase and is given a single argument when called:

request
: An object of the SOAP::SOM class, containing the deserialized request from the client.

find_target   ($class, $uri, $name) = $server->find_target($req)

Taking as its argument an object of the SOAP::SOM class that contains the deserialized request, this method returns a three-element list describing the method that is to be called. The elements are:

class
: The class into which the method call should be made. This may come back as either a string or an object reference, if the dispatching is configured using an object instance.

uri
: The URN associated with the request method. This is the value that was used when configuring the method routing on the server object.

name
: The name of the method to call.

handle   `$server->handle($request_text);`

Implements the main functionality of the serving process, in which the server takes an incoming request and dispatches it to the correct server-side subroutine. The parameter taken as input is either plain XML or MIME-encoded content (if MIME-encoding support is enabled).

make_fault   `return $server->makefault($code, $message);`

Creates a SOAP::Fault object from the data passed in. The order of arguments is: code, message, detail, actor. The first two are required (because they must be present in all faults), but the last two may be omitted unless needed.

SOAP::Server::Parameters

This class provides two methods, but the primary purpose from the developer's point of view is to allow classes that a SOAP server exposes inherit from it. When a class inherits from the SOAP::Server::Parameters class, the list of parameters passed to a called method includes the deserialized request in the form of a SOAP::SOM object. This parameter is passed at the end of the arguments list, giving methods the option of ignoring it unless it is needed.

The class provides two subroutines (not methods), for retrieving parameters from the SOAP::SOM object. These are designed to be called without an object reference in the parameter list, but with an array reference instead (as the first parameter). The remainder of the arguments list is expected to be the list from the method-call itself, including the SOAP::SOM object at the end of the list. The routines may be useful to understand if an application wishes to subclass SOAP::Server::Parameters and inherit from the new class instead.

byNameOrOrder(*order, parameter list, envelope*)   `@args = SOAP::Server::Parameters::`
                                                      `byNameOrOrder ([qw(a b)], @_);`

Using the list of argument names passed in the initial argument as an array reference, this routine returns a list of the parameter values for the parameters matching those names, in that order. If none of the names given in the initial array-reference exist in the parameter list, the values are returned in the order in which they already appear within the list of parameters. In this case, the number of returned values may differ from the length of the requested-parameters list.

byName(*order, parameter list, envelope*)   `@args = SOAP::Server::Parameters::byName`
                                                `([qw(a b c)], @_);`

Acts in a similar manner to the previous, with the difference that it always returns as many values as requested, even if some (or all) don't exist. Parameters that don't exist in the parameter list are returned as undef values.

SOAP::Trace

As was detailed in Chapter 6, this class has no methods or objects. It is used only to manage and manipulate the run-time tracing of execution within the toolkit. In absence of methods, this section reviews the events that may be configured and the ways of configuring them.

Tracing is enabled by the SOAP::Lite import method. This is usually done at compile-time, though it may be done explicitly by calling import directly. The commands for setting up tracing start with the keyword +trace. Alternately, +debug may be used; the two are interchangeable. After the initial keyword, one or more of the signals detailed here may be specified, optionally with a callback to handle them. When specifying multiple signals to be handled by a single callback, it is sufficient to list all of them first, followed finally by the callback, as in:

```
use SOAP::Lite +trace =>
              method => fault => \&message_level,
              trace => objects => \&lower_level;
```

In the fragment, the reference to message_level is installed as the callback for both method and fault signals, while lower_level is installed for trace and object events. If callbacks aren't explicitly provided, the default tracing action is to log a message to Perl's STDOUT file descriptor. Callbacks should expect a one or more arguments passed in, though the nature of the arguments varies based on the signal.

Any signal can be disabled by prefacing the name with a hyphen, such as -result. This is useful with the pseudo-signal "all," which is shorthand for the full list of signals. The following fragment disables only the two signals, while still enabling the rest:

```
SOAP::Lite->import(+trace => all => -result => -parameters);
```

If the keyword +trace (or +debug) is used without any signals specified, it enables all signals (as if all were implied).

The signals and their meaning follow. Each also bears a note as to whether the signal is relevant to a server application, client application, or both.

transport   *Client only*
    Triggered in the transport layer just before a request is sent and immediately after a response is received. Each time the signal is sent, the sole argument to the callback is the relevant object. On requests, this is a HTTP::Request object; for responses, it's a HTTP::Response object.

dispatch   *Server only*
    Triggered with the full name of the method being dispatched, just before execution is passed to it. It is currently disabled in SOAP::Lite 0.55.

result   *Server only*
>   Triggered after the method has been dispatched and is passed the results returned from the method as a list. The result values have not yet been serialized when this signal is sent.

parameters   *Server only*
>   Triggered before a method call is actually dispatched, with the data that is intended for the call itself. The parameters for the method call are passed in as a list, after having been deserialized into Perl data.

headers   *Server only*
>   This signal should be for triggering on the headers of an incoming message, but it isn't implemented as of SOAP::Lite 0.55.

objects   *Client or server*
>   Highlights when an object is instantiated or destroyed. It is triggered in the new and DESTROY methods of the various SOAP::Lite classes.

method   *Client or server*
>   Triggered with the list of arguments whenever the envelope method of SOAP::Serializer is invoked with an initial argument of method. The initial string itself isn't passed to the callback.

fault   *Client or server*
>   As with the method signal earlier, except that this signal is triggered when SOAP::Serializer::envelope is called with an initial argument of fault.

freeform   *Client or server*
>   Like the two previous, this signal is triggered when the method SOAP::Serializer::envelope is called with an initial parameter of freeform. This syntax is used when the method is creating SOAP::Data objects from free-form input data.

trace   *Client or server*
>   Triggered at the entry-point of many of the more-significant functions. Not all the functions within the SOAP::Lite classes trigger this signal. Those that do are primarily the highly visible functions described in the interface descriptions for the various classes.

debug   *Client or server*
>   Used in the various transport modules to track the contents of requests and responses (as ordinary strings, not as objects) at different points along the way.

SOAP Transport Classes

Because the bulk of the work is done within the SOAP::Lite module itself, many of the transport-level modules are very simple in their implementations. Transport modules are expected to define both client and server classes within their files. If a module defines only one of the types, it is assumed that the transport protocol itself supports only that side of the conversation. An example is SOAP::Transport::FTP, which provides only a SOAP::Transport::FTP::Client class.

Each class is expected to declare (or inherit, if it is subclassing another transport class) at least two methods. Any newly developed transport classes is also expected to adhere to this interface. Here are the methods:

new(*optional key/value pairs***)** $object = $class->new(%params);
  Creates a new object instance and returns it. Like the constructors for both SOAP::Lite and SOAP::Server classes, all arguments passed in are treated as key/value pairs, where the key is expected to be one of the methods the class supports, and the value is the argument (or list reference of arguments) to the method.

send_receive(*key/value pairs***)** $client->send_recieve(%hash_table);
  (Required for client classes only) When the SOAP::Lite objects attempt to send out requests, the means for doing so is to attempt to call this method on the object held within the SOAP::Transport object contained within the client itself. All clients are expected to provide this, and the call to this method always passes four values for the hash keys:

  action
    The URI specifying the action being performed, usually the result from the on_action hook on the client object.

  encoding
    The URI of the encoding scheme that governs the message being sent.

  endpoint
    The URI specifying the endpoint to which the message is being sent.

  envelope
    The XML content of the message to be sent. It is generally the return value of the envelope method from the SOAP::Serializer object instance that the client object maintains.

handle $server->handle;
  (Required for server classes only.) This method is the central point for the various server classes to provide an interface to handling requests. The exact set and nature of parameters generally varies based on the classes themselves.

Each individual transport module is now examined, and their provision of client and/or server classes is outlined. Each class detailed also includes notes on which of the classes from SOAP::Lite they inherit from, for reference.

SOAP::Transport::FTP

The SOAP::Transport::FTP module is automatically loaded by the SOAP::Transport portion of the client structure. It is brought in when an endpoint is specified via the proxy method that starts with the characters, ftp://. This module provides only a client class.

SOAP::Transport::FTP::Client

Inherits from: SOAP::Client.

Support is provided for clients to connect to FTP servers using SOAP. The methods defined within the class are just the basic new and send_receive.

SOAP::Transport::HTTP

The most commonly used transport module is the HTTP implementation. This is loaded whenever an endpoint is given that starts with the characters, http:// or https://. This is also the most involved of the transport modules, defining not only a client class but several different server classes as well.

SOAP::Transport::HTTP::Client

Inherits from: SOAP::Client, LWP::UserAgent (from the LWP package).

With this class, clients are able to use HTTP for sending messages. This class provides just the basic new and send_receive methods. Objects of this class understand the compress_threshold option and use it if the server being communicated to also understands it.

SOAP::Transport::HTTP::Server

Inherits from: SOAP::Server.

This is the most basic of the HTTP server implementations. It provides the basic methods, new and handle. The handle method's behavior is defined here, along with other methods specific to this class. The role of this class is primarily to act as a superclass for the other HTTP-based server classes.

handle $server->handle;
Expects the request method to have been used to associate a HTTP::Request object with the server object prior to being called. This method retrieves that object reference to get at the request being handled.

request(*optional value*) $server->request($req_object)
Gets or sets the HTTP::Request object reference that the server will process within the handle method.

response(*optional value*) $server->response(HTTP::Response->new(...));
Gets or sets the HTTP::Response object reference that the server has prepared for sending back to the client.

make_response(*code, body*)   `$server->make_response(200, $body_xml);`
Constructs and returns an object of the `HTTP::Response` class, using the response code and content provided.

make_fault(*fault arguments*)   `$server->response($server->make_fault(@data));`
Creates a `HTTP::Response` object reference using a predefined HTTP response code to signify that a fault has occurred. The arguments are the same as those for the `make_fault` method of the `SOAP::Server` class.

product_tokens
This method takes no arguments and simply returns a string identifying the elements of the server class itself. It is similar to the `product_tokens` methods in the `HTTP::Daemon` and `Apache` classes.

SOAP::Transport::HTTP::CGI

Inherits from: `SOAP::Transport::HTTP::Server`.

This class is a direct subclass of `SOAP::Transport::HTTP::Server` and defines no additional methods. It includes logic in its implementation of the `handle` method that deals with the request headers and parameters specific to a CGI environment.

SOAP::Transport::HTTP::Daemon

Inherits from: `SOAP::Transport::HTTP::Server`.

The `SOAP::Transport::HTTP::Daemon` class encapsulates a reference to an object of the `HTTP::Daemon` class (from the `LWP` package). The class catches methods that aren't provided locally or by the superclass and attempts to call them on the `HTTP::Daemon` object. Thus, all methods defined in the documentation for that class are available to this class as well. Any that conflict with methods in `SOAP::Transport::HTTP::Server` (such as `product_tokens`) go to the superclass. Additionally, the behavior of the `handle` method is specific to this class:

handle
When invoked, this method enters into the typical accept loop in which it waits for a request on the socket that the daemon object maintains and deals with the content of the request. When all requests from the connection returned by the accept method of the `HTTP::Daemon` object have been processed, this method returns.

SOAP::Transport::HTTP::Apache

Inherits from: `SOAP::Transport::HTTP::Server`.

This class provides an integration of the `SOAP::Server` base class with the `mod_perl` extension for Apache. To work as a location handler, the package provides a method called `handler`, for which `handle` is made an alias. The `new` method isn't functionally different from the superclass. Here are the other methods provided by this class:

handler(*Apache request*)   `$server->handler($r)`

Defines the basis for a location handler in the `mod_perl` fashion. The method expects an Apache request object as the parameter, from which it pulls the body of the request and calls the superclass `handle` method. Note that in this class, the local method named `handle` is aliased to this method.

configure(*Apache request*)   `$server->configure(Apache->request);`

Per-location configuration information can be provided to the server object using the Apache `DirConfig` directive and calling this method on the object itself. When invoked, the method reads the directory configuration information from Apache and looks for lines of the form:

    method => param

Each line that matches the pattern is regarded as a potential method to call on the server object, with the remaining token taken as the parameter to the method. Methods that take hash references as arguments may be specified as:

    method => key => param, key => param

The key/value pairs will be made into a hash reference on demand. If the server object doesn't recognize the named method as valid, it ignores the line.

SOAP::Transport::HTTP::FCGI

Inherits from: `SOAP::Transport::HTTP::CGI`.

This is an extension of the `SOAP::Transport::HTTP::CGI` that implements the differences needed for the FastCGI protocol. None of the methods are functionally different.

SOAP::Transport::IO

The `SOAP::Transport::IO`-based class allows for a sort of I/O proxying by allowing the application to configure what files or filehandles are used. This module supplies only a server class.

SOAP::Transport::IO::Server

Inherits from: `SOAP::Server`.

The server class defined here inherits all methods from `SOAP::Server`, and adds two additional methods specific to the nature of the class:

in   `$server->in(IO::File->new($file));`

Gets or sets the current filehandle being used as the input source.

out   `$server->out(\*STDERR);`

Gets or sets the filehandle being used as the output destination.

SOAP::Transport::JABBER

This class uses the Net::Jabber classes to abstract the Jabber protocol away from the direct notice of the application. Besides maintaining any needed objects internally, the package also uses a separate class as a proxy between communication layers, SOAP::Transport::JABBER::Query. The Jabber support provides both client and server classes.

SOAP::Transport::JABBER::Client

Inherits from: SOAP::Client, Net::Jabber::Client.

This class provides localized implementations for both the new and send_receive methods, neither of which are changed in terms of interface. The only difference is that the send_receive method doesn't directly use the action hash key on the input it receives. In addition to these two basic methods, the server class overrides the endpoint method it would otherwise inherit from SOAP::Client:

endpoint
 In the general sense, this still acts as a basic accessor method, with the same get value/set value behavior used consistently through the SOAP::Lite module. The difference between this version and most others is that when the endpoint is initially set or is changed, the client object makes the connection to the Jabber endpoint, sending the proper authentication credentials and setting up the conversation mechanism using the SOAP::Transport::JABBER::Query class as a delegate. It then calls the superclass endpoint method to ensure that all other related elements are taken care of.

SOAP::Transport::JABBER::Server

Inherits from: SOAP::Server.

The server class provided for Jabber support defines a slightly different interface to the constructor. The server manages the Jabber communication by means of an internal Net::Jabber::Client instance. In a fashion similar to that used by SOAP::Transport::HTTP::Daemon, the server class catches methods that are meant for the Jabber client and treats them as if the class inherits directly from that class, without actually doing so. In doing so, the handle method is implemented as a frontend to the Process method of the Jabber client class. The difference in the interface to the constructor is:

new(*URI, optional server key/value options*)   `$srv = SOAP::Transport::JABBER::Server->`
                                                                         `new($uri);`
 The constructor for the class expects that the first argument will be a Jabber-style URI, followed by the standard set of optional key/value pairs of method names and their parameters. All the method/parameter pairs are delegated to the

superclass constructor; only the Jabber URI is handled locally. It's used to set up the `Net::Jabber::Client` instance that manages the actual communications.

SOAP::Transport::LOCAL

The `SOAP::Transport::LOCAL` module is designed to provide a no-transport client class for tracing and debugging communications traffic. It links `SOAP::Client` and `SOAP::Server` so that the same object that "sends" the request also "receives" it.

SOAP::Transport::LOCAL::Client

Inherits from: `SOAP::Client`, `SOAP::Server`.

The implementations of the `new` and `send_receive` methods aren't noticeably different in their interface. Their behavior warrants description, however:

new
When the constructor creates a new object of this class, it sets up a few things beyond the usual `SOAP::Client` layout. The `is_success` method is set to a default value of 1. The `dispatch_to` method inherited from `SOAP::Server` is called with the current value of the global array `@INC`, allowing the client to call any methods that can be found in the current valid search path. And as with most of the constructors in this module, the optional key/value pairs are treated as method names and parameters.

send_receive
The implementation of this method simply passes the envelope portion of the input data to the `handle` method of `SOAP::Server`. While no network traffic results (directly) from this, it allows for debug signals to be sent through the `SOAP::Trace` facility.

SOAP::Transport::MAILTO

This transport class manages SMTP-based sending of messages from a client perspective. It doesn't provide a server class. The class gets selected when a client object passes a URI to proxy or endpoint that starts with the characters, `mailto:`.

SOAP::Transport::MAILTO::Client

Inherits from: `SOAP::Client`.

The client class for this protocol doesn't define any new methods. The constructor functions in the same style as the others class constructors. The functionality of the `send_receive` method is slightly different from other classes, however.

When invoked, the `send_receive` method uses the `MIME::Lite` package to encapsulate and transmit the message. Because mail messages are one-way communications (the reply being a separate process), there is no response message to be returned by the method. Instead, all the status-related attributes (code, message, status, is_success) are set, and no value is explicitly returned.

SOAP::Transport::MQ

This class provides implementations of both client and server frameworks built on IBM's Message Queue set of classes. The SOAP objects encapsulate additional objects from these classes, creating and using them behind the scenes as needed.

SOAP::Transport::MQ::Client

Inherits from: SOAP::Client.

The client class provides two methods specific to it, as well as specialized versions of the endpoint and send_receive methods. It also provides a localized new method, but the interface isn't changed from the superclass method. The new methods are:

requestqueue $client->requestqueue->Put(message => $request);
> Manages the MQSeries::Queue object the client uses for enqueuing requests to the server. In general, an application shouldn't need to directly access this attribute, let alone set it. If setting it, the new value should be an object of (or derived from) the MQSeries::Queue class.

replyqueue $client->replyqueue(MQSeries::Queue->new(%args));
> Manages the queue object used for receiving messages back from the designated server (endpoint). It is also primarily for internal use, though if the application needs to set it explicitly, the new value should be an object of (or derived from) the MQSeries::Queue class.

The two previous methods are mainly used by the localized versions of the methods:

endpoint
> This accessor method has the same interface as other similar classes but is worth noting for the internal actions that take place. When the endpoint is set or changed, the method creates a queue-manager object (from the MQSeries::QueueManager class) and references this object when creating queues for replies and requests using the methods described earlier. The URI structure used with these classes (strings beginning with the characters mq://user@host:port) contains the information needed for these operations.

send_receive
> This method uses the same interface as other classes, but makes use of only the endpoint and envelope keys in the hash-table input data. The endpoint key is needed only if the client wishes to switch endpoints prior to sending the message. The message (the value of the envelope key) is inserted into the queue stored in the requestqueue attribute. The client then waits for a reply to the message to appear in the queue stored in the replyqueue attribute.

SOAP::Transport::MQ::Server

Inherits from: SOAP::Server.

The server class also defines requestqueue and replyqueue methods under the same terms as the client class. Of course, the server reads from the request queue and writes to the reply queue, the opposite of the client's behavior. The methods whose functionality are worth noting are:

new(*URI, optional parameters*)
: When called, the constructor creates the MQSeries::QueueManager object and the two MQSeries::Queue objects, similar to what the client does inside its endpoint method. Like the Jabber server described earlier, the first argument to this constructor is expected to be the URI that describes the server itself. The remainder of the arguments are treated as key/value pairs, as with other class constructors previously described.

handle
: When this method is called, it attempts to read a pending message from the request-queue stored on the requestqueue attribute. The message itself is passed to the handle method of the superclass, and the result from that operation is enqueued to the replyqueue object. This process loops until no more messages are present in the request queue. The return value is the number of messages processed. The reads from the request queue are done in a nonblocking fashion, so if there is no message pending, the method immediately returns with a value of zero.

SOAP::Transport::POP3

POP3 support is limited to a server implementation. Just as the MAILTO class detailed earlier operates by sending requests without expecting to process a response, the server described here accepts request messages and dispatches them without regard for sending a response other than that which POP3 defines for successful delivery of a message.

SOAP::Transport::POP3::Server

Inherits from: SOAP::Server.

The new method of this class creates an object of the Net::POP3 class to use internally for polling a specified POP3 server for incoming messages. When an object of this class is created, it expects an endpoint to be specified with a URI that begins with the characters pop:// and includes user ID and password information as well as the hostname itself.

The handle method takes the messages present in the remote mailbox and passes them (one at a time) to the superclass handle method. Each message is deleted after being routed. All messages in the POP3 mailbox are presumed to be SOAP messages.

Methods for the Net::POP3 object are detected and properly routed, allowing operations such as $server->ping(). This means that the endpoint string doesn't need to provide the user ID and password because the login method from the POP3 API may be used directly.

SOAP::Transport::TCP

The classes provided by this module implement direct TCP/IP communications methods for both clients and servers. The connections don't use HTTP or any other higher-level protocol. These classes are selected when the client or server object being created uses an endpoint URI that starts with tcp://. Both client and server classes support using Secure Socket Layer if it is available. If any of the parameters to a new method from either of the classes begins with SSL_ (such as SSL_server in place of Server), the class attempts to load the IO::Socket::SSL package and use it to create socket objects.

Both of the following classes catch methods that are intended for the socket objects and pass them along, allowing calls such as $client->accept() without including the socket class in the inheritance tree.

SOAP::Transport::TCP::Client

Inherits from: SOAP::Client.

The TCP client class defines only two relevant methods beyond new and send_receive. These methods are:

SSL(*optional new boolean value*)   if ($client->SSL) # Execute only if in SSL mode
    Reflects the attribute that denotes whether the client object is using SSL sockets for communications.

io_socket_class   ($client->io_socket_class)->new(%options);
    Returns the name of the class to use when creating socket objects for internal use in communications. As implemented, it returns one of IO::Socket::INET or IO::Socket::SSL, depending on the return value of the previous SSL method.

If an application creates a subclass that inherits from this client class, either method is a likely target for overloading. The new method behaves identically to most other classes, except that it detects the presence of SSL-targeted values in the parameter list and sets the SSL method appropriately if they are present.

The send_receive method creates a socket of the appropriate class and connects to the configured endpoint. It then sets the socket to nonblocking I/O, sends the message, shuts down the client end of the connection (preventing further writing), and reads the response back from the server. The socket object is discarded after the response and appropriate status codes are set on the client object.

SOAP::Transport::TCP::Server

Inherits from: `SOAP::Server`.

The server class also defines the same two additional methods as in the client class:

SSL(*optional new boolean value*)   `if ($client->SSL) # Execute only if in SSL mode`
   Reflects the attribute that denotes whether the client object is using SSL sockets for communications.

io_socket_class   `($client->io_socket_class)->new(%options);`
   Returns the name of the class to use when creating socket objects for internal use in communications. As implemented, it returns one of `IO::Socket::INET` or `IO::Socket::SSL`, depending on the return value of the previous SSL method.

The new method also manages the automatic selection of SSL in the same fashion as the client class does.

The handle method in this server implementation isn't designed to be called once with each new request. Rather, it is called with no arguments, at which time it enters into an infinite loop of waiting for a connection, reading the request, routing the request and sending back the serialized response. This continues until the process itself is interrupted by an untrapped signal or similar means.

The Apache Wrapper

Part of the overall SOAP support in the `SOAP::Lite` module is a wrapper to allow easy deployment of objects of the Apache-based HTTP transport class detailed earlier as location handlers under Apache with `mod_perl`:

Apache::SOAP

Inherits from: `SOAP::Transport::HTTP::Apache`.

This class defines only one method, `handler`, which is the name that `mod_perl` expects to find in a class defined as a location handler:

handler   `# In httpd.conf, within <Location>:PerlHandler Apache::SOAP`
   Uses a single instance of an `Apache::SOAP` object (created at compile-time from the new method inherited from the superclass) to route the request contained in the Apache request record that gets passed in to the handler as the sole parameter. The configure method is called on the object (see the `SOAP::Transport::HTTP::Apache` section), followed by the superclass `handler` method.

The SOAP server in this case relies entirely on configuration by means of the `DirConfig` lines in the Apache configuration file.

UDDI::Lite

The UDDI support that `SOAP::Lite` provides is accomplished through subclassing the basic SOAP components, much as `XMLRPC::Lite` does to provide the XML-RPC functionality. This section will be less detailed as a result, focusing on the aspects of the methods and class behavior that are different from the parent classes.

UDDI::Lite

The `UDDI::Lite` class itself is a subclass of `SOAP::Lite` and inherits all the transport and related functionality from its parent. For the basic utility methods (new, proxy, etc.) refer back to that section earlier in this appendix. What this class does offer that goes beyond the basic SOAP capability is predefined class methods for the various UDDI elements. Since UDDI has a much stricter grammar than the more generalized SOAP, the class is able to cater to that in the functionality it offers.

The methods are named directly after the UDDI XML element they represent. They are also importable and may be used as normal function calls rather than object methods. Table B-1 lists the methods grouped by the import tag applications can use to get access to them:

Table B-1. UDDI::Lite importable functions

Import tag	Functions
auth	get_authToken
	discard_authToken
	get_registeredInfo
delete	delete_binding
	delete_business
	delete_service
	delete_tModel
find	find_binding
	find_business
	find_service
	find_tModel
get	get_bindingDetail
	get_businessDetail
	get_businessDetailExt
	get_serviceDetail
	get_tModelDetail

Table B-1. UDDI::Lite importable functions (continued)

Import tag	Functions
save	save_binding
	save_business
	save_service
	save_tModel
validate	validate_categorization

Besides these tags, `inquiry` imports the combined lists from `find` and `get`, while `publish` returns the combination of `auth`, `delete`, `save`, and `validate`. As with most modules that export, the special tag `all` pulls in the complete set.

The class uses the same style and syntax for error handling (`on_fault`) and debugging (the `SOAP::Trace` facility) as the previous classes.

UDDI::Data

As with the `SOAP::Data` class from which this derives, the purpose of `UDDI::Data` is to provide explicit typing and namespace control over values that the application is passing to other methods. The usage and style are identical to `SOAP::Data`.

Like `UDDI::Lite`, this class exports a large number of names that can be used as shortcuts in creating structures for a UDDI message. The names are identical to the UDDI element names as defined in the schema for UDDI. There are too many to list here, but the distribution includes some examples in the manpage, as well as some example code.

UDDI::SOM

The `UDDI::SOM` package is identical to `SOAP::SOM`, except that it overrides the result method to use an XPath expression specific to UDDI responses.

UDDI::Serializer and UDDI::Deserializer

These two classes are derived from their SOAP counterparts, with UDDI-specific functionality added. Given the much more strictly defined nature of UDDI syntax, neither class is recommended for subclassing or replacement on the `UDDI::Lite` object.

APPENDIX C
XML-RPC Example Code

This appendix presents the full versions of the example code from Chapters 3 and 4. The versions shown here have additional code commentary inserted to aid in understanding.

Basic Meerkat Client (Chapter 3)

Chapter 3 presented this single example program. It illustrates developing an XML-RPC application from scratch, without the benefit of toolkits. The purpose of this is to provide a basis of comparison with the sample clients in Chapter 4, in which the various toolkits are demonstrated.

Example C-1. meer2html.pl

```perl
#!/usr/bin/perl -w

use strict;
use vars qw($chan $cat $num $data $UA $request);

use LWP::UserAgent;
use HTTP::Request;
use XML::XPath;

use constant MEERKAT =>
    'http://www.oreillynet.com/meerkat/xml-rpc/server.php';
use constant XPATH_TO_STRUCTS =>
    '/methodResponse/params/param/value/array/data/value' .
    '/struct';

# Read and test the command-line arguments.
if ($ARGV[0] =~ /^-ch/) {
    $chan = $ARGV[1];
    $num  = $ARGV[2] || 15;
} elsif ($ARGV[0] =~ /^-ca/) {
    $cat = $ARGV[1];
    $num = $ARGV[2] || 15;
```

Example C-1. meer2html.pl (continued)

```perl
}
unless (($chan or $cat) and ($num =~ /^\d+$/)) {
    die "USAGE: $0 { -channel str | -category str } [ n ]";
}

# Create a user-agent object, and pre-create the HTTP
# Request object. Also, set the Content-Type to the standard
# value, as that will never need to be changed.
$UA = LWP::UserAgent->new();
$request = HTTP::Request->new(POST => MEERKAT);
$request->content_type('text/xml');

# This could be done with just one data-retrieval routine,
# but this way is easier to follow, and tests $chan/$cat
# less-often.
$data = $chan ? data_from_chan($chan, $num) :
                data_from_cat($cat, $num);
show_data($data);

exit;

# Retrieve data from a 'Channel' source
sub data_from_chan {
    my ($chan, $num) = @_;

    # If $chan is not already numeric, convert it by using
    # an intermediate XML-RPC call
    $chan = resolve_name($chan, 'Channels')
        unless ($chan =~ /^\d+$/);
    get_data(channel => $chan, $num);
}

# Retrieve data from a 'Category' source
sub data_from_cat {
    my ($cat, $num) = @_;

    # If $cat is not already numeric, convert it by using
    # an intermediate XML-RPC call
    $cat = resolve_name($cat, 'Categories')
        unless ($cat =~ /^\d+$/);
    get_data(category => $cat, $num);
}

# Output the HTML fragment for the data. Note that the way
# the data is treated is independant of whether the source
# was a category or a channel
sub show_data {
    my $data = shift;

    # The data in was a scalar reference pointing to the
    # XML returned from Meerkat. Feed it straight to the
    # XML::XPath engine, then start by retrieving all the
```

Example C-1. meer2html.pl (continued)

```perl
    # 'struct' nodes.
    my $xp = XML::XPath->new(xml => $$data);
    my $nodes = $xp->find(XPATH_TO_STRUCTS);

    my @stories = ();
    for my $struct ($nodes->get_nodelist) {
        # Each story record is built by finding the
        # <member> within the <struct> that has a <name>
        # matching the given key (the loop value). When
        # that is found, the <value>/<string> part is
        # extracted and saved on the hash-reference.
        my $tmp = {};
        for my $key (qw(title link description)) {
            my $node = $xp->find(qq(member[name="$key"]),
                                    $struct);
            $tmp->{$key} =
                $xp->find('value/string',
                            $node->get_node(1))
                    ->string_value;
        }
        push(@stories, $tmp);
    }
    print STDOUT qq(<span class="meerkat">\n<dl>\n);
    for (@stories) {
        print STDOUT <<"END_HTML";
<dt class="title"><a href="$_->{link}">$_->{title}</a></dt>
<dd class="description">$_->{description}</dd>
END_HTML
    }
    print STDOUT qq(</dl>\n</span>\n);
}

# Resolve a substring name-fragment into the numeric ID that
# the call later on in get_data requires
sub resolve_name {
    my ($str, $name) = @_;

    # Fortunately, the calling syntax is the same for
    # categories or channels, the only difference being
    # the name of the remote procedure
    $name = "meerkat.get${name}BySubstring";
    # Make the XML for the request
    my $xml = <<"END_XML";
<?xml version="1.0"?>
<methodCall>
  <methodName>$name</methodName>
  <params>
    <param><value>$str</value></param>
  </params>
</methodCall>
END_XML
```

Example C-1. meer2html.pl (continued)

```perl
    # Set the content of the request object to the XML
    $request->content($xml);
    # Make the request and get the HTTP::Response object
    my $resp = $UA->request($request);
    die "resolve_name: transport error: " . $resp->message
        if $resp->is_error;
    # Feed the XML of the result to XML::XPath
    my $xp = XML::XPath->new(xml => $resp->content);
    # Grab the <struct> block(s) within the <array>
    my $nodeset = $xp->find(XPATH_TO_STRUCTS);
    # We aren't doing multi-channels (yet), so report an
    # error if the substring returns more than one hit
    die "resolve_name: $str returned more than 1 match"
        if ($nodeset->size > 1);
    my $node = $nodeset->get_node(1);
    $node = $xp->find('member[name="id"]', $node);

    # The only value needed is the <int> ID for the
    # <struct>
    $xp->find('value/int', $node->get_node(1))
        ->string_value;
}

# Get the data-- will return a scalar reference to the
# XML text.
sub get_data {
    my ($key, $val, $num) = @_;

    # Create the XML message for the request
    my $xml = <<"END_XML";
<?xml version="1.0"?>
<methodCall>
  <methodName>meerkat.getItems</methodName>
  <params>
    <param><value>
      <struct>
        <member>
          <name>$key</name>
          <value><int>$val</int></value>
        </member>
        <member>
          <name>time_period</name>
          <value><string>7DAY</string></value>
        </member>
        <member>
          <name>num_items</name>
          <value><int>$num</int></value>
        </member>
        <member>
          <name>descriptions</name>
          <value><int>200</int></value>
        </member>
```

Example C-1. meer2html.pl (continued)

```
      </struct>
    </value></param>
  </params>
</methodCall>
END_XML

    # Set the content on the request object to the XML
    $request->content($xml);
    # Get the HTTP::Response object back
    my $resp = $UA->request($request);
    die "resolve_name: transport error: " . $resp->message
        if $resp->is_error;
    my $content = $resp->content;
    # Return the XML body of the response
    \$content;
}
```

XML-RPC Toolkit Samples (Chapter 4)

Chapter 4 presents the three XML-RPC toolkits available to the Perl developer. For each module the earlier Meerkat client was reimplemented as an example of a client; a simple server that provided quotes from the popular fortune program demonstrated server development. The examples are broken down by toolkit used, with the base code for the fortune interface presented last, because it was kept toolkit-independent.

The RPC::XMLSimple Examples

The client example was the first look at reengineering the Meerkat example from Chapter 3 with a toolkit. The result was a script less than half the size of the original sample.

Example C-2. meer2html-Frontier.pl

```
#!/usr/bin/perl -w

use strict;
use vars qw($chan $cat $num $data $client);

use Frontier::Client;
use constant MEERKAT =>
    'http://www.oreillynet.com/meerkat/xml-rpc/server.php';

# Read and test the command-line arguments.
if ($ARGV[0] =~ /^-ch/) {
    $chan = $ARGV[1];
    $num  = $ARGV[2] || 15;
} elsif ($ARGV[0] =~ /^-ca/) {
    $cat  = $ARGV[1];
```

Example C-2. meer2html-Frontier.pl (continued)

```perl
    $num = $ARGV[2] || 15;
}
unless (($chan or $cat) and ($num =~ /^\d+$/)) {
    die "USAGE: $0 { -channel str | -category str } [ n ]";
}

$client = Frontier::Client->new(url => MEERKAT);

# This could be done with just one data-retrieval routine,
# but this way is easier to follow, and tests $chan/$cat
# less-often.
$data = $chan ? data_from_chan($chan, $num) :
                data_from_cat($cat, $num);
show_data($data);

exit;

# Retrieve data from a 'Channel' source
sub data_from_chan {
    my ($chan, $num) = @_;

    # If $chan is not already numeric, convert it by using
    # an intermediate XML-RPC call
    $chan = resolve_name($chan, 'Channels')
        unless ($chan =~ /^\d+$/);
    get_data(channel => $chan, $num);
}

# Retrieve data from a 'Category' source
sub data_from_cat {
    my ($cat, $num) = @_;

    # If $cat is not already numeric, convert it by using
    # an intermediate XML-RPC call
    $cat = resolve_name($cat, 'Categories')
        unless ($cat =~ /^\d+$/);
    get_data(category => $cat, $num);
}

# Output the HTML fragment for the data. Note that the way
# the data is treated is independant of whether the source
# was a category or a channel
sub show_data {
    my $data = shift;

    print STDOUT qq(<span class="meerkat">\n<dl>\n);
    for (@$data) {
        print STDOUT <<"END_HTML";
<dt class="title"><a href="$_->{link}">$_->{title}</a></dt>
<dd class="description">$_->{description}</dd>
END_HTML
    }
```

Example C-2. meer2html-Frontier.pl (continued)

```perl
    print STDOUT qq(</dl>\n</span>\n);
}

# Resolve a substring name-fragment into the numeric ID that
# the call later on in get_data requires
sub resolve_name {
    my ($str, $name) = @_;

    # Fortunately, the calling syntax is the same for
    # categories or channels, the only difference being
    # the name of the remote procedure
    $name = "meerkat.get${name}BySubstring";
    my $resp = $client->call($name, $str);
    # We aren't doing multi-channels (yet), so report an
    # error if the substring returns more than one hit
    die "resolve_name: $str returned more than 1 match"
        if (@$resp > 1);

    $resp->[0]{id};
}

# Get the data-- the result of the method call below happens
# to return the data in the exact format needed by show_data
sub get_data {
    my ($key, $val, $num) = @_;

    $client->call('meerkat.getItems',
                  { $key         => $val,
                    time_period  => '7DAY',
                    num_items    => $num,
                    descriptions => 200 });
}
```

The server example presented the RPC::XMLSimple::Daemon class as the basis for writing servers. It's a lightweight class, as this example shows. The server uses the XRFortune.pm module, which is presented at the end of this appendix.

Example C-3. fortune-Frontier.pl

```perl
#!/usr/bin/perl -w

use strict;

use XRFortune;
use RPC::XMLSimple::Daemon;

# The way the Daemon class in RPC::XMLSimple is set up, the
# constructor actually drops directly into the socket-accept
# loop, so there is no need to call any other method. The
# local routines are specified via the "methods" key on the
# input parameters. This package calls local routines as
# ordinary routines, not class methods, so there is no need
```

Example C-3. fortune-Frontier.pl (continued)

```
# for a wrapper class.
RPC::XMLSimple:Daemon->new(LocalPort => 9000,
                           ReuseAddr => 1,
                           methods =>
                           { books    => \&XRFortune::books,
                             fortune =>
                             \&XRFortune::fortune,
                             weighted_fortune =>
                             \&XRFortune::weighted_fortune
                           });

exit;
```

The XMLRPC::Lite Examples

The XMLRPC::Lite version of the Meerkat client weighs in at just five lines longer than the RPC::XMLSimple version. The following example illustrates the way in which the XMLRPC::Lite clients return data to the caller, as well as the methods used to specify the server URL and make the actual calls.

Example C-4. meer2html-Lite.pl

```
#!/usr/bin/perl -w

use strict;
use vars qw($chan $cat $num $data $client);

use XMLRPC::Lite;
use constant MEERKAT =>
    'http://www.oreillynet.com/meerkat/xml-rpc/server.php';

# Read and test the command-line arguments.
if ($ARGV[0] =~ /^-ch/) {
    $chan = $ARGV[1];
    $num  = $ARGV[2] || 15;
} elsif ($ARGV[0] =~ /^-ca/) {
    $cat  = $ARGV[1];
    $num  = $ARGV[2] || 15;
}
unless (($chan or $cat) and ($num =~ /^\d+$/)) {
    die "USAGE: $0 { -channel str | -category str } [ n ]";
}

# Creating a client object happens automatically when one of
# the methods such as proxy() is called. The on_fault call
# sets up a handler call-back for transport errors.
$client = XMLRPC::Lite->proxy(MEERKAT)
          ->on_fault(sub { die "Transport error: " .
                           $_[1]->faultstring });
```

Example C-4. meer2html-Lite.pl (continued)

```perl
# This could be done with just one data-retrieval routine,
# but this way is easier to follow, and tests $chan/$cat
# less-often.
$data = $chan ? data_from_chan($chan, $num) :
                data_from_cat($cat, $num);
show_data($data);

exit;

# Retrieve data from a 'Channel' source
sub data_from_chan {
    my ($chan, $num) = @_;

    # If $chan is not already numeric, convert it by using
    # an intermediate XML-RPC call
    $chan = resolve_name($chan, 'Channels')
        unless ($chan =~ /^\d+$/);
    get_data(channel => $chan, $num);
}

# Retrieve data from a 'Category' source
sub data_from_cat {
    my ($cat, $num) = @_;

    # If $cat is not already numeric, convert it by using
    # an intermediate XML-RPC call
    $cat = resolve_name($cat, 'Categories')
        unless ($cat =~ /^\d+$/);
    get_data(category => $cat, $num);
}

# Output the HTML fragment for the data. Note that the way
# the data is treated is independant of whether the source
# was a category or a channel
sub show_data {
    my $data = shift;

    print STDOUT qq(<span class="meerkat">\n<dl>\n);
    for (@$data) {
        print STDOUT <<"END_HTML";
<dt class="title"><a href="$_->{link}">$_->{title}</a></dt>
<dd class="description">$_->{description}</dd>
END_HTML
    }
    print STDOUT qq(</dl>\n</span>\n);
}

# Resolve a substring name-fragment into the numeric ID that
# the call later on in get_data requires
sub resolve_name {
    my ($str, $name) = @_;
```

Example C-4. meer2html-Lite.pl (continued)

```perl
    # Fortunately, the calling syntax is the same for
    # categories or channels, the only difference being
    # the name of the remote procedure
    $name = "meerkat.get${name}BySubstring";
    my $resp = $client->call($name, $str)->result;
    # We aren't doing multi-channels (yet), so report an
    # error if the substring returns more than one hit
    die "resolve_name: $str returned more than 1 match"
        if (@$resp > 1);

    $resp->[0]{id};
}

# Get the data-- the result of the method call below happens
# to return the data in the exact format needed by show_data
sub get_data {
    my ($key, $val, $num) = @_;

    $client->call('meerkat.getItems',
                  { $key          => $val,
                    time_period   => '7DAY',
                    num_items     => $num,
                    descriptions  => 200 })->result;
}
```

The example server under XMLRPC::Lite is a little more complicated than its RPC::XMLSimple counterpart. The most notable difference is that this package calls the local routines as if they were static class methods, with the package name as the first element of the parameter list. Because the code in XRFortune.pm is procedural rather than object-oriented, it requires a small amount of extra work up front to provide wrappers for the functions.

Example C-5. fortune-Lite.pl

```perl
#!/usr/bin/perl -w

use strict;

use XRFortune;
use XMLRPC::Transport::HTTP;

# For each of the three routines from the XRFortune package
# that will be made available to clients, the server needs a
# front-end wrapper that strips the first argument from the
# parameters list. This is because XMLRPC::Lite calls the
# routines as if they were static class methods.
BEGIN {
    no strict 'refs';

    for my $method qw(books fortune weighted_fortune) {
        eval "sub $method";
```

Example C-5. fortune-Lite.pl (continued)

```perl
        *$method =
            eval "sub { shift; XRFortune::$method(\@_) }";
    }
}

# The constructor returns the object reference, which is
# then used to chain a call to dispatch_to() that sets up
# the three local routines to be made available to clients.
# That also returns the object ref, which is used to
# chain along to the handle() method, which doesn't return
# until a signal interrupts the program.
XMLRPC::Transport::HTTP::Daemon
    ->new(LocalPort => 9000, ReuseAddr => 1)
    ->dispatch_to(qw(books fortune weighted_fortune))
    ->handle;

exit;
```

The RPC::XML Examples

The RPC::XML version of the Meerkat client is one line longer than its XMLRPC::Lite counterpart. This toolkit offers different ways to call the remote methods that return either an object wrapper around the return value or straight Perl data. In this example, the method used returns simple Perl data.

Example C-6. meer2html-RPC::XML.pl

```perl
#!/usr/bin/perl -w

use strict;
use vars qw($chan $cat $num $data $client);

use RPC::XML::Client;
use constant MEERKAT =>
    'http://www.oreillynet.com/meerkat/xml-rpc/server.php';

# Read and test the command-line arguments.
if ($ARGV[0] =~ /^-ch/) {
    $chan = $ARGV[1];
    $num  = $ARGV[2] || 15;
} elsif ($ARGV[0] =~ /^-ca/) {
    $cat  = $ARGV[1];
    $num  = $ARGV[2] || 15;
}
unless (($chan or $cat) and ($num =~ /^\d+$/)) {
    die "USAGE: $0 { -channel str | -category str } [ n ]";
}

# Create a client object. The error_handler key specifies a
# callback to be invoked when a transport error occurs. If
# desired, a fault_handler could be installed for catching
```

Example C-6. meer2html-RPC::XML.pl (continued)

```perl
# server-side errors, as well.
$client = RPC::XML::Client
            ->new(MEERKAT,
                  error_handler =>
                  sub { die "Transport error: $_[0]" });

# This could be done with just one data-retrieval routine,
# but this way is easier to follow, and tests $chan/$cat
# less-often.
$data = $chan ? data_from_chan($chan, $num) :
                data_from_cat($cat, $num);
show_data($data);

exit;

# Retrieve data from a 'Channel' source
sub data_from_chan {
    my ($chan, $num) = @_;

    # If $chan is not already numeric, convert it by using
    # an intermediate XML-RPC call
    $chan = resolve_name($chan, 'Channels')
        unless ($chan =~ /^\d+$/);
    get_data(channel => $chan, $num);
}

# Retrieve data from a 'Category' source
sub data_from_cat {
    my ($cat, $num) = @_;

    # If $cat is not already numeric, convert it by using
    # an intermediate XML-RPC call
    $cat = resolve_name($cat, 'Categories')
        unless ($cat =~ /^\d+$/);
    get_data(category => $cat, $num);
}

# Output the HTML fragment for the data. Note that the way
# the data is treated is independant of whether the source
# was a category or a channel
sub show_data {
    my $data = shift;

    print STDOUT qq(<span class="meerkat">\n<dl>\n);
    for (@$data) {
        print STDOUT <<"END_HTML";
<dt class="title"><a href="$_->{link}">$_->{title}</a></dt>
<dd class="description">$_->{description}</dd>
END_HTML
    }
    print STDOUT qq(</dl>\n</span>\n);
}
```

Example C-6. meer2html-RPC::XML.pl (continued)

```perl
# Resolve a substring name-fragment into the numeric ID that
# the call later on in get_data requires
sub resolve_name {
    my ($str, $name) = @_;

    # Fortunately, the calling syntax is the same for
    # categories or channels, the only difference being
    # the name of the remote procedure
    $name = "meerkat.get${name}BySubstring";
    my $resp = $client->simple_request($name, $str);
    # We aren't doing multi-channels (yet), so report an
    # error if the substring returns more than one hit
    die "resolve_name: $str returned more than 1 match"
        if (@$resp > 1);

    $resp->[0]{id};
}

# Get the data-- the result of the method call below happens
# to return the data in the exact format needed by show_data
sub get_data {
    my ($key, $val, $num) = @_;

    $client->simple_request('meerkat.getItems',
                            { $key         => $val,
                              time_period  => '7DAY',
                              num_items    => $num,
                              descriptions => 200 });
}
```

This server example appears to be the most complex of the three. This is due mainly to the fact that the RPC::XML::Server class is designed for explicit definition of server-side procedures; this prevents accidentally exposing parts of a class or namespace that weren't mean to be published. Thus, the three routines being exported from this sample server must each be explicitly named, one at a time.

Example C-7. fortune-RPC::XML.pl

```perl
#!/usr/bin/perl -w

use strict;

use XRFortune;
use RPC::XML::Server;

# The object created by the constructor will be used to
# chain on a set of calls to add_proc() (which means it
# isn't necessary to deal with the local routines being
# called as methods), and then drop directly into the
# server_loop() method.
RPC::XML::Server->new(port => 9000)
```

Example C-7. fortune-RPC::XML.pl (continued)

```
    # add_proc can take a pre-created RPC::XML::Procedure
    # object, or a hash reference.
    ->add_proc({ name => 'books',
                 signature => [ 'array',
                                'array string',
                                'array array' ],
                 code => \&XRFortune::books })
    # It gets called once for each routine being made
    # public by the server.
    ->add_proc({ name => 'fortune',
                 signature => [ 'array',
                                'array string',
                                'array array' ],
                 code => \&XRFortune::fortune })
    # There are other ways of specifying the server-side
    # procedures, but for an example of this size, this way
    # is just as efficient.
    ->add_proc({ name => 'weighted_fortune',
                 signature => [ 'array',
                                'array string',
                                'array array' ],
                 code => \&XRFortune::weighted_fortune })
    # This method will only return after a signal interrupts
    # it.
    ->server_loop;

exit;
```

The XRFortune.pm Module

The code in the following example is used as the basis for writing the sample servers. It exposes some part of the functionality of the well-known fortune command, which produces quotes at random from a set of files (sometimes referred to as "books").

Example C-8. XRFortune.pm

```
package XRFortune;

use 5.6.0;
use strict;
use vars qw($FORTUNE %BOOKS);
use subs qw(books fortune weighted_fortune);

BEGIN {
    # Locate the fortune program. Look in some standard
    # places, then loop over the user's PATH.
    for my $path (qw(/bin /usr/bin /usr/games),
                  split(':', $ENV{PATH})) {
        if (-e "$path/fortune" && -x _) {
            $FORTUNE = "$path/fortune";
```

Example C-8. XRFortune.pm (continued)

```perl
                last;
            }
        }
        die "No 'fortune' command found!\n"
            unless $FORTUNE;

        # Calling fortune -f lists the books it knows, but the
        # output goes to STDERR for some reason.
        my @books = qx($FORTUNE -f 2>&1); shift(@books);
        chomp(@books);
        $BOOKS{(reverse split(/ /))[0]}++ for (@books);
}

1;

# If called with no arguments, returns the list of known
# books as a list reference. If one or more book names were
# passed, then take the list and return only the elements
# from it that are known books (pruning operation).
sub books {
    my $list = shift || '';

    my @prune = $list ? (ref $list ? @$list : ($list)) : ();
    my @books;

    if (@prune) {
        @books = sort grep($BOOKS{$_}, @prune);
    } else {
        @books = sort keys %BOOKS;
    }

    \@books;
}

# Get and return one fortune. With no arguments, just call
# the command. With one or more books, limit the selection
# of quotes to those books. When the fortune is extracted,
# take off the OS-dependent newlines and return the lines
# of text as a list reference.
sub fortune {
    my $book = shift || '';

    my @lines;
    my $exec = $FORTUNE;
    my @books = $book ? (ref $book ? @$book : ($book)) : ();
    if (@books) {
        my @bad;
        if (@bad = grep(! $BOOKS{$_}, @books)) {
            local $" = ', ';
            die "fortune: Unknown books (@bad)";
        } else {
            $exec .= " @books";
```

Example C-8. XRFortune.pm (continued)

```perl
        }
    }

    chomp(@lines = `$exec`);
    \@lines;
}

# This also retrieves one fortune. However, the arguments
# here are more than just a list of books to restrict the
# search to. If a list reference is passed, use those books
# but weight them all equally in the search. If a hash
# reference is passed, its keys should be books and the
# corresponding values are the integer weights for each
# book. The weights must add up to 100.
sub weighted_fortune {
    my $weights = shift;

    die 'weighted_fortune: Must be called with array of ' .
        "books or struct of weights and books\n"
        unless ref $weights;

    my @lines;
    my $exec = $FORTUNE;
    if (ref($weights) eq 'ARRAY') {
        # Use our own books() call to ensure all the passed
        # books are valid
        $weights = books($weights);
        # The -e flag makes all books equal in weight
        $exec .= " -e @$weights";
    } else {
        # Trickier: must ensure that the weights add up to
        # 100%, even though pruning the list may mean that
        # one or more are dropped.
        my $total_weight;
        my $books = books([ keys %$weights ]);
        $total_weight += $weights->{$_} for (@$books);
        die 'weighted_fortune: Weights must add up to 100' .
            " (total is $total_weight)\n"
            unless ($total_weight == 100);
        $exec .= " $weights->{$_}% $_" for (@$books);
    }

    # As with fortune() above, drop the OS-dependent
    # newline characters and return a list reference.
    chomp(@lines = `$exec`);
    \@lines;
}
```

The listMethods.xpl File

The following example illustrates the XPL file format. In the module, this file is generated at build-time.

Example C-9. listMethods.pl

```
<?xml version="1.0"?>
<!DOCTYPE methoddef SYSTEM "rpc-method.dtd">
<!--
    Generated automatically by make_method v1.09,
    Thu Aug 15 03:48:27 2002
    Any changes made here will be lost.
-->
<methoddef>
<name>system.listMethods</name>
<version>1.1</version>
<signature>array</signature>
<signature>array string</signature>
<help>
List all the methods known to the server. If the STRING
parameter is passed, it is used as a substring to match
against, with only those matching methods being returned.
Note that the STRING parameter is not a regular expression,
but rather just a simple substring.
</help>
<code language="perl">
<![CDATA[
#!/usr/bin/perl
sub listMethods
{
    use strict;

    my $srv = shift;
    my $pat = shift;

    my @list = sort $srv->list_methods;

    # Exclude any that are hidden from introspection APIs
    @list = grep(! $srv->get_method($_)->hidden, @list);
    @list = grep(index($_, $pat) != -1, @list) if ($pat);

    \@list;
}

__END__
]]></code>
</methoddef>
```

APPENDIX D
SOAP Example Code

This appendix contains the collected Perl source code for the SOAP client and server examples presented in Chapters 7 and 8. The code presented here contains more commentary than in the chapters. The functionality of the code remains unchanged.

HTTP SOAP Code (Chapter 7)

The code from Chapter 7 is presented in the same order in which it was introduced in the chapter.

WishListCustomer

This is the basic container class for the catalog and user classes that are to be presented as a unified interface.

Example D-1. WishListCustomer.pm

```perl
#
# The WishListCustomer package is the basis for the SOAP
# example in Chapters 7 and 8. It is a container class for
# two other interfaces, SoapExBook and SoapExUser.
#
package WishListCustomer;

use strict;
use subs qw(new GetBook BooksByAuthor BooksByTitle Wishlist
            AddBook RemoveBook CanPurchase PurchaseBooks
            SetUser make_cookie);

use Digest::MD5 'md5_hex';
use SoapExBook;
use SoapExUser;

1;
```

Example D-1. WishListCustomer.pm (continued)

```perl
#
# The class constructor
#
sub new {
    my ($class, $user, $passwd) = @_;

    my $self = bless {}, $class;

    die "$!"
        unless $self->{_catalog} = SoapExBook::connect;

    if ($user and $passwd) {
        return undef
            unless $self->SetUser(user     => $user,
                                  password => $passwd);
    }

    $self;
}

#
# Initialize and load specific user information into the
# main object.
#
sub SetUser {
    my ($self, %args) = @_;

    $self->{_user} = SoapExUser->new();
    unless (ref($self) and $args{user} and
            $self->{_user}->get_user($args{user})) {
        undef $self->{_user};
        return "Could not load data for $args{user}";
    }

    # User data is loaded beforehand, so that the password
    # is available for testing. If the validation fails,
    # user object is destroyed before the error is sent, so
    # that the caller does not accidentally get the user
    # data.
    if ($args{password}) {
        unless ($args{password} eq $self->{_user}->passwd) {
            undef $self->{_user};
            return "Bad password for $args{user}";
        }
    } elsif ($args{cookie}) {
        unless ($args{cookie} eq
                make_cookie($args{user},
                            $self->{_user}->{passwd})) {
            undef $self->{_user};
            return "Auth token for $args{user} invalid";
        }
```

Example D-1. WishListCustomer.pm (continued)

```perl
    } else {
        undef $self->{_user};
        return "No authentication present for $args{user}";
    }

    $self;
}

#
# Retrieve information on one specific book. May be called
# as a static method.
#
sub GetBook {
    my ($self, $isbn) = @_;

    # If this is called as a static method, then get a fresh
    # book-database connection. Otherwise, use the one that
    # is already available.
    my $bookdb = ref($self) ? $self->{_catalog} :
                              SoapExBook::connect();
    return 'Unable to connect to catalog' unless $bookdb;
    # If there is a valid user record, set the flag to
    # return extra information
    my $fullinfo = $self->{_user} ? 1 : 0;

    my $book = SoapExBook::get_book($bookdb, $isbn);
    return "No book found for key $isbn" unless $book;

    return { title => $book->{title},
             isbn  => $book->{isbn},
             url   => $book->{url},
             $fullinfo ?
             ( authors  => $book->{authors},
               us_price => $book->{us_price} ) :
             () };
}

#
# Retrieve a list of keys of books whose authors field
# contains the requested substring. May be called as a
# static method.
#
sub BooksByAuthor {
    my ($class, $author) = @_;

    # If this is called as a static method, then get a fresh
    # book-database connection. Otherwise, use the one that
    # is already available.
    my $bookdb = ref($class) ? $class->{_catalog} :
```

Example D-1. WishListCustomer.pm (continued)

```perl
                                    SoapExBook::connect();
    return 'Unable to connect to catalog' unless $bookdb;

    my @books =
        SoapExBook::get_books_by_author($bookdb, $author);
    \@books;
}

#
# Retrieve a list of keys of books whose title field
# contains the requested substring. May be called as a
# static method.
#
sub BooksByTitle {
    my ($class, $title) = @_;

    # If this is called as a static method, then get a fresh
    # book-database connection. Otherwise, use the one that
    # is already available.
    my $bookdb = ref($class) ? $class->{_catalog} :
                               SoapExBook::connect();
    return 'Unable to connect to catalog' unless $bookdb;

    my @books =
        SoapExBook::get_books_by_title($bookdb, $title);
    \@books;
}

#
# Return the current contents of the user's wish-list. The
# list contains abbreviated book information.
#
sub Wishlist {
    my $self = shift;

    # This is not callable as a static method, so it must
    # have a value user object stored within.
    return 'The object is missing user data'
        unless (ref($self) and my $user = $self->{_user});
    return 'The object is missing catalog data'
        unless (my $bdb = $self->{_catalog});

    my $books = $user->wishlist;
    # At this point, @$books is full of keys, not data
    my ($book, @books);
    for (@$books)
    {
        return "ISBN $_ unknown to catalog"
            unless ($book = SoapExBook::get_book($bdb, $_));
        push(@books, { isbn   => $book->{isbn},
```

Example D-1. WishListCustomer.pm (continued)

```perl
                    title => $book->{title},
                    url   => $book->{url} });
    }

    \@books;
}

#
# Add the specified book to the user's wish-list. Returns an
# error if the key/ISBN is unknown to the catalog.
#
sub AddBook {
    my ($self, $isbn) = @_;

    # This is not callable as a static method, so it must
    # have a value user object stored within.
    return 'The object is missing user data'
        unless (my $user = $self->{_user});
    return "ISBN $isbn unknown to catalog"
        unless $user->add_book($isbn);
    $user->write_user;

    $self;
}

#
# Remove a specified book from the wish-list. Note that this
# does NOT return an error if the book was not on the list.
# That case is silently ignored.
#
sub RemoveBook {
    my ($self, $isbn) = @_;

    # This is not callable as a static method, so it must
    # have a value user object stored within.
    return 'The object is missing user data'
        unless (my $user = $self->{_user});
    $user->drop_book($isbn);
    $user->write_user;

    $self;
}

#
# Return a true/false value indicating whether the user is
# approved to purchase books directly off their wish-list.
#
sub CanPurchase {
    my $self = shift;
```

Example D-1. WishListCustomer.pm (continued)

```perl
    # This is not callable as a static method, so it must
    # have a value user object stored within.
    return 'Object is missing user data'
        unless (ref($self) and my $user = $self->{_user});

    $user->can_purchase;
}

#
# Attempt to purchase one or more books on the wish-list.
# The parameter $list contains either a single key, or a
# list-reference of keys.
#
sub PurchaseBooks {
    my ($self, $list) = @_;

    # This is not callable as a static method, so it must
    # have a value user object stored within.
    return 'Object is missing user data'
        unless (ref($self) and my $user = $self->{_user});
    return 'User cannot make direct purchases'
        unless ($user->can_purchase);

    # Handle a single ISBN as just a one-item list
    my @books = ref($list) ? @$list : ($list);

    # Here would normally be lots of convoluted glue code to
    # interact with enterprise systems, CRM, etc. For this
    # example, just remove the books from the wishlist and
    # update the user.
    $user->drop_book($_) for (@books);
    $user->write_user;

    $self;
}

#
# This is the code that is used to generate cookies based on
# the user name and password. It is not cryptographically
# sound, it is just a simple form of obfuscation, used as an
# example.
#
# Courtesy of the Slash codebase
#
sub make_cookie {
    my ($user, $passwd) = @_;
    my $cookie = $user . '::' . md5_hex($passwd);
    $cookie =~ s/(.)/sprintf("%%%02x", ord($1))/ge;
    $cookie =~ s/%/%25/g;
    $cookie;
}
```

SoapExUser

The first of the two classes encapsulated by WishListCustomer, this example manages the user data as a class, interfacing with a DB_File store.

Example D-2. SoapExUser.pm

```perl
package SoapExUser;

use 5.005;
use strict;
use vars qw($DBNAME);
use subs qw(import new get_user write_user name wishlist
            can_purchase add_book drop_book dbconnect);

use DB_File;
use Storable qw(freeze thaw);
use SoapExBook;

sub import {
    my ($proto, %args) = @_;

    # Right now, only $args{database} is recognized
    $DBNAME = $args{database} || '';
}

sub new {
    my ($class, @args) = @_;

    my (%hash, $k, $v);
    @hash{qw(name passwd wishlist purchase_ok)} = ('', '', [], 0);
    while (@args)
    {
        ($k, $v) = splice(@args, 0, 2);
        $hash{lc $k} = $v;
    }

    bless \%hash, $class;
}

sub get_user {
    my ($self, $user) = @_;

    my ($db, $val);
    $db = dbconnect;
    return undef if ($db->get($user, $val));
    $val = thaw $val;
    %$self = %$val;

    $self;
}
```

Example D-2. SoapExUser.pm (continued)

```perl
sub write_user {
    my $self = $_[0];

    return undef unless $self->{name};
    my $db = dbconnect;
    # Pass freeze() a hashref to a COPY of $self, unblessed
    return undef
        if ($db->put($self->{name}, freeze({ %$self })));

    $self;
}

sub name { $_[0]->{name}; }

sub passwd {
    my ($self, $newpass) = @_;

    $self->{passwd} = $newpass if $newpass;
    $self->{passwd};
}

sub wishlist {
    my $list = $_[0]->{wishlist};

    # Return a listref that is a copy, not the main list
    $list ? [ @$list ] : [];
}

sub can_purchase { $_[0]->{purchase_ok}; }

sub add_book {
    my ($self, $book) = @_;

    my $bookdb = SoapExBook::connect;
    return undef unless ($bookdb and
                         SoapExBook::get_book($bookdb, $book));
    $book =~ s/-//g;
    push(@{$self->{wishlist}}, $book);

    $self;
}

sub drop_book {
    my ($self, $book) = @_;

    $book =~ s/-//g;
    @{$self->{wishlist}} =
        grep($_ ne $book, @{$self->{wishlist}});
```

Example D-2. SoapExUser.pm (continued)

```perl
    $self;
}

sub dbconnect {
    $DBNAME ||
        ($DBNAME = __FILE__) =~ s|[^/]+$|users.db|;
    my %hash;

    tie %hash, 'DB_File', $DBNAME;
}

1;
```

SoapExBook

The second of the two interfaces encapsulated by `WishListCustomer`, this manages connections to the book catalog using a `DB_File` store.

Example D-3. SoapExBook.pm

```perl
package SoapExBook;

use 5.005;
use strict;
use subs qw(connect get_book get_books_by_title
            get_books_by_author);

use DB_File;
use Storable qw(freeze thaw);

sub connect {
    my $dbfile = $_[0];

    $dbfile ||
        ($dbfile = __FILE__) =~ s|[^/]+$|catalog.db|;
    my ($tied, %hash);
    return unless ($tied = tie(%hash, 'DB_File', $dbfile));

    $tied;
}

sub get_book {
    my ($db, $key) = @_;

    my $val;
    $key =~ s/-//g;
    return undef if $db->get($key, $val);

    thaw $val;
}
```

Example D-3. SoapExBook.pm (continued)

```perl
sub get_books_by_title {
    my ($db, $pat) = @_;

    my ($key, $val, @matches);

    return () if ($db->seq($key, $val, R_FIRST));
    do {
        $val = thaw $val;
        push(@matches, $key)
            if (index(lc $val->{title}, lc $pat) != -1);
    } until ($db->seq($key, $val, R_NEXT));

    @matches;
}

sub get_books_by_author {
    my ($db, $pat) = @_;

    my ($key, $val, @matches);

    return () if ($db->seq($key, $val, R_FIRST));
    do {
        $val = thaw $val;
        push(@matches, $key)
            if (index(lc $val->{authors}, lc $pat) != -1);
    } until ($db->seq($key, $val, R_NEXT));

    @matches;
}

1;
```

The First HTTP::Daemon Server

The first of the servers based on SOAP::Transport::HTTP::Daemon provides the most basic linkage between WishListCustomer and SOAP::Lite, with no authentication layer.

Example D-4. Server-HTTP::Daemon-1

```perl
#!/usr/bin/perl -w

#
# A simple server that does not yet do access-control on
# requests.
#

use strict;
```

Example D-4. Server-HTTP::Daemon-1 (continued)

```
use SOAP::Transport::HTTP;
# Loading this class here keeps SOAP::Lite from having to
# load it on demand.
use WishListCustomer;

my $port = pop(@ARGV) || 9000;
my $host = shift(@ARGV) || 'localhost';

SOAP::Transport::HTTP::Daemon
    ->new(LocalAddr => $host, LocalPort => $port,
          Reuse => 1)
    ->dispatch_with({ 'urn:/WishListCustomer' =>
                      'WishListCustomer' })
    ->objects_by_reference('WishListCustomer')
    ->handle;

exit;
```

WishListCustomer::Daemon

This subclass of SOAP::Transport::HTTP::Daemon is the first half of the solution that provides user authentication in the SOAP environment.

Example D-5. WishListCustomer::Daemon.pm

```
#
# The sample daemon class derived by sub-classing the
# SOAP::Transport::HTTP::Daemon class, which is in turn
# derived from HTTP::Daemon.
#
package WishListCustomer::Daemon;

use strict;
use vars qw(@ISA);

use SOAP::Transport::HTTP;
@ISA = qw(SOAP::Transport::HTTP::Daemon);

1;

#
# This is the only method that needs to be overloaded in
# order for this daemon class to handle the authentication.
# All cookie headers on the incoming request get copied to
# a hash table local to the WishListCustomer::SOAP
# package. The request is then passed on to the original
# version of this method.
#
sub request {
    my $self = shift;
```

Example D-5. WishListCustomer::Daemon.pm (continued)

```
    if (my $request = $_[0]) {
        my @cookies = $request->headers->header('cookie');
        %WishListCustomer::SOAP::COOKIES = ();
        for my $line (@cookies) {
            for (split(/; /, $line)) {
                next unless /(.*?)=(.*)/;
                $WishListCustomer::SOAP::COOKIES{$1} = $2;
            }
        }
    }

    $self->SUPER::request(@_);
}
```

WishListCustomer::SOAP

This class provides a SOAP-oriented layer over the basic WishListCustomer class and combines with the previous class to manage user-level authentication via cookies.

Example D-6. WishListCustomer::SOAP.pm

```
#
# This is the sample SOAP layer built over the
# WishListCustomer class, as part of the exercises of
# chapters 7 and 8.
#
package WishListCustomer::SOAP;

use strict;
use vars qw(@ISA %COOKIES);

use SOAP::Lite;
use WishListCustomer;

@ISA = qw(WishListCustomer);

BEGIN {
    no strict 'refs';

    #
    # This block creates local versions of the methods
    # in the list. The local versions catch errors that
    # would otherwise be simple text, and turn them into
    # SOAP::Fault objects.
    #
    for my $method qw(GetBook BooksByAuthor BooksByTitle
                      Wishlist AddBook RemoveBook
                      PurchaseBooks) {
        eval "sub $method";
        *$method = sub {
            my $self = shift->new;
```

Example D-6. WishListCustomer::SOAP.pm (continued)

```perl
            die SOAP::Fault
                    ->faultcode('Server.RequestError')
                    ->faultstring('Could not get object')
                unless $self;

            my $smethod = "SUPER::$method";
            my $res = $self->$smethod(@_);
            die SOAP::Fault
                    ->faultcode('Server.ExecError')
                    ->faultstring("Execution error: $res")
                unless ref($res);

            $res;
        };
    }
}

1;

#
# The class constructor. It is designed to be called by each
# invocation of each other method. As such, it returns the
# first argument immediately if it is already an object of
# the class. This lets users of the class rely on constructs
# such as cookie-based authentication, where each request
# calls for a new object instance.
#
sub new {
    my $class = shift;
    return $class if ref($class);

    my $self;
    # If there are no arguments, but available cookies, then
    # that is the signal to work the cookies into play
    if ((! @_) and (keys %COOKIES)) {
        # Start by getting the basic, bare object
        $self = $class->SUPER::new();
        # Then call SetUser. It will die with a SOAP::Fault
        # on any error
        $self->SetUser;
    } else {
        $self = $class->SUPER::new(@_);
    }

    $self;
}

#
# This derived version of SetUser hands off to the parent-
# class version if any arguments are passed. If none are,
# it looks for cookies to provide the authentication. The
# user name is extracted from the cookie, and the "user"
```

Example D-6. WishListCustomer::SOAP.pm (continued)

```perl
# and "cookie" arguments are passed to the parent-class
# SetUser method with these values.
#
sub SetUser {
    my $self = shift->new;
    my %args = @_;

    return $self->SUPER::SetUser(%args) if (%args);

    my $user;
    my $cookie = $COOKIES{user};
    return $self unless $cookie;
    ($user = $cookie) =~ s/%([0-9a-f]{2})/chr(hex($1))/ge;
    $user =~ s/%([0-9a-f]{2})/chr(hex($1))/ge;
    $user =~ s/:::.*//;

    my $res = $self->SUPER::SetUser(user   => $user,
                                    cookie => $cookie);
    die SOAP::Fault
            ->faultcode('Server.AuthError')
            ->faultstring("Authorization failed: $res")
        unless ref($res);

    $self;
}

#
# This method could not be relegated to the loop-construct
# in the BEGIN block above, because SOAP::Lite cannot tell
# instinctively that this method returns a boolean rather
# than an integer. So the value from the parent-class
# method is coerced into the correct encoding via the
# SOAP::Data class.
#
sub CanPurchase {
    my $self = shift->new;
    die SOAP::Fault->faultcode('Server.RequestError')
                   ->faultstring('Could not get object')
        unless $self;

    SOAP::Data->name('return', $self->SUPER::CanPurchase)
              ->type('xsd:boolean');
}
```

The Second HTTP::Daemon Server

This is the same server as used initially, only now it uses the two new classes in place of the original ones.

Example D-7. server-HTTP::Daemon-2

```perl
#!/usr/bin/perl -w

#
# Version 2 of the daemon, this time using a SOAP layer for
# the methods to expose, and a daemon class that derives
# from the original HTTP::Daemon-based class for the server
# layer. Combined, these allow for basic authentication of
# user operations.
#
use strict;

# Again, loading this now saves effort for SOAP::Lite
use WishListCustomer::SOAP;
use WishListCustomer::Daemon;

my $port = pop(@ARGV) || 9000;
my $host = shift(@ARGV) || 'localhost';

WishListCustomer::Daemon
    ->new(LocalAddr => $host, LocalPort => $port,
          Reuse => 1)
    ->dispatch_with({ 'urn:/WishListCustomer' =>
                      'WishListCustomer::SOAP' })
    ->objects_by_reference('WishListCustomer::SOAP')
    ->handle;

exit;
```

The SOAP::Lite Client to Format a Wish List

This client tested the server presented earlier by retrieving the wish list for a specified user and displaying the formatted data to the console.

Example D-8. client-wishlist-1

```perl
#!/usr/bin/perl -w

#
# This is a sample client that calls the SOAP interface on
# the specified endpoint (defaulting to a local address)
# gets the wishlist for the specified user. The data is
# given a simple formatting by means of a format-picture.
# This client needed no updating even as the server was
# moved from HTTP::Daemon to Apache/mod_perl.
#
use strict;

use URI;
use HTTP::Cookies;
use SOAP::Lite;
```

Example D-8. client-wishlist-1 (continued)

```perl
# This is included only to avoid re-copying the cookie
# code.
use WishListCustomer; # for make_cookie

my ($user, $passwd) = (shift, shift);
die "USAGE: $0 username passwd [ endpoint ]\n"
    unless ($user and $passwd);

# To allow more flexibility in specifying the endpoint, the
# URI class is used on the URL to properly extract the host
# and port values for creating the cookies.
my $endpoint = shift || 'http://localhost.localdomain:9000';
my $uri = URI->new($endpoint);
my $cookie = WishListCustomer::make_cookie($user, $passwd);
my $cookie_jar = HTTP::Cookies->new();
$cookie_jar->set_cookie(0, user => $cookie, '/', $uri->host,
                        $uri->port);

#
# Create the SOAP handle, with access to the cookie...
#
my $soap = SOAP::Lite->uri('urn:/WishListCustomer')
              ->proxy($endpoint,
                      cookie_jar => $cookie_jar);

# ...and call the Wishlist method, checking for errors
my $result = $soap->Wishlist;
if ($result->fault) {
    die "$0: Operation failed: " . $result->faultstring;
}
my $books = $result->result;

format =
@<<<<<<<<<<<<<<<<<<<<<<<<<<<<<<<<<<<<<<<          @>>>>>
$result->{title},                             $result->{us_price}
@<<<<<<<<<<<<<<<<<<<<<<<<<<<<<<<<<<<<<<< @>>>>>>>>>>>>>>>
$result->{authors},                       $result->{isbn}
.

for (sort { $a->{title} cmp $b->{title} } @$books) {
    $result = $soap->GetBook($_->{isbn});
    # Quietly skip books that cause faults
    next if ($result->fault);
    $result = $result->result;
    write;
}

exit;
```

WishListCustomer::Apache

This class subclasses the SOAP::Transport::HTTP::Apache class to provide the authentication cookies in the same manner as the previous server class.

Example D-9. WishListCustomer::Apache.pm

```
#
# The sample Apache-binding layer for the Chapter 7 SOAP
# example.
#
package WishListCustomer::Apache;

use strict;
use vars qw(@ISA);

#
# In addition to loading the SOAP::Transport::HTTP module,
# The WishListCustomer::SOAP module is loaded here so that
# it is available immediately, without SOAP::Lite having
# to load it on-demand.
#

use SOAP::Transport::HTTP;
use WishListCustomer::SOAP;
@ISA = qw(SOAP::Transport::HTTP::Apache);

1;

#
# The only routine that needs to be overloaded to use the
# existing Apache code is this one. This version looks for
# any cookies in the incoming request and stores them in a
# hash table local to the WishListCustomer::SOAP module.
# It then passes the request on to the original version of
# this method.
#
sub handler ($$) {
    my ($self, $request) = @_;

    my $cookies = $request->header_in('cookie');
    my @cookies = ref $cookies ? @$cookies : $cookies;
    %WishListCustomer::SOAP::COOKIES = ();
    for my $line (@cookies) {
        for (split(/; /, $line)) {
            next unless /(.*?)=(.*)/;
            $WishListCustomer::SOAP::COOKIES{$1} = $2;
        }
    }

    $self->SUPER::handler($request);
}
```

WishListCustomer::SOAP2

The revised interface design in this class replaces the two search functions with a single interface that uses the parameter's name within the SOAP envelope to control the search.

Example D-10. WishListCustomer::SOAP2.pm

```
#
# This is the sample SOAP layer as presented in the
# WishListCustomer::SOAP class, but with the FindBooks
# method instead of the BooksByAuthor and BooksByTitle
# methods. Hence, it cannot inherit from that class
# without exposing them. Only the changes parts of the
# code are documented.
#
package WishListCustomer::SOAP2;

use strict;
use vars qw(@ISA %COOKIES);

use SOAP::Lite;
use WishListCustomer;

#
# Adding SOAP::Server::Parameters to the inheritance
# tree enables the FindBooks method to access the
# deserialized request object.
#
@ISA = qw(WishListCustomer SOAP::Server::Parameters);

BEGIN {
    no strict 'refs';

    #
    # Note the absence of BooksByAuthor and BooksByTitle
    # from this list.
    #
    for my $method qw(GetBook Wishlist AddBook RemoveBook
                      PurchaseBooks) {
        eval "sub $method";
        *$method = sub {
            my $self = shift->new;
            die SOAP::Fault
                    ->faultcode('Server.RequestError')
                    ->faultstring('Could not get object')
                unless $self;

            my $smethod = "SUPER::$method";
            my $res = $self->$smethod(@_);
            die SOAP::Fault
                    ->faultcode('Server.ExecError')
```

Example D-10. WishListCustomer::SOAP2.pm (continued)

```perl
                    ->faultstring("Execution error: $res")
                unless ref($res);

            $res;
        };
    }
}

1;

sub new {
    my $class = shift;
    return $class if ref($class);

    my $self;
    # If there are no arguments, but available cookies, then
    # that is the signal to work the cookies into play
    if ((! @_) and (keys %COOKIES)) {
        # Start by getting the basic, bare object
        $self = $class->SUPER::new();
        # Then call SetUser. It will die with a SOAP::Fault
        # on any error
        $self->SetUser;
    } else {
        $self = $class->SUPER::new(@_);
    }

    $self;
}

sub SetUser {
    my $self = shift->new;
    my %args = @_;

    return $self->SUPER::SetUser(%args) if (%args);

    my $user;
    my $cookie = $COOKIES{user};
    return $self unless $cookie;
    ($user = $cookie) =~ s/%([0-9a-f]{2})/chr(hex($1))/ge;
    $user =~ s/%([0-9a-f]{2})/chr(hex($1))/ge;
    $user =~ s/:::.*//;

    my $res = $self->SUPER::SetUser(user   => $user,
                                    cookie => $cookie);
    die SOAP::Fault
            ->faultcode('Server.AuthError')
            ->faultstring("Authorization failed: $res")
        unless ref($res);

    $self;
}
```

Example D-10. WishListCustomer::SOAP2.pm (continued)

```
#
# This replaces BooksBy{Author,Title} with a single
# interface that uses the name given to the input parameter
# to choose the type of search to execute.
#
sub FindBooks {
    my ($class, $arg, $env) = @_;

    #
    # Using the SOAP envelope of the request, get the
    # SOAP::Data object that wraps the value $arg was
    # assigned.
    #
    my $argname = $env->match(SOAP::SOM::paramsin)->dataof;
    my $hook = ($argname->name eq 'author') ?
                    \&SoapExBook::get_books_by_author :
                    \&SoapExBook::get_books_by_title;
    #
    # As with the originals, this can be a static method,
    # so the test to use a new book-database handle versus
    # the self-stored one is still present.
    #
    my $bookdb = ref($class) ? $class->{_catalog} :
                                SoapExBook::connect();
    return 'Unable to connect to catalog' unless $bookdb;

    my @books = $hook->($bookdb, $arg);
    \@books;
}

sub CanPurchase {
    my $self = shift->new;
    die SOAP::Fault->faultcode('Server.RequestError')
                    ->faultstring('Could not get object')
        unless $self;

    SOAP::Data->name('return', $self->SUPER::CanPurchase)
            ->type('xsd:boolean');
}
```

The Third HTTP::Daemon Server

The final version of the HTTP::Daemon–based server differs from the previous only in that it uses the revised SOAP interface presented in the previous section.

Example D-11. server-HTTP::Daemon-3

```perl
#!/usr/bin/perl -w

#
# The third version of the HTTP::Daemon-based server uses
# the SOAP layer with the FindBooks method in place of the
# two original search methods. Note that this will not
# correctly handle the authentication because of the
# coupling between the WishListCustomer::Daemon and the
# WishListCustomer::SOAP classes.
#
use strict;

use WishListCustomer::SOAP2;
use WishListCustomer::Daemon;

my $port = pop(@ARGV) || 9000;
my $host = shift(@ARGV) || 'localhost';

WishListCustomer::Daemon
    ->new(LocalAddr => $host, LocalPort => $port,
          Reuse => 1)
    ->dispatch_with({ 'urn:/WishListCustomer' =>
                      'WishListCustomer::SOAP2' })
    ->objects_by_reference('WishListCustomer::SOAP2')
    ->handle;

exit;
```

The SOAP::Lite Client to Test FindBooks

This client is a simplified version of the first client, designed to test the FindBooks method defined in the revised SOAP interface.

Example D-12. client-wishlist-2

```perl
#!/usr/bin/perl -w

#
# This sample client is much simpler than the previous one,
# as it is only intended to demonstrate the flexibility of
# having the single-entry search interface that uses the
# parameter name to help in forming the search.
#
use strict;

use SOAP::Lite;

my ($type, $string) = (shift, shift);
die "USAGE: $0 { author | title } pattern [ endpoint ]\n"
    unless ($type and $string);
```

Example D-12. client-wishlist-2 (continued)

```perl
my $endpoint = shift || 'http://localhost.localdomain:9000';

# Simple creation of the SOAP handle
my $soap = SOAP::Lite->uri('urn:/WishListCustomer')
              ->proxy($endpoint);

#
# Instead of just passing the value, encode it with the
# SOAP::Data class and give it a specific name. As always,
# check for errors.
#
my $result = $soap->FindBooks(SOAP::Data->name($type,
                                               $string));
if ($result->fault) {
    die "$0: Operation failed: " . $result->faultstring;
}
my $books = $result->result;

# This is a simpler format because we called it as a static
# method, which means less data returned.
format =
@<<<<<<<<<<<<<<<<<<<<<<<<<<<<<<<<<<<<<< @>>>>>>>>>>>>>>
$result->{title},                       $result->{isbn}
.

for (@$books) {
    $result = $soap->GetBook($_);
    # Quietly skip books that cause faults
    next if ($result->fault);
    $result = $result->result;
    write;
}

exit;
```

SOAP with Other Protocols (Chapter 8)

Many server examples in this chapter are functionally identical except for the declaration of a different transport protocol at an early point in the code.

The Generic Transport Class

This class is used by the non-HTTP daemon examples to both provide an overloading of a method to accomplish the task of reading authentication header data and to allow compile-time (or runtime, even) specification of the protocol to use.

Example D-13. WishListCustomer::Transport.pm

```perl
package WishListCustomer::Transport;

use strict;
use vars qw(@ISA);
use subs qw(import find_target);

use SOAP::Lite;

# For lack of a better default, SOAP::Server is given here.
# In fact, the expectation is that import() will change this
# at compile-time or run-time.
@ISA = qw(SOAP::Server);

1;

# Set the parent class that this class inherits from for
# all the server functionality. The purpose here is just
# to overload find_target (below).
sub import {
    my $class = shift;
    my $new_parent = shift;

    @ISA = ($new_parent);
}

# This overloading of the find_target method takes the
# (now) deserialized request object and looks for a header
# named "authenticate". If found, the value is stuffed into
# the same %WishListCustomer::SOAP::COOKIES hash table that
# the code already uses.
#
# This remains coupled to WishListCustomer::SOAP by virtue
# of the use of the %WishListCustomer::SOAP hash table.
sub find_target {
    my $self = shift;
    my $request = shift;

    %WishListCustomer::SOAP::COOKIES = ();
    my $header = $request->match(SOAP::SOM::header .
                                 '/authenticate')->dataof;
    if ($header) {
        my $key = $header->attr->{name} || 'user';
        my $value = $header->value;

        $value =~ s/\n\r\s//g;
        $WishListCustomer::SOAP::COOKIES{$key} = $value;
    }

    $self->SUPER::find_target($request);
}
```

The Subclass of SOAP::Lite

The client examples use the `WishListCustomer::Client` class to automate the inclusion of a SOAP header that bears the authentication data into each request. Without this, the application is responsible for including a header in all outgoing requests.

Example D-14. WishListCustomer::Client.pm

```
package WishListCustomer::Client;

use strict;
use vars qw(@ISA);
use subs qw(setAuth call);

use WishListCustomer; # For make_cookie
use SOAP::Lite;
@ISA = qw(SOAP::Lite);

1;

# Create a SOAP::Header instance and store it on the object.
# If called with no parameters at all, the the header is
# cleared out. The header will contain the cookie data in
# the format that the existing WishListCustomer code is
# expecting.
sub setAuth {
    my ($self, $user, $passwd, @rest) = @_;

    if ($user and $passwd) {
        my $cookie =
            WishListCustomer::make_cookie($user, $passwd);
        $self->{__auth_header} =
            SOAP::Header->name(authenticate => $cookie)
                        ->uri('urn:/WiahListCustomer');
        if (@rest) {
            # This extra block allows the user to specify
            # extra parts such as forcing mustUnderstand
            # or setting the namespace URI for the header.
            my %attr = @rest;
            $self->{__auth_header}->attr(%attr);
        }
    } else {
        delete $self->{__auth_header};
    }

    $self;
}

# This overloading of call() allows the calling object to
# insert the authentication header, if one is set. The
# argument set is simple, and the only concern is adding
# a header to @args.
sub call {
```

Example D-14. WishListCustomer::Client.pm (continued)

```
    my ($self, $method, @args) = @_;

    unshift(@args, $self->{__auth_header})
        if $self->{__auth_header};
    $self->SUPER::call($method, @args);
}
```

A TCP-Based Server

The first server example given is essentially identical to the basic daemon from Chapter 7, differing mainly in the use of the generic transport class. The daemon has to specify the base server class, and it has to load the module that contains the class.

Example D-15. server-TCP-1

```
#!/usr/bin/perl -w

#
# This daemon uses the SOAP-layer for WishListCustomer and
# the SOAP::Transport::TCP::Server class by way of the
# WishListCustomer::Transport generic class for a transport
# method.
#
use strict;

use SOAP::Transport::TCP;
# Loading this now saves effort for SOAP::Lite
use WishListCustomer::SOAP;
use WishListCustomer::Transport
        'SOAP::Transport::TCP::Server';

my $port = pop(@ARGV) || 9000;
my $host = shift(@ARGV) || 'localhost';

# The constructor has to give a Listen argument with a
# value, something that HTTP::Daemon did automatically.
# Other than that, the only real difference is the use
# of WishListCustomer::Transport as the class to create
# the object from.
WishListCustomer::Transport
    ->new(LocalAddr => $host, LocalPort => $port,
          Listen => 5, Reuse => 1)
    ->dispatch_with({ 'urn:/WishListCustomer' =>
                      'WishListCustomer::SOAP' })
    ->objects_by_reference('WishListCustomer::SOAP')
    ->handle;

exit;
```

A Generic Client (TCP by Default)

The client that connect to the earlier server is even more generic in nature than the server, because clients don't have to directly load their own transport code. This example is also strongly based on one of the clients from Chapter 7. It defaults to an endpoint value that indicates a TCP server, but it can just as easily be one of the other protocols.

Example D-16. client-general-1

```perl
#!/usr/bin/perl -w

#
# This is a sample client that calls the SOAP interface on
# the specified endpoint (defaulting to a local address) and
# gets the wishlist for the specified user. The data is
# given a simple formatting by means of a format-picture.
#
use strict;

use WishListCustomer::Client;

my ($user, $passwd) = (shift, shift);
die "USAGE: $0 username passwd [ endpoint ]\n"
    unless ($user and $passwd);

my $endpoint = shift || 'tcp://localhost:9000';

# Create the SOAP handle, using the class that manages the
# authentication data
my $soap = WishListCustomer::Client
             ->uri('urn:/WishListCustomer')
             ->proxy($endpoint);
# Set the authentication credentials
$soap->setAuth($user, $passwd);
# ...and call the Wishlist method, checking for errors
my $result = $soap->Wishlist;
if ($result->fault) {
    die "$0: Operation failed: " . $result->faultstring;
}
my $books = $result->result;

format =
@<<<<<<<<<<<<<<<<<<<<<<<<<<<<<<<<<<<<<              @>>>>>>
$result->{title},                          $result->{us_price}
@<<<<<<<<<<<<<<<<<<<<<<<<<<<<<<<<<<<<  @>>>>>>>>>>>>>>>>
$result->{authors},                        $result->{isbn}

.

for (sort { $a->{title} cmp $b->{title} } @$books) {
    $result = $soap->GetBook($_->{isbn});
    # Quietly skip books that cause faults
```

Example D-16. client-general-1 (continued)

```perl
        next if ($result->fault);
        $result = $result->result;
        write;
    }

exit;
```

A Jabber-Based Server

For the Jabber example, only a server was written, because, by specifying an endpoint on the command line that starts with the sequence jabber://, the generic client (shown previously) can connect to the Jabber server without modification.

Example D-17. server-JABBER-1

```perl
#!/usr/bin/perl -w

# This daemon uses the SOAP-layer for WishListCustomer and
# the SOAP::Transport::JABBER::Server class by way of the
# WishListCustomer::Transport generic class for a transport
# method.
use strict;

use SOAP::Transport::JABBER;
# Loading this now saves effort for SOAP::Lite
use WishListCustomer::SOAP;
use WishListCustomer::Transport
        'SOAP::Transport::JABBER::Server';

my ($user, $passwd, $host, $port) = @ARGV;
$host = 'jabber.org' unless $host;
$port = 5222          unless $port;
my $jabber_url = "jabber://$user:$passwd\@$host:$port";

# The constructor expects a string that looks like a URL,
# but with a leading sequence of "jabber://". The string
# will provide the connection and authentication data for
# reaching the Jabber server.
my $server = WishListCustomer::Transport
    ->new($jabber_url)
    ->dispatch_with({ 'urn:/WishListCustomer' =>
                      'WishListCustomer::SOAP' })
    ->objects_by_reference('WishListCustomer::SOAP');

while (1) {
    $server->handle;
    sleep 10;
}

exit;
```

The MQ-Based Server

This server closely resembles the Jabber server because a URI-style string is built up from command-line parameters and because the handle method isn't designed to run as an endless loop; the daemon itself provides the loop construct.

Example D-18. server-MQ-1

```perl
#!/usr/bin/perl -w

# This daemon uses the SOAP-layer for WishListCustomer and
# the SOAP::Transport::MQ::Server class by way of the
# WishListCustomer::Transport generic class for a transport
# method.
use strict;

use SOAP::Transport::MQ;
# Loading this now saves effort for SOAP::Lite
use WishListCustomer::SOAP;
use WishListCustomer::Transport
        'SOAP::Transport::MQ::Server';

my ($chan, $mgr, $reqest, $reply, $host, $port) = @ARGV;
# Putting these last on the command-line allowed for default
# values to be used.
$host = 'localhost' unless $host;
$port = 9000        unless $port;
die "USAGE: $0 channel manager request_queue reply_queue " .
    '[ host port ]'
    unless ($chan and $mgr and $request and $reply);

my $mq_url = "mq://$host:$port?Channel=$chan;" .
    "QueueManager=$mgr;RequestQueue=$request;" .
    "ReplyQueue=$reply";

# The constructor expects a string that looks like a URL,
# but with a leading sequence of "jabber://". The string
# will provide the connection and authentication data for
# reaching the Jabber server.
my $server = WishListCustomer::Transport
    ->new($mq_url)
    ->dispatch_with({ 'urn:/WishListCustomer' =>
                    'WishListCustomer::SOAP' })
    ->objects_by_reference('WishListCustomer::SOAP');

do { $server->handle } while sleep 1;

exit;
```

The POP3-Based Server

The POP3 server example was the first of the applications to be one-way in the communication model. The server class it uses doesn't directly reply to the requests it receives. Thus, any clients that sent those requests must also have been designed to not expect replies. Aside from this behavior, the server resembles those written for Jabber and MQ.

Example D-19. server-POP3-1

```perl
#!/usr/bin/perl -w

#
# This daemon uses the SOAP-layer for WishListCustomer and
# the SOAP::Transport::POP3::Server class by way of the
# WishListCustomer::Transport generic class for a transport
# method.
#
use strict;

use SOAP::Transport::TCP;
# Loading this now saves effort for SOAP::Lite
use WishListCustomer::SOAP;
use WishListCustomer::Transport
        'SOAP::Transport::POP3::Server';

my ($user, $passwd, $host) = @ARGV;
$host ||= 'localhost';
my $pop3_url = "pop://$user:$passwd\@$host";

# The constructor takes a URL string that contains all the
# the needed information for connecting and authenticating
# with the POP3 server.
WishListCustomer::Transport
    ->new($pop3_url)
    ->dispatch_with({ 'urn:/WishListCustomer' =>
                      'WishListCustomer::SOAP' })
    ->objects_by_reference('WishListCustomer::SOAP');

do { $server->handle ) while sleep 10;

exit;
```

The MAILTO Client

Presented as a compliment to the previous POP3 server, this client doesn't expect an actual reply from the transmission of the request. The success or failure of transmitting is as close to a result as can be presented to the user.

Example D-20. client-mailto-1

```perl
#!/usr/bin/perl -w

#
# This is a sample client that calls the SOAP interface on
# the specified endpoint using the MAILTO protocol. It sends
# a request to purchase one or more books from the wish-
# list.
#
use strict;

use WishListCustomer::Client;
use Sys::Hostname 'hostname';

my ($user, $passwd, $mailto) = (shift, shift, shift);
die "USAGE: $0 username passwd endpoint ISBN [ ISBN... ]\n"
    unless ($user and $passwd and $mailto and @ARGV);

my $hostname = eval { hostname };
$hostname = 'localhost' if $@;
my $endpoint = sprintf("maito:%s?From=%s&Subject=SOAP",
                       $mailto,
                       "$user\@$hostname");

# Create the SOAP handle, using the class that manages the
# authentication data
my $soap = WishListCustomer::Client
               ->uri('urn:/WishListCustomer')
               ->proxy($endpoint);
# Set the authentication credentials
$soap->setAuth($user, $passwd);
# ...and call the PurchaseBooks method, checking for errors
my $result = $soap->PurchaseBooks(\@ARGV);
if ($result->fault) {
    die "$0: Operation failed: " . $result->faultstring;
} else {
    print "Request sent\n";
}

exit;
```

The IO-Based Filter

The example presented for the SOAP::Transport::IO::Server class is designed as a filter, reading a request from Perl's STDIN file handle and writing the response to the STDOUT file handle.

Example D-21. server-IO-1

```perl
#!/usr/bin/perl -w

# This example uses the SOAP-layer for WishListCustomer and
```

Example D-21. server-IO-1 (continued)

```perl
# the SOAP::Transport::IO::Server class by way of the
# WishListCustomer::Transport generic class for a transport
# method.
use strict;

use SOAP::Transport::IO;
# Loading this now saves effort for SOAP::Lite
use WishListCustomer::SOAP;
use WishListCustomer::Transport
        'SOAP::Transport::IO::Server';

# The constructor could take parameters for the input and
# output filehandles, but this application is going to act
# as an ordinary filter, so the defaults of STDIN and STDOUT
# are fine.
my $server = WishListCustomer::Transport
    ->new( )
    ->dispatch_with({ 'urn:/WishListCustomer' =>
                      'WishListCustomer::SOAP' })
    ->objects_by_reference('WishListCustomer::SOAP')
    ->handle;

exit;
```

The FTP Client

The example FTP client is actually a reengineered version of the MAILTO client (client-mailto-1). This version is designed to accept endpoint strings for either MAILTO or FTP. Because FTP is also a one-way client implementation, the functionality of the application is independent of the specific protocol used.

Example D-22. client-general-2

```perl
#!/usr/bin/perl -w

#
# This is a sample client that calls the SOAP interface on
# the specified endpoint using a one-way protocol. It sends
# a request to purchase one or more books from the wish-
# list.
#
use strict;

use WishListCustomer::Client;
use Sys::Hostname 'hostname';

my ($user, $passwd, $endpoint) = (shift, shift, shift);
die "USAGE: $0 username passwd endpoint ISBN [ ISBN... ]\n"
    unless ($user and $passwd and $endpoint and @ARGV);
```

Example D-22. client-general-2 (continued)

```perl
if (substr($endpoint, 0, 3) eq 'ftp') {
    my @time = localtime;
    my $file = sprintf("%s-%02d%02d%02d:%02d%02d.xml",
                       $user,
                       $time[5] % 100, # year
                       $time[4] + 1,   # month
                       $time[3],       # day
                       $time[2],       # hour
                       $time[1]);      # minute
    $endpoint .= '/'
        unless (substr($endpoint, -1, 1) eq '/');
    $endpoint .= $file;
} elsif (substr($endpoint, 0, 6) eq 'mailto') {
    my $hostname = eval { hostname };
    $hostname = 'localhost' if $@;
    $endpoint = "$endpoint?From=$user\@$hostname&Subject=" .
        'SOAP';
} else {
    die "$0: endpoint only supports ftp: and mailto: ";
}

# Create the SOAP handle, using the class that manages the
# authentication data
my $soap = WishListCustomer::Client
              ->uri('urn:/WishListCustomer')
              ->proxy($endpoint);
# Set the authentication credentials
$soap->setAuth($user, $passwd);
# ...and call the PurchaseBooks method, checking for errors
my $result = $soap->PurchaseBooks(\@ARGV);
if ($result->fault) {
    die "$0: Operation failed: " . $result->faultstring;
} else {
    print "Request sent\n";
}

exit;
```

The LOCAL Example

The example used to illustrate the SOAP::Transport::LOCAL module is in fact a client that acts as its own server. The example is simple but noteworthy for the way one object acts in both roles. An example of this is the need to call the dispatch_with method for the server aspect of the object. Calling this directly on the object created from the SOAP::Lite class results in an attempt to treat dispatch_with as a remote call itself. To avoid confusion, the code uses the transport method of SOAP::Lite to gain access to the underlying SOAP::Transport object. That object reference then calls the method and sets up the dispatch table.

Example D-23. server+client-LOCAL-1

```perl
#!/usr/bin/perl -w

# This example uses the SOAP-layer for WishListCustomer and
# the SOAP::Transport::LOCAL::Client class by way of the
# WishListCustomer::Transport generic class for a transport
# method.
use strict;

use SOAP::Lite +trace => 'method';
# Loading this now saves effort for SOAP::Lite
use WishListCustomer::SOAP;

my $pattern = shift || 'perl';
my $soap = SOAP::Lite->uri('urn:/WishListCustomer')
                    ->proxy('local:');
$soap->transport
        ->dispatch_with({ 'urn:/WishListCustomer',
                          'WishListCustomer::SOAP' });

my $result = $soap->BooksByTitle($pattern);
if ($result->fault) {
    die "$0: Operation failed: " . $result->faultstring;
}
my $books = $result->result;

format =
@<<<<<<<<<<<<<<<<<<<<<<<<<<<<<<<<<<<<< @>>>>>>>>>>>>>>>
$result->{title},                      $result->{isbn}
.

print "Books whose title matches '$pattern':\n\n";
for (@$books) {
    $result = $soap->GetBook($_);
    # Quietly skip books that cause faults
    next if ($result->fault);
    $result = $result->result;
    write;
}

exit;
```

The Sample Transport Module

The code in this module is an example of writing and subclassing modules for client-transport or general SOAP::Transport replacement. Note that the code hasn't actually been tested in a sample application and that some ciphers it supports aren't considered strong encryption. It's meant as an exercise; don't use it if you need to keep data secure!

Example D-24. Crypt::SOAP.pm

```perl
package Crypt::SOAP;

use strict;
use vars qw(%known_cbc);

use SOAP::Lite;
use Crypt::CBC;

# A mapping table of the cyphers that can be used with the
# Crypt::CBC module. The key is the lc'd name for matching
# and the value is what must get passed to Crypt::CBC::new
%known_cbc = ( des      => 'DES',
               idea     => 'IDEA',
               blowfish => 'Blowfish',
               rc6      => 'RC6',
               rijndael => 'Rijndael' );

package Crypt::SOAP::Transport;

use strict;
use vars qw(@ISA);
use subs qw(new proxy cipher key iv padding prepend_iv
            as_hex encrypt decrypt crypt);

@ISA = qw(SOAP::Transport);

sub new {
    my ($class, @args) = @_;
    return $class if ref $class;

    # While SOAP::Transport::new takes no arguments, there
    # are a number of attributes in this class, any of
    # which can be set in the constructor.
    my $self = $class->SUPER::new();
    my ($method, $value);
    while (@args) {
        ($method, $value) = splice(@args, 0, 2);
        $self->can($method) ?
            $self->$method($value) :
            die "$class: Unknown parameter $method in new";
    }

    $self;
}
sub proxy {
    my $self = shift->new;
    my $class = ref $self;

    return $self->{_proxy} unless @_;

    my ($cipher, $proto);
    my $endpoint = shift;
```

Example D-24. Crypt::SOAP.pm (continued)

```perl
    if ($endpoint =~ /^(\w+):/) {
        ($cipher, $proto) = split(/-/, $1);
        $endpoint =~ s/^$cipher-//;
    } else {
        die "$class: No transport protocol in proxy";
    }
    if ($cipher = $Crypt::SOAP::known_cbc{lc $cipher}) {
        $self->cipher($cipher);
    } else {
        die "$class: Cipher $cipher unknown or unsupported "
            . 'in proxy';
    }

    $self->SUPER::proxy($endpoint, @_);
    # This is cheating, using knowledge of SOAP::Transport
    # internal keys. But it is necessary as long as the
    # super-class proxy method only takes string arguments.
    $self->{_proxy} =
        Crypt::SOAP::Client->new($self, $self->{_proxy});
}

sub encrypt { shift->crypt('E', shift) }
sub decrypt { shift->crypt('D', shift) }

sub crypt {
    my ($self, $direction, $text) = @_;

    die ref($self) . ": both 'direction' and 'text' must " .
        'be passed to crypt'
            unless ($direction and $text);

    # This relies on the application having set most of
    # these attributes already
    my $cipher = Crypt::CBC->new({
                                  key => $self->key,
                                  cipher => $self->cipher,
                                  $self->iv ?
                                  (iv => $self->iv) : (),
                                  $self->padding ?
                                  (padding =>
                                   $self->padding) : (),
                                  prepend_iv =>
                                  $self->prepend_iv || 0
                                });

    my $method =
        ($direction =~ /^e/i) ? 'encrypt' : 'decrypt';
    $method .= '_hex' if $self->as_hex;

    $cipher->$method($text);
}
```

Example D-24. Crypt::SOAP.pm (continued)

```perl
BEGIN {
    no strict 'refs';
    for my $method (qw(cipher key iv padding prepend_iv
                       as_hex)) {
        my $field = "_$method";
        *$method = sub {
            my $self = shift->new;
            @_ ? ($self->{$field} = shift, return $self) :
                return $self->{$field};
        }
    }
}

package Crypt::SOAP::Server;

use strict;
use vars qw(@ISA);
use subs qw(import subclass new handle);

sub import {
    my ($class, $new_parent, $load_class) = @_;

    @ISA = ($new_parent);

    # Attempt to load the module that provides the parent
    # class, unless expressly told not to
    return $class if (defined($load_class) and
                      ("$load_class" eq '0'));
    if ($load_class) {
        eval { require $load_class };
        die "$class: Error loading $load_class: $@" if $@;
    } else {
        # First we try the parent name directly
        eval { require $new_parent };
        # If that failed and the last 8 character of the
        # classname are "::Server", trim that and try again
        if ($@ and substr($new_parent, -8) eq '::Server') {
            substr($new_parent, -8) = '';
            eval { require $new_parent };
            die "$class: Error loading $new_parent " .
                "(derived from ${new_parent}::Server: $@"
                    if $@;
        } else {
            die "$class: Error loading $new_parent: $@";
        }
    }

    $class;
}

# Just a little alias to avoid confusing people not used to
# thinking of import() as just another function. Allows an
# application to say "->subclass($new_parent)" instead.
```

Example D-24. Crypt::SOAP.pm (continued)

```perl
sub subclass {
    shift->import(@_);
}

sub new {
    my ($class, %args) = @_;
    return $class if ref $class;

    die "$class: Cannot create objects without a parent " .
        'class specified first'
            unless (@ISA);

    # Save any arguments intended for the transport object
    # so they can be passed to new() later.
    my $transport_args;
    if ($args{transport}) {
        $transport_args = $args{transport};
        delete $args{transport};
    }
    my $self = $class->SUPER::new(%args);
    # The CSS in the key is to hopefully avoid collision
    $self->{_CSS_transport} =
        Crypt::SOAP::Transport->new($transport_args ?
                                    @$transport_args : ());

    $self;
}

sub handle {
    my ($self, $message) = @_;

    $message = $self->{_CSS_transport}->decrypt($message);
    $self->SUPER::handle($message);
}

package Crypt::SOAP::Client;

use strict;
use vars qw(@ISA);
use subs qw(new send_receive);

sub new {
    my ($class, $transport, $client) = @_;
    return $class if ref $class;

    # The only purpose of this new() method is to hang a
    # reference to $transport on the object and re-bless it
    # into this class, after setting the @ISA path to
    # include the original class.
    die "$class: new() must be called with a transport " .
        'object and an existing client object'
            unless (UNIVERSAL::can($transport, 'new') &&
                    UNIVERSAL::can($client, 'new'));
```

Example D-24. Crypt::SOAP.pm (continued)

```
    # The key here hopes to avoid collisions
    $client->{_CSC_transport} = $transport;
    @ISA = (ref $client);
    bless $client, $class;
}

sub send_receive {
    my $self = shift;
    my %args = @_;

    $args{envelope} = $self->{_CSC_transport}
                            ->encrypt($args{envelope});
    $self->SUPER::send_receive(%args);
}

1;
```

APPENDIX E
WSDL and UDDI Examples

This appendix collects the WSDL files from Chapter 9, shown here complete with documentation elements to help you understand the logical flow.

Following these is the show_biz sample application of Chapter 10 (annotated with inline comments), demonstrating the UDDI::Lite classes.

The wishlist.wsdl File

This WSDL description covers the functionality from the application as it was designed in Chapter 7, with the SOAP bindings.

Example E-1. wishlist.wsdl

```
<?xml version="1.0"?>
<definitions name="WishListCustomer"
    targetNamespace="urn:WishListCustomer"
    xmlns="http://schemas.xmlsoap.org/wsdl/"
    xmlns:tns="urn:WishListCustomer"
    xmlns:wsdl="http://schemas.xmlsoap.org/wsdl/"
    xmlns:soap="http://schemas.xmlsoap.org/wsdl/soap/"
    xmlns:enc="http://schemas.xmlsoap.org/soap/encoding/"
    xmlns:xsd="http://www.w3.org/2001/XMLSchema">
  <documentation>
      The WSDL Specification for WishListCustomer
  </documentation>

  <types>
    <documentation>
      This section defines the types that will be used by
      the rest of the WSDL document to describe the data
      that describes books. Only the types not already
      available from XML Schema are defined here.
    </documentation>
    <xsd:schema targetNamespace="urn:WishListCustomer">
      <xsd:complexType name="PartialBook">
        <xsd:annotation>
```

Example E-1. wishlist.wsdl (continued)

```xml
        <xsd:documentation>
          Partial book information, returned when a
          wish-list is fetched, or when a non-validated
          request for a single book is received.
        </xsd:documentation>
      </xsd:annotation>
      <xsd:all>
        <xsd:annotation>
          <xsd:documentation>
            The "all" construct allows arbitrary ordering,
            which preferable to forcing SOAP::Lite to
            serialize the hashref in a special way. But,
            it also allows the elements to appear 0 times,
            which must be overridden with minOccurs.
          </xsd:documentation>
        </xsd:annotation>
        <xsd:element name="isbn"   type="xsd:string"
                     minOccurs="1" />
        <xsd:element name="title"  type="xsd:string"
                     minOccurs="1" />
        <xsd:element name="url"    type="xsd:anyURI"
                     minOccurs="1" />
      </xsd:all>
    </xsd:complexType>
    <xsd:complexType name="Book">
      <xsd:annotation>
        <xsd:documentation>
          Extends the PartialBook type with the rest of
          the fields that are returned for a full-info
          request by a validated user.
        </xsd:documentation>
      </xsd:annotation>
      <xsd:extension base="tns:PartialBook">
        <xsd:annotation>
          <xsd:documentation>
            Note that minOccurs is not needed here, since
            the GetBook operation isn't guaranteed to
            return these two fields.
          </xsd:documentation>
        </xsd:annotation>
        <xsd:all>
          <xsd:element name="authors" type="xsd:string" />
          <xsd:element name="us_price" type="xsd:string"/>
        </xsd:all>
      </xsd:extension>
    </xsd:complexType>
    <xsd:complexType name="ArrayOfPartialBook">
      <xsd:annotation>
        <xsd:documentation>
          An array of the PartialBook type, defined above.
          This draws on the definition of "Array" from the
          SOAP encoding document (namespace "enc"), and
```

Example E-1. wishlist.wsdl (continued)

```xml
              extends it by associating the arrayType attr
              from WSDL.
          </xsd:documentation>
        </xsd:annotation>
        <xsd:complexContent>
          <xsd:restriction base="enc:Array">
            <xsd:attribute ref="enc:arrayType"
                 wsdl:arrayType="tns:PartialBook[]" />
          </xsd:restriction>
        </xsd:complexContent>
      </xsd:complexType>
      <xsd:complexType name="ArrayOfString">
        <xsd:annotation>
          <xsd:documentation>
            An array of xsd:string data, the return value
            for operations such as BooksByTitle.
          </xsd:documentation>
        </xsd:annotation>
        <xsd:complexContent>
          <xsd:restriction base="enc:Array">
            <xsd:attribute ref="enc:arrayType"
                 wsdl:arrayType="xsd:string[]" />
          </xsd:restriction>
        </xsd:complexContent>
      </xsd:complexType>
    </xsd:schema>
  </types>

  <!-- The service is being presented as an RPC model,
       without going into the object-based features.
       Instead, the SOAP binding will define header
       requirements. Thus, only the the operational
       parts are given operations.                        -->

  <message name="BookRequest">
    <documentation>
      A request for a single book, passing the ISBN and
      the user information
    </documentation>
    <part name="user" type="xsd:string" />
    <part name="isbn" type="xsd:string" />
  </message>

  <message name="BookResponse">
    <documentation>
      For operations that return a single Book
    </documentation>
    <part name="return" type="tns:Book" />
  </message>

  <message name="ISBNListResponse">
    <documentation>
```

Example E-1. wishlist.wsdl (continued)

```
      For operations that return a list of ISBN strings
    </documentation>
    <part name="return" type="tns:ArrayOfString" />
  </message>

  <message name="BooksByAuthorRequest">
    <documentation>
      A request for all books whose authors field matches
      the pattern in "author", also passed user information
    </documentation>
    <part name="user" type="xsd:string" />
    <part name="author" type="xsd:string" />
  </message>

  <message name="BooksByTitleRequest">
    <documentation>
      A request for all books whose title field matches the
      pattern in "title", also passed user information
    </documentation>
    <part name="user" type="xsd:string" />
    <part name="title" type="xsd:string" />
  </message>

  <message name="SimpleRequest">
    <documentation>
      Requests that do not explicitly pass arguments still
      may need the "user" element for authentication
    </documentation>
    <part name="user" type="xsd:string" />
  </message>

  <message name="SimpleResponse">
    <documentation>
      Responses from methods that do not return specific
      data (where non-fault return means success) need a
      generic message
    </documentation>
    <part name="return" type="xsd:anyType" />
  </message>

  <message name="BookListResponse">
    <documentation>
      A list of partial-book structures, as defined in the
      schema, for routines like BooksByAuthor, etc.
    </documentation>
    <part name="return" type="tns:ArrayOfPartialBook" />
  </message>

  <message name="BooleanResponse">
    <documentation>Simple T/F response type</documentation>
    <part name="result" type="xsd:boolean" />
  </message>
```

Example E-1. wishlist.wsdl (continued)

```xml
<message name="PurchaseBooksRequest">
  <documentation>
    The PurchaseBooks method requires a list of one or
    more books (by ISBN), and the user information
  </documentation>
  <part name="user" type="xsd:string" />
  <part name="list" type="tns:ArrayOfString" />
</message>

<portType name="WishListCustomerPort">
  <documentation>
    This port exposes the WishListCustomer::SOAP
    operations
  </documentation>

  <operation name="GetBook">
    <documentation>
      Retrieve information on one book, specified by the
      BookRequest message
    </documentation>
    <input message="tns:BookRequest" />
    <output message="tns:BookResponse" />
  </operation>

  <operation name="BooksByAuthor">
    <documentation>
      Retrieve a list of books searched by the author
      field against the substring passed in the input
      message
    </documentation>
    <input message="tns:BooksByAuthorRequest" />
    <output message="tns:ISBNListResponse" />
  </operation>

  <operation name="BooksByTitle">
    <documentation>
      Retrieve a list of books searched by the title
      field against the substring passed in the input
      message
    </documentation>
    <input message="tns:BooksByTitleRequest" />
    <output message="tns:ISBNListResponse" />
  </operation>

  <operation name="Wishlist">
    <documentation>
      Returns the current wish-list for the user whose
      authentication information is contained in the
      request
    </documentation>
    <input message="tns:SimpleRequest" />
```

Example E-1. wishlist.wsdl (continued)

```
      <output message="tns:BookListResponse" />
    </operation>

    <operation name="AddBook">
      <documentation>
        Add the specified book to the user's wish-list
      </documentation>
      <input message="tns:BookRequest" />
      <output message="tns:SimpleResponse" />
    </operation>

    <operation name="RemoveBook">
      <documentation>
        Remove a specified book from the wish-list
      </documentation>
      <input message="tns:BookRequest" />
      <output message="tns:SimpleResponse" />
    </operation>

    <operation name="CanPurchase">
      <documentation>
        Return a true/false value whether the user is set
        up to purchase directly from the wish-list
      </documentation>
      <input message="tns:SimpleRequest" />
      <output message="tns:BooleanResponse" />
    </operation>

    <operation name="PurchaseBooks">
      <documentation>
        Request to purchase one or more books from the
        user's wish-list
      </documentation>
      <input message="tns:PurchaseBooksRequest" />
      <output message="tns:SimpleResponse" />
    </operation>

  </portType>

  <binding name="SOAP" type="tns:WishListCustomerPort">
    <documentation>
      This binding is used to define the SOAP-level parts
      of the operations, which will later be joined with
      the portType within a service declaration.
    </documentation>
    <soap:binding style="rpc"
        transport="http://schemas.xmlsoap.org/soap/http" />
    <operation name="GetBook">
      <soap:operation soapAction=
                    "urn:WishListCustomer#GetBook" />
      <input>
        <soap:body use="encoded" parts="isbn"
```

Example E-1. wishlist.wsdl (continued)

```
              namespace="urn:WishListCustomer"
              encodingStyle=
              "http://schemas.xmlsoap.org/soap/encoding/" />
          <soap:header use="encoded" part="user"
              message="tns:BookRequest" wsdl:required="0"
              namespace="urn:WishListCustomer"
              encodingStyle=
              "http://schemas.xmlsoap.org/soap/encoding/" />
      </input>
      <output>
          <soap:body use="encoded"
              namespace="urn:WishListCustomer"
              encodingStyle=
              "http://schemas.xmlsoap.org/soap/encoding/" />
      </output>
  </operation>
  <operation name="BooksByAuthor">
    <soap:operation soapAction=
                    "urn:WishListCustomer#BooksByAuthor"/>
      <input>
          <soap:body use="encoded" part="author"
              namespace="urn:WishListCustomer"
              encodingStyle=
              "http://schemas.xmlsoap.org/soap/encoding/" />
          <soap:header use="encoded" part="user"
              message="tns:BooksByAuthorRequest"
              wsdl:required="0"
              namespace="urn:WishListCustomer"
              encodingStyle=
              "http://schemas.xmlsoap.org/soap/encoding/" />
      </input>
      <output>
          <soap:body use="encoded"
              namespace="urn:WishListCustomer"
              encodingStyle=
              "http://schemas.xmlsoap.org/soap/encoding/" />
      </output>
  </operation>
  <operation name="BooksByTitle">
    <soap:operation soapAction=
                    "urn:WishListCustomer#BooksByTitle" />
      <input>
          <soap:body use="encoded" part="title"
              namespace="urn:WishListCustomer"
              encodingStyle=
              "http://schemas.xmlsoap.org/soap/encoding/" />
          <soap:header use="encoded" part="user"
              message="tns:BooksByTitleRequest"
              wsdl:required="0"
              namespace="urn:WishListCustomer"
              encodingStyle=
              "http://schemas.xmlsoap.org/soap/encoding/" />
```

Example E-1. wishlist.wsdl (continued)

```xml
      </input>
      <output>
        <soap:body use="encoded"
            namespace="urn:WishListCustomer"
            encodingStyle=
            "http://schemas.xmlsoap.org/soap/encoding/" />
      </output>
    </operation>
    <operation name="Wishlist">
      <soap:operation soapAction=
                    "urn:WishListCustomer#Wishlist" />
      <input>
        <soap:body use="encoded" part=""
            namespace="urn:WishListCustomer"
            encodingStyle=
            "http://schemas.xmlsoap.org/soap/encoding/" />
        <soap:header use="encoded" part="user"
            message="tns:SimpleRequest"
            namespace="urn:WishListCustomer"
            encodingStyle=
            "http://schemas.xmlsoap.org/soap/encoding/" />
      </input>
      <output>
        <soap:body use="encoded"
            namespace="urn:WishListCustomer"
            encodingStyle=
            "http://schemas.xmlsoap.org/soap/encoding/" />
      </output>
    </operation>
    <operation name="AddBook">
      <soap:operation soapAction=
                    "urn:WishListCustomer#AddBook" />
      <input>
        <soap:body use="encoded" part="isbn"
            namespace="urn:WishListCustomer"
            encodingStyle=
            "http://schemas.xmlsoap.org/soap/encoding/" />
        <soap:header use="encoded" part="user"
            message="tns:BookRequest"
            namespace="urn:WishListCustomer"
            encodingStyle=
            "http://schemas.xmlsoap.org/soap/encoding/" />
      </input>
      <output>
        <soap:body use="encoded"
            namespace="urn:WishListCustomer"
            encodingStyle=
            "http://schemas.xmlsoap.org/soap/encoding/" />
      </output>
    </operation>
    <operation name="RemoveBook">
      <soap:operation soapAction=
```

Example E-1. wishlist.wsdl (continued)

```
                     "urn:WishListCustomer#RemoveBook" />
    <input>
      <soap:body use="encoded" part="isbn"
          namespace="urn:WishListCustomer"
          encodingStyle=
          "http://schemas.xmlsoap.org/soap/encoding/" />
      <soap:header use="encoded" part="user"
          message="tns:BookRequest"
          namespace="urn:WishListCustomer"
          encodingStyle=
          "http://schemas.xmlsoap.org/soap/encoding/" />
    </input>
    <output>
      <soap:body use="encoded"
          namespace="urn:WishListCustomer"
          encodingStyle=
          "http://schemas.xmlsoap.org/soap/encoding/" />
    </output>
  </operation>
  <operation name="CanPurchase">
    <soap:operation soapAction=
                     "urn:WishListCustomer#CanPurchase" />
    <input>
      <soap:body use="encoded" part=""
          namespace="urn:WishListCustomer"
          encodingStyle=
          "http://schemas.xmlsoap.org/soap/encoding/" />
      <soap:header use="encoded" part="user"
          message="tns:SimpleRequest"
          namespace="urn:WishListCustomer"
          encodingStyle=
          "http://schemas.xmlsoap.org/soap/encoding/" />
    </input>
    <output>
      <soap:body use="encoded"
          namespace="urn:WishListCustomer"
          encodingStyle=
          "http://schemas.xmlsoap.org/soap/encoding/" />
    </output>
  </operation>
  <operation name="PurchaseBooks">
    <soap:operation soapAction=
                     "urn:WishListCustomer#PurchaseBooks"/>
    <input>
      <soap:body use="encoded" part="list"
          namespace="urn:WishListCustomer"
          encodingStyle=
          "http://schemas.xmlsoap.org/soap/encoding/" />
      <soap:header use="encoded" part="user"
          message="tns:PurchaseBooksRequest"
          namespace="urn:WishListCustomer"
          encodingStyle=
```

Example E-1. wishlist.wsdl (continued)

```
            "http://schemas.xmlsoap.org/soap/encoding/" />
      </input>
      <output>
        <soap:body use="encoded"
            namespace="urn:WishListCustomer"
            encodingStyle=
            "http://schemas.xmlsoap.org/soap/encoding/" />
      </output>
    </operation>
  </binding>

  <service name="WishListCustomer">
    <documentation>
      The WishListCustomer service defines the combinations
      of portTypes and bindings to provide the functionality
      of the WishListCustomer class to the outside world.
    </documentation>
    <port name="WishListCustomerPort" binding="tns:SOAP">
      <documentation>
        For the binding of the portType to the SOAP-level
        bindings, the address uses HTTP and will point to
        a server providing the WishListCustomer::SOAP
        interface.
      </documentation>
      <soap:address location="http://localhost:9000" />
    </port>
  </service>

</definitions>
```

The useperlorg.wsdl File

The second WSDL example presented here describes the alpha-version interface to the use.perl.org journal system.

Example E-2. useperlorg.wsdl

```
<?xml version="1.0"?>
<definitions name="UsePerlJournal"
    targetNamespace="http://use.perl.org/Slash/Journal/SOAP"
    xmlns="http://schemas.xmlsoap.org/wsdl/"
    xmlns:tns="http://use.perl.org/Slash/Journal/SOAP"
    xmlns:wsdl="http://schemas.xmlsoap.org/wsdl/"
    xmlns:soap="http://schemas.xmlsoap.org/wsdl/soap/"
    xmlns:enc="http://schemas.xmlsoap.org/soap/encoding/"
    xmlns:xsd="http://www.w3.org/2001/XMLSchema">

  <types>
    <documentation>
      This section defines the types that will be used by
      the rest of the WSDL document to describe the data
```

Example E-2. useperlorg.wsdl (continued)

```
      that describes journal entries. Only the types not
      already available from XML Schema are defined here.
   </documentation>
   <xsd:schema targetNamespace=
               "http://use.perl.org/Slash/Journal/SOAP">
     <xsd:complexType name="PartialEntry">
       <xsd:annotation>
         <xsd:documentation>
           Partial journal entry information, this is
           what gets returned by get_entries.
         </xsd:documentation>
       </xsd:annotation>
       <xsd:all>
         <xsd:element name="url" type="xsd:anyURI" />
         <xsd:element name="id" type="xsd:int" />
         <xsd:element name="subject" type="xsd:string" />
       </xsd:all>
     </xsd:complexType>
     <xsd:complexType name="Entry">
       <xsd:annotation>
         <xsd:documentation>
           Full journal entry information, this is
           what gets returned by get_entry.
         </xsd:documentation>
       </xsd:annotation>
       <xsd:extension base="PartialEntry">
         <xsd:all>
           <xsd:element name="nickname" type="xsd:string"/>
           <xsd:element name="body" type="xsd:string"/>
           <xsd:element name="discussion_id"
                        type="xsd:int" />
           <xsd:element name="discussion_url"
                        type="xsd:anyURI" />
           <xsd:element name="posttype" type="xsd:int" />
           <xsd:element name="date" type="xsd:string" />
           <xsd:element name="tid" type="xsd:int" />
           <xsd:element name="uid" type="xsd:int" />
         </xsd:all>
       </xsd:extension>
     </xsd:complexType>
     <xsd:complexType name="CreationEntry">
       <xsd:annotation>
         <xsd:documentation>
           This is an abbreviated form of the Entry above,
           which is used when creating an entry using full-
           form, or when modifying an entry.
         </xsd:documentation>
       </xsd:annotation>
       <xsd:all>
         <xsd:element name="subject" type="xsd:string" />
         <xsd:element name="body" type="xsd:string"/>
         <xsd:element name="discuss" type="xsd:boolean" />
```

Example E-2. useperlorg.wsdl (continued)

```xml
            <xsd:element name="posttype" type="xsd:int" />
            <xsd:element name="tid" type="xsd:int" />
        </xsd:all>
      </xsd:complexType>
      <xsd:complexType name="ArrayOfPartialEntry">
        <xsd:complexContent>
          <xsd:restriction base="enc:Array">
            <xsd:attribute ref="enc:arrayType"
                  wsdl:arrayType="tns:PartialEntry[]" />
          </xsd:restriction>
        </xsd:complexContent>
      </xsd:complexType>
    </xsd:schema>
</types>

<!-- The message names reflect the types that are passed
     or returned, as the case may be. See the operation
     tags in the portType below for where the messages are
     actually used.                                       -->
<message name="SubjectBody">
  <part name="subject" type="xsd:string" />
  <part name="body" type="xsd:string" />
</message>
<message name="CreationEntry">
  <part name="entry" type="tns:CreationEntry" />
</message>
<message name="IDCreationEntry">
  <part name="id" type="xsd:int" />
  <part name="entry" type="tns:CreationEntry" />
</message>
<message name="ID">
  <part name="id" type="xsd:int" />
</message>
<message name="UidLimit">
  <part name="uid" type="xsd:int" />
  <part name="limit" type="xsd:int" />
</message>
<message name="IntOutput">
  <part name="return" type="xsd:int" />
</message>
<message name="Boolean">
  <part name="return" type="xsd:boolean" />
</message>
<message name="Entry">
  <part name="return" type="tns:Entry" />
</message>
<message name="ListOfPartialEntry">
  <part name="return" type="tns:ArrayOfPartialEntry" />
</message>

<portType name="UsePerlJournalPort">
  <operation name="add_entry">
```

Example E-2. useperlorg.wsdl (continued)

```
    <documentation>
      add_entry creates a new journal entry on the server
      and returns the ID number of the entry. This form
      of the call takes two strings, subject and body.
    </documentation>
    <input name="SubjectBodyCall"
          message="tns:SubjectBody" />
    <output message="tns:IntOutput" />
  </operation>
  <operation name="add_entry">
    <documentation>
      add_entry creates a new journal entry on the server
      and returns the ID number of the entry. This form
      of the call takes a structure with up to six
      elements.
    </documentation>
    <input name="CreationEntryCall"
          message="tns:CreationEntry" />
    <output message="tns:IntOutput" />
  </operation>
  <operation name="modify_entry">
    <documentation>
      Make changes to an existing entry. Takes the ID of
      the entry to change, and an entry structure like
      the second form of add_entry takes. Only the fields
      being changes should be present in the entry
      parameter. Returns the entry ID on success.
    </documentation>
    <input message="tns:IDCreationEntry" />
    <output message="tns:IntOutput" />
  </operation>
  <operation name="delete_entry">
    <documentation>
      Delete the entry specified by ID. Returns true or
      false on success or failure.
    </documentation>
    <input message="tns:ID" />
    <output message="tns:Boolean" />
  </operation>
  <operation name="get_entry">
    <documentation>
      Get the full entry indicated by the ID number in
      the parameter.
    </documentation>
    <input message="tns:ID" />
    <output message="tns:Entry" />
  </operation>
  <operation name="get_entries">
    <documentation>
      Returns an array of partial entries for the user
      referenced by UID, up to a maximum of LIMIT entries
      in all. If the user has fewer than LIMIT entries,
```

Example E-2. useperlorg.wsdl (continued)

```
          only that number will be returned.
        </documentation>
        <input message="tns:UidLimit" />
        <output message="tns:ListOfPartialEntry" />
      </operation>
    </portType>

    <binding name="UsePerlJournalSOAP"
             type="tns:UsePerlJournalPort">
      <documentation>
        Provide the concrete binding of the operations given
        in the port-type to the SOAP protocol. This binding
        does not address the need for user authentication by
        means of HTTP cookies for all operations that alter
        entries (create, modify, delete).
      </documentation>
      <soap:binding style="rpc"
                    transport=
                    "http://schemas.xmlsoap.org/soap/http" />
      <operation name="add_entry"
                 parameterOrder="subject body">
        <soap:operation soapAction=
          "http://use.perl.org/Slash/Journal/SOAP#get_entry"
        />
        <input name="SubjectBodyCall">
          <soap:body use="encoded"
              namespace=
              "http://use.perl.org/Slash/Journal/SOAP"
              encodingStyle=
              "http://schemas.xmlsoap.org/soap/encoding/" />
        </input>
        <output>
          <soap:body use="encoded"
              namespace=
              "http://use.perl.org/Slash/Journal/SOAP"
              encodingStyle=
              "http://schemas.xmlsoap.org/soap/encoding/" />
        </output>
      </operation>
      <operation name="add_entry">
        <soap:operation soapAction=
          "http://use.perl.org/Slash/Journal/SOAP#add_entry"
        />
        <input name="CreationEntryCall">
          <soap:body use="encoded"
              namespace=
              "http://use.perl.org/Slash/Journal/SOAP"
              encodingStyle=
              "http://schemas.xmlsoap.org/soap/encoding/" />
        </input>
        <output>
          <soap:body use="encoded"
```

Example E-2. useperlorg.wsdl (continued)

```
            namespace=
            "http://use.perl.org/Slash/Journal/SOAP"
            encodingStyle=
            "http://schemas.xmlsoap.org/soap/encoding/" />
      </output>
    </operation>
    <operation name="modify_entry">
      <soap:operation soapAction=
        "http://use.perl.org/Slash/Journal/SOAP#modify_entry"
      />
      <input>
        <soap:body use="encoded"
            namespace=
            "http://use.perl.org/Slash/Journal/SOAP"
            encodingStyle=
            "http://schemas.xmlsoap.org/soap/encoding/" />
      </input>
      <output>
        <soap:body use="encoded"
            namespace=
            "http://use.perl.org/Slash/Journal/SOAP"
            encodingStyle=
            "http://schemas.xmlsoap.org/soap/encoding/" />
      </output>
    </operation>
    <operation name="delete_entry">
      <soap:operation soapAction=
        "http://use.perl.org/Slash/Journal/SOAP#delete_entry"
      />
      <input>
        <soap:body use="encoded"
            namespace=
            "http://use.perl.org/Slash/Journal/SOAP"
            encodingStyle=
            "http://schemas.xmlsoap.org/soap/encoding/" />
      </input>
      <output>
        <soap:body use="encoded"
            namespace=
            "http://use.perl.org/Slash/Journal/SOAP"
            encodingStyle=
            "http://schemas.xmlsoap.org/soap/encoding/" />
      </output>
    </operation>
    <operation name="get_entry">
      <soap:operation soapAction=
        "http://use.perl.org/Slash/Journal/SOAP#get_entry"/>
      <input>
        <soap:body use="encoded"
            namespace=
            "http://use.perl.org/Slash/Journal/SOAP"
            encodingStyle=
```

Example E-2. useperlorg.wsdl (continued)

```
              "http://schemas.xmlsoap.org/soap/encoding/" />
      </input>
      <output>
        <soap:body use="encoded"
            namespace=
            "http://use.perl.org/Slash/Journal/SOAP"
            encodingStyle=
            "http://schemas.xmlsoap.org/soap/encoding/" />
      </output>
    </operation>
    <operation name="get_entries">
      <soap:operation soapAction=
        "http://use.perl.org/Slash/Journal/SOAP#get_entries"
      />
      <input>
        <soap:body use="encoded"
            namespace=
            "http://use.perl.org/Slash/Journal/SOAP"
            encodingStyle=
            "http://schemas.xmlsoap.org/soap/encoding/" />
      </input>
      <output>
        <soap:body use="encoded"
            namespace=
            "http://use.perl.org/Slash/Journal/SOAP"
            encodingStyle=
            "http://schemas.xmlsoap.org/soap/encoding/" />
      </output>
    </operation>
  </binding>

  <service name="UsePerlJournal">
    <documentation>
      Describe a service using the SOAP binding given above,
      bound to the URL that corresponds to the use.perl.org
      web server.
    </documentation>
    <port name="UsePerlJournalPort"
          binding="tns:UsePerlJournalSOAP">
      <soap:address location=
                    "http://use.perl.org/soap.pl" />
    </port>
  </service>

</definitions>
```

The show_biz UDDI Application

This application was presented in Chapter 10 to illustrate the usage of the UDDI::Lite classes that are a part of the SOAP::Lite package. In particular, it outlines how the

UDDI::Data class provides an object-model view of the UDDI data structures, as returned by UDDI registry servers in response to queries.

The application takes any of three optional command-line switch arguments and a string representing a business name (or partial name) to search for. All matching business records are dumped to the terminal in a fairly readable layout that goes down to the level of the bindingTemplate structures. For brevity, the application stops at that point, though adding functionality to follow tModel references and deconstruct the identifierBag or categoryBag lists would be fairly easy.

Example E-3. show_biz

```perl
#!/usr/bin/perl

use strict;
use vars qw(%opts $name @qualifiers @params $SHOWKEYS);
use subs qw(dump_business dump_service dump_template);

# Text::Wrap will be used to format <description> blocks
use Text::Wrap qw(wrap $columns);
use Getopt::Long 'GetOptions';
# This example will make use of the autodispatch ability
use UDDI::Lite +autodispatch =>
                proxy => 'http://uddi.microsoft.com/inquire',
                import => 'UDDI::Data';

# --case:     Do the matching in a case-sensitive manner
# --exact:    Match a string exactly
# --showkeys: Display record UUIDs right after the name
GetOptions(\%opts, qw(case exact showkeys)) and
    $name = shift or
    die "USAGE: $0 [ --case ] [ --exact ] [ --showkeys ] " .
        "name\n";
$SHOWKEYS++ if ($opts{showkeys});

# Building up the qualifiers this way makes it cleaner to
# create the <findQualifiers> structure. And since the
# parameters are being pre-constructed, throw the search
# string on at the end for convenience.
@qualifiers = ('sortByNameAsc');
push(@qualifiers, 'exactNameMatch')       if ($opts{exact});
push(@qualifiers, 'caseSensitiveMatch') if ($opts{case});
push(@params,
     findQualifiers(findQualifier(@qualifiers)),
     name($name));

# First UDDI call: find all businesses that match the
# criteria, then loop over them passing each to the
# dump_business routine.
my $result = find_business(@params);
dump_business($_)
```

Example E-3. show_biz (continued)

```perl
    for ($result->businessInfos->businessInfo);

exit;

# Dump the contents of a <businessInfo> (an abbreviated
# form of a <businessEntity>) record.
sub dump_business {
    my $business = shift;

    print $business->name, "\n";
    print 'uuid:', $business->businessKey, "\n"
        if $SHOWKEYS;
    print "\n";
    if (my $description = $business->description) {
        $columns = 72;
        print wrap("\t", "\t", $description), "\n\n";
    }
    # Hand off each service entry to the dump_service
    # routine.
    dump_service($_)
        for ($business->serviceInfos->serviceInfo);
}

# Dump the contents of a <businessService> record. What
# gets passed in is just a brief overview, however.
sub dump_service {
    my $svc = shift;

    my ($key, $service);

    # First order of business (so to speak) is to get the
    # full <businessService> record, since what was passed
    # in was a <serviceInfo>, that lacks a lot of data.
    $key = $svc->serviceKey;
    # Call get_serviceDetail using the serviceKey attribute
    # from the short-form data.
    return unless
        $service = get_serviceDetail($key);
    $service = $service->businessService;
    print '   Service: ', $service->name, "\n";
    print '      uuid:', $service->serviceKey, "\n"
        if $SHOWKEYS;
    if (my $description = $service->description) {
        $columns = 64;
        print wrap("\t    ", "\t    ", $description), "\n";
    }
    print "\n";
    # Hand off a third time to handle <bindingTemplate>
    # records.
    dump_template($_)
        for ($service->bindingTemplates->bindingTemplate);
}
```

Example E-3. show_biz (continued)

```perl
# Dump the contents of a <bindingTemplate> record. This
# doesn't need an extra call, because all the needed data
# was retrieved in the earlier get_serviceDetail call.
sub dump_template {
    my $template = shift;

    print "\tTemplate:\n";
    print "\tuuid:", $template->bindingKey, "\n"
        if $SHOWKEYS;
    if (my $description = $template->description) {
        $columns = 60;
        print wrap("\t\t", "\t\t", $description), "\n";
    }
    # Display either the access point (with a parenthetical
    # comment about the URLType) or the redirector key.
    # If neither are present, well, the registry should
    # never have permitted that, but we can't count on it.
    if (my $access = $template->accessPoint) {
        printf "\t   Access point (%s): %s\n",
            $access->attr->URLType, $access->value;
    } elsif (my $redir = $template->hostingRedirector) {
        print "\t   Hosting redirect to ",
            $redir->value, "\n";
    } else {
        print "\t   No access point or hosting " ,
            "redirector?\n";
    }
    print "\n";
}
```

APPENDIX F
Bibliography and References

This appendix collects the various books, web pages, and other references that were used to research this book. Printed books are presented first; the web sites and other references are grouped by their focus and topical relevance.

Bibliography

HTTP Pocket Reference, Clinton Wong. O'Reilly & Associates, Inc. ISBN 1-56592-862-8.

Learning XML, Erik T. Ray. O'Reilly. ISBN 0-596-00046-4.

Power Programming with RPC, John Bloomer. O'Reilly. ISBN 0-937175-77-3.

Programming Web Services with SOAP, James Snell, Doug Tidwell, and Pavel Kulchenko. O'Reilly. ISBN 0-596-00095-2.

Programming Web Services with XML-RPC, Simon St. Laurent, Joe Johnston, and Edd Dumbill. O'Reilly. ISBN 0-596-00119-3.

SOAP: Cross Platform Web Service Development Using XML, Scott Seely. Prentice Hall PTR. ISBN 0-13-090763.

XML Pocket Reference, Robert Eckstein. O'Reilly. ISBN 1-56592-709-5.

XML Schema, Eric van der Vlist, O'Reilly. ISBN 0-596-00252-1.

Additional Recommended Books

Some of the following titles were released while this book was in development. The rest are books that provide similar information to some references in the previous section but in a different style or format that may be more useful depending on what kind of reference you seek. Though not used for research here, they may be of interest if you work with HTTP-oriented applications, XML applications, and web service tools.

HTTP: The Definitive Guide, Brian Totty and David Gourley. O'Reilly. ISBN 1-56592-509-2.

Perl and LWP, Sean M. Burke. O'Reilly. ISBN 0-596-00178-9.

XML in a Nutshell: A Desktop Quick Reference, Elliote Rusty Harold and W. Scott Means. O'Reilly. ISBN 0-596-00058-8.

Web Pages

As would be expected in a book about web services, the majority of the research done for this project was on the Web itself. Many, but not all, are on the home page of the World Wide Web Consortium (W3C). The links here aren't an exhaustive set; more information can always be found through judicious use of search engines. Web sites have been divided by the general subject area, though some sites might cover more than the listed topic.

General XML and XML Schema

http://www.w3.org/TR/REC-xml
  The formal specification for the Extensible Markup Language (XML).

http://www.w3.org/TR/REC-xml-names/
  Defines the concepts and rules governing XML namespaces.

http://www.w3.org/XML/Schema
  The work on XML Schema covers more than one specification. This page is the W3C group's central point of information for the work on XML Schema. All parts of the current specification are linked from this site.

http://www.xml.com
  Part of the O'Reilly Network family of information servers. It hosts a range of writers and columnists who explore new and newsworthy topics regarding XML and its application to business interests and areas.

http://www.xmlhack.com/
  A news portal geared to the XML developer community. News items that impact either XML directly or developer tools with XML relevance (such as scripting languages) are gathered and sorted by general topic.

http://xml.coverpages.org/
  Another portal, sponsored by the OASIS group, an international nonprofit consortium that develops standards and specifications based on XML.

XML-RPC

http://www.xmlrpc.com/
> The primary home for XML-RPC. This page links to the formal specification and a directory of other related information. Included are pointers to all known implementations in various languages.

http://www.soaplite.com/
> The home page for the SOAP::Lite Perl module, listed here because the XMLRPC::Lite module is a part of SOAP::Lite. Information on the progress of the software, as well as download links, can be found here.

http://www.blackperl.com/RPC::XML
> The home page for the RPC::XML Perl module, one of the three implementations for Perl. The page links to downloads of the module and HTML versions of the manpages.

http://xmlrpc-epi.sourceforge.net/specs/rfc.fault_codes.php
> The effort to define an accepted standardization of error codes and messages for XML-RPC toolkit interoperability is maintained at this page.

http://www.oreillynet.com/pub/a/rss/2000/11/14/meerkat_xmlrpc.html
> The Meerkat Open Wire Service provides a XML-RPC interface to the searching and filtering capabilities it sports. This article details the interface for developers.

http://groups.yahoo.com/group/xml-rpc
> The mailing list that discusses all manner of XML-RPC issues, ranging from how-to questions to announcements of tools and developer toolkits. Hosted by the Yahoo! Groups mailing list manager.

SOAP

http://www.w3.org/TR/SOAP/
> The SOAP specification Version 1.1.

http://www.w3.org/2002/ws/
> The W3C primary page for web-services activities. Links from this pages lead to several topics besides SOAP, but the most recent activity on SOAP standards and protocols are announced here.

http://www.w3.org/TR/soap12-part0/
http://www.w3.org/TR/soap12-part1/
http://www.w3.org/TR/soap12-part2/
> The SOAP 1.2 specification is divided into three parts: Part 0 is the primer, Part 1 covers the messaging framework, and Part 2 covers adjuncts (concrete descriptions of transport, serialization, and so forth).

http://www.soaplite.com/
> The home page for the `SOAP::Lite` Perl module is also mentioned here because the focus is more on SOAP than XML-RPC.

There are considerable references and resources on the Web concerning SOAP. This list represents what is most relevant to the material covered in this book.

WSDL

http://www.w3.org/TR/wsdl
> The formal specification for WSDL 1.1. All the WSDL materials in this book are based on this version of WSDL.

http://www.w3.org/TR/wsdl12/
http://www.w3.org/TR/wsdl12-bindings/
> As of this writing, these two documents are the working drafts for WSDL 1.2. The specification is broken into two parts: WSDL itself; a second part covers bindings (SOAP, HTTP, etc.).

WSDL support is also found in the `SOAP::Lite` toolkit.

UDDI

http://www.uddi.org/
> This site is the central headquarters for the development and specification of UDDI. Copies of the specification (both versions), XML Schema descriptions, and links to tools may be found here.

As with WSDL, the `SOAP::Lite` toolkit also offers some degree of support for UDDI.

REST

http://www.ics.uci.edu/~fielding/pubs/dissertation/top.htm
> The original doctoral thesis by Roy Fielding, in which REST is defined and described.

http://www.w3.org/TR/2001/NOTE-uri-clarification-20010921/
> The W3C organization's paper clarifying the distinctions between URN, URL, and URI. Though not directly related to REST, the fact that REST uses URIs makes this recommended reading.

http://www.prescod.net/rest/wrdl/wrdl.html
> Paul Prescod's article on the Web Resource Description Language, an alternative to WSDL that is popular in REST circles.

Index

Symbols

&eacute entity, 18, 23
& (ampersand), 17, 202
< (angle bracket), 14
: (colon), 15, 26, 37, 189
, (comma), 102
!DOCTYPE element, 18
$@ variable (Perl), 62, 69
! (exclamation point), 18
$header variable, 164
- (hyphen), 127
() parentheses, 11
% (percent sign), 202
. (period), 37, 107
#!perl start-up line, 77
? (question mark), 11, 18
" (quotation marks), 16
; (semicolon), 17
/ (slash)
   hierarchical boundaries, 243
   URI and, 254
   user element, 202
   XML elements, 14
   XML-RPC requests, 37
[] (square brackets), 102
_ (underscore)
   attributes and, 16
   key name, 178
   XML element, 14
   XML-RPC requests, 37

A

absolute URIs, 241, 250, 264
abstract element
   message specifications, 192
   WSDL documents, 187
   WS-Inspection, 287
abstract operation, 198, 206
abstraction
   basic classes, 124
   bindings, 196
   client objects, 128
   REST, 238
Accept header (REST), 252, 253
Accept-Encoding header (REST), 252
Accept-Language header (REST), 252
access control, 272, 280
access control lists (ACLs), 272
access method (SOAP::Schema), 340
accessor methods, 74, 125, 327, 336, 352
accessors
   data elements, 98
   generic compound types and, 104
   references, 100
   RPC over SOAP, 109
   structures and, 100, 104
accessPoint element (UDDI bindingTemplate structure), 215, 222
ACID properties, 293
acknowledgements, 289
ACLs (access control lists), 272
action method (SOAP::Server), 342
activation service (WS-Coordination), 294
ActiveState, 300

We'd like to hear your suggestions for improving our indexes. Send email to *index@oreilly.com*.

actor attribute (SOAP)
    features, 90–91
    global attribute, 88
    message body, 96
    message routing, 263
actor method (SOAP::Data), 333
actors
    anonymous actors, 89, 90, 96
    current actor, 90
    transition of messages, 84
    WS-Referral and, 266
    (see also roles)
add_default_methods
        (RPC::XML::Server), 319
add_header method
        (SOAP::EnvelopeMaker), 118
add_method method
        (RPC::XML::Server), 74, 80, 319
add_methods_in_dir method
        (RPC::XML::Server), 75, 320
add_proc method (RPC::XML::Server),
        73, 74
add_publisherAssertions call (UDDI),
        229, 230
address element (UDDI), 219
addressLine element (UDDI), 219
add_signature method (RPC::XML), 322
ADS specification, 287
AI (artificial intelligence), 5
all construct (XML Schema), 190
annotation element, 31
anonymous actors, 89, 90, 96
anyType type (XML Schema), 192
anyURI type (XML Schema), 26
AOL Instant Messaging, 167
Apache environment
    configuring server objects, 78–81
    content handling, 67
    mod_perl combined with, 145
    moving SOAP servers to, 153–155
    NTLM authentication, 274
    RPC::XML::Server class and, 73
    server introspection interface, 78
    server side and, 53
    SOAP::Lite options, 120
    XMLRPC::Lite support, 65
Apache::AuthenNTLM module
        (CPAN), 274
Apache::Registry system, 78, 145
Apache::RPC::Server class, 78, 324, 325
Apache::RPC::Status monitor, 81, 325

Apache::SOAP wrapper module, 145,
        153, 357
apache_status_attach method
        (Apache::RPC::Status), 326
APIs
    documenting for REST services, 259
    SAX and, 21
    UDDI, 229
    (see also interfaces)
applications
    defined, 14
    developing REST, 253–255
    method signatures, 42
    querying routine models, 226
    security and, 271
    SOAP server example, 139
application/soap+xml type (SOAP), 261
args method (RPC::XML::request), 314
arguments
    accessor methods and, 125
    controlling with parameterOrder, 209
    hash references as, 134
    lack of ordering, 206
    languages and, 41
    overlapping, 110
    (see also parameters)
array of bytes type (SOAP), 98
array reference
        (RPC::XMLSimple::Client), 54, 56
array type (XML Schema), 99
array type (XML-RPC), 34, 38
arrays
    accessors and, 100
    array datatype, 34
    partial, 103
    RPC::XMLSimple data classes and, 56
    SOAP messages, 101–104
    sparse, 103
    WSDL specification and, 191
arrayType attribute (SOAP), 101, 102, 191
artificial intelligence (AI), 5
ASCII character set, 275, 299
assertions, 282, 285
assign activity (BPEL), 298
as_string method (RPC::XML), 71, 313
asymmetric cryptography, 278
asynchronous environment, 292, 294–296
atomic transactions, 293, 295
attachments, messages and, 270
attr method (SOAP::Data), 232, 332
attribute element (XML Schema), 26, 191

attributes
    DTD declaring, 19
    placement in Header elements, 92–95
    SAML, 282
    simple/complex types, 27
    validation, 19
    XML building block, 16, 17
    XML Schema, 26, 98
    XML Signature, 278
    XML-RPC datatypes, 34
auditing, 273
authentication
    cookie-based, 144
    defined, 272
    digest, 274
    digest tokens, 31
    digit-authentication tokens, 31
    Header element, 86, 88
    HTTP and, 246
    improving code/service, 155
    REST and, 237
    SAML, 276, 282
    SetUser method, 143
    SOAP and, 84, 161–165
    SOAP server example, 147
    SSL/TLS, 275
    static methods and, 149
    UDDI API calls, 229
    user element and, 192
    WishListCustomer class, 147, 148, 387, 398, 400
    WishListCustomer example, 388–390, 393, 401
    WS-Security, 284
    (see also basic authentication)
authentication tokens, 164, 229
authInfo element (UDDI), 229, 230
authority component (URI), 241
authorization
    defined, 272
    HTTP and, 246
    REST and, 237
    SAML, 276, 282
    SOAP mustUnderstand attribute, 91
    WS-Authorization, 286
    XACML, 276, 283
Authorize element (SOAP), 86
authorizedName attribute (UDDI), 218, 223
autodispatching
    dispatch_with method, 177
    RPC::XML::Client class and, 71
    special characters and, 64

    UDDI::Lite and, 234–236
    XMLRPC::Lite and, 63
AUTOLOAD routine (SOAP::Lite), 126, 129
auto-loading feature (Perl), 127, 129
autotype method (SOAP::Lite), 328

B

BA (business activities) coordination types, 295
Base64 algorithm
    base64 datatype and, 33
    basic authentication and, 274
    new method, 71
    value method, 71
    XML Schema and, 267
    XML-RPC and, 50
base64 method (RPC::XMLSimple), 55, 304, 306
base64 type (XML-RPC), 33, 56
base64Binary type (XML Schema), 26
basic authentication, 274, 289
BEA, 296, 297
BEEP (Blocks Extensible Exchange Protocol), 50, 112
binary data, 267, 268, 270
BinarySecurityToken element (WS-Security), 284
binding attribute (WSDL port element), 200
binding element (WSDL), 196, 197, 207
bindingKey attribute (UDDI), 222
bindings
    hostnames and ports, 165
    HTTP and, 112
    HTTP bindings, 201–203
    overloaded operations and, 207–209
    servers to ports, 58
    SMTP and, 112
    SOAP, 282, 415–424
    TCP transport example, 166, 167
    UDDI businessService structure, 220
    WSDL, 201–205
    WSDL documents, 187, 196–199
    WS-Inspection, 288
    WS-Routing and, 265
bindingTemplate structure (UDDI)
    defined, 215
    delete_binding call, 230
    example, 220, 430
    save_binding call, 229
    specifics, 221, 222
BizTalk Server, 297

blocks
    actor responsibility for, 89
    header element components, 88
    placement of global attributes, 92–95
    WSDL example, 191, 192
Blocks Extensible Exchange Protocol (see BEEP)
Body element (SOAP)
    declaring URN, 117
    Fault element and, 105
    message component, 85
    namespaces and, 86
    root attribute, 105
    soap:body element, 198
    specifics, 95, 97
body method (SOAP::SOM), 335
BOM (Byte Order Mark), 299
boolean method (RPC::XMLSimple), 55, 304, 306
boolean type (XML Schema), 25
boolean type (XML-RPC), 33, 56, 62
BPEL (Business Process Execution Language), 297, 298
BPEL4WS (Business Processing Execution Language for Web Services), 296
BPML (Business Process Modeling Language), 296
BPSS (Business Process Specification Schema), 296
br element, 14
BTP (Business Transaction Protocol), 296
Business Activity protocols, 295
Business Process Execution Language (see BPEL)
business process management, 291–298
Business Process Management Initiative, 296
Business Process Modeling Language (BPML), 296
Business Process Specification Schema (BPSS), 296
Business Processing Execution Language for Web Services (BPEL4WS), 296
business services
    classifications, 217
    publishing information, 228–230
    UDDI tModel structure and, 223
Business Transaction Protocol (BTP), 296
BusinessAgreement protocol (WS-Transaction), 295
BusinessAgreementWithComplete protocol (WS-Transaction), 295

businessEntity structure (UDDI)
    API calls, 229
    delete_business call, 230
    relationships, 216
    save_business call, 229
    specifics, 215, 217–220
    WS-Inspection, 288
businessEntityExt structure (UDDI), 218
businessInfo element (UDDI), 232
businessKey attribute
    UDDI businessEntity structure, 217, 218
    UDDI businessService structure, 221
businessList element (UDDI), 232, 233
businessService structure (UDDI)
    delete_service call, 230
    relationships, 216
    save_service call, 229
    specifics, 215, 220, 221
    WS-Inspection, 288
byName routine (SOAP::Server::Parameters), 345
byNameOrOrder routine (SOAP::Server::Parameters), 345
Byte Order Mark (BOM), 299

C

C language
    arguments list and, 41
    array dimensions, 103
    void type, 50
C++ language, 42
C# language, 298
call method
    client authentication and, 164
    RPC::XML server classes, 323
    RPC::XMLSimple::Client class, 54, 55, 306
    SOAP::Lite class, 330
    XMLRPC::Lite class, 7, 60, 61, 62, 307
callbacks
    fault_handler method and, 69
    RPC::XML example, 68
    trace signals and, 63
    tracing events, 127
    XMLRPC::Lite, 60, 61
canonicalization, 278, 279
capability, 246
case sensitivity, 14, 235
categoryBag element (UDDI), 220, 223, 224
CDATA section (XML), 19, 77, 268
certificates, 275, 281

442 | Index

CGI (Common Gateway Interface), 65, 145, 252
chaffing, 272
character sets
    ASCII, 275, 299
    international, 299, 300
    non-English, 299
chatty interfaces, 292
checkSignature element, SOAP Header block, 93
child_started method (Apache::RPC::Server), 325
choreography, 291
chunky interfaces, 292
class methods
    authentication data and, 162
    paramsin method and, 156
    SOAP servers and, 146
    WSDL::Generator module and, 212
    XMLRPC::Lite class, 61
classes
    headers and, 161
    SOAP::Lite toolkit, 124–127
    subclassing, 147–150
    (see also server classes)
Class::Hook module, 212
client certificates, 275
client classes (see specific classes)
Client fault code (SOAP 1.1), 107
clients
    certificates, 275
    client authentication, 163–165
    CPAN resource, 239
    example of generic, 402, 403
    following link example, 250
    FTP-based, 407, 408
    introspection interface, 77
    LWP toolkit and, 52
    MAILTO example, 405, 406
    NTLM authentication, 274
    RPC::XML example, 68–72
    RPC::XMLSimple example, 53–55
    sample transport module, 409–414
    simple access with SOAP::Lite, 151, 152
    SOAP::Lite and WSDL, 211, 213
    SOAP::Lite toolkit, 120–136
    SOAP::Transport::LOCAL example, 408
    SOAP::Transport::MAILTO example, 172, 173
    state changes, 239
    transport protocols, 165–173

WishListCustomer example, 391, 397, 398
WSDL capabilities, 185
XML-RPC request/response, 40, 41
XMLRPC::Lite example, 59–64
(see also specific client classes)
client/server model
    MAILTO module, 170–173
    POP3 protocol, 170, 172
    REST principles, 241
    RPC system and, 2
    SOAP and, 3, 89
    SOAP::Transport::JABBER module, 167–169
    SOAP::Transport::LOCAL::Client, 173
    SOAP::Transport::LOCAL::Client class, 176
    SOAP::Transport::MQ classes, 169, 170
    SOAP::Transport::TCP classes, 165–167
    UDDI and, 4
    XML-RPC and, 40, 41, 50
clone method (RPC::XML), 322
Code element (SOAP 1.2), 106
collaboration, 291
collisions, avoiding, 178
COM (Component Object Model), 2
combined_handler method (RPC::XML::Client), 70, 316
comments, 18
commit
    conditional commitment, 296
    two-phase commit, 293
Common Gateway Interface (see CGI)
Common Object Request Broker Architecture (see CORBA)
communication
    HTTP requests, 3
    one-way, 174
    store-and-forward, 171
    web services and, 1
    (see also client/server model)
compatibility, 49
compensate activity (BPEL), 298
compensating transaction, 294
compensation handlers, 298
Completion protocol (WS-Coordination), 295
CompletionWithAck protocol (WS-Coordination), 295
complex types (XML Schema), 27, 28, 142
complexity, 23
Component Object Model (COM), 2

Index | 443

composition, 291
compound types, 99, 104
Comprehensive Perl Archive Network
    (see CPAN)
compression
    CPAN uploads example, 134
    GNU Zip algorithm, 49
    packaging, 262
    SOAP::Lite options, 120
    XML and, 268
    XML Signature, 279
compress_requests method
    (RPC::XML::Client), 316
compress_thresh method
    (RPC::XML::Client), 316
Compress::Zlib module (CPAN), 66, 75
concrete elements (WSDL), 187
Concurrent Version Control (CVS), 29–31
confidentiality
    defined, 272
    SSL/TLS, 275
    WS-Security, 284
    XML Encryption, 276, 285
configuration
    Apache server objects, 78–81
    SOAP::Lite options, 120
    WS-Referral and, 267
configure method, (SOAP::Transport::
    HTTP::Apache), 351
consistency (transactions), 293
constants (SOAP), 339
contact element (UDDI), 218
containers
    actor roles, 89
    BPEL and, 298
    complex types and, 28
    DTD example, 20
    hash table as, 99
    MIME and, 269
    requirements, 35
    schema documents, 24
content
    data as, 17
    digital content, 278
    handling, 67
    MIME extensions and, 203
    result method and, 123
    validation, 19
    WSDL abstract element, 187
    XML Schema, 20, 23
Content-ID header (MIME), 269

Content-Length header (HTTP)
    chunked transfer encoding, 49
    request/response, 13
    streaming media, 11
    XML-RPC communication, 40
    XML-RPC limitations, 50
Content-Location header (MIME), 269
Content-Range header (REST), 245, 255
Content-Transfer-Encoding header
    (HTTP), 11
Content-Type header (HTTP)
    request/response, 13
    streaming media, 11
    transporting messages and, 112
    XML-RPC communication, 40
    XML-RPC Meerkat example, 48
Content-Type header (MIME), 270
control data (REST data element), 238, 239
conversion
    integer to text, 115–122
    RPC::XMLSimple toolkit, 55
cookies
    Apache transport, 153
    authentication and, 144
    authentication headers and, 164
    CPAN uploads example, 132
    extension element limitations, 209
    improving code/service, 155
    username and password, 151
    WishListCustomer example, 147, 148,
        388–390
Coordinated Universal Time (UTC), 34
coordination, 291, 294, 295
copy_methods (RPC::XML::Server), 75
CORBA (Common Object Request Broker
    Architecture), 2, 4
Costello, Roger, 237
cover page service, 258, 259
Cozen, Simon, 300
CPAN (Comprehensive Perl Archive
    Network)
    Apache::AuthenNTLM module, 274
    Compress::Zlib module, 75
    cryptographic algorithms, 278
    Crypt::SOAP::Transport class, 182
    Digest::HMAC module, 273
    installing SSL modules, 120
    Net::Jabber module, 168, 169
    Net::Server module, 53, 67, 73
    resource defined, 239
    REST principles, 239
    RPC::XML Simple toolkit, 53

SOAP::MIME package, 270
toolkits for Perl, 114
uploads example, 132–136
WSDL::Generator package, 212
XML::LibXML module, 21
XML::Parser module, 21, 52, 67
XML::RSS module, 123
CreateCoordinationContext operation
    (WS-Coordination), 294
credentials method (RPC::XML::Client), 316
cron jobs, 48, 174
cryptographic algorithms
    hash functions, 273
    integrity and, 272
    symmetric/asymmetric, 278
    XML security standards and, 276
    XML Signature and, 278
    (see also encryption)
Crypt::SOAP::Transport class, 182
Crypt::SSLeay module, 120
current actor, 90
CVS (Concurrent Version Control), 29–31

D

data
    complex types and, 27
    managing with SOAP, 130, 131
    processing instructions, 18
    reading example, 232–234
    saving, 229
    UDDI registries, 216, 230
    XML building block, 17, 18
data confidentiality (see confidentiality)
DATA element (DIME), 270
data element (SOAP Header), 93
data encapsulation, 123, 136, 176
data encoding
    enc label and, 188
    HTTP bindings and, 202
    IPC and, 155
    remote method, 130
    serializing data, 35, 60
    S/MIME and, 275
    SOAP encodingStyle attribute, 89
    SOAP messages, 97–105
    SOAP-ENC label, 87
    SOAP::Header class, 164
    transforms and, 279
    UTF-8, 299
    XML Signature and, 278
    XML-RPC and, 33, 34
data integrity (see integrity)

data representation
    complex types and, 28
    XML and, 3, 13, 13–19
DataEncodingUnknown fault code
    (SOAP 1.2), 108
dataof method (SOAP::SOM), 334
dataTime.iso8601 type (XMLRPC::Lite), 62
datatypes
    SOAP, 31, 124
    WSDL, 187, 189
    XML Schema, 25
    XML-RPC supported, 33
dates/times, 34
date_time method, (RPC::XMLSimple::
    Client), 55, 306
dateTime type (XML Schema), 26
dateTime.iso8601 type (XML-RPC), 33,
    34, 56
DB_File module (Perl), 140, 383–386
DBI module (SOAP), 136
DCOM (Distributed Component Object
    Model), 2
debug signal (SOAP::Trace), 347
debugging
    SOAP::Lite and, 126
    SOAP::Trace class, 126, 127
    XMLRPC::Lite and, 62, 63
decimal type (XML Schema), 26
declaring
    complex types, 28
    namespaces, 15, 86, 87
decode method (RPC::XMLSimple), 304
decoding, 279
decryption, 280, 285
definitions element (WSDL), 188, 189
DELETE method (HTTP/REST), 244, 245,
    255, 256, 258
DELETE operation, 242, 246
delete_binding call (UDDI), 230
delete_business call (UDDI), 230
delete_method (RPC::XML::Server), 75, 320
delete_publisherAssertions call (UDDI), 230
delete_service call (UDDI), 230
delete_signature (RPC::XML), 323
delete_tModel call (UDDI), 230
deleting
    data from UDDI registries, 230
    resources, 245
    routing entries, 265
desc element (WS-Referral), 266

description element
  UDDI bindingTemplate structure, 222
  UDDI businessEntity structure, 215, 218
  UDDI businessService structure, 215, 220
  UDDI tModel structure, 223
  WS-Inspection, 287, 288
deserializer method
  SOAP::Server class, 342
  XMLRPC::Lite class, 308
detached signatures, 279
detail element (SOAP), 106
DevelopMentor, 115
die keyword (Perl), 60
die statement (RPC::XMLSimple), 55, 56
digest authentication, 274
Digest::HMAC module (CPAN), 273
digital rights management, 273, 276
digital signatures
  defined, 273
  error notification and, 94
  message validation and, 96
  XML Signature, 277–279
digital watermarking, 272
DIME (Direct Internet Message Encapsulation), 268, 270, 271
DIME header, 270
discard_authToken call (UDDI), 229
DISCO specification, 287
discovery, web services, 287–289
discoveryURL element (UDDI), 218
dispatch method (RPC::XML::Server), 321
dispatch signal (SOAP::Trace), 346
dispatch_from setting (SOAP::Lite), 126, 128
dispatch_to method
  SOAP::Server class, 343
  XMLRPC::Lite, 65, 66
dispatch_with method
  SOAP::Server class, 343
  SOAP::Transport::LOCAL, 408
Distributed Component Object Model (DCOM), 2
!DOCTYPE element, 18
Document Object Model (see DOM)
document style, 291–293
Document Type Declaration (see DTD)
documentation
  SOAP::Lite signals, 62, 63
  system.methodHelp method, 51
documentation element (WSDL), 189
DOM (Document Object Model), 21, 189
domain model (REST), 248–251

double method (RPC::XMLSimple), 55, 304
double type (XML-RPC), 33, 56, 62
DTD (Document Type Declaration)
  replacement argument, 23, 24
  SOAP messages, 84
  XML and, 19, 20
  XML-RPC specification, 38
D-U-N-S number (Dun & Bradstreet), 217, 224
durability (transactions), 293
Dylan, toolkit for, 32

E

&eacute entity, 18, 23
ebXML (Electronic Business XML), 31, 296, 297
editing, business information, 228–230
EDOC (Enterprise Distributed Object Computing), 296
effects, 283
Eiffel, toolkit for, 32
Electronic Business XML (see ebXML)
electronic mail (see email)
element type (arrays), 102
elements
  accessors, 98, 100
  array elements, 35
  attributes and, 16
  complex types, 28
  complex types and, 27
  DTD declaring, 19
  empty elements, 14, 34
  empty structs and, 36
  namespaces and, 15, 17
  namespaces within, 15
  REST, 238
  WSDL, 187, 209–211
  XML building block, 14–15
  in XML documents, 36
  XML Schema, 23, 27
  XML Schema primary components and, 26
email
  for announcements, 132
  CPAN uploads example, 133
  HTTP request/response cycle, 10
  POP3 and, 160
  transport mechanisms and, 170
embedding
  recursive, 34
  XML documents, 267

empty activity (BPEL), 298
empty elements, 14, 34
enc label
    SOAP-ENC label, 87
    WSDL documents, 188
encapsulation, data, 123, 136, 176
Encode module, 299
encode_call method
    (RPC::XMLSimple), 304
encode_fault method
    (RPC::XMLSimple), 304
encode_response method
    (RPC::XMLSimple), 304
encoding method (SOAP::Lite), 300, 329
encoding (see data encoding)
encodingStyle attribute (SOAP)
    Body element, 96
    data encoding, 89, 97
    detail block and, 106
    Envelope element, 87
    purpose, 88
    soap:body element, 198
    soap:header element, 199
encodingStyle method (SOAP::Data),
    130, 333
encprefix method
    SOAP::Lite class, 329
    SOAP::Serializer class, 338
EncryptedData element (XML), 280, 285
EncryptedKey element (XML), 285
encryption
    confidentiality and, 272
    decryption, 280, 285
    HTTP messages and, 86
    sample transport module, 409
    Security header and, 285
    transport module example, 181, 182
    WS-Policy, 286
    XML Encryption specification, 279–281
    (see also cryptographic algorithms)
__END__ token, 77
endpoint method
    SOAP::Lite class, 181, 328
    SOAP::Transport class, 124, 352, 354
    XMLRPC::Lite class, 307
Enterprise Distributed Object Computing
    (EDOC), 296
entities
    DTD declaring, 19
    MIME specification and, 269
    XML predefined, 17, 18
    XML Schema limitations, 23

entity reference (XML), 17
env namespace label (SOAP-ENV label), 87
env:DataEncodingUnknown fault code
    (SOAP 1.2), 111
Envelope element (SOAP)
    Fault element, 105
    message closing, 95
    namespaces, 85, 86, 87, 89
    URNs, 117
envelope method
    SOAP::Serializer class, 338
    SOAP::SOM class, 334
    XMLRPC::SOM class, 309
enveloped signatures, 278
envelopes
    authentication data in, 161
    SOAP headers, 161, 162
enveloping signatures, 279
envprefix method
    SOAP::Lite class, 329
    SOAP::Serializer class, 338
env:Server fault code (SOAP 1.2), 111
error handling
    digital signatures and, 94
    Fault element, 96
    HTTP error codes, 41
    RPC::XML, 68
    RPC::XMLSimple, 56
    SOAP Fault element, 105–108
    SOAP::Fault and, 150
    subclassing and, 147
    well-formed XML documents and, 19
    XML-RPC, 4, 39, 50
    (see also exception handling; fault
    handling)
error_handler method
    (RPC::XML::Client), 70, 316
escape characters, 202
events
    disabling, 127
    SOAP::Trace class, 126, 127
exception handling
    die calls, 56
    die statements, 55
    encoding exceptions, 3
    languages and, 42
    XMLRPC::Lite and, 60
    (see also error handling)
EXCHANGE command (HTTPR), 290
extensibility, 2
Extensible Markup Language (see XML)

Extensible Rights Markup Language
    (see XrML)
Extensible Stylesheet Language Template
    (see XSLT)

F

FastCGI protocol, 145, 300
fault element
    fault method, 61
    two-way models and, 195
    WSDL, 194, 196, 198
Fault element (SOAP), 96, 105–108, 110
fault handling
    BPEL and, 298
    decryption failure, 285
    news service example, 7
    REST and, 260
    (see also error handling)
fault method
    SOAP::SOM class, 131, 335
    XMLRPC::SOM class, 61, 309
fault signal (SOAP::Trace), 347
faultactor element (SOAP Fault
    element), 106
faultactor method
    SOAP::Fault class, 336
    SOAP::SOM class, 131, 335
faultcode element (SOAP), 106, 118, 199
faultcode method
    SOAP::Fault class, 336
    SOAP::Lite module, 122
    SOAP::SOM class, 131, 335
    XMLRPC::SOM class, 61, 309
faultdetail method
    SOAP::Fault class, 336
    SOAP::SOM class, 131, 335
fault_handler method
    (RPC::XML::Client), 69, 70, 316
faults
    CPAN uploads example, 134
    problem communication, 41
    return elements and, 118
    RPC over SOAP, 110, 111
    RPC::XML::fault class, 72
    RPC::XMLSimple::Client class and, 56
    soap:fault element, 199
    XML-RPC syntax, 39
faultstring element (SOAP), 106, 118, 199
faultstring method
    SOAP::Fault class, 336
    SOAP::Lite module, 122

SOAP::SOM class, 131, 335
XMLRPC::SOM class, 61, 62
file extensions, 252
filters, IO-based, 406
find operation, 227, 228
find_binding call (UDDI), 226, 233
find_business call (UDDI), 226, 232–234
findQualifier routine (UDDI::Data), 235
findQualifiers element (UDDI), 226, 228
findQualifiers routine (UDDI::Data), 235
find_relatedBusinesses call (UDDI), 226, 234
find_service call (UDDI), 226, 234
find_target method (SOAP::Server), 344
find_tModel call (UDDI), 226, 234
firewalls, 246, 275
flexibility, 160, 260
float type (SOAP), 98
for element (WS-Referral), 265
formatting text, 235
fragment identifier (REST), 241, 242
freeform signal (SOAP::Trace), 347
fromKey element (UDDI), 219, 220
Frontier content management system, 52
Frontier::RPC2 toolkit, 52
FTP, 112, 222, 407, 408
    (see also SOAP::Transport::FTP::Client
        class)
ftp://, 169
functions
    RPC::XML::Function, 74
    RPC::XML::Server class, 73
    XML-RPC process, 33
fwd element (WS-Routing), 263, 264

G

GET method (HTTP/REST), 244, 257, 259
GET operation (REST), 242, 246
GET request (HTTP), 11, 12, 201
get_assertionStatusReport call (UDDI), 229
get_authToken call (UDDI), 229
get_basic_credentials method
    (SOAP::Lite), 274
get_bindingDetail query routine
    (UDDI), 226
get_businessDetail query routine
    (UDDI), 226
get_businessDetailExt query routine
    (UDDI), 226
get_entries method (SOAP), 123
get_method (RPC::XML::Server), 75, 320
Getopt::Long method (UDDI::Lite), 235
Getopt::Std method, 132

get_publisherAssertions call (UDDI), 229
get_registeredInfo call (UDDI), 229
GET-RESPONDER-INFO command
    (HTTPR), 290
get_server method
    (Apache::RPC::Server), 325
get_serviceDetail query routine (UDDI), 226
get_tModelDetail call (UDDI), 226, 230
GIF, 241
global attributes, 88, 92–95
global positioning system (GPS), 171
global variables, 132, 147
GNU Zip compression algorithm, 49
go element (WS-Referral), 265
Google, 261
GPS (global positioning system), 171
granularity of interface, 292

H

handle method
    Jabber-based servers, 168
    server classes and, 139
    SOAP::Server, 181
    SOAP::Server class, 176, 179, 345
    SOAP::Transport, 348
    SOAP::Transport::HTTP::Daemon, 350
    SOAP::Transport::HTTP::Server, 349
    SOAP::Transport::IO::Server, 173
    SOAP::Transport::MQ::Server, 355
    SOAP::Transport::POP3::Server, 356
    SOAP::Transport::TCP::Server, 165, 357
    writing localized, 178, 179
    XMLRPC::Lite, 67
handler method
    Apache transport, 153
    Apache::RPC::Server, 78, 324
    Apache::RPC::Status, 325
    Apache::SOAP, 357
    SOAP::Transport::HTTP::Apache, 351
hash functions, 272, 273
hash references
    as arguments, 134
    autogenerated XML example, 118
    fault method, 61
    leading underscore, 178
    RPC::XMLSimple::Client, 54, 56
    RPC::XMLSimple::Daemon, 58
    simple_request method, 70
    SOAP::Server, 178
hash tables
    arguments to proxy method, 180
    array datatype, 34

CPAN upload example, 132
ordering of, 190
returned data, 142
send_receive method, 180
structure type as, 99
XML::Simple, 22
HEAD method (REST), 244
HEAD request (HTTP), 11
Header element (SOAP)
    Fault element and, 105
    message component, 85
    references example, 101
    RPC over SOAP and, 110
    specifics, 88–95
header method (SOAP::SOM), 334
$header variable, 164
headerof method (SOAP::SOM), 334
headers
    authentication tokens, 229
    SOAP envelope, 161, 162
    SOAP::Header class, 164
    WishListCustomer example, 400, 401
    WS-Routing and, 263
headers method (SOAP::SOM), 335
headers signal (SOAP::Trace), 347
hexadecimal representation, 267, 271
Host header (HTTP), 40
hostingRedirector element (UDDI), 222
hostnames, 11, 165
hr element, 14
href attribute (Content-ID header), 269
HTML
    entity reference, 17
    HTTP and, 9
    REST principles, 241
    screenscraping, 1
HTTP (Hypertext Transfer Protocol), as
    standard, 160
http://, 166, 169
HTTP GET request (see GET method)
HTTP (Hypertext Transfer Protocol)
    authentication and authorization, 246
    authentication tokens, 229
    basic authentication, 289
    binding in WSDL, 201–205
    cookie data example, 132
    message structure, 10–13
    MIME extensions and, 203
    port used, 275
    proxy method and, 125
    request delivery, 178
    REST and, 237, 239, 241

Index | 449

HTTP (*continued*)
  RPC fault codes, 111
  selecting transport, 145
  SOAP and, 115, 146–152
  SOAPAction header, 198
  transporting messages, 112
  ubiquity of, 9
  UDDI URLType attribute, 222
  URLs as endpoints, 134
  web services and, 3
  WSDL binding declaration, 196
  WS-Routing and, 263
  XML-RPC communication, 40, 41
  XMLRPC::Lite support, 65
HTTP over SSL, 86
HTTP over SSL/TLS (HTTPS), 222, 275
HTTP POST request (see POST request)
http:address element, 201, 202
http:binding element, 201
HTTP::Cookies package, 133
HTTP::Daemon class
  example, 396, 397
  LWP, 53, 58, 146
  RPC::XML::Server class, 67, 73
  WishListCustomer example, 386, 390, 391
http:operation element, 201, 202
HTTPR, 289, 291
HTTP::Request module, 48
https://, 166
HTTPS (HTTP over SSL/TLS), 222, 275
http:urlEncoded element, 201, 202
http:urlReplacement element, 201, 202, 203
Hypertext Transfer Protocol (see HTTP)

I

i4type (XML-RPC), 33
IBM
  BPEL, 297
  BPEL4WS, 296
  HTTPR, 289
  MQSeries software, 169, 289
  standards process, 5
  UDDI partnership, 214
  WS-Attachments specification, 271
  WSDL authoring, 185
  WSFL, 297
  WS-Inspection specification, 287
  WS-Security specification, 283
ID element (DIME), 270
id element (WS-Routing), 264
identification, 272

identifierBag element, UDDI tModel structure, 223, 224
IDL (Interface Design Language), 2
if element (WS-Referral), 265
If-Match header (REST), 245, 258
If-None-Match header (REST), 245, 258
img element, 14
import element (WSDL), 189, 210, 211
in method (SOAP::Transport::IO::Server), 351
inflation, 279
inheritance
  server classes and, 162
  SOAP::Server class, 178
  SOAP::Transport::LOCAL::Client class, 177
  UDDI::Lite classes, 231
  use attribute and, 27
init_handler method
  Apache::RPC::Server class, 78, 324
  Apache::RPC::Status class, 326
in/out parameters, 210
inspection element (WS-Inspection), 287
installation, SOAP::Lite module, 119, 120
instanceParms element (UDDI), 225
instant messaging, 3, 167
int method (RPC::XMLSimple::Client), 55
int type
  RPC::XMLSimple, 56
  SOAP, 98
  XML Schema, 26
  XML-RPC, 33, 37
  XMLRPC::Lite, 62
Int type (SOAP), 103
Intalio, 296
integer type (XML Schema), 26
integers, converting to text, 115–122
integrity
  defined, 272
  SSL/TLS, 275
  WS-Security, 284, 285
  XML Signature, 276
intellectual property, 214
Interface Design Language (IDL), 2
interfaces
  chatty, 292
  chunky, 292
  DCOM, 2
  granularity of, 292
  improving code, 152–158
  introspection, 67, 77
  managing, 140–144

SOAP servers and, 146–152
SOAP::Transport::LOCAL::Client
    class, 176
UDDI, 225–231
WSDL, 4, 187, 424–430
XML::Simple module and, 22
intermediaries
    defined, 263
    message forwarding and, 265
    message routing and, 262
    REST and, 239
    WS-Policy, 286
    WS-Routing, 264, 265
    (see also nodes)
international character sets, 299, 300
Internet Relay Chat, 167
interoperability
    COM and, 2
    drawbacks, 6
    fault code consistency and, 107
    REST principles and, 241
    XML-RPC and, 50, 51
interprocess communication (IPC), 155
introspection interface, 67, 77
invocation model, 226
invoke activity (BPEL), 298
IO::Socket class family, 165
io_socket_class method
        (SOAP::Transport::TCP), 356
IO::Socket::INET class, 58
IO::Socket::SSL module, 120
IPC (interprocess communication), 155
IPSec (IP Security Protocol), 275
ISBN number, 140, 142
is_fault method (RPC::XML), 72, 313, 314
ISO 8601 standard, 34
isolation (transactions), 293
is_valid method (RPC::XML), 322

J

jabber://, 168, 169, 179, 403
Jabber protocol
    acceptance of, 161
    proxy method and, 125
    server example, 403, 404
    SOAP and, 112
    transport classes, 167–169
Java language
    arguments list and, 41
    BPEL documents, 298
    Object type equivalent, 103
    overloaded methods, 42

journal system
    posting entries, 132, 134
    use.perl.org, 122, 127, 128, 132
JPG, 241

K

Kerberos tickets, 284
keyed hash, 273
keyedReference element (UDDI), 219, 224
KeyInfo element (XML Signature), 276
keyName attribute (UDDI), 219, 220, 224
keys
    avoiding collisions, 178
    private keys, 278
    public keys, 281
    search keys, 227
    secret-key, 278
    send_receive method hash table, 180
    UDDI registries, 216
    XKMS, 276
    X-KRSS, 281
keyValue attribute (UDDI), 219, 220, 224
key/value pairs
    add_entry method, 134
    order of, 35
    struct datatype, 35
    structure type, 99
Kulchenko, Pavel, 52, 59, 119

L

Library for WWW Programming in Perl
        (see LWP)
libxml2 library, 21
libxslt library, 21
link element (WS-Inspection), 287, 288
linking
    import element, 210
    XML documents, 267
Lisp, 32
list_methods (RPC::XML::Server), 320
list_servers method
        (Apache::RPC::Server), 325
load method (SOAP::Schema), 340
local types, 26
location attribute
    http:urlReplacement element, 202
    soap:address element, 200
    WS-Inspection description element, 288
location handler, 53, 67, 80
loose coupling, 4

LWP (Library for WWW Programming in Perl)
  additional resources, 13
  HTTP::Daemon, 53, 58, 67, 73
  HTTP::Daemon class, 146
  modules in, 48
  PRC::XMLSimple toolkit and, 53
  XML::Parser toolkit and, 52
  XML-RPC Meerkat example, 44
  XML::RSS and, 22
LWP::UserAgent class
  authentication, 274
  CPAN uploads, 134
  Meerkat example, 48
  REST example, 256
  wrapping, 118

M

MAC (message authentication code), 246
mailboxes, REST principles and, 242, 243
MAILTO (see specific classes)
mail-transfer agent (MTA), 172
make_fault method
  SOAP::Server class, 345
  SOAP::Transport::HTTP::Server class, 350
make_method tool, 77
make_response method, (SOAP::Transport::HTTP::Server), 350
make_url method, (Apache::RPC::Status), 326
match method
  SOAP::SOM, 157, 333
  XMLRPC::SOM, 309
match_signature method (RPC::XML), 323
maxOccurs attribute (XML Schema), 27
MD5-based algorithm, 144
Meerkat news service
  defined, 43
  example, 7
  RPC::XML example, 68–69, 370–373
  RPC::XMLSimple example, 53–55, 364–367
  XML-RPC and REST, 261
  XML-RPC example, 42–49, 360–364
  XMLRPC::Lite example, 6, 59–61, 367–370
message authentication code (MAC), 246
message element (WSDL), 189, 210
Message Exchange Pattern (SOAP), 261

messages
  attachments and, 270
  compressing, 49
  full web services and, 262
  HTTP structure, 10–13
  MQ connections and, 169
  packaging, 262
  piping to scripts, 134
  REST principles and, 243
  routing capabilities, 263–267
  security and, 271
  SOAP functionality, 84
  transport protocols and, 112
  UDDI registries, 215
  WSDL document component, 187
  WS-Routing and, 263, 265
  (see also requests; responses; SOAP messages; XML messages)
messaging style (see document style)
META element (HTML), 288
Meta package, 137
Meta::Comm::Soap::Client class, 137
Meta::Comm::Soap::Server class, 137
metadata
  DIME headers, 270
  representation metadata, 238, 239, 252
  SOAP Header element, 88
  transition of messages, 84
method method
  SOAP::SOM class, 131, 335
  XMLRPC::SOM class, 309
method signal (SOAP::Trace), 347
method signatures
  RPC::XMLSimple::Daemon class, 58
  system.methodSignature method, 51
  XML-RPC and, 41, 42
methodCall element (XML-RPC), 36
methodName element (XML-RPC), 36
methodResponse element (XML-RPC), 38
methods
  accessor methods, 125
  dispatching, 127–129
  making requests and, 36
  overloaded, 42
  overloading, 147
  overriding, 79
  procedure name as, 109
  REST, 244–245
  return value restrictions, 42
  RPC style and, 292
  RPC::XML::Method, 74
  RPC::XML::Server class and, 73

search methods, 155
sharing, 79
Microsoft
   BPEL, 297
   BPEL4WS, 296
   Component Object Model, 2
   DCOM, 2
   NTLM authentication, 274
   standards process, 5
   UDDI partnership, 214
   WS-Attachments, 271
   WSDL authoring, 185
   WS-Inspection, 287
   WS-Routing, 263
   WS-Security, 283
   XLANG, 297
Microsoft Message Queuing, 289
Microsoft .NET framework, 112, 185, 211
MIME (Multipurpose Internet Mail Extensions)
   binding in WSDL, 201–205
   packaging and, 268, 269, 270
   soap:body and soap:header, 199
   SOAP::Lite options, 120
   WSDL binding declaration, 196
MIME::Base64 module, 33
mime:content element, 203, 205
mime:mimeXml element, 204
mime:multipartRelated element, 204
mime:part element, 204
minOccurs attribute (XML Schema), 27, 190
mod_perl
   ActiveState, 300
   Apache combined with, 145
   content handling, 67
   enabling, 41
   improving code/service, 154
   interface, 158
   location handlers and, 67
   server side and, 53
   SOAP servers and, 153
mq://, 169
MQ protocol, 178, 404, 405
MTA (mail-transfer agent), 172
Multipurpose Internet Mail Extensions (see MIME)
multirefinplace method (SOAP::Lite), 330
mustUnderstand attribute (SOAP)
   actors/roles, 89
   authentication headers, 164
   global attribute, 88
   Header blocks, 92

message body, 96
message routing, 263
purpose, 91
server authentication, 162
MustUnderstand fault code (SOAP), 107, 108
mustUnderstand method (SOAP::Data), 333
myuri method (SOAP::Server), 342

N

NAICS (North American Industry Code Standard), 217
name attribute
   authentication headers and, 164
   binding element, 197
   definitions element, 189
   fault element and, 196
   input/output elements (WSDL), 195
   operation element, 197
   part element and, 192
   port element, 200
   service element, 200, 212
   soap:body and soap:header, 199
   soap:fault element, 199
   soap:headerfault element, 199
   XML Schema, 26, 27
name element
   member container and, 35
   SOAP::Header class, 164
   UDDI businessEntity structure, 215, 218
   UDDI businessService structure, 215, 220
   UDDI tModel structure, 223
   WS-Inspection, 287
name method
   RPC::XML server classes, 322
   RPC::XML::request class, 314
   SOAP::Data class, 130, 157, 332
name routine (UDDI::Data), 235
namespace attribute
   import element, 211
   soap:body element, 198
   soap:fault element, 199
   soap:header element, 199
namespace element (SOAP::Header), 164
namespaces
   arrayType attribute, 101
   attributes and, 16
   declaring, 86, 87
   declaring default, 15
   declaring elements, 17
   declaring within elements, 15
   elements in, 98

namespaces (*continued*)
　Envelope element, 85
　Fault element within, 105
　header element blocks and, 88
　import element and, 210
　labels for, 188
　mustUnderstand attribute, 91
　parsing and, 84
　period in, 37
　predefined for encoding, 89
　referencedNamespace attribute, 288
　REST and, 239
　RPC::XML::Server class, 72
　schema documents and, 24
　SOAP Body element, 86, 96
　SOAP messages, 96
　SOAP standard and, 4
　SOAP::Lite module, 129
　SOAP::payload module, 136
　target, 198
　WSDL binding declarations, 196
　WSDL documentation element, 189
　WSDL documents, 188
　XML and, 14–15
　XML::Parser tool, 21
namespaceuriof method (SOAP::SOM), 334
naming conventions
　abbreviated names, 118
　client classes, 179, 180
　Jabber-based servers, 168
　leading underscore, 178
　parameter name as selector, 155
　slashes, 243
　URI strings for TCP transport, 166
　WSDL document operations, 195
　XML-RPC elements, 37
negativeInteger type (SOAP), 98
negotiation
　file extensions and, 252
　full web services, 262
　headers and, 253
　HTTPR, 290
Net::Jabber module (CPAN), 168, 169
Net::Server package (CPAN), 53, 67, 73
new method
　Apache::RPC::Server class, 324
　Apache::RPC::Status class, 325
　client transport classes, 180
　RPC::XML classes, 69, 71, 312, 315, 317, 318, 321
　RPC::XMLSimple class, 55, 303, 305, 306
　SOAP::Data class, 332

SOAP::EnvelopeMaker class, 118
SOAP::Fault class, 336
SOAP::Lite class, 125, 327
SOAP::Schema class, 340
SOAP::Serializer class, 338
SOAP::Server class, 342
SOAP::SOM class, 333
SOAP::Transport class, 337, 348, 353, 355, 357
　specialized constructors, 178
　WishListCustomer class, 142, 148, 149
　WSDL, 192
　XMLRPC::Data class, 308
　XMLRPC::Lite class, 60, 61, 307
news service (see Meerkat news service)
NMTOKEN (XML Schema type), 26
Node element (SOAP 1.2), 106
nodes
　actor attribute, 88
　defined, 89
　intermediaries as, 264
　null actor, 90
　providing for next URI, 91
　SOAP Node element, 106
　userUpdate block and, 93
　(see also intermediaries; servers)
nonrepudiation, 272
North American Industry Code Standard (NAICS), 217
notification model (WSDL), 194, 195
NTLM challenge/response authentication, 274
null actor, 90, 94
NumToWords_English element (SOAP), 117

O

OASIS (Organization for the Advancement of Structured Information Standards), 276, 296
Object element (XML Signature), 279
Object Management Group, 296
Object Request Broker (ORB), 2
objects by reference, 151, 154, 192
objects signal (SOAP::Trace), 347
objects_by_reference method (SOAP::Server), 139, 154, 343
obligations, 283
on_action method
　SOAP::Lite class, 331
　SOAP::Server class, 344

on_debug method (SOAP::Lite), 331
on_dispatch method (SOAP::Server), 344
one-way model (WSDL), 194, 195
on_fault method
  auto-dispatching and, 63
  SOAP::Lite class, 331
  XMLRPC::Lite class, 60, 61, 308
on_nonserialized method (SOAP::Lite), 331
opacity, 242
open standards, 1, 3
operation element
  binding, 212
  name attribute, 199
  parameterOrder attribute, 209, 210
  portType block, 193
operations
  idempotent, 244
  overloaded, 207–209
  overloading, 205–209
  REST and, 241, 261
  transforms and, 279
  WSDL and, 187, 193–196
operator attribute
  UDDI businessEntity structure, 218
  UDDI tModel structure, 223
optimization, web services, 300
OPTIONS element (DIME), 270
options method
  SOAP::Server class, 342
  XMLRPC::Lite and, 66
ORB (Object Request Broker), 2
orchestration, 291
Organization for the Advancement of
    Structured Information Standards
    (see OASIS)
out method, (SOAP::Transport::IO::
    Server), 351
OutcomeNotification protocol
    (WS-Coordination), 295
outputxml method (SOAP::Lite), 328
overloaded methods, 42
overloaded operations, 207–209
overloading operations, 205–209
overviewDoc element (UDDI), 223
overviewURL element (UDDI), 223

P

P3P (Platform for Privacy Preferences), 276
packaging, web services, 267–271
param container (XML-RPC), 37, 38
parameterOrder attribute (WSDL operation
    element), 209, 210

parameters
  arbitrary, 41
  authInfo element, 230
  client/server interaction, 2
  defining order, 209
  empty, 37
  findQualifiers element, 226, 228
  HTTP extension bindings, 202
  in/out parameters, 110, 210
  languages and, 41
  name as selector, 155
  named, 98
  name=value pairs, 201
  new method, 55
  overlapping arguments, 110
  params element and, 37
  returning objects, 130
  UDDI query routines, 226
  WSDL documents and, 4
parameters signal (SOAP::Trace), 347
params element (XML-RPC), 37, 38
paramsall method
  SOAP::SOM class, 131, 336
  XMLRPC::SOM class, 310
paramsin method
  SOAP::SOM class, 131, 156, 336
  XMLRPC::SOM class, 310
paramsout method (SOAP::SOM), 131, 336
parse method (SOAP::Schema), 340
parsers/parsing
  command-line, 235
  entities and, 18
  MIME messages, 270
  regexp-based parsing, 302
  schema documents and, 20
  SOAP messages, 84
  SOAP standard and, 4
  XML documents and, 19
  XML::LibXML module, 21
  (see also XML::Parser module; XML
      parsers)
part attribute
  soap:body element, 198
  soap:header element, 199
partial arrays, 103
parts attribute (soap:body element), 198
passwords
  basic authentication and, 274
  cookies and, 151
  digital authentication and, 274
  MAC-based, 246
  secure transport, 86

Index | 455

path component (URI), 241
PAUSE (Perl Authors Upload Server)
    daemon, 132
PDF format, 251, 253
performance
    web services, 298, 300
    XML parsers, 22
Perl Authors Upload Server (PAUSE)
    daemon, 132
<Perl> configuration block, 153, 154
Perl language
    arbitrary parameters, 41
    array dimensions, 103
    auto-loading, 127, 129
    BPEL documents, 298
    CPAN toolkit, 114
    DB_File module, 140
    LWP and, 13
    overloading operations, 209
    special variables, 62, 69
    undef type, 50
    Unicode support, 298
    -w flag, 129
    XML modules and tools, 21, 22
    XML-RPC toolkit, 3, 32, 52, 53
#!perl start-up line, 77
PerlChildInitHandler, 78, 158
PerlEx (ActiveState), 300
PerlHandler, 78
PhaseZero protocol (WS-Coordination), 295
PHP language, 32, 41, 51
pick activity (BPEL), 298
pipelining, 134, 290
PKI (Public Key Infrastructure), 281
Platform for Privacy Preferences (P3P), 276
pop://, 171
POP3 protocol
    client replies, 179
    email and, 160
    request delivery, 178
    server example, 405
    transports for client/server, 170, 172
    XMLRPC::Lite, 59, 65
portability, 298
ports
    binding, 58, 165
    HTTP, 275
    Jabber service, 169
    W3C specifications, 200
    WSDL document component, 187
portType block (WSDL), 193–196

POST method (HTTP/REST), 244, 245, 255, 256, 257
POST operation (REST), 242, 246
POST request (HTTP)
    clients, 40
    example, 11
    extending WSDL, 201
    HTTPR commands, 290
    purpose, 11, 12
    URL encoding, 203
    XML-RPC limitations, 50
postfix (MTA), 172
prefix method (SOAP::Data), 332
prefixes
    attributes and, 17
    namespaces and, 15
privacy
    defined, 273
    P3P and, 276
    WS-Policy, 286
    WS-Privacy, 286
private-key cryptography, 278
problem domains, REST and, 242
procedure calls
    client/server interaction, 2
    encoding, 3
    mapping, 3
    RPC::XML::Procedure, 74
    RPC::XML::Server class, 73
    (see also RPC)
processing instructions
    SOAP 1.2, 84
    XML, 18
procmail (mail-filter program), 134
product_tokens method
    RPC::XML::Server class, 318
    SOAP::Transport::HTTP::Server
        class, 350
programming
    BPEL specification, 297
    granularity of interfaces, 292
    LWP and, 13
    new transport modules, 177–182
    REST, 246–261
    UDDI::Lite, 231–236
    WSDL, 211–213
protocols
    choosing, 160, 161
    coordination, 294, 295
    full web services, 262
    HTTP requests, 11
    HTTP response lines, 12

security and, 271
two-phase commit, 293
(see also specific protocols; transport protocols)
proxy method
auto-dispatching, 63
constructors, 180
CPAN uploads, 134
SOAP::Lite, 123, 125, 328
SOAP::Transport, 124, 179, 180, 337
transport module, 181
XMLRPC::Lite, 60, 61, 307
Public Key Infrastructure (PKI), 281
public keys, 281
public-key cryptography, 278
publisherAssertion structure (UDDI)
API calls, 229
keyedReference element, 224
specifics, 215, 217–220
publisherAssertions structure (UDDI), 229, 230
publishing, business information, 225–231
PULL command (HTTPR), 290
purchase order service, 256–258
PUSH command (HTTPR), 290
PUT method (HTTP/REST), 244, 245, 255, 256, 257
PUT operation (REST), 242, 246
Python scripting language, 3

Q

queries
format information, 252
SAML, 282
XPath, 39, 48
query component (URI), 241
query referral message (WS-Referral), 266
query routines, 232–234

R

random access, 267, 268
rapid application development, 2, 5
Ray, Randy J., 67
readable method
SOAP::Lite class, 329
XMLRPC::Lite class, 308
Reason element (SOAP 1.2), 106
receive activity (BPEL), 298
Receiver fault code (SOAP 1.2), 108
recursive embedding, 34
ref attribute (XML Schema), 27

ref element (WS-Referral), 265
Reference element (XML Signature), 279
ReferenceList element (XML Signature), 285
references
aggregating, 287
arrays and, 104
assuming valid, 123
external resources, 101
location handler as, 80
on_fault method and, 61
RPC::XML::Server class methods, 73
XMLRPC::SOM class, 61
referral header messages (WS-Referral), 266
referral statement (WS-Referral), 265, 266
refld element (WS-Referral), 266
Register operation (WS-Coordination), 294
register referral messages (WS-Referral), 266
registration service (WS-Coordination), 294
registries (see UDDI registries)
relatedTo element (WS-Routing), 264
relatesTo element (WS-Routing), 264
reliability, 257
reliable HTTP (see HTTPR)
reliable messaging, 289–291, 295
reload method (RPC::XML), 323
Remote Procedure Call (see RPC)
reply activity (BPEL), 298
replyqueue method, (SOAP::Transport::MQ::Client), 354
REPORT command (HTTPR), 290
representation
changing resource, 245
creating multiple, 251–252
defined, 238
REST definition, 238, 239
REST principles, 241
transformation of, 256
XML as, 249
representation metadata (REST), 238, 239, 252
Representational State Transfer (see REST)
request lines (HTTP), 11, 12
request method
global variables, 147
RPC::XML::Client class, 315
SOAP::Transport::HTTP class, 147, 349
requestqueue method, (SOAP::Transport::MQ::Client), 354
request-response model (WSDL), 194, 195

requests
    HTTP headers required by XML-RPC, 40
    HTTP message structure, 10–13
    MAILTO and, 170
    protocols and delivery of, 178
    RPC::XMLSimple::Daemon class, 58
    SOAP and, 3
requests method (RPC::XML::Server), 318
resource identifiers (see URIs)
resource metadata (REST data
        element), 238, 239
resource modeling (REST), 241–244,
        248–251
resource (REST), 238
resources
    addressable, 246
    deleting, 245
    determining contents, 242
    HTTP requests, 11
    modeling, 248
    modifying, 244, 245
    REST, 239, 241, 243, 261
response lines, 12
response method
    RPC::XML::Server class, 318
    SOAP::Transport::HTTP::Server
        class, 349
responses
    Content-Length header (HTTP), 40
    delivery considerations, 179
    HTTP error codes, 41
    HTTP message structure, 10–13
    return elements, 118
    SOAP and, 3
    (see also messages)
REST (Representational State Transfer)
    defined, 237–239
    documenting service APIs, 259
    methods, 244–245
    principles, 240–244
    programming, 246–261
    reliable messaging, 289
    shortcomings, 4
    web sites, 437
restriction
    complex types and, 28
    simple types and, 27
result method
    CPAN uploads example, 134
    Meerkat news service example, 7
    SOAP::Lite class, 123, 128
    SOAP::SOM class, 131, 336

XMLRPC::Lite and, 61
XMLRPC::SOM class, 61, 310
result signal (SOAP::Trace), 347
return values
    client/server interaction, 2
    complex types, 142
    cookies and, 147
    method restrictions, 42
    objects in, 130
    remote procedures, 50
    RPC over SOAP responses, 110
    RPC::XMLSimple, 54, 56
    send_request method, 70
    XML-RPC responses, 38
    XMLRPC::SOM class, 61
rev element (WS-Routing), 264
reverse paths, 264, 265
RFC 2246, 275
role attribute (SOAP 1.2), 89, 90
Role element (SOAP 1.2), 106
roles
    access control, 272
    transition of messages, 84
    WS-Referral, 266
    (see also actors)
root attribute (SOAP), 105
root method
    SOAP::Data class, 130, 333
    SOAP::SOM class, 334
routers, SOAP, 265–267
rpc namespace label, 111
RPC over SOAP, 108–111
RPC (Remote Procedure Call)
    converting integers to text, 115
    dispatch_with method, 408
    encapsulation within SOAP, 97
    Meerkat example, 48
    parameter order, 209
    request/response, 36, 38
    REST and, 4, 246
    RPC::XMLSimple::Client Class, 55
    send_request method, 70
    SOAP over HTTP, 125
    SOAP support, 84
    web services history, 2
    WSDL and, 192, 210
    XML-RPC and, 32, 50
    XMLRPC::Lite, 60, 61
    (see also methods; RPC over SOAP)
RPC style, 291–293
rpc:BadArguments fault code
        (SOAP 1.2), 111

RPC_BASE64 function (RPC::XML), 314
RPC_BOOLEAN function (RPC::XML), 314
RPC_DATETIME_ISO8601 function
    (RPC::XML), 314
RPC_DOUBLE function (RPC::XML), 314
RPC_I4 function (RPC::XML), 314
RPC_INT function (RPC::XML), 314
rpc:ProcedureNotPresent fault code
    (SOAP 1.2), 111
RpcServerDir directives, 79
RpcServerMethod directives, 79
RPC_STRING function (RPC::XML), 314
RPC::XML module
    CPAN upload example, 133
    examples, 370–373
    message compression, 49
    programming reference, 312–326
    requirements, 52
    XML-RPC and, 67–81
RPC::XML::Client class, 69–72, 315–317
RPC::XML::fault class, 72
RPC::XML::Function class, 74, 323
RPC::XML::Method class, 74, 323
RPC::XML::Procedure class, 74, 323
RPC::XML::Server class, 67, 72–77, 317–321
RPC::XMLSimple toolkit
    data classes in, 56
    origin of, 52
    programming reference, 303–306
    sample code, 364–367
    XML-RPC examples, 53–58
RPC::XMLSimple::Client class
    client example, 54
    example details, 55, 56
    methods, 305, 306
    toolkit example, 53
RPC::XMLSimple::Daemon class, 53,
    56–58, 306
RSS
    client feed, 158
    dispatching method, 128
    representation format, 251
    use.perl.org journal stream, 122–124
Ruby language, 32

S

SAML (Security Assertion Markup
    Language), 276, 282, 283
SAP, 296
save_binding call (UDDI), 229
save_business call (UDDI), 229
save_service call (UDDI), 229

save_tModel call (UDDI), 229
SAX (Simple API for XML), 21, 301
SAX2, 21
schema method (SOAP::Schema), 340
Scheme, toolkit for, 32
screenscraping, 1
searching
    search engines, 4, 239
    search qualifiers, 226
    UDDI query routines, 226
    WishListCustomer, 394–396
secret-key cryptography, 278
Secure SHell (SSH), 31
Secure Socket Layer (SSL), 86
Secured/Multipurpose Internet Mail
    Extensions (S/MIME), 275
security
    capability, 246
    defined, 272
    full web services, 262
    HTTP over SSL, 86
    inspection documents, 288
    levels addressed, 271
    SOAP support, 84
    specifications, 283–287
    transport level, 274–275
    web services and, 271–273
    XML standards, 275–283
Security Assertion Markup Language
    (see SAML)
Security element (WS-Security), 284
Security header (WS-Security), 285
security tokens, 285, 286
self method (SOAP::Lite), 330
Sender fault code (SOAP 1.2), 108
sendmail MTA, 172
send_receive method
    SOAP::Lite, 180, 181
    SOAP::Transport, 348
    SOAP::Transport::HTTP::Client, 118
    SOAP::Transport::LOCAL::Client, 353
    SOAP::Transport::MQ::Client, 354
    SOAP::Transport::TCP::Client, 356
send_request method
    (RPC::XML::Client), 69, 70, 316
sequence activity (BPEL), 298
serialization (see data encoding)
serializer method
    SOAP::Lite class, 328
    SOAP::Server class, 342
    XMLRPC::Lite class, 308
serve method (RPC::XMLSimple), 304

server classes
    authentication and, 161
    creating generic, 162, 163
    generic, 162, 163
    handle method and, 178
    Jabber-based, 168
    reasons for writing new, 177
    RPC::XML module, 321–323
    SOAP::Lite, 138, 139
    SOAP::Transport::IO::Server, 173
    (see also specific classes)
Server fault code (SOAP 1.1), 107
Server header (HTTP), 13, 40
server_loop method
        (RPC::XML::Server), 75, 320
servers
    absolute vs. relative URLs, 249
    clients as, 408
    determining representation format, 252
    discover interface, 51
    HTTP ubiquity, 3
    HTTP::Daemon class example, 386, 387,
        390, 391, 396
    Jabber protocol requirements, 168
    Jabber-based example, 403, 404
    method signatures, 42
    MQ-based example, 404, 405
    POP3-based example, 405
    proxying services, 136
    RPC::XML example, 72–81
    RPC::XMLSimple example, 53, 56–58
    server authentication, 161–163
    signatures and, 109
    SOAP support for conversations, 84
    SOAP::Lite and, 121, 138, 139
    TCP-based example, 401, 402
    transport protocols, 165–173
    XML::Parser module, 300
    XML-RPC request/response, 41
    XMLRPC::Lite example, 64–67
    (see also SOAP servers)
service element
    add_entry operation, 207
    characteristics, 199, 200
    name attribute, 212
    WS-Inspection, 287
service level agreement, 263
service method (SOAP::Lite), 328
serviceKey attribute (UDDI), 221, 222
services method (SOAP::Schema), 340
set_body method
        (SOAP::EnvelopeMaker), 117, 118

set_publisherAssertions call (UDDI),
        229, 230
SetUser method (WSDL), 192
SGML, 20, 23
share_methods
    Apache::RPC::Server class, 80
    RPC::XML::Server class, 320
share_methods (RPC::XML::Server), 75
shutdown call, 173
signals (SOAP::Lite), 62, 63
Signature element (XML Signature),
        278, 285
signatures
    detached, 279
    enveloped, 278
    enveloping, 279
    invalid, 285
    languages and, 41
    portType blocks and, 193
    RPC over SOAP and, 109
    RPC::XML::Method, 74
    RPC::XML::Server, 72
    Signature element, 285
    X-KISS, 281
    (see also digital signatures; method
        signatures)
Simple API for XML (see SAX)
Simple Mail Transport Protocol (see SMTP)
Simple Object Access Protocol (see SOAP)
simple types (XML Schema), 27
simple_request method
        (RPC::XML::Client), 69, 70, 316
SmallTalk, 103
smart_encode function (RPC::XML), 314
S/MIME (Secured/Multipurpose Internet
        Mail Extensions), 275
SMTP (Simple Mail Transport Protocol)
    email, 170
    proxy method, 125
    RPC fault codes, 111
    SOAP binding, 112
SOAP 1.1
    envelope end, 95
    fault codes and, 107
    labels, 87
    predefined faults for, 107
    return values, 110
    RPC faults in, 111
SOAP 1.2
    envelope end, 95
    fault codes and, 107
    labels, 87

predefined faults for, 108
processing instructions, 84
return values, 110
RPC faults in, 111
specification for faults, 106
SOAP bindings
 SAML and, 282
 WSDL example, 415–424
SOAP messages
 common namespaces, 86
 data encoding, 97–105
 DTD declarations and, 84
 Fault element, 105–108
 Header element, 85, 88–95
 $header variable, 164
 payloads of, 291
 RPC over SOAP and, 110
 WS-Attachments specification and, 271
 XrML licenses, 285
SOAP Messages with Attachments
   (SwA), 269
SOAP over HTTP, 125
SOAP servers
 commonly used elements, 138, 139
 designing, 140–145
 freeing from maintenance, 145
 HTTP transport, 146–152
 improving code and service, 152–158
 revising server code, 150, 151
SOAP (Simple Object Access Protocol)
 Accept header, 253
 arrayType attribute, 191
 authentication, 161–165
 Body element, 198
 creating transport modules, 177–182
 features, 3
 MIME extensions and, 205
 packaging and, 269, 270
 REST and, 261
 routers, 265–267
 shortcomings, 4
 toolkits, 5, 114
 transporting, 111–113
 transports with server/client, 165–173
 UDDI and, 214, 225
 W3C design, 83
 web sites, 436, 437
 WSDL binding declaration, 196
 WSDL port elements and, 200
 WS-Security, 284
 XKMS and, 281
 XML definitions, 84–108

XML Schema, 20, 22, 31
XML-RPC, 3, 32, 51, 84
SOAPAction header, 198, 275
soap:address element, 200
soap:binding element, 197, 198, 210
soap:body element, 198, 204, 205, 208
SOAP::Client class, 341, 342
SOAP::Constants class, 339
SOAP::Data class
 accessing SOAP envelope, 156, 157
 managing data, 130, 131
 methods, 332–333
 purpose, 124
 SOAP::Header subclass, 164
SOAP-ENC label, 86, 87
SOAP-ENV label, 86, 87, 88
SOAP::EnvelopeMaker class, 116, 118
SOAP::Fault class
 error handling, 150
 error messages as, 147
 error reports, 149
 methods, 336, 337
soap:fault element, 199
SOAP::Header class, 164, 339
soap:header element, 199, 208
soap:headerfault element, 199
SOAP::Lite module
 basic authentication, 274
 client authentication and, 164
 client class names, 179
 client communications, 120–136
 client support for WSDL, 211, 213
 converting integers to text, 115–118
 designing servers, 140–145
 encoding method, 300
 global objects, 125
 improving code and service, 152–158
 installing, 119, 120
 loading client class, 166
 manipulating messages, 84
 messages with attachments, 270
 methods, 327–331
 performance, 301
 Perl and, 52
 programming reference, 327–347
 proxy method, 60
 purpose, 124
 server classes, 138, 139
 signals, 62, 63
 tracing, 176
 transport method, 177
 tying interface code, 146–152

Index | 461

SOAP::Lite module (*continued*)
    UDDI query routines, 226
    UDDI::Lite class and, 231
    web service example, 7
    web site, 119
    WS-Security example, 284
    (see also XMLRPC::Lite class;
        XMLRPC::Lite toolkit)
SOAP::Lite::SmartProxy module, 136
SOAP::MIME package, 270
SOAP::Parser class, 118
SOAP::payload module, 136
SOAP-RP (SOAP Routing Protocol), 263
SOAP::Schema class, 211, 212, 213, 340
SOAP::Schema::WSDL class, 341
SOAP::Serializer class, 337, 339
SOAP::Server class
    accessing SOAP envelope, 156, 157
    arguments and, 66
    authentication, 161
    handle method, 176, 179
    methods, 342–345
    overloading methods, 147
    server classes and, 162
SOAP::Server::Parameters class
    routines, 345
    server authentication and, 161
    SOAP envelope, 147, 156
SOAP::SOM class
    accessing SOAP envelope, 156
    CPAN uploads, 134
    managing data, 130, 131
    match method, 157
    methods, 333–336
    purpose, 124
    RSS example, 123
    XMLRPC::SOM class, 61
SOAP::Struct class, 116
SOAP::Trace class
    debugging/tracing facility, 126, 127
    programming reference, 346–347
    UDDI::Lite and, 234
SOAP::Transport class
    methods, 337
    programming reference, 347–357
    proxy method, 179
    purpose, 124
    transport binding, 122
    transport objects, 179
SOAP::Transport::FTP::Client class, 173,
    174, 175, 176, 349

SOAP::Transport::HTTP class, 148, 153,
    349–351
SOAP::Transport::HTTP::Apache class, 145,
    153, 350
SOAP::Transport::HTTP::CGI class,
    145, 350
SOAP::Transport::HTTP::Client class,
    118, 349
SOAP::Transport::HTTP::Daemon
    class, 145, 147, 350
    (see also HTTP::Daemon class)
SOAP::Transport::HTTP::FCGI class,
    145, 351
SOAP::Transport::HTTP::Server class, 349
SOAP::Transport::IO class, 173, 174, 351
SOAP::Transport::IO::Server class, 173,
    351, 406
SOAP::Transport::JABBER class, 167–169,
    352, 353
SOAP::Transport::JABBER::Client class, 352
SOAP::Transport::JABBER::Server class, 352
SOAP::Transport::JABBER::URI class, 169
SOAP::Transport::LOCAL class, 353
SOAP::Transport::LOCAL module, 408,
    409–414
SOAP::Transport::LOCAL::Client
    class, 173, 176, 181, 353
SOAP::Transport::MAILTO class, 170,
    194, 353
SOAP::Transport::MAILTO::Client
    class, 353
SOAP::Transport::MQ class, 169, 170,
    354, 355
SOAP::Transport::MQ::Client class, 354
SOAP::Transport::MQ::Server class, 355
SOAP::Transport::POP3 class, 170, 355
SOAP::Transport::POP3::Server class,
    171, 355
SOAP::Transport::TCP class, 165–167,
    356, 357
SOAP::Transport::TCP::Client class, 166,
    167, 356
SOAP::Transport::TCP::Server class, 165,
    166, 357
soapversion method
    SOAP::Lite, 329
    SOAP::Serializer, 338
sockets
    IO::Socket class family, 165
    request delivery, 178
    shutdown call, 173
solicit-response model (WSDL), 194, 195

SonicMQ, 289
spaces, 11, 14, 202
    (see also whitespace)
sparse arrays, 103
SSH (Secure SHell), 31
SSL method
    SOAP::Transport::TCP::Client class, 356
    SOAP::Transport::TCP::Server class, 357
SSL (Secure Sockets Layer), 275
SSL/TLS, 275
standards
    complaints about process, 5
    error systems, 4
    HTTP protocol, 9
    REST addressing principles, 241
    XML-RPC and, 50
started method (RPC::XML::Server), 318
static methods
    authentication and, 149
    class methods as, 123
    object creation and, 130
    SOAP::Lite and, 125
    XMLRPC::Lite assumptions, 65
    (see also class methods)
status codes, 12, 13
STDERR file handle, 127
STDIN file handle, 133, 406
STDOUT file handle, 406
steganography, 272
store-and-forward management, 167, 171
string method (RPC::XMLSimple::Client), 55, 306
string type
    RPC::XMLSimple, 56
    SOAP, 98, 103
    XML Schema, 25
    XML-RPC, 33, 34, 37
    XMLRPC::Lite, 62
strings
    converting integers to text, 120–122
    converting numbers to text, 115–118
    proxy method and, 125
    TCP transport, 166
    UUIDs, 216
    (see URI strings)
struct type
    arrays and, 101
    compound type, 99
    key/value pairs, 99
    XML-RPC request example, 37
    XML-RPC responses and, 38, 39
    XML-RPC supported, 34

structures
    accessors and, 104
    autogenerated XML example, 118
    document structure vs., 23
    operations as named, 193
    RPC over SOAP, 109
    RPC::XMLSimple data classes, 56
    struct datatype, 34
    for UDDI, 215–225
stubmaker.pl tool, 213
style attribute (soap:binding element), 197, 210
subclassing
    classes, 147–150
    client authentication, 164
    complex types and, 28
    sample transport module, 409
    server authentication, 161
    server classes, 159
    simple types and, 27
    SOAP::Transport, 180
    transport classes, 180
Sun, 2, 296
SwA (SOAP Messages with Attachments), 269
switch activity (BPEL), 298
system.identify procedure, 78
system.introspection procedure, 78
system.listMethods method (PHP), 51
system.listMethods procedure, 78
system.methodHelp method (PHP), 51
system.methodHelp procedure, 78
system.methodSignature method (PHP), 51
system.methodSignature procedure, 78
system.multicall procedure, 78
system.status method, 80
system.status procedure, 78

T

targets, 18, 283
tcp://, 166, 169
TCP protocol
    binding example, 167
    generic client example, 402, 403
    HTTP and, 9
    request delivery, 178
    server example, 401, 402
    SOAP::Transport::IO module and, 173
    URI strings, 166
    WS-Routing and, 263
    XML-RPC limitations and, 50

Index | 463

TCP/IP protocol
    SOAP transport, 112
    SOAP::Transport::TCP, 165–167
    web services, 160
    XMLRPC::Lite, 59, 65
Technical Recommendation (TR) (see W3C
        Technical Recommendation)
terminate activity (BPEL), 298
testing
    interface code, 176
    interoperability, 6
    SOAP::Lite module, 120
text
    converting from integers, 120–122
    converting integers to, 115–118
    formatting, 235
throw activity (BPEL), 298
time zones, 34
time2iso8601 function (RPC::XML), 314
timeouts, 296
TLS (Transport Layer Security) protocol, 275
tModel structure (UDDI)
    API calls, 229
    bindingTemplate structure, 221
    delete_tModel call, 230
    save_tModel call, 229
    specifics, 215, 222–225
tModelInstanceDetails element (UDDI), 224
tModelInstanceInfo structure (UDDI), 222,
        224, 225
tModelKey attribute
    UDDI address element, 219
    UDDI keyedReference element, 220
    UDDI tModel structure, 223, 224
    UDDI tModelInstanceInfo structure, 225
to element (WS-Routing), 263, 264
toKey element (UDDI), 219, 220
toolkits
    command-line arguments, 48
    indentation levels, 37
    method signatures, 42
    news service example, 6
    testing interoperability, 6
    value of, 44
TR (Technical Recommendation) (see W3C
        Technical Recommendation)
trace signal (SOAP::Trace), 347
tracing
    SOAP::Lite, 126, 176
    SOAP::Trace class, 126, 127
    YATT tool, 271

transactions
    atomic, 293, 295
    compensating, 294
    distributed, 293, 294
    full web services and, 262
    nonrepudiation, 272
    SOAP Header element, 88
    SOAP support, 84
    two-phase commit, 294
Transform mechanism, 279
transport class, generic, 401, 402
transport method (SOAP::Lite), 177, 327
transport protocols
    creating modules, 177–182
    security, 274–275
    server and client classes, 165–173
    SOAP and, 112
    standalone, 173–177
    UDDI and, 214
transport signal (SOAP::Trace), 346
trust relationships, 281, 286
two-phase commit (2PC) protocol, 293
type attribute
    binding element, 197
    memo:content element, 204
    SOAP messages, 98
    XML Schema, 26, 27
TYPE element (DIME), 270
type element (SOAP), 164
type method
    RPC::XML classes, 71, 313
    SOAP::Data class, 130, 332
    XMLRPC::Data class, 308
typelookup method (SOAP::Lite), 330
types element (WSDL), 189

U

UCS (Universal Character Set), 299
UDDI registries
    generating URLs, 218
    messages and, 215
    persistent data, 216
    publishing data, 225
    removing data, 230
    sample application, 234
UDDI (Universal Description, Discovery, and
        Integration)
    artificial intelligence and, 5
    basic data structures, 215–225
    capabilities, 214
    element hierarchy, 17
    one-man test, 297

publish and query interfaces, 225–231
services discovery, 287
standard for advertisement, 237
web sites, 437
WS-Inspection, 288
WS-Inspection and, 289
XML Schema, 22
UDDI::Data class
    connecting, 232–234
    example, 430–433
    interface and, 231
    programming reference, 359
UDDI::Deserializer class, 231, 359
UDDI::Lite class
    example, 430–433
    programming reference, 358–359
    programming with, 231–236
UDDI::Serializer class, 231, 359
UDDI::SOM class, 231, 359
UDDI::SOM::result method, 232
UDP protocol, 173
UN/CEFACT, 296
Unicode Transformation Standard, 299
Unicode::Map8 module, 299
Unicode::String module, 299
uniform resource identifiers (see URIs)
uniform resource locators (see URLs)
uniform resource names (see URNs)
United Nations/Standard Products and
        Services Classification
        (UN/SPC), 217
units of work, 290, 296
Universal Character Set (UCS), 299
Universal Description, Discovery, and
        Integration (see UDDI)
UNIVERSAL namespace, 126
universally unique identifiers (see UUIDs)
Unix protocol, 48, 173, 174
UN/SPC (United Nations/Standard Products
        and Services Classification), 217
uri method
    RPC::XML::Client class, 70
    SOAP::Data class, 332
    SOAP::Lite class, 123, 125, 330
    SOAP::Transport class, 124
URI strings
    Jabber protocol, 168, 169, 179
    MQ connections, 169
    POP3, 171
    transport classes, 166

URIs (uniform resource identifiers)
    declaring namespace example, 15
    defining actor roles, 90
    DIME and, 270
    httpx, 137
    opacity of, 242
    remote procedure calls using, 125
    resource modeling, 248
    REST and, 237, 238, 241, 243, 260
    slash in, 254
    standard for referencing, 237
    unguessable, 246
    URNs and URLs, 241
url method
    RPC::XML::Client class, 315
    RPC::XML::Server class, 318
URLs (uniform resource locators)
    absolute vs. relative, 249
    CPAN resource, 239
    http and, 9
    as HTTP endpoints, 134
    HTTP requests, 11
    resource modeling, 248
    server identification, 3
    UDDI registries and, 218
    URI subset, 241
URNs (uniform resource names)
    Envelope element and, 117
    URI subset, 241
    WSDL binding declarations, 196
use attribute
    message element, 210
    soap:body element, 198
    soap:fault element, 199
    soap:header element, 199
    XML Schema, 27
use Perl; discussion site, 122, 144
use statement (Perl), 116, 121
use.perl.org journal system, 122, 127, 128,
        132, 424–430
User-Agent header (HTTP), 13, 40
UserAgent header (REST), 252
useragent method (RPC::XML::Client), 315
usernames, 151, 274
UsernameToken element, 284
userUpdate element (SOAP Header), 93
useType attribute (UDDI), 218, 219
UTC (Coordinated Universal Time), 34
UTF-16 encoding, 299
UTF-8 encoding, 299, 300

UUIDs (universally unique identifiers)
    businessKey attribute, 217
    removing data from UDDI registries, 230
    special data, 216
    UDDI query routines, 226
    UDDI tModelKey attribute, 225

V

value element
    attribute placement, 93
    member container and, 35
    param container and, 37
value method
    RPC::XML classes, 71, 313
    RPC::XML::response class, 314
    RPC::XMLSimple class, 305
    RPC::XMLSimple::Client class, 55
    SOAP::Data class, 130, 332
    XMLRPC::Data class, 308
valueof method
    SOAP::SOM class, 334
    XMLRPC::SOM class, 309
variables
    global, 132, 147
    Perl language, 62
    special Perl, 69
verification, 280
version method
    Apache::RPC::Server class, 325
    RPC::XML::Server class, 318
VersionMismatch fault code (SOAP), 107, 108
via element (WS-Routing), 264
VPNs (Virtual Private Networks), 275

W

W3C Technical Recommendation, 83, 214
W3C (World Wide Web Consortium)
    criticism of, 5
    HTTP standards, 9
    information links, 435
    parameterOrder attribute, 210
    port specifications, 200
    security specifications, 276
    SOAP and, 83
    standardization process, 277
    web site, 13
    WSDL specification, 185
    XML Schema, 20, 22, 24
    XPath definition, 22
    XPath query syntax, 48

wait activity (BPEL), 298
Wall, Larry, 21
Web Resource Description Language
    (see WRDL)
Web Service Choreography Interface
    (WSCI), 296
Web Service Description Language
    (see WSDL)
web services
    advantages/drawbacks, 5
    complex functionality, 262
    considerations, 302
    discovery, 287–289
    features, 3–4
    firewalls, 275
    history, 2
    implementation, 5, 298–302
    improving, 152–158
    message routing, 263–267
    overloading operations, 205
    packaging, 267–271
    performance and optimization, 300
    practical applications, 6
    registration service, 294
    reliable messaging, 289–291
    REST and SOAP, 261
    security, 271–273
    security specifications, 283–287
    TCP/IP and, 160
    transport level security, 274–275
    WSDL, 185
    XML standards, 275–283
Web Services Coordination
    (see WS-Coordination)
Web Services Description Language
    (see WSDL)
Web Services Flow Language (WSFL), 297
Web Services Inspection Language
    (see WS-Inspection)
web services protocols (see specific protocols)
Web Services Referral Protocol
    (see WS-Referral)
Web Services Routing Protocol
    (see WS-Routing)
Web Services Security, 283–287
Web Services Transaction
    (see WS-Coordination)
web sites
    Fielding dissertation, 237
    general XML and XML Schema, 435
    MQSeries software, 169
    REST, 437

SOAP, 436, 437
SOAP::Lite module, 119
UDDI, 437
use Perl; discussion site, 122
W3C, 13, 24
WSDL, 437
XLink specification, 249
XML-RPC, 32, 49, 436
WebMethod feature (SOAP), 261
while activity (BPEL), 298
whitespace
   Base64 data and, 33
   parsers and, 16
   server class removing, 162
   XML Signature and, 278
   (see also spaces)
WishListCustomer class
   example code, 377–383
   HTTP::Daemon class, 386, 390, 391, 396, 397
   make_cookie method, 164
   managing connections, 385–386
   managing user data, 383–385
   methods for, 142–144
   search example, 394–396
   search methods, 155
   SOAP::Lite client example, 391, 393
   static methods, 141
   testing FindBooks method, 397, 398
WishListCustomer::Apache class, 393, 394
WishListCustomer::Client class
   client authentication, 164, 165
   example, 400, 401
   MAILTO example, 173
   as subclass, 179
WishListCustomer::Daemon class, 147, 148, 158, 387
WishListCustomer::SOAP class, 148–150, 158, 388–390
WishListCustomer::Transport class, 177, 398, 400
workflow, 262, 291, 296
Workflow Management Coalition, 297
World Wide Web Consortium (see W3C)
WRDL (Web Resource Description Language), 237, 259
writing
   client transports, 179–181
   server transports, 177–179
WS-Attachments specification, 270, 271
WS-Authorization specification, 286
WSCI (Web Service Choreography Interface), 296
WS-Coordination (Web Services Coordination), 294, 295, 297
WSDL documents, 187–200
WSDL (Web Services Description Language)
   APIs and, 259
   code generation based on, 213
   document components, 187–200
   features, 4, 185–187
   HTTP and MIME bindings, 201–205
   other elements, 209–211
   overloading operations, 205–209
   programming, 211–213
   resource access, 237
   SOAP bindings example, 415–424
   use.perl.org journal system, 424–430
   web sites, 437
   XKMS and, 281
   XML Schema and, 20, 22, 24, 31
WSDL::Generator package (CPAN), 212
WS-Federation specification, 286
WSFL (Web Services Flow Language), 297
WS-Inspection (Web Services Inspection Language), 237, 287–289
WS-Policy specification, 286
WS-Privacy specification, 286
WS-Referral (Web Services Referral Protocol), 265–267
WS-Routing (Web Services Routing Protocol), 263–265, 267
WS-SecureConversations, 286
WS-Security (Web Services Security Language), 276, 283–286, 297
WS-Transaction specification, 295, 297
WS-Trust specification, 286

X

X.509 certificates, 284, 285
XACML (XML Access Control Markup Language), 276, 283
XHTML, 14, 15
X-KISS (XML Key Information Service Specification), 281
XKMS (XML Key Management), 276, 281
X-KRSS (XML Key Registration Service Specification), 281
XLANG (Microsoft), 297
XLink (XML Linking Language), 16, 237, 249, 267
xlink:href attribute, 249

XML Access Control Markup Language
    (see XACML)
XML Canonicalization specification, 278
XML Decryption Transform
    specification, 280
XML definitions, 84–108
XML documents
    document style, 291
    elements in, 36
    embedding, 267
    initial line required, 38
    linking to external sources, 267
    multiple signatures, 279
    SOAP messages as, 85
    validation and, 19
    WSDL example, 185–187
    XML security and, 276
    XPath syntax, 22
XML Encryption
    confidentiality, 285
    KeyInfo element, 276
    specifics, 279–281
    W3C, 276
XML (Extensible Markup Language)
    Accept header and, 253
    compression and, 268
    CVS example, 29–31
    data representation, 3, 13
    DTD and, 19, 20
    indentation levels, 37
    Jabber protocol and, 167
    modules and tools, 21, 22
    packaging and, 267
    random access and, 267
    requests expressed in, 36
    security standards, 275–283
    self-describing data and, 13–19
    SOAP expression in, 84
    standard document structure, 237
    UDDI and, 214, 215
    web sites, 435
    WSDL, 4, 185
    XML Schema, 20
    XML-RPC and, 33, 34
XML Fragment Interchange
    specification, 267
XML Inclusions specification, 268
XML Key Information Service Specification
    (X-KISS), 281
XML Key Management (see XKMS)
XML Key Management specification, 276

XML Key Registration Service Specification
    (X-KRSS), 281
XML Linking Language (see XLink)
XML messages
    autogenerated, 117–118
    parsing, 302
XML parsers
    performance and, 22
    RPC::XML and, 67
    ubiquity of, 3
    UTF-8 encoding, 299
    whitespace and, 16
    XML messages and, 302
    XML::LibXML::SAX::Parser module, 301
    XML::Parser::Lite, 301
    XML-RPC and, 52
    XMLRPC::Lite and, 59
    XML::SAX::PurePerl parser, 301
    (see also XML::Parser module)
XML Processing Description Language
    (XPDL), 297
XML Schema language
    all construct, 190
    anyType datatype, 192
    anyType type, 103
    attributes, 26
    compound types, 99
    data encoding schemes, 267
    describing XML, 20
    DTD benefits, 23
    embedded XML and, 225
    encoding and, 97
    import element and, 210
    mustUnderstand attribute value and, 91
    namespaces in SOAP messages, 87
    one-man test, 297
    overview, 22–31
    simple SOAP types, 98
    SOAP and, 31
    SOAP standard and, 4
    validation, 279
    W3C web site, 24
    web sites, 435
    WSDL and, 31
    WSDL documents and, 189
    xsd label and, 188
XML security, 275–283
XML Signature (XML Signature Syntax
    and Processing), 276, 277–279,
    281, 285
XML Stylesheet Language Transforms
    (see XSLT)

468 | Index

xml:attributes attribute (XML), 16
xml:lang attribute (XML), 16
XML::LibXML tool, 21
XML::LibXML::SAX::Parser module, 301
XML::LibXSLT tool, 21
xml:link attribute (XML), 16
XML::Parser module
   comparisons to, 44
   CPAN package, 67
   RPC::XMLSimple toolkit, 53
   SOAP::Lite, 300
   tool features, 21
   toolkits and, 52
   XMLRPC::Lite and, 59
   XML::XPath module and, 22
XML::Parser::Lite, 301
XML-RPC requests, 33, 36–38, 78
XML-RPC responses, 33, 38, 78
XML-RPC toolkit
   arrays and structures, 34, 36
   basis of types, 31
   client/server communication, 40, 41
   convenience, 5
   creating responses, 38
   data encoding, 33, 34
   fault as error response, 39
   first web service protocol, 3
   history of, 32
   introspection routines, 77
   limitations, 49–51
   making requests, 36–38
   Meerkat client sample code, 360–364
   Meerkat example, 42–49
   Meerkat news service, 6, 261
   Perl toolkits, 52, 53
   requests, 37
   RPC over SOAP comparison, 109
   RPC::XML examples, 370–373
   RPC:XML toolkit, 67–77
   RPC::XMLSimple examples, 364–367
   RPC::XMLSimple toolkit, 53–58
   sending error responses, 39
   SOAP comparison, 3, 51, 84
   as SOAP spinoff, 83
   standardized errors, 4
   transport protocols, 112
   web sites, 32, 436
   XMLRPC::Lite examples, 367–370
   (see also XMLRPC::Lite toolkit)
XMLRPC::Data class, 62, 308, 309
XMLRPC::Deserializer class, 310

XMLRPC::Lite module
   examples, 367–370
   Meerkat news service, 6
   message compression, 49
   programming reference, 306–312
   server classes, 65–67
   XML-RPC and, 59–67
   XML-RPC support, 52
XMLRPC::Lite::Transport module, 64
XMLRPC::Serializer class, 310
XMLRPC::Server class, 310
XMLRPC::Server::Parameters class, 310
XMLRPC::SOM class, 61, 309, 310
XMLRPC::Transport::HTTP module, 66
   classes, 311
XMLRPC::Transport::HTTP::Apache
   class, 66, 311
XMLRPC::Transport::HTTP::CGI class,
   66, 311
XMLRPC::Transport::HTTP::Daemon
   class, 66, 311
XMLRPC::Transport::POP3 module, 66, 311
XMLRPC::Transport::POP3::Server
   class, 311
XMLRPC::Transport::TCP module, 66, 312
XMLRPC::Transport::TCP::Server class, 312
XML::RSS module (CPAN), 22, 123
XML::SAX::PurePerl parser, 301
xmlschema method (SOAP::Serializer), 339
XML::Simple module, 22
xml:space attribute (XML), 16
XML::XPath module, 22, 44, 48
XPath language
   query syntax, 48
   reusing query paths, 39
   signatures and, 279
   validation, 279
   W3C definition, 22
   WSDL documents and, 189
   XML Signature specification and, 276
   XML-RPC Meerkat example, 44
XPDL (XML Processing Description
   Language), 297
XPL files
   Apache::RPC::Server and, 79
   listMethods.xpl file, 376
   managing server-side code, 76, 77
xpl_path method (RPC::XML::Server), 321
XPointer, 237
XRFortune.pm module, 56, 64, 373–376
XrML (Extensible Rights Markup
   Language), 276, 285

xs namespace label, 97
xs:boolean type attribute, 105
xsd namespace label, 97, 188
xsi namespace label, 97
xsi:type attribute, 102, 104
XSLT (Extensible Stylesheet Language
 Template)
  libxslt library, 21
  processing instructions, 18
  SOAP messages and, 84
  validation, 279

Y

YATT (tracing tool), 271

About the Authors

Randy J. Ray has been programming in Perl since 1992. He has contributed to perl5-porters, presented at various conferences, and written for *The Perl Journal*. Randy has a BSc in Computer Science from the University of Oklahoma and is now a software engineer with Tellme Networks in Mountain View, California, working on Perl components for VoiceXML applications.

Randy is the author and maintainer of several CPAN modules including `RPC::XML`, `Image::Size`, Perl-RPM, and `Devel::Modlist`. When not hacking Perl or reading about it, Randy builds and paints historical miniatures, reads about military history, and plays butler to two very demanding cats.

Pavel Kulchenko is an open source developer, best known for his `SOAP::Lite`, `XMLRPC::Lite`, and `UDDI::Lite` modules for Perl. After graduating and discovering Perl in 1993, he has consulted for a variety of companies in both the United States and abroad.

With years of software architecture and development experience, including involvement with web services since early 2000, he is a frequent writer and speaker on web services and XML technologies. Pavel lives in always sunny Seattle with his wife, Alena, and his son, Daniil.

Colophon

Our look is the result of reader comments, our own experimentation, and feedback from distribution channels. Distinctive covers complement our distinctive approach to technical topics, breathing personality and life into potentially dry subjects.

The animal on the cover of *Programming Web Services with Perl* is a flying dragon (genus *draco*). Found in the tropical rainforests of the East Indies and Southern Asia, this small lizard has five or six hind ribs on each side that are prolonged and covered with weblike skin, forming "wings." While jumping, the lizard spreads its wings and glides to the ground; it can generally glide almost nine yards. Gliding is used only as a means of locomotion and not for predator escape; to escape danger, the lizard always climbs. The lizard also never glides when it's raining or windy.

A flying dragon feeds mostly on small ants and termites and is described as a sit-and-wait feeder. It will sit next to a tree trunk waiting for insects to come to it.

A female flying dragon builds a nest for her eggs by forcing her head into the soil to create a small hole. She then lays five eggs into the hole and covers them with dirt, packing the soil on top with a patting motion of her head. The eggs take approximately 32 days to incubate.

Humans don't eat flying dragons, and they aren't currently listed as threatened.

Mary Anne Weeks Mayo was the production editor and proofreader, and Sarah Jane Shangraw was the copyeditor for *Programming Web Services with Perl*. Colleen Gorman and Jane Ellin provided quality control. Ellen McHale provided production assistance. Lucie Haskins wrote the index.

Pam Spremulli designed the cover of this book, based on a series design by Edie Freedman. The cover image is a 19th-century engraving from the Dover Pictorial Archive. Emma Colby produced the cover layout with QuarkXPress 4.1 using Adobe's ITC Garamond font.

David Futato designed the interior layout. This book was converted to FrameMaker 5.5.6 with a format conversion tool created by Erik Ray, Jason McIntosh, Neil Walls, and Mike Sierra that uses Perl and XML technologies. The text font is Linotype Birka; the heading font is Adobe Myriad Condensed; and the code font is LucasFont's TheSans Mono Condensed. The illustrations that appear in the book were produced by Robert Romano and Jessamyn Read using Macromedia FreeHand 9 and Adobe Photoshop 6. The tip and warning icons were drawn by Christopher Bing. This colophon was compiled by Mary Anne Weeks Mayo.

Made in the USA
Lexington, KY
19 January 2011